P9-EJU-000

THE POEMS OF CATULLUS

A Teaching Text

Phyllis Young Forsyth

UNIVERSITY
PRESS OF
AMERICA

LANHAM • NEW YORK • LONDON

WITHDRAWN
PROPERTY OF
CLACKAMAS COMMUNITY COLLEGE
LIBRARY

Copyright © 1986 by

University Press of America,® Inc.

4720 Boston Way
Lanham, MD 20706

3 Henrietta Street
London WC2E 8LU England

All rights reserved

Printed in the United States of America

Co-published by arrangement with the
Classical Association of Atlantic States

Library of Congress Cataloging-in-Publication Data

Forsyth, Phyllis Young.
  The poems of Catullus.

  "Co-published by arrangement with the Classical
Association of Atlantic States"—T.p. verso.
  Bibliography: p.
  1. Catullus, Gaius Valerius—Criticism and
interpretation. I. Catullus, Gaius Valerius.
Selections. 1986. II. Classical Association of the
Atlantic States. III. Title.
PA6276.F57   1986   874.01   85-26439
ISBN 0-8191-5150-5 (alk. paper)
ISBN 0-8191-5151-3 (pbk. : alk. paper)

All University Press of America books are produced on acid-free
paper which exceeds the minimum standards set by the National
Historical Publications and Records Commission.

For my husband: James J. Forsyth

For my teacher: Betty Nye Quinn

For my grandmother: Mary Echlov Rosenthal

Acknowledgments

I would like to thank the University of Waterloo for granting me a sabbatical leave which made possible the writing of this text, and for a grant in aid of publication through the Social Sciences and Humanities Research Council of Canada.

Thanks also to Herbert Benario and Harry Rutledge of the *CW* Special Series; to Ann Hodgins; and to James J. Forsyth. All in their different ways contributed greatly to this endeavor.

TABLE OF CONTENTS

This text is intended for use at the undergraduate level and is a result of my own experience at the University of Waterloo since 1969. Over the years, students have increasingly been entering university with little or no Latin, and now commonly arrive in a course on Catullus with just one or two years of instruction in the language. For these students texts of Catullus presently on the market (*e.g.*, Merrill, Fordyce, and Quinn) have proved a hindrance rather than a help, for their approach and their notes tend to leave bewildered students behind. One major problem stems from these texts' frequent references to Greek parallels (totally meaningless to the majority of students) or to emulations of Catullus in later Latin poets (with whom most students are not familiar). These texts are, to be sure, appropriate for a very senior or graduate student, but in my experience have deterred many a promising beginner from further pursuing an interest in Latin literature.

For these reasons I have developed what I call a "Teaching Text", that is, a text and commentary specifically designed for the neophyte Latin student. The commentary concentrates on the poems themselves—on what makes them poetry, on what themes the poet is examining, and (importantly) on how the poems relate to each other. References to literary parallels have been removed in favor of more direct help with the Latin language; more attention has been given to assisting the student in recognizing the literary features of a poem, *e.g.*, the use of sound and image; references to modern scholarly literature have been kept to a minimum, appearing only where an English-speaking undergraduate would benefit from a concise article in a readily accessible classical journal; and help with vocabulary has been incorporated directly into the commentary on each poem.

In regard to vocabulary, my approach to Catullus needs to be made clear at once. As any teacher who has studied the complete text of this poet well knows, Catullus can at times (especially in the epigrams) employ raw, even obscene language. It seems insulting to modern undergraduates (most of whom are in their twenties when they come to Catullus) to gloss over the more graphic words with delicate euphemisms. But, more importantly, such glossing of the text prevents these students from coming to know (and appreciate) the real Catullus; after all, his poetry was radical in its own time (indeed it shocked many of his contemporaries), and we do him a great injustice by our attempts to sanitize his poems. We should let the modern student meet the poet directly, and then judge for himself/herself the merit of the poems. To obscure on purpose vital aspects of Catullan verse is a disservice to both ancient poet and modern student.

P.Y.F.
1985

Catullus

Gaius Valerius Catullus (ca. 84-54 B.C.) was without doubt one of the greatest poets produced by either Greece or Rome. He stood in the front ranks of the so-called *Novi Poetae* ("New Poets" or "Neoterics"): Roman literary revolutionaries who were determined to resuscitate a poetic tradition they considered stale and stagnant. Prior to their advent, serious poets of Rome had concentrated their efforts on the epic genre, and lyric and epigrammatic forms had been the preserve of amateur dilettantes. The *Novi Poetae*, however, took the art of lyric and epigram seriously and approached it innovatively.

Catullus and his colleagues brought a freshness and vitality to their verse that may have seemed shocking to more conservative Romans; and yet, this vitality was not gained at the expense of artistry, for the poems of Catullus are carefully crafted, indeed worked out so meticulously as to deny any rash image of the poet as an impetuous, art-less emoter of passions. In the poems of Catullus, perhaps as nowhere else, *ars* and *ingenium* are perfectly united, and it is, in fact, this union which makes his poetry as important and as appealing today as it was in antiquity.

About the private life of Catullus relatively little is known, although much conjecture has been put forward. Born in Verona to a prominent family (his father apparently was on friendly terms with Julius Caesar himself; *cf.* Suetonius' *Life of Julius Caesar*, 73), Catullus travelled south to Rome sometime around 60 B.C., and it was there that he pursued the love affair which was to play such a central role in his poetry. The object of his passion bore the pseudonym of "Lesbia"; her real name (according to Apuleius in *Apology*, 10) was Clodia, and she was one of the three daughters of Appius Claudius Pulcer (consul in 79 B.C.), and thus sister to the infamous Roman rabble-rouser, P. Clodius Pulcer. As all three sisters, however, were called "Clodia", there has been some debate as to which woman was the beloved of Catullus. What facts are now known seem to favor the Clodia who was the wife of Q. Caecilius Metellus Celer (the governor of Cisalpine Gaul in 62-61 B.C.) and the object of Cicero's scorn, for her scandalous behavior, in the *Pro Caelio*.

It was also in Rome that Catullus mixed and matched wits with other like-minded poetic rebels, men such as Calvus and Cinna, and with them honed his art to a fine edge (as witnessed by poem 50). At some period, however, probably from 57-56 B.C., Catullus left Rome for a year's stay in the province of Bithynia. There he was apparently attached to the general staff of the provincial governor, C. Memmius. Apart from this journey (which may have included a side trip to Troy to visit the tomb of his brother; *cf.* poem 101), fixed dates in Catullus' life are notoriously difficult to determine. It is not clear, for example, when his love affair with Lesbia-Clodia actually began, when his book of poems was published, or when, indeed, he died. All that can be said with regard to this last problem is that no extant poem can be securely dated later than 54 B.C.

The Poems

The text of Catullus as we now have it falls easily

2

into three distinct parts: 1) the polymetrics (1-60), *i.e.*, short poems in various lyric meters; 2) the long poems (61-68); and 3) the epigrams (69-116) in the elegiac meter. Taken together, these poems bear witness to the versatility of Catullus as a poet, and, taken in turn, each group of poems illuminates a particular aspect of his achievement.

The Polymetrics (1-60):

It is in the polymetric poems that Catullus displays his mastery of a genre with a very distinguished ancestry. Lyric poetry had begun in antiquity as verse that was meant to be sung to the accompaniment of the lyre. Its ultimate origin remains obscure, but lyric appears as a formal literary genre in Greece in the seventh century B.C., and it flourished thereafter for some two centuries. Greek lyric poetry succeeded the epic genre (best represented today by the *Iliad* and *Odyssey* of Homer) and differed greatly from it in being of a more introspective nature: this was verse of a personal sort, expressing the individual thoughts and emotions of the poet. Also unlike epic, lyric poems were generally short, some only a few lines in length, and the meters in which they were composed did not include the epic's stately dactylic hexameter.

Within the overall genre of lyric verse, the Greeks developed several distinct types of poetry. There was, for example, iambic verse (commonly associated today with the name of Archilochus) which featured satire, ridicule and invective, often with a touch of the obscene. There was also lyric monody: songs in various meters, usually arranged in stanzas, designed for a single singer and generally sung at private gatherings. This type of lyric finds its best Greek representatives today in the extant fragments of

3

Sappho and Alcaeus. For a group of singers there was choral lyric: longer pieces, often quite complex in their meters, performed at public ceremonies or festivities, and thematically rich, often incorporating a significant amount of myth. Indeed, so complex was choral lyric that it itself could be subdivided into such types as *epithalamia* (wedding songs), *epinicia* (victory odes), or *partheneia* (maiden songs). The extant poems of Pindar are perhaps the finest examples of Greek choral lyric in all its complexity and variety.

Not surprisingly, given the overwhelming influence that Greek culture exercised on the Romans, Greek lyric was eventually brought to Rome, where it began to thrive in the first century B.C. The poet most responsible for the development of Latin lyric verse was Catullus, even though in the Augustan Age the poet Horace attempted to claim this honor for himself (*Odes* III.30).

Catullus' achievement, however, lay not in simply adapting Greek lyric for a Roman audience, but in blending the old form with a newer literary style which we today refer to as "Alexandrian", since it arose in Alexandria in the third century B.C., when that city was winning renown for its great museum and extensive library. Scholarship was valued here, and so it is not surprising that the poetry written in Alexandria tended to be scholarly in tone, intended not for a wide public audience, but for an intellectual elite. Indeed, so scholarly was this verse that much of it seems to have been pedantically obscure.

The greatest exponent of the Alexandrian style was the poet-scholar Callimachus (ca. 310-240 B.C.), to whom Catullus pays tribute in several poems (*cf.* 7.6; 65.16; and 116.2; moreover, poem 66 is in fact a translation of a

4

Callimachean poem). Callimachus was not only a prolific poet (writing, for example, hymns, epigrams, elegiacs, and miniature epics), he was also an arbiter of literary style, encouraging the composition of short, elegant, and learned poetry. To Callimachus' concern for form and learning (*doctrina*), Catullus would add his own passionate personality and his own fertile imagination; the result was a lyric verse unlike any that had yet been written (for a more detailed analysis, *cf.* K. Quinn's *The Catullan Revolution* [1959] and D. O. Ross' *Style and Tradition in Catullus* [1969]).

The Lyric Libellus

One of the most controversial aspects of Catullan studies, especially in regard to poems 1-60, pertains to the arrangement of his poems. That Catullus published a volume of poetry seems clearly attested by poem 1: the dedication by the poet of a *lepidum novum libellum / arida modo pumice expolitum* to Cornelius Nepos. But, what did this *libellus* contain? Was it in fact identical with the entire Catullan corpus as we have it today? Or, was it identical to only one segment, *i.e.*, the polymetrics? Or, is our text a posthumous compilation which bears little or no resemblance to Catullus' own publication? In modern Catullan studies, few questions have been debated with as much vigor as these, and answers have ranged all the way from Ellis' disbelief that the present order of poems reflects the original plan of the poet (*cf.* R. Ellis, *A Commentary on Catullus* [1889] xlv-1; and 1-5) to Wilamowitz' famous assertion that Catullus himself was responsible for the entire text as we know it (*cf.* U. von Wilamowitz-Moellendorf, *Sappho und Simonides* [1913] 292).

In dealing with this problem, some help is afforded by three poems of Martial: 1.7; 4.14; and 11.6. In the last piece, a poem set in the time of the Saturnalia festival, Martial states (lines 12-16):

> Possum nil ego sobrius; bibenti
> succurrent mihi quindecim poetae.
> da nunc *basia*, sed Catulliana:
> quae si tot fuerint quot ille dixit,
> donabo tibi *passerem* Catulli.

> "I can do nothing at all when I'm sober; but when I'm drinking, fifteen poets will come to my aid. Now give me kisses, but make them Catullan ones; if these be as many as he said, I will give you the *passer* of Catullus."

The references here (in italics above) to *basia* and *passerem* turn the reader's mind to Catullus' poems 2, 3, 5, and 7; *passer* in fact is the initial word of the second poem which, if one excludes the prefatory dedication to Nepos, is really the poem that begins the Catullan corpus. It thus seems possible that Martial in this poem is actually referring to a collection of poems known in antiquity as the *Passer* of Catullus and which contained at least some of the initial poems of our modern text.

That this is indeed the case is well supported by another poem of Martial, 4.14: again the setting is the Saturnalia, and Martial invites another poet, Silius Italicus, to relax by reading some of Martial's verse, stating (lines 11-14):

nec torva lege fronte, sed remissa
lascivis madidos iocis *libellos*;
sic forsan tener ausus est Catullus
magno mittere *passerem* Maroni.

"and not with a grim, but with a
relaxed brow, read *libelli* dripping
with wanton jokes; so perhaps tender
Catullus dared to send his *passer*
to great Maro [*i.e.*, Vergil]."

In addition to the appearance of *passerem* in this poem,
note the use of *libellos*, a word used by Catullus in his
first poem to describe his collection.

Finally, in 1.7 Martial writes:

Stellae delicium mei columba,
Verona licet audiente dicam,
vicit, Maxime, *passerem* Catulli;
tanto Stella meus tuo Catullo
quanto *passere* maior est columba.

"The dove of my Stella
[*i.e.*, L. Arruntius Stella,
the patron of Martial] — a favorite
pet - let me say it even if
Verona is listening—has surpassed,
o Maximus, the *passer* of Catullus;
my Stella is so much greater than
your Catullus, just as a dove is
greater than a *passer*."

In sum, the most logical interpretation of all three of these poems is that a collection of Catullus' poems, popularly known as the *Passer*, was familiar to Martial and his contemporaries. Our next task, then, is to relate that volume to the present text of Catullus.

First of all, it would seem reasonable to assume that any hypothetical later editor of Catullus intent on publishing a "complete edition" of the poems would *not* tamper with an already well known *libellus* in circulation; rather, as M. B. Skinner has written, "a *libellus* already in circulation at the time of the poet's death would serve as the point of departure for a posthumous edition: unpublished poems, scraps, and fragments would naturally be tacked on to the end of an extant volume. We should therefore look to the beginning of the collection for that material which was arranged and published by Catullus himself" (*Catullus' Passer* [1981] 11). Our problem, then, is to determine just exactly where the original *Passer* ends in our modern text, and where any "posthumous collection" begins.

There is at present a wide range of opinions on this matter. A few scholars, most prominently T. P. Wiseman, argue that the *whole* corpus as we have it (poems 1-116) was precisely the volume (the *Passer*) arranged and published by Catullus himself (*cf.* T. P. Wiseman, *Catullan Questions* [1969]). Others have been less venturesome: Kenneth Quinn, for example, has stated that "on internal grounds only, the most likely (but quite unprovable) hypothesis is that Poems 1-60 were published by Catullus, whereas Poems 69-116 (a scrappier and shorter collection) are the work of somebody who gathered together complete poems and fragments" (*Catullus: The Poems* [1970] xxi). Where this hypothesis would leave the so-called Long Poems (poems 61-68) is rather unclear.

Recent scholarship, however, seems rather more inclined to Quinn's view than to Wiseman's: W. Clausen, for example, has argued that poem 1 would be most appropriate as a dedication to poems 2-60, although he also sees in poem 50 a "perfect ending" for the original *libellus*; for Clausen, a second *libellus*, compiled by a later editor, begins at poem 61 and includes poems 62, 63, and 64; while a third *libellus* (also the editor's) includes poems 65-116, all in the elegiac meter (*cf.* W. Clausen, "Catulli Veronensis Liber", in *Classical Philology* 71 [1976] 37-43). Somewhat similarly, M.B. Skinner has put forth the hypothesis that the original *libellus*, the *Passer*, is to be found in poems 1-51 of our text (Skinner, *op. cit.*, 86-92), an hypothesis which this editor finds most plausible given the internal unity and coherence of poems 1-51 (*cf.* commentary on individual poems). Poems 52-60, on this interpretation, would be scraps of verse found by an editor and tacked onto the end of the *Passer*.

As for the corpus as a whole, a bit of speculation may be allowed at this point. Years of work on the poems of Catullus have convinced this editor that meaningful juxtapositions of poems are to be found not only in the polymetrics, but also in the long poems and epigrams. Poems 65-116 seem to me an especially "neat package" (*cf.* my articles "The Gellius Cycle of Catullus" in *Classical Journal* 68 [1972-3] 175-177; "Comments on Catullus 116" in *Classical Quarterly* 27 [1977] 352-353; "Order and Meaning in Catullus 97-99" in *Classical World* 72 [1979] 403-408; and "Quintius and Aufillena in Catullus" in *Classical World* 74 [1981] 220-223), and if they were in fact compiled by a later editor, he was certainly concerned about the order of the individual poems in his edition. I would indeed go so far as to present the following hypothesis: perhaps Catullus himself, after the publication of his *Passer*, set about preparing his next (and complementary) volumes of verse—one containing poems 61-64; the other poems 65-116. The poet, however, never lived to see these volumes actually published, but a later editor incorporated them into a "complete" edition. To echo Quinn, this hypothesis is at present unprovable, but it does not seem entirely without foundation. Certainly more work is needed on poems 61-116, and especially on the elegiac poems, to help solve this still outstanding Catullan question.

The Long Poems (61-68):

Poems 61-68 were once considered labored, artificial ("Alexandrian" in the worst sense), and unsuccessful poetic experiments. While the polymetrics and epigrams were said to reflect the "real Catullus", the long poems were dismissed as uninspired oddities. Closer examination of these poems in recent years, however, has shown such a simplistic view to be untenable: far from being artificial exercises, poems 61-68 are as authentically "Catullan" as any in the corpus, incorporating themes and concepts also present in the shorter poems. "Experimental" they are indeed, as the poet sought to express his thoughts and feelings in a more expansive form, but "unsuccessful" they are not; the poetic quality of these poems, as seen in the poet's skilled manipulation of language, imagery, and sounds, is the equal of that displayed in the shorter pieces. The difference is that of form and quantity, not quality.

The present order of the long poems in the text does not seem to be without design. Poem 61, for example, shares in the lyric meters of the preceding polymetrics, and poem 65, the first elegiac piece we meet in the corpus,

10

contains a programmatic statement that establishes the elegiac meter of all the ensuing poems (*cf.* commentary on poem 65). This selection of meter for the long poems by itself separates the group into two halves of four poems each: first, poems 61, 62, 63, and 64; then, poems 65/66 (taken as one; *cf.* commentary on poem 65), 67, 68A, and 68B (for the division of poem 68 into two distinct pieces, *cf.* commentary on each). While the latter group all share the elegiac meter, the former group displays an alternation of lyric and hexameter meters.

Moreover, poems 61-64 share a common theme which binds them together—that of "union achieved". Poems 61 and 62, for example, are both wedding songs (*epithalamia*) and as such obviously celebrate the union of a man and woman; poem 63 then presents a variation on the theme, as a man (Attis) successfully unites with a goddess (Cybele) in a perverted form of marriage which ultimately strips him of his reason; poem 64 then features a more positive union of god (Thetis) and mortal (Peleus), complete with a formal *epithalamium* sung by the goddesses of Fate (*cf.* poems 61 and 62). Thus, this group of poems comes full circle, with its final member completing the movement begun in its initial piece.

Poem 64, however, is also transitional to the following group (poems 65-68), for its tragic tale of Ariadne's ill-fated love for Theseus foreshadows the ensuing theme of "union thwarted" or "separation", that is, a theme directly opposed to that of poems 61-64. Poem 65/66, for example, in each of its components participates in this theme: poem 65 dwells upon the separation (by death) of Catullus from his brother, while poem 66 in turn tells the more lighthearted tale of Queen Berenice's separation first from her husband, and then from her dedicated lock of hair (*cf.* commentary on poem 66). Poem 67 varies the theme (as poem 63 had offered variation in the first group of long poems) by focusing on a somewhat different type of separation or union thwarted—the marital disloyalty of a wife to her spouse. As the talking door of the house makes clear in the dialogue of the poem (*cf.* the use of the dialogue form in the first group, at poem 62), the mistress of the house had been totally disloyal in her many adulteries; such a "disunion" contrasts greatly with the unions central to the first four long poems.

Poem 68A then returns to the theme of the poet's separation from his brother (*cf.* poem 65), while poem 68B echoes the separation-as-disloyalty theme of poem 67: here the poet and his mistress, despite their physical union, are spiritually far apart because of her adulteries. Indeed, poem 68B serves as a fitting conclusion to the entire cycle of long poems by combining the themes of union and separation, with the latter theme including not only the poet's separation from his unfaithful mistress, but also his irreversible separation from his dead brother (*cf.* poems 65 and 68A).

The present arrangement of the long poems thus displays a thematic rhythm throughout, while, at the same time, it offers a transition between the polymetrics and the elegiac epigrams. The patterns and parallels are not, however, mechanical or rigid; just as patterns and parallels in the polymetrics and epigrams show imagination and flexibility, so too those found in poems 61-68B.

The Epigrams (69-116):

An epigram may be defined simply as a short poem in the elegiac meter, often having a caustic point or "sting" at the end. Of the Catullan poems in the elegiac meter, only poems 69-116 are properly considered epigrams, while the much longer poems 65-68 are usually termed "elegiacs".

The elegiac form as seen in epigram had had a lengthy history in Greek literature, in which it had been employed for a variety of themes, both sacred and secular: prominent subjects, for example, included martial and political deeds, moralizing advice, laments for the deceased, and praises of love and hedonism. Early Greek poets especially famous for their epigrams were Callinus, Tyrtaeus, Mimnermus, Theognis, and Solon (whose extant epigrams shed much light on early Athens). In the Alexandrian age, Callimachus himself was a prolific writer of both long elegiacs and epigrams, but only a small portion of his work is still extant. It is not surprising, however, that the Alexandrian poets appreciated the epigram, given their general interest in compactness of form. What *is* surprising is that Catullan epigram, on close examination, reflects less influence from Alexandria than do the polymetrics and long poems.

In his epigrams, Catullus employs a vocabulary quite different from that used in the rest of the corpus; his language, indeed, is often vulgar, even to the point of gross obscenity. Moreover, there is little of the imagery found in the polymetrics and long poems; in their blunt directness, the epigrams seem to reflect a native Latin poetic tradition which had taken root in Italy long before Catullus, a tradition which placed heavy emphasis on invective, and which has been studied by D. O. Ross, Jr., in his *Style and*

13

Tradition in Catullus (1969). Ross has convincingly demonstrated that it was this native tradition that formed the foundation of the Catullan epigrams.

Yet, despite their differences from the polymetrics and long poems, the Catullan epigrams are still "poetry" thanks to the poet's overriding artistry. In these poems Catullus effectively reveals the wide range of the emotions flowing through his verse; here one finds piquant wit, tender affections, wry observations, as well as savage invective—all co-existing within the compact epigrammatic form. If some epigrams seem offensive, so they were meant to be; they are our windows to another aspect of Catullus, and they complete our picture of the poet.

The Manuscripts (MSS.)

That we today have the poems of Catullus at all is mainly due to the existence in the thirteenth century of the so-called *Veronensis* manuscript, commonly referred to as V. This manuscript has now been lost, but while it was still available at least two copies of it were made: one is now known as O (because it is at Oxford), and the other, no longer extant, has traditionally been called X. Before X disappeared, two copies of it were apparently made: G (in Paris) and R (in the Vatican); both of these were most likely composed in the fourteenth century. Thus, manuscripts O, G and R form the basis of our modern text, and, while there are indeed some later manuscripts extant, they all appear to be less reliable copies of these three.

The problem for an editor of Catullus is, of course, to determine as well as possible what the readings of V were. This involves close study of the variant readings in the extant manuscripts and, sometimes, a bit of Sherlockian intuition. In places where the text is clearly corrupt, generations of scholars have made interpolations and emendations. And yet, an element of uncertainty must remain, for even if we can ultimately recover the readings of V, we are still faced with the problem of how accurate a text *that* manuscript was in the first place. This question can only be answered by the future discovery of a manuscript of Catullus made prior to the thirteenth century.

The Meters of Catullus

One of Catullus' major contributions to the development of Latin verse was his skillful adaptation of complex Greek metrical patterns. These Greek patterns were based on the quantity of a syllable, that is, on whether a syllable was long or short. It has become conventional to indicate a long syllable by the sign _ and a short syllable by the sign ∪ ; the sign ∪̲ is used to indicate that a syllable may be either long or short. Another conventional sign is ´, which indicates the metrical stress (*ictus*) which normally falls on one syllable in every foot. Thus, for example, in iambic verse the individual foot is symbolized by ∪ _́ .

In the polymetric poems of Catullus, the dominant meter is the *hendecasyllabic* (also known as "phalaecian"). As its name implies, the hendecasyllabic meter consists of verses of eleven syllables each, divided into five feet in the following pattern:

$$\underline{\prime} \_ \mid \underline{\prime} \cup \cup \mid \underline{\prime} \cup \mid \underline{\prime} \cup \mid \underline{\prime} \underline{\cup}.$$

While an opening foot of two long syllables (a spondee) is most common, on occasion Catullus varies his initial foot by employing a trochee ($\_\cup$) or iamb ($\cup\_$); the second foot, however, is always a dactyl ($\_\cup\cup$).

Another common Catullan meter is the *choliambic* (also known as "limping iambics" or as "scazons"). This meter features a verse with six feet of a basically iambic nature, in the following pattern:

$$\underline{\cup}\_\mid\cup\_\mid\underline{\cup}\_\mid\cup\_\mid\cup\_\mid\_\underline{\cup}.$$

While the fifth foot is regularly iambic, the first and third feet may at times be spondaic in nature; the sixth foot can be either a trochee or a spondee, and the fact that it bears the metrical stress on its initial syllable, immediately following the stressed syllable of the fifth foot, gives this verse its halting or "limping" movement.

Two Catullan polymetrics (11 and 51) feature the *Sapphic stanza*, in which the first three lines follow this pattern:

$$\_\cup\mid\_\underline{\cup}\mid\_\cup\cup\mid\_\cup\mid\_\_.$$

This line is essentially trochaic, except for the fact that the third foot is always dactylic. The final line in the stanza is shorter, and runs:

$$\_\cup\cup\mid\_\underline{\cup}.$$

Other meters in the polymetrics are:

1) *iambic trimeter*: six iambic feet in the following pattern:

$$\underline{\cup}\_\mid\cup\_\mid\underline{\cup}\_\mid\cup\_\mid\cup\_\mid\cup\_.$$

16

2) *iambic tetrameter catalectic*: an essentially iambic eight-foot verse with a truncated final foot:

$$\underline{\text{u}}\, {\diagup} \mid \text{u}\, {\diagup} \mid \text{u}\, {\diagup} \mid \text{u}\, {\diagup} \mid \underline{\text{u}}\, {\diagup} \mid \text{u}\, {\diagup} \mid \underline{\text{u}}\, {\diagup} \mid \underline{\acute{\text{u}}} \,.$$

3) *greater asclepiadic*: a basically trochaic verse with eight feet, dactylic substitution, and truncated feet:

$${\diagup}\,\_ \mid {\diagup}\,\text{u u} \mid {\diagup} \mid {\diagup}\,\text{u u} \mid {\diagup} \mid {\diagup}\,\text{u u} \mid {\diagup}\,\text{u} \mid \underline{\acute{\text{u}}}\,.$$

4) *glyconic and pherecratic combinations*: a glyconic (${\diagup}\,\underline{\text{u}} \mid {\diagup}\,\text{u u} \mid {\diagup}\,\text{u} \mid {\diagup}$) plus a pherecratic (${\diagup}\,\underline{\text{u}} \mid {\diagup}\,\text{u u} \mid {\diagup} \mid {\diagup}$) comprises the so-called *priapean* meter:

$${\diagup}\,\underline{\text{u}} \mid {\diagup}\,\text{u u} \mid {\diagup}\,\text{u} \mid {\diagup} \mid {\diagup}\,\underline{\text{u}} \mid {\diagup}\,\text{u u} \mid {\diagup} \mid {\diagup}\,;$$

this appears only in poem 17. A similar combination can be found in poem 34, where each stanza is composed of three glyconic lines and a fourth, concluding pherecratic:

(lines 1-3) $\quad {\diagup}\,\underline{\text{u}} \mid {\diagup}\,\text{u u} \mid {\diagup}\,\text{u} \mid {\diagup}\,,$

(line 4) $\quad {\diagup}\,\underline{\text{u}} \mid {\diagup}\,\text{u u} \mid {\diagup} \mid {\diagup}\,.$

In the long poems, poem 61 continues the combination of glyconics and pherecratics with stanzas of four glyconics and a final pherecratic.

Two of the long poems, 62 and 64, are written in the *dactylic hexameter* meter, in which six feet are normally structured as follows:

$${\diagup}\,\underline{\text{u u}} \mid {\diagup}\,\underline{\text{u u}} \mid {\diagup}\,\underline{\text{u u}} \mid {\diagup}\,\underline{\text{u u}} \mid {\diagup}\,\text{u u} \mid {\diagup}\,\underline{\text{u}}\,,$$

although in places Catullus employs a spondee in the fifth foot (such a verse is commonly termed "spondaic").

Poem 63 features the rare and complicated *galliambic* meter, with a general scheme as follows:

$$\cup \cup \underline{\angle} \mid \cup \underline{\angle} \mid \cup \underline{\angle} \mid \underline{\angle} \mid \cup \cup \underline{\angle} \mid \cup \cup \cup \mid \cup \cup,$$

although a long syllable may at times be substituted for two short ones.

From poem 65 on, the corpus is composed of *elegiac couplets*, in which the first verse is a dactylic hexameter, and the second verse a dactylic pentameter, arranged as follows:

$$\angle \underline{\cup \cup} \mid \angle \underline{\cup \cup} \mid \angle \mid\mid \angle \cup \cup \mid \angle \cup \cup \mid \acute{\underline{\cup}}.$$

It should be noted that the pentameter line is treated as being composed of two halves of two and one-half feet each.

References

In the commentary, reference is at times made to the following scholars:

ELLIS ....Robinson Ellis, *A Commentary on Catullus* (Oxford, 1889).

FORDYCE ....C. J. Fordyce, *Catullus* (Oxford, 1961).

KROLL.............Wilhelm Kroll, *Catull* (Leipzig and Berlin, 1959).

MERRILL.........E. T. Merrill, *Catullus* (Cambridge, MA., 1893).

NEUDLING......C.L. Neudling, *A Prosopography to Catullus* (Oxford, 1955).

QUINN.............Kenneth Quinn, *Catullus: The Poems* (London, 1970).

ROSS................D. O. Ross, Jr., *Style and Tradition in Catullus* (Cambridge, MA., 1969).

SKINNER.........M.B. Skinner, *Catullus' Passer* (New York, 1981).

THOMSON.......D. F. S. Thomson, *Catullus: A Critical Edition* (Chapel Hill, 1978).

WISEMAN........T. P. Wiseman, *Catullan Questions* (Leicester, 1969).

Cui dono lepidum novum libellum
arida modo pumice expolitum?
Corneli, tibi; namque tu solebas
meas esse aliquid putare nugas
iam tum, cum ausus es unus Italorum   5
omne aevum tribus explicare cartis
doctis, Iuppiter, et laboriosis.
quare habe tibi quidquid hoc libelli
qualecumque, quod, <o> patrona virgo,
plus uno maneat perenne saeclo.   10

2A

Passer, deliciae meae puellae
quicum ludere, quem in sinu tenere,
cui primum digitum dare appetenti
et acris solet incitare morsus,
cum desiderio meo nitenti   5
carum nescio quid lubet iocari,
ut solaciolum sui doloris,
credo, ut tum gravis acquiescat ardor;
tecum ludere sicut ipsa possem
et tristis animi levare curas.   10

2B

tam gratum est mihi quam ferunt puellae
pernici aureolum fuisse malum,
quod zonam soluit diu ligatam.

3

Lugete, o Veneres Cupidinesque
et quantum est hominum venustiorum:
passer mortuus est meae puellae,
passer, deliciae meae puellae,
quem plus illa oculis suis amabat;   5
nam mellitus erat suamque norat
ipsam tam bene quam puella matrem,
nec sese a gremio illius movebat,
sed circumsiliens modo huc modo illuc
ad solam dominam usque pipiabat;   10
qui nunc it per iter tenebricosum
illuc, unde negant redire quemquam.
at vobis male sit, malae tenebrae
Orci, quae omnia bella devoratis:
tam bellum mihi passerem abstulistis.   15
o factum male, quod, miselle passer,
tua nunc opera meae puellae
flendo turgiduli rubent ocelli.

4

Phaselus ille, quem videtis, hospites,
ait fuisse navium celerrimus,
neque ullius natantis impetum trabis
nequisse praeterire, sive palmulis
opus foret volare sive linteo.   5
et hoc negat minacis Hadriatici
negare litus insulasve Cycladas
Rhodumque nobilem horridamque Thraciam
Propontida trucemve Ponticum sinum,
ubi iste post phaselus antea fuit   10
comata silva; nam Cytorio in iugo

loquente saepe sibilum edidit coma.
Amastri Pontica et Cytore buxifer,
tibi haec fuisse et esse cognitissima
ait phaselus, ultima ex origine 15
tuo stetisse dicit in cacumine,
tuo imbuisse palmulas in aequore,
et inde tot per impotentia freta
erum tulisse, laeva sive dextera
vocaret aura, sive utrumque Iuppiter 20
simul secundus incidisset in pedem;
neque ulla vota litoralibus deis
sibi esse facta, cum veniret a mari
novissime hunc ad usque limpidum lacum.
sed haec prius fuere; nunc recondita 25
senet quiete seque dedicat tibi,
gemelle Castor et gemelle Castoris.

5

Vivamus, mea Lesbia, atque amemus,
rumoresque senum severiorum
omnes unius aestimemus assis.
soles occidere et redire possunt;
nobis, cum semel occidit brevis lux, 5
nox est perpetua una dormienda.
da mi basia mille, deinde centum,
dein mille altera, dein secunda centum,
deinde usque altera mille, deinde centum;
dein, cum milia multa fecerimus, 10
conturbabimus, illa ne sciamus,
aut ne quis malus invidere possit
cum tantum sciat esse basiorum.

6

Flavi, delicias tuas Catullo,
ni sint illepidae atque inelegantes,
velles dicere nec tacere posses.
verum nescio quid febriculosi
scorti diligis: hoc pudet fateri.   5
nam te non viduas iacere noctes
nequiquam tacitum cubile clamat,
sertis ac Syrio fragrans olivo,
pulvinusque peraeque et hic et ille
attritus, tremulique quassa lecti   10
argutatio inambulatioque.
nam nil stupra valet, nihil, tacere.
cur? non tam latera ecfututa pandas,
ni tu quid facias ineptiarum.
quare, quidquid habes boni malique,   15
dic nobis. volo te ac tuos amores
ad caelum lepido vocare versu.

7

Quaeris quot mihi basiationes
tuae, Lesbia, sint satis superque.
quam magnus numerus Libyssae harenae
lasarpiciferis iacet Cyrenis
oraclum Iovis inter aestuosi   5
et Batti veteris sacrum sepulcrum,
aut quam sidera multa, cum tacet nox,
furtivos hominum vident amores;
tam te basia multa basiare
vesano satis et super Catullo est,   10
quae nec pernumerare curiosi
possint nec mala fascinare lingua.

8

Miser Catulle, desinas ineptire,
et quod vides perisse perditum ducas.
fulsere quondam candidi tibi soles,
cum ventitabas quo puella ducebat
amata nobis quantum amabitur nulla.   5
ibi illa multa cum iocosa fiebant,
quae tu volebas nec puella nolebat,
fulsere vere candidi tibi soles.
nunc iam illa non vult; tu quoque inpote<ns noli>,
nec quae fugit sectare, nec miser vive,   10
sed obstinata mente perfer, obdura.
vale, puella. iam Catullus obdurat,
nec te requiret nec rogabit invitam.
at tu dolebis, cum rogaberis nulla.
scelesta, vae te! quae tibi manet vita?   15
quis nunc te adibit? cui videberis bella?
quem nunc amabis? cuius esse diceris?
quem basiabis? cui labella mordebis?
at tu, Catulle, destinatus obdura.

9

Verani, omnibus e meis amicis
antistans mihi milibus trecentis,
venistine domum ad tuos penates
fratresque unanimos anumque matrem?
venisti. o mihi nuntii beati!   5
visam te incolumem audiamque Hiberum
narrantem loca, facta, nationes,
ut mos est tuus, applicansque collum
iucundum os oculosque saviabor.
o quantum est hominum beatiorum,   10

quid me laetius est beatiusve?

10

Varus me meus ad suos amores
visum duxerat e foro otiosum,
scortillum, ut mihi tum repente visum est,
non sane illepidum neque invenustum.
huc ut venimus, incidere nobis   5
sermones varii: in quibus, quid esset
iam Bithynia; quo modo se haberet;
et quonam mihi profuisset aere.
respondi, id quod erat, nihil neque ipsis
nec praetoribus esse nec cohorti,   10
cur quisquam caput unctius referret,
praesertim quibus esset irrumator
praetor, nec faceret pili cohortem.
"at certe tamen" inquiunt "quod illic
natum dicitur esse, comparasti   15
ad lecticam homines." ego, ut puellae
unum me facerem beatiorem,
"non" inquam "mihi tam fuit maligne,
ut, provincia quod mala incidisset,
non possem octo homines parare rectos."   20
at mi nullus erat nec hic neque illic,
fractum qui veteris pedem grabati
in collo sibi collocare posset.
hic illa, ut decuit cinaediorem,
"quaeso" inquit mihi "mi Catulle, paulum   25
istos commoda; nam volo ad Serapim
deferri." "mane" inquii puellae
"istud quod modo dixeram me habere,
fugit me ratio: meus sodalis -
Cinna est Gaius - is sibi paravit.   30

verum, utrum illius an mei, quid ad me?
utor tam bene quam mihi pararim.
sed tu insulsa male et molesta vivis,
per quam non licet esse neglegentem."

11

Furi et Aureli, comites Catulli,
sive in extremos penetrabit Indos,
litus ut longe resonante Eoa
     tunditur unda,

sive in Hyrcanos Arabasve molles,   5
seu Sagas sagittiferosve Parthos,
sive quae septemgeminus colorat
     aequora Nilus,

sive trans altas gradietur Alpes,
Caesaris visens monimenta magni,   10
Gallicum Rhenum horribilesque ulti-
     mosque Britannos,

omnia haec, quaecumque feret voluntas
caelitum, temptare simul parati,
pauca nuntiate meae puellae   15
     non bona dicta.

cum suis vivat valeatque moechis,
quos simul complexa tenet trecentos,
nullum amans vere, sed identidem omnium
     ilia rumpens;   20

nec meum respectet, ut ante, amorem,
qui illius culpa cecidit velut prati

ultimi flos, praetereunte postquam
    tactus aratro est.

12

Marrucine Asini, manu sinistra
non belle uteris: in ioco atque vino
tollis lintea neglegentiorum.
hoc salsum esse putas? fugit te, inepte;
quamvis sordida res et invenusta est.   5
non credis mihi? crede Pollioni
fratri, qui tua furta vel talento
mutari velit: est enim leporum
differtus puer ac facetiarum.
quare aut hendecasyllabos trecentos   10
exspecta, aut mihi linteum remitte,
quod me non movet aestimatione,
verum est mnemosynum mei sodalis.
nam sudaria Saetaba ex Hiberis
miserunt mihi muneri Fabullus   15
et Veranius; haec amem necesse est
ut Veraniolum meum et Fabullum.

13

Cenabis bene, mi Fabulle, apud me
paucis, si tibi di favent, diebus,
si tecum attuleris bonam atque magnam
cenam, non sine candida puella
et vino et sale et omnibus cachinnis.   5
haec si, inquam, attuleris, venuste noster,
cenabis bene - nam tui Catulli
plenus sacculus est aranearum.
sed contra accipies meros amores

seu quid suavius elegantiusve est: 10
nam unguentum dabo quod meae puellae
donarunt Veneres Cupidinesque,
quod tu cum olfacies, deos rogabis
totum ut te faciant, Fabulle, nasum.

14A

Ni te plus oculis meis amarem,
iucundissime Calve, munere isto
odissem te odio Vatiniano:
nam quid feci ego quidve sum locutus,
cur me tot male perderes poetis?   5
isti di mala multa dent clienti,
qui tantum tibi misit impiorum.
quod si, ut suspicor, hoc novum ac repertum
munus dat tibi Sulla litterator,
non est mi male, sed bene ac beate,   10
quod non dispereunt tui labores.
di magni, horribilem et sacrum libellum!
quem tu scilicet ad tuum Catullum
misti continuo, ut die periret
Saturnalibus optimo dierum!   15
non non hoc tibi, salse, sic abibit.
nam, si luxerit, ad librariorum
curram scrinia; Caesios, Aquinos,
Suffenum, omnia colligam venena,
ac te his suppliciis remunerabor.   20
vos hinc interea valete abite
illuc, unde malum pedem attulistis,
saecli incommoda, pessimi poetae.

Si qui forte mearum ineptiarum
lectores eritis manusque vestras
non horrebitis admovere nobis,

....

15

Commendo tibi me ac meos amores,
Aureli. veniam peto pudentem,
ut, si quicquam animo tuo cupisti,
quod castum expeteres et integellum,
conserves puerum mihi pudice,   5
non dico a populo - nihil veremur
istos, qui in platea modo huc modo illuc
in re praetereunt sua occupati -
verum a te metuo tuoque pene
infesto pueris bonis malisque.   10
quem tu qua lubet, ut lubet, moveto
quantum vis, ubi erit foris paratum;
hunc unum excipio, ut puto, pudenter.
quod si te mala mens furorque vecors
in tantam impulerit, sceleste, culpam,   15
ut nostrum insidiis caput lacessas,
a tum te miserum malique fati!
quem attractis pedibus patente porta
percurrent raphanique mugilesque.

16

Pedicabo ego vos et irrumabo,
Aureli pathice et cinaede Furi,
qui me ex versiculis meis putastis,

quod sunt molliculi, parum pudicum.
nam castum esse decet pium poetam   5
ipsum, versiculos nihil necesse est;
qui tum denique habent salem ac leporem,
si sunt molliculi ac parum pudici,
et quod pruriat incitare possunt,
non dico pueris, sed his pilosis   10
qui duros nequeunt movere lumbos.
vos, quod milia multa basiorum
legistis, male me marem putatis?
pedicabo ego vos et irrumabo.

17

O Colonia, quae cupis ponte ludere longo,
et salire paratum habes, sed vereris inepta
crura ponticuli axulis stantis in redivivis,
ne supinus eat cavaque in palude recumbat:
sic tibi bonus ex tua pons libidine fiat,   5
in quo vel Salisubsali sacra suscipiantur,
munus hoc mihi maximi da, Colonia, risus.
quendam municipem meum de tuo volo ponte
ire praecipitem in lutum per caputque pedesque,
verum totius ut lacus putidaeque paludis   10
lividissima maximeque est profunda vorago.
insulsissimus est homo, nec sapit pueri instar
bimuli tremula patris dormientis in ulna.
cui cum sit viridissimo nupta flore puella
et puella tenellulo delicatior haedo,   15
adservanda nigerrimis diligentius uvis,
ludere hanc sinit ut lubet, nec pili facit uni,
nec se sublevat ex sua parte; sed velut alnus
in fossa Liguri iacet suppernata securi,
tantundem omnia sentiens quam si nulla sit usquam, 20

talis iste meus stupor nil videt, nihil audit;
ipse qui sit, utrum sit an non sit, id quoque nescit.
nunc eum volo de tuo ponte mittere pronum,
si pote stolidum repente excitare veternum,
et supinum animum in gravi derelinquere caeno,   25
ferream ut soleam tenaci in voragine mula.

21

Aureli, pater esuritionum,
non harum modo, sed quot aut fuerunt
aut sunt aut aliis erunt in annis,
pedicare cupis meos amores.
nec clam: nam simul es, iocaris una,   5
haerens ad latus omnia experiris.
frustra: nam insidias mihi instruentem
tangam te prior irrumatione.
atque id si faceres satur, tacerem;
nunc ipsum id doleo, quod esurire   10
a te mi puer et sitire discet.
quare desine, dum licet pudico,
ne finem facias, sed irrumatus.

22

Suffenus iste, Vare, quem probe nosti,
homo est venustus et dicax et urbanus,
idemque longe plurimos facit versus.
puto esse ego illi milia aut decem aut plura
perscripta, nec sic ut fit in palimpsesto   5
relata: cartae regiae, novi libri,
novi umbilici, lora rubra, membranae,
derecta plumbo et pumice omnia aequata.
haec cum legas tu, bellus ille et urbanus

Suffenus unus caprimulgus aut fossor   10
rursus videtur: tantum abhorret ac mutat.
hoc quid putemus esse?   qui modo scurra
aut si quid hac re scitius videbatur,
idem inficeto est inficetior rure,
simul poemata attigit, neque idem umquam   15
aeque est beatus ac poema cum scribit:
tam gaudet in se tamque se ipse miratur.
nimirum idem omnes fallimur, neque est quisquam
quem non in aliqua re videre Suffenum
possis. suus cuique attributus est error;   20
sed non videmus manticae quod in tergo est.

23

Furi, cui neque servus est neque arca
nec cimex neque araneus neque ignis,
verum est et pater et noverca, quorum
dentes vel silicem comesse possunt,
est pulcre tibi cum tuo parente   5
et cum coniuge lignea parentis.
nec mirum: bene nam valetis omnes,
pulcre concoquitis, nihil timetis,
non incendia, non graves ruinas,
non facta impia, non dolos veneni,   10
non casus alios periculorum.
atqui corpora sicciora cornu
aut siquid magis aridum est habetis
sole et frigore et esuritione.
quare non tibi sit bene ac beate?   15
a te sudor abest, abest saliva,
mucusque et mala pituita nasi.
hanc ad munditiem adde mundiorem,
quod culus tibi purior salillo est,

nec toto decies cacas in anno; 20
atque id durius est faba et lapillis,
quod tu si manibus teras fricesque,
non umquam digitum inquinare posses.
haec tu commoda tam beata, Furi,
noli spernere nec putare parvi, 25
et sestertia quae soles precari
centum desine, nam sat es beatus.

24

O qui flosculus es Iuventiorum,
non horum modo, sed quot aut fuerunt
aut posthac aliis erunt in annis,
mallem divitias Midae dedisses
isti, cui neque servus est neque arca, 5
quam sic te sineres ab illo amari.
"qui? non est homo bellus?" inquies. est:
sed bello huic neque servus est neque arca.
hoc tu quam lubet abice elevaque:
nec servum tamen ille habet neque arcam. 10

25

Cinaede Thalle, mollior cuniculi capillo
vel anseris medullula vel imula oricilla
vel pene languido senis situque araneoso,
idemque, Thalle, turbida rapacior procella
cum laeva + mulier aries + offendit oscitantes, 5
remitte pallium mihi meum, quod involasti,
sudariumque Saetabum catagraphosque Thynos,
inepte, quae palam soles habere tamquam avita.
quae nunc tuis ab unguibus reglutina et remitte,
ne laneum latusculum manusque mollicellas 10

inusta turpiter tibi flagella conscribillent,
et insolenter aestues, velut minuta magno
deprensa navis in mari, vesaniente vento.

26

Furi, villula vestra non ad Austri
flatus opposita est neque ad Favoni
nec saevi Boreae aut Apheliotae,
verum ad milia quindecim et ducentos.
o ventum horribilem atque pestilentem!   5

27

Minister vetuli puer Falerni,
inger mi calices amariores,
ut lex Postumiae iubet magistrae
ebrioso acino ebriosioris.
at vos quo lubet hinc abite, lymphae,   5
vini pernicies, et ad severos
migrate. hic merus est Thyonianus.

28

Pisonis comites, cohors inanis,
aptis sarcinulis et expeditis,
Verani optime tuque mi Fabulle,
quid rerum geritis? satisne cum isto
vappa frigoraque et famem tulistis?   5
ecquidnam in tabulis patet lucelli
expensum, ut mihi, qui meum secutus

praetorem refero datum lucello:
'o Memmi, bene me ac diu supinum
tota ista trabe lentus irrumasti.'   10
sed, quantum video, pari fuistis
casu: nam nihilo minore verpa
farti estis. pete nobiles amicos!
at vobis mala multa di deaeque
dent, opprobia Romuli Remique.   15

29

Quis hoc potest videre, quis potest pati,
nisi impudicus et vorax et aleo,
Mamurram habere quod Comata Gallia
habebat ante et ultima Britannia?
cinaede Romule, haec videbis et feres?   5
et ille nunc superbus et superfluens
perambulabit omnium cubilia,
ut albulus columbus aut Adoneus?
cinaede Romule, haec videbis et feres?
es impudicus et vorax et aleo.   10
eone nomine, imperator unice,
fuisti in ultima occidentis insula,
ut ista vestra diffututa mentula
ducenties comesset aut trecenties?
quid est alid sinistra liberalitas?   15
parum expatravit an parum helluatus est?
paterna primum lancinata sunt bona,
secunda praeda Pontica, inde tertia
Hibera, quam scit amnis aurifer Tagus:
nunc Gallicae timetur et Britannicae.   20
quid hunc malum fovetis? aut quid hic potest
nisi uncta devorare patrimonia?
eone nomine, urbis o potissimi

36

socer generque, perdidistis omnia?

30

Alfene immemor atque unanimis false sodalibus,
iam te nil miseret, dure, tui dulcis amiculi?
iam me prodere, iam non dubitas fallere, perfide?
nec facta impia fallacum hominum caelicolis placent.
quae tu neglegis ac me miserum deseris in malis.   5
eheu quid faciant, dic, homines cuive habeant fidem?
certe tute iubebas animam tradere, inique, <me>
inducens in amorem, quasi tuta omnia mi forent.
idem nunc retrahis te ac tua dicta omnia factaque
ventos irrita ferre ac nebulas aerias sinis.   10
si tu oblitus es, at di meminerunt, meminit Fides,
quae te ut paeniteat postmodo facti faciet tui.

31

Paene insularum, Sirmio, insularumque
ocelle, quascumque in liquentibus stagnis
marique vasto fert uterque Neptunus,
quam te libenter quamque laetus inviso,
vix mi ipse credens Thyniam atque Bithynos   5
liquisse campos et videre te in tuto.
o quid solutis est beatius curis,
cum mens onus reponit, ac peregrino
labore fessi venimus larem ad nostrum,
desideratoque acquiescimus lecto?   10
hoc est quod unum est pro laboribus tantis.
salve, o venusta Sirmio, atque ero gaude
gaudente, vosque o Lydiae lacus undae
ridete quidquid est domi cachinnorum.

Amabo, mea dulcis Ipsitilla,
meae deliciae, mei lepores,
iube ad te veniam meridiatum.
et si iusseris, illud adiuvato,
ne quis liminis obseret tabellam,   5
neu tibi lubeat foras abire,
sed domi maneas paresque nobis
novem continuas fututiones.
verum si quid ages, statim iubeto:
nam pransus iaceo et satur supinus   10
pertundo tunicamque palliumque.

33

O furum optime balneariorum
Vibenni pater et cinaede fili
(nam dextra pater inquinatiore,
culo filius est voraciore),
cur non exilium malasque in oras   5
itis? quandoquidem patris rapinae
notae sunt populo, et natis pilosas,
fili, non potes asse venditare.

34

Dianae sumus in fide
puellae et pueri integri:
Dianam pueri integri
    puellaeque canamus.

o Latonia, maximi   5
magna progenies Iovis,

quam mater prope Deliam
    deposivit olivam,

montium domina ut fores
silvarumque virentium   10
saltuumque reconditorum
    amniumque sonantum:

tu Lucina dolentibus
Iuno dicta puerperis,
tu potens Trivia et notho es   15
    dicta lumine Luna;

tu cursu, dea, menstruo
metiens iter annuum
rustica agricolae bonis
    tecta frugibus exples.   20

sis quocumque tibi placet
sancta nomine, Romulique,
antique ut solita es, bona
    sospites ope gentem.

35

Poetae tenero, meo sodali,
velim Caecilio, papyre, dicas
Veronam veniat, Novi relinquens
Comi moenia Lariumque litus:
nam quasdam volo cogitationes   5
amici accipiat sui meique.
quare, si sapiet, viam vorabit,
quamvis candida milies puella
euntem revocet, manusque collo

ambas iniciens roget morari.   10
quae nunc, si mihi vera nuntiantur,
illum deperit impotente amore:
nam quo tempore legit incohatam
Dindymi dominam, ex eo misellae
ignes interiorem edunt medullam.   15
ignosco tibi, Sapphica puella
musa doctior: est enim venuste
Magna Caecilio incohata Mater.

36

Annales Volusi, cacata carta,
votum solvite pro mea puella.
nam sanctae Veneri Cupidinique
vovit, si sibi restitutus essem
desissemque truces vibrare iambos,   5
electissima pessimi poetae
scripta tardipedi deo daturam
infelicibus ustulanda lignis,
et hoc pessima se puella vidit
iocose lepide vovere divis.   10
nunc, o caeruleo creata ponto,
quae sanctum Idalium Uriosque apertos
quaeque Ancona Cnidumque harundinosam
colis quaeque Amathunta quaeque Golgos
quaeque Dyrrhachium Hadriae tabernam,   15
acceptum face redditumque votum,
si non illepidum neque invenustum est.
at vos interea venite in ignem,
pleni ruris et inficetiarum
annales Volusi, cacata carta.   20

Salax taberna vosque contubernales,
a pilleatis nona fratribus pila,
solis putatis esse mentulas vobis,
solis licere, quidquid est puellarum,
confutuere et putare ceteros hircos?   5
an, continenter quod sedetis insulsi
centum an ducenti, non putatis ausurum
me una ducentos irrumare sessores?
atqui putate: namque totius vobis
frontem tabernae sopionibus scribam.   10
puella nam mi, quae meo sinu fugit,
amata tantum quantum amabitur nulla,
pro qua mihi sunt magna bella pugnata,
consedit istic. hanc boni beatique
omnes amatis, et quidem, quod indignum est,   15
omnes pusilli et semitarii moechi;
tu praeter omnes une de capillatis,
cuniculosae Celtiberiae fili,
Egnati, opaca quem bonum facit barba
et dens Hibera defricatus urina.   20

38

Malest, Cornifici, tuo Catullo,
malest, me hercule, et laboriose,
et magis magis in dies et horas.
quem tu, quod minimum facillimumque est,
qua solatus es allocutione?   5
irascor tibi. sic meos amores?
paulum quid lubet allocutionis,
maestius lacrimis Simonideis.

Egnatius, quod candidos habet dentes,
renidet usque quaque, si ad rei ventum est
subsellium, cum orator excitat fletum,
renidet ille; si ad pii rogum fili
lugetur, orba cum flet unicum mater,   5
renidet ille; quidquid est, ubicumque est,
quodcumque agit, renidet: hunc habet morbum,
neque elegantem, ut arbitror, neque urbanum.
quare monendum est <te> mihi, bone Egnati.
si urbanus esses aut Sabinus aut Tiburs   10
aut pinguis Umber aut obesus Etruscus
aut Lanuvinus ater atque dentatus
aut Transpadanus, ut meos quoque attingam,
aut quilubet, qui puriter lavit dentes,
tamen renidere usque quaque te nollem: 15
nam risu inepto res ineptior nulla est.
nunc Celtiber <es>; Celtiberia in terra,
quod quisque minxit, hoc sibi solet mane
dentem atque russam defricare gingivam;
ut, quo iste vester expolitior dens est,   20
hoc te amplius bibisse praedicet loti.

40

Quaenam te mala mens, miselle Ravide,
agit praecipitem in meos iambos?
quis deus tibi non bene advocatus
vecordem parat excitare rixam?
an ut pervenias in ora vulgi?   5
quid vis? qualubet esse notus optas?
eris, quandoquidem meos amores
cum longa voluisti amare poena.

Ameana puella defututa
tota milia me decem poposcit,
ista turpiculo puella naso,
decoctoris amica Formiani.
propinqui, quibus est puella curae,   5
amicos medicosque convocate:
non est sana puella, nec rogare
qualis sit solet aes imaginosum.

42

Adeste, hendecasyllabi, quot estis
omnes undique, quotquot estis omnes.
iocum me putat esse moecha turpis,
et negat mihi vestra redditturam
pugillaria, si pati potestis.   5
persequamur eam et reflagitemus.
quae sit, quaeritis? illa, quam videtis
turpe incedere, mimice ac moleste
ridentem catuli ore Gallicani.
circumsistite eam et reflagitate: 10
"moecha putida, redde codicillos,
redde, putida moecha, codicillos!"
non assis facis? o lutum, lupanar,
aut si perditius potest quid esse.
sed non est tamen hoc satis putandum.   15
quod si non aliud potest, ruborem
ferreo canis exprimamus ore.
conclamate iterum altiore voce
"moecha putida, redde codicillos,
redde, putida moecha, codicillos!"   20
sed nil proficimus, nihil movetur.

mutanda est ratio modusque vobis,
siquid proficere amplius potestis:
"pudica et proba, redde codicillos."

43

Salve, nec minimo puella naso
nec bello pede nec nigris ocellis
nec longis digitis nec ore sicco
nec sane nimis elegante lingua.
decoctoris amica Formiani,   5
ten provincia narrat esse bellam?
tecum Lesbia nostra comparatur?
o saeclum insapiens et inficetum!

44

O funde noster seu Sabine seu Tiburs
(nam te esse Tiburtem autumant, quibus non est
cordi Catullum laedere; at quibus cordi est,
quovis Sabinum pignore esse contendunt),
sed seu Sabine sive verius Tiburs,   5
fui libenter in tua suburbana
villa, malamque pectore expuli tussim,
non inmerenti quam mihi meus venter,
dum sumptuosas appeto, dedit, cenas.
nam, Sestianus dum volo esse conviva,   10
orationem in Antium petitorem
plenam veneni et pestilentiae legi.
hic me gravedo frigida et frequens tussis
quassavit usque, dum in tuum sinum fugi,
et me recuravi otioque et urtica.   15
quare refectus maximas tibi grates
ago, meum quod non es ulta peccatum.

44

nec deprecor iam, si nefaria scripta
Sesti recepso, quin gravedinem et tussim
non mi, sed ipsi Sestio ferat frigus,   20
qui tunc vocat me, cum malum librum legi.

45

Acmen Septimius suos amores
tenens in gremio "mea" inquit "Acme,
ni te perdite amo atque amare porro
omnes sum assidue paratus annos,
quantum qui pote plurimum perire,   5
solus in Libya Indiaque tosta
caesio veniam obvius leoni."
hoc ut dixit, Amor sinistra ut ante
dextra sternuit approbationem.
at Acme leviter caput reflectens   10
et dulcis pueri ebrios ocellos
illo purpureo ore saviata,
"sic," inquit "mea vita Septimille,
huic uni domino usque serviamus,
ut multo mihi maior acriorque   15
ignis mollibus ardet in medullis."
hoc ut dixit, Amor sinistra ut ante
dextra sternuit approbationem.
nunc ab auspicio bono profecti
mutuis animis amant amantur.   20
unam Septimius misellus Acmen
mavult quam Syrias Britanniasque;
uno in Septimio fidelis Acme
facit delicias libidinesque.
quis ullos homines beatiores   25
vidit, quis Venerem auspicatiorem?

Iam ver egelidos refert tepores,
iam caeli furor aequinoctialis
iucundis Zephyri silescit aureis.
linquantur Phrygii, Catulle, campi
Nicaeaeque ager uber aestuosae: 5
ad claras Asiae volemus urbes.
iam mens praetrepidans avet vagari,
iam laeti studio pedes vigescunt.
o dulces comitum valete coetus,
longe quos simul a domo profectos   10
diversae varie viae reportant.

47

Porci et Socration, duae sinistrae
Pisonis, scabies famesque mundi,
vos Veraniolo meo et Fabullo
verpus praeposuit Priapus ille?
vos convivia lauta sumptuose   5
de die facitis, mei sodales
quaerunt in trivio vocationes?

48

Mellitos oculos tuos, Iuventi,
si quis me sinat usque basiare,
usque ad milia basiem trecenta
nec mi umquam videar satur futurus,
non si densior aridis aristis   5
sit nostrae seges osculationis.

Disertissime Romuli nepotum,
quot sunt quotque fuere, Marce Tulli,
quotque post aliis erunt in annis,
gratias tibi maximas Catullus
agit pessimus omnium poeta, 5
tanto pessimus omnium poeta
quanto tu optimus omnium patronus.

Hesterno, Licini, die otiosi
multum lusimus in meis tabellis,
ut convenerat esse delicatos:
scribens versiculos uterque nostrum
ludebat numero modo hoc modo illoc, 5
reddens mutua per iocum atque vinum.
atque illinc abii tuo lepore
incensus, Licini, facetiisque,
ut nec me miserum cibus iuvaret
nec somnus tegeret quiete ocellos, 10
sed toto indomitus furore lecto
versarer, cupiens videre lucem,
ut tecum loquerer simulque ut essem.
at defessa labore membra postquam
semimortua lectulo iacebant, 15
hoc, iucunde, tibi poema feci,
ex quo perspiceres meum dolorem.
nunc audax cave sis, precesque nostras,
oramus, cave despuas, ocelle,
ne poenas Nemesis reposcat a te. 20
est vemens dea: laedere hanc caveto.

Ille mi par esse deo videtur,
ille, si fas est, superare divos,
qui sedens adversus identidem te
   spectat et audit

dulce ridentem, misero quod omnis   5
eripit sensus mihi: nam simul te,
Lesbia, aspexi, nihil est super mi
   ....

lingua sed torpet, tenuis sub artus
flamma demanat, sonitu suopte   10
tintinant aures, gemina teguntur
   lumina nocte.

otium, Catulle, tibi molestum est;
otio exsultas nimiumque gestis;
otium et reges prius et beatas   15
   perdidit urbes.

Quid est, Catulle? quid moraris emori?
sella in curuli struma Nonius sedet;
per consulatum peierat Vatinius;
quid est, Catulle? quid moraris emori?

Risi nescio quem modo e corona,
qui, cum mirifice Vatiniana
meus crimina Calvus explicasset,

admirans ait haec manusque tollens:
"di magni, salaputium disertum!"   5

54

Othonis caput oppido est pusillum,
+et eri+ rustica semilauta crura,
subtile et leve peditum Libonis;
si non omnia, displicere vellem
tibi et Sufficio seni recocto.   5
irascere iterum meis iambis
inmerentibus, unice imperator.

55

Oramus, si forte non molestum est,
demonstres ubi sint tuae tenebrae.
te in Campo quaesivimus minore,
te in Circo, te in omnibus libellis,
te in templo summi Iovis sacrato.   5
in Magni simul ambulatione
femellas omnes, amice, prendi,
quas vultu vidi tamen sereno.
+avelte+ (sic ipse flagitabam)
"Camerium mihi, pessimae puellae!"   10
quaedam inquit, nudum reduc...
"en hic in roseis latet papillis."
sed te iam ferre Herculei labos est;
tanto te in fastu negas, amice?
dic nobis ubi sis futurus, ede   15
audacter, committe, crede luci.
nunc te lacteolae tenent puellae?
si linguam clauso tenes in ore,
fructus proicies amoris omnes;

verbosa gaudet Venus loquella.   20
vel, si vis, licet obseres palatum,
dum vestri sim particeps amoris.

56

O rem ridiculam, Cato, et iocosam,
dignamque auribus et tuo cachinno!
ride quidquid amas, Cato, Catullum:
res est ridicula et nimis iocosa.
deprendi modo pupulum puellae   5
trusantem; hunc ego, si placet Dionae,
pro telo rigida mea cecidi.

57

Pulcre convenit improbis cinaedis,
Mamurrae pathicoque Caesarique.
nec mirum: maculae pares utrisque,
urbana altera et illa Formiana,
impressae resident nec eluentur: 5
morbosi pariter, gemelli utrique,
uno in lecticulo erudituli ambo,
non hic quam ille magis vorax adulter,
rivales socii et puellularum.
pulcre convenit improbis cinaedis.   10

58A

Caeli, Lesbia nostra, Lesbia illa,
illa Lesbia, quam Catullus unam
plus quam se atque suos amavit omnes,
nunc in quadriviis et angiportis
glubit magnanimi Remi nepotes.   5

Non custos si fingar ille Cretum,
non si Pegaseo ferar volatu,
non Ladas ego pinnipesve Perseus,
non Rhesi niveae citaeque bigae;
adde huc plumipedas volatilesque,   5
ventorumque simul require cursum,
quos cunctos, Cameri, mihi dicares;
defessus tamen omnibus medullis
et multis languoribus peresus
essem te mihi, amice, quaeritando.   10

59

Bononiensis Rufa Rufulum fellat,
uxor Meneni, saepe quam in sepulcretis
vidistis ipso rapere de rogo cenam,
cum devolutum ex igne prosequens panem
ab semiraso tunderetur ustore.   5

60

Num te leaena montibus Libystinis
aut Scylla latrans infima inguinum parte
tam mente dura procreavit ac taetra
ut supplicis vocem in novissimo casu
contemptam haberes, a nimis fero corde?   5

61

Collis o Heliconii
cultor, Uraniae genus,
qui rapis teneram ad virum

virginem, o Hymenaee Hymen,
    o Hymen Hymenaee;   5

cinge tempora floribus
suave olentis amaraci,
flammeum cape, laetus huc
huc veni, niveo gerens
    luteum pede soccum;   10

excitusque hilari die,
nuptialia concinens
voce carmina tinnula,
pelle humum pedibus, manu
    pineam quate taedam.   15

namque Iunia Manlio,
qualis Idalium colens
venit ad Phrygium Venus
iudicem, bona cum bona
    nubet alite virgo,   20

floridis velut enitens
myrtus Asia ramulis
quos Hamadryades deae
ludicrum sibi roscido
    nutriunt umore.   25

quare age, huc aditum ferens,
perge linquere Thespiae
rupis Aonios specus,
nympha quos super irrigat
    frigerans Aganippe.   30

ac domum dominam voca

coniugis cupidam novi,
mentem amore revinciens,
ut tenax hedera huc et huc
    arborem implicat errans. 35

vosque item simul, integrae
virgines, quibus advenit
par dies, agite in modum
dicite, o Hymenaee Hymen,
    o Hymen Hymenaee. 40

ut lubentius, audiens
se citarier ad suum
munus, huc aditum ferat
dux bonae Veneris, boni
    coniugator amoris. 45

quis deus magis anxiis
est petendus amantibus?
quem colent homines magis
caelitum, o Hymenaee Hymen,
    o Hymen Hymenaee? 50

te suis tremulus parens
invocat, tibi virgines
zonula soluunt sinus,
te timens cupida novus
    captat aure maritus. 55

tu fero iuveni in manus
floridam ipse puellulam
dedis a gremio suae
matris, o Hymenaee Hymen,
    o Hymen Hymenaee. 60

nil potest sine te Venus,
fama quod bona comprobet,
commodi capere, at potest
te volente. quis huic deo
    compararier ausit? 65

nulla quit sine te domus
liberos dare, nec parens
stirpe nitier; at potest
te volente. quis huic deo
    compararier ausit? 70

quae tuis careat sacris,
non queat dare praesides
terra finibus; at queat
te volente. quis huic deo
    compararier ausit? 75

claustra pandite ianuae;
virgo, ades. viden ut faces
splendidas quatiunt comas?
    ....
      ....

    ....
    ....
tardet ingenuus pudor.
quem tamen magis audiens, 80
    flet quod ire necesse est.

flere desine. non tibi, Aurunculeia, periculum est
ne qua femina pulcrior
clarum ab Oceano diem 85

viderit venientem.

talis in vario solet
divitis domini hortulo
stare flos hyacinthinus.
sed moraris, abit dies.   90
    <prodeas, nova nupta.>

prodeas, nova nupta, si
iam videtur, et audias
nostra verba. viden? faces
aureas quatiunt comas;   95
    prodeas, nova nupta.

non tuus levis in mala
deditus vir adultera,
probra turpia persequens,
a tuis teneris volet   100
    secubare papillis,

lenta sed velut adsitas
vitis implicat arbores,
implicabitur in tuum
complexum. sed abit dies;   105
    prodeas, nova nupta.

o cubile, quod omnibus
    ....
    ....
    ....
    candido pede lecti,

quae tuo veniunt ero,
quanta gaudia, quae vaga   110

nocte, quae medio die
gaudeat! sed abit dies;
    prodeas, nova nupta.

tollite, <o> pueri, faces:
flammeum video venire.   115
ite concinite in modum
"io Hymen Hymenaee io,
    io Hymen Hymenaee."

ne diu taceat procax
Fescennina iocatio,   120
nec nuces pueris neget
desertum domini audiens
    concubinus amorem.

da nuces pueris, iners
concubine; satis diu   125
lusisti nucibus; lubet
iam servire Talasio.
    concubine, nuces da.

sordebant tibi vilicae,
concubine, hodie atque heri;   130
nunc tuum cinerarius
tondet os. miser a miser
    concubine, nuces da.

diceris male te a tuis
unguentate glabris, marite,   135
abstinere, sed abstine.
io Hymen Hymenaee io,
    io Hymen Hymenaee.

scimus haec tibi quae licent
sola cognita, sed marito   140
ista non eadem licent.
io Hymen Hymenaee io,
    io Hymen Hymenaee.

nupta, tu quoque quae tuus
vir petet cave ne neges,   145
ni petitum aliunde eat.
io Hymen Hymenaee io,
    io Hymen Hymenaee.

en tibi domus ut potens
et beata viri tui,   150
quae tibi sine serviat
(io Hymen Hymenaee io,
    io Hymen Hymenaee)

usque dum tremulum movens
cana tempus anilitas   155
omnia omnibus annuit.
io Hymen Hymenaee io,
    io Hymen Hymenaee.

transfer omine cum bono
limen aureolos pedes,   160
rasilemque subi forem.
io Hymen Hymenaee io,
    io Hymen Hymenaee.

aspice intus ut accubans
vir tuus Tyrio in toro   165
totus immineat tibi.
io Hymen Hymenaee io,

io Hymen Hymenaee.

illi non minus ac tibi
pectore uritur intimo
flamma, sed penite magis.
io Hymen Hymenaee io,
    io Hymen Hymenaee.

mitte brachiolum teres,
praetextate, puellulae:
iam cubile adeat viri.
io Hymen Hymenaee io,
    io Hymen Hymenaee.

<vos> bonae senibus viris
cognitae bene feminae
collocate puellulam.
io Hymen Hymenaee io,
    io Hymen Hymenaee.

iam licet venias, marite:
uxor in thalamo tibi est,
ore floridulo nitens
alba parthenice velut
    luteumve papaver.

at, marite, ita me iuvent
caelites, nihilo minus
pulcer es, neque te Venus
neglegit. sed abit dies;
    perge, ne remorare.

non diu remoratus es:
iam venis. bona te Venus

170

175

180

185

190

195

iuverit, quoniam palam
quod cupis cupis, et bonum
    non abscondis amorem.

ille pulveris Africi
siderumque micantium   200
subducat numerum prius,
qui vestri numerare vult
    multa milia ludi.

ludite ut lubet, et brevi
liberos date. non decet   205
tam vetus sine liberis
nomen esse, sed indidem
    semper ingenerari.

Torquatus volo parvulus
matris e gremio suae   210
porrigens teneras manus
dulce rideat ad patrem
    semihiante labello.

sit suo similis patri
Manlio et facile omnibus   215
noscitetur ab insciis,
et pudicitiam suae
    matris indicet ore.

talis illius a bona
matre laus genus approbet,   220
qualis unica ab optima
matre Telemacho manet
    fama Penelopaeo.

claudite ostia, virgines:
lusimus satis. at, boni   225
coniuges, bene vivite et
munere assiduo valentem
    exercete iuventam.

62

Vesper adest; iuvenes, consurgite; Vesper Olympo
exspectata diu vix tandem lumina tollit.
surgere iam tempus, iam pinguis linquere mensas;
iam veniet virgo, iam dicetur hymenaeus.
Hymen o Hymenaee, Hymen ades o Hymenaee!   5

Cernitis, innuptae, iuvenes? consurgite contra;
nimirum Oetaeos ostendit Noctifer ignes.
sic certest; viden ut perniciter exsiluere?
non temere exsiluere; canent quod vincere par est.
Hymen o Hymenaee, Hymen ades o Hymenaee!   10

Non facilis nobis, aequales, palma parata est;
aspicite, innuptae secum ut meditata requirunt.
non frustra meditantur: habent memorabile quod sit;
nec mirum, penitus quae tota mente laborant.
nos alio mentes, alio divisimus aures;   15
iure igitur vincemur: amat victoria curam.
quare nunc animos saltem convertite vestros;
dicere iam incipient, iam respondere decebit.
Hymen o Hymenaee, Hymen ades o Hymenaee!

Hespere, quis caelo fertur crudelior ignis?   20
qui natam possis complexu avellere matris,
complexu matris retinentem avellere natam,
et iuveni ardenti castam donare puellam.

quid faciunt hostes capta crudelius urbe?
Hymen o Hymenaee, Hymen ades o Hymenaee!   25

Hespere, quis caelo lucet iucundior ignis?
qui desponsa tua firmes conubia flamma,
quae pepigere viri, pepigerunt ante parentes,
nec iunxere prius quam se tuus extulit ardor.
quid datur a divis felici optatius hora?   30
Hymen o Hymenaee, Hymen ades o Hymenaee!

Hesperus e nobis, aequales, abstulit unam.
....

....
namque tuo adventu vigilat custodia semper.
nocte latent fures, quos idem saepe revertens,
Hespere, mutato comprendis nomine Eous.   35
at lubet innuptis ficto te carpere questu.
quid tum, si carpunt, tacita quem mente requirunt?
Hymen o Hymenaee, Hymen ades o Hymenaee!

Ut flos in saeptis secretus nascitur hortis,
ignotus pecori, nullo convulsus aratro,   40
quem mulcent aurae, firmat sol, educat imber;
multi illum pueri, multae optavere puellae;
idem cum tenui carptus defloruit ungui,
nulli illum pueri, nullae optavere puellae:
sic virgo, dum intacta manet, dum cara suis est;   45
cum castum amisit polluto corpore florem,
nec pueris iucunda manet, nec cara puellis.
Hymen o Hymenaee, Hymen ades o Hymenaee!

Ut vidua in nudo vitis quae nascitur arvo,
numquam se extollit, numquam mitem educat uvam,   50

sed tenerum prono deflectens pondere corpus
iam iam contingit summum radice flagellum;
hanc nulli agricolae, nulli coluere iuvenci;
at si forte eadem est ulmo coniuncta marito,
multi illam agricolae, multi coluere iuvenci: 55
sic virgo dum intacta manet, dum inculta senescit;
cum par conubium maturo tempore adepta est,
cara viro magis et minus est invisa parenti.
<Hymen o Hymenaee, Hymen ades o Hymenaee!>   58B

Et tu ne pugna cum tali coniuge, virgo.
non aequum est pugnare, pater cui tradidit ipse,   60
ipse pater cum matre, quibus parere necesse est.
virginitas non tota tua est, ex parte parentum est,
tertia pars patris est, pars est data tertia matri,
tertia sola tua est: noli pugnare duobus,
qui genero sua iura simul cum dote dederunt.   65
Hymen o Hymenaee, Hymen ades o Hymenaee!

63

Super alta vectus Attis celeri rate maria,
Phrygium ut nemus citato cupide pede tetigit
adiitque opaca silvis redimita loca deae,
stimulatus ibi furenti rabie, vagus animis,
devovit ili acuto sibi pondera silice.   5
itaque ut relicta sensit sibi membra sine viro,
etiam recente terrae sola sanguine maculans,
niveis citata cepit manibus leve typanum,
typanum tuum, Cybebe, tua, mater, initia,
quatiensque terga tauri teneris cava digitis   10
canere haec suis adorta est tremebunda comitibus.
"agite ite ad alta, Gallae, Cybeles nemora simul,
simul ite, Dindymenae dominae vaga pecora,

aliena quae petentes velut exules loca
sectam meam exsecutae duce me mihi comites   15
rapidum salum tulistis truculentaque pelagi,
et corpus evirastis Veneris nimio odio;
hilarate erae citatis erroribus animum.
mora tarda mente cedat: simul ite, sequimini
Phrygiam ad domum Cybebes, Phrygia ad nemora deae,   20
ubi cymbalum sonat vox, ubi tympana reboant,
tibicen ubi canit Phryx curvo grave calamo,
ubi capita Maenades vi iaciunt hederigerae,
ubi sacra sancta acutis ululatibus agitant,
ubi suevit illa divae volitare vaga cohors,   25
quo nos decet citatis celerare tripudiis."
simul haec comitibus Attis cecinit notha mulier,
thiasus repente linguis trepidantibus ululat,
leve tympanum remugit, cava cymbala recrepant,
viridem citus adit Idam properante pede chorus.   30
furibunda simul anhelans vaga vadit animam agens
comitata tympano Attis per opaca nemora dux,
veluti iuvenca vitans onus indomita iugi;
rapidae ducem sequuntur Gallae properipedem.
itaque, ut domum Cybebes tetigere lassulae,   35
nimio e labore somnum capiunt sine Cerere.
piger his labante languore oculos sopor operit;
abit in quiete molli rabidus furor animi.
sed ubi oris aurei sol radiantibus oculis
lustravit aethera album, sola dura, mare ferum,   40
pepulitque noctis umbras vegetis sonipedibus,
ibi Somnus excitam Attin fugiens citus abiit;
trepidante eum recepit dea Pasithea sinu.
ita de quiete molli rapida sine rabie
simul ipsa pectore Attis sua facta recoluit,   45
liquidaque mente vidit sine quis ubique foret,
animo aestuante rusum reditum ad vada tetulit.

ibi maria vasta visens lacrimantibus oculis
patriam allocuta maestast ita voce miseriter.
"patria o mei creatrix, patria o mea genetrix,   50
ego quam miser relinquens, dominos ut erifugae
famuli solent, ad Idae tetuli nemora pedem,
ut apud nivem et ferarum gelida stabula forem,
et earum opaca adirem furibunda latibula,
ubinam aut quibus locis te positam, patria, reor?   55
cupit ipsa pupula ad te sibi derigere aciem,
rabie fera carens dum breve tempus animus est.
egone a mea remota haec ferar in nemora domo?
patria, bonis, amicis, genitoribus abero?
abero foro, palaestra, stadio et gyminasiis?   60
miser a miser, querendum est etiam atque etiam, anime.
quod enim genus figurae est, ego non quod obierim?
ego mulier, ego adolescens, ego ephebus, ego puer,
ego gymnasi fui flos, ego eram decus olei:
mihi ianuae frequentes, mihi limina tepida,   65
mihi floridis corollis redimita domus erat,
linquendum ubi esset orto mihi sole cubiculum.
ego nunc deum ministra et Cybeles famula ferar?
ego Maenas, ego mei pars, ego vir sterilis ero?
ego viridis algida Idae nive amicta loca colam?   70
ego vitam agam sub altis Phrygiae columinibus,
ubi cerva silvicultrix, ubi aper nemorivagus?
iam iam dolet quod egi, iam iamque paenitet."
roseis ut hinc labellis sonitus <citus> abiit,
geminas deorum ad aures nova nuntia referens,   75
ibi iuncta iuga resolvens Cybele leonibus
saevumque pecoris hostem stimulans ita loquitur:
"agedum," inquit "age ferox <i>, fac ut hunc furor
                                             <agitet>,
fac uti furoris ictu reditum in nemora ferat,
mea libere nimis qui fugere imperia cupit.   80

age caede terga cauda, tua verbera patere,
fac cuncta mugienti fremitu loca retonent,
rutilam ferox torosa cervice quate iubam."
ait haec minax Cybebe religatque iuga manu.
ferus ipse sese adhortans rabidum incitat animo, 85
vadit, fremit, refringit virgulta pede vago.
at ubi umida albicantis loca litoris adiit,
tenerumque vidit Attin prope marmora pelagi,
facit impetum. illa demens fugit in nemora fera;
ibi semper omne vitae spatium famula fuit. 90

dea magna, dea Cybebe, dea domina Dindymi,
procul a mea tuus sit furor omnis, era, domo:
alios age incitatos, alios age rabidos.

64

Peliaco quondam prognatae vertice pinus
dicuntur liquidas Neptuni nasse per undas
Phasidos ad fluctus et fines Aeetaeos,
cum lecti iuvenes, Argivae robora pubis,
auratam optantes Colchis avertere pellem 5
ausi sunt vada salsa cita decurrere puppi,
caerula verrentes abiegnis aequora palmis.
diva quibus retinens in summis urbibus arces
ipsa levi fecit volitantem flamine currum,
pinea coniungens inflexae texta carinae. 10
illa rudem cursu prima imbuit Amphitriten;
quae simul ac rostro ventosum proscidit aequor
tortaque remigio spumis incanuit unda,
emersere feri candenti e gurgite vultus
aequoreae monstrum Nereides admirantes. 15
illa, atque <haud> alia, viderunt luce marinas
mortales oculis nudato corpore Nymphas

65

nutricum tenus exstantes e gurgite cano.
tum Thetidis Peleus incensus fertur amore,
tum Thetis humanos non despexit hymenaeos,   20
tum Thetidi pater ipse iugandum Pelea sensit.
o nimis optato saeclorum tempore nati
heroes, salvete, deum genus! o bona matrum
progenies, salvete! iter<um salvete, bonarum!>   23b
vos ego saepe, meo vos carmine compellabo.
teque adeo eximie taedis felicibus aucte,   25
Thessaliae columen Peleu, cui Iuppiter ipse,
ipse suos divum genitor concessit amores;
tene Thetis tenuit pulcerrima Nereine?
tene suam Tethys concessit ducere neptem,
Oceanusque, mari totum qui amplectitur orbem?   30
quae simul optatae finito tempore luces
advenere, domum conventu tota frequentat
Thessalia, oppletur laetanti regia coetu;
dona ferunt prae se, declarant gaudia vultu.
deseritur Cieros; linquunt Pthiotica Tempe   35
Crannonisque domos ac moenia Larisaea;
Pharsalum coeunt, Pharsalia tecta frequentant.
rura colit nemo, mollescunt colla iuvencis,
non humilis curvis purgatur vinea rastris,
non glebam prono convellit vomere taurus,   40
non falx attenuat frondatorum arboris umbram;
squalida desertis robigo infertur aratris.
ipsius at sedes, quacumque opulenta recessit
regia, fulgenti splendent auro atque argento:
candet ebur soliis; collucent pocula mensae;   45
tota domus gaudet regali splendida gaza.
pulvinar vero divae geniale locatur
sedibus in mediis, Indo quod dente politum
tincta tegit roseo conchyli purpura fuco.
haec vestis priscis hominum variata figuris   50

66

heroum mira virtutes indicat arte.
namque fluentisono prospectans litore Diae
Thesea cedentem celeri cum classe tuetur
indomitos in corde gerens Ariadna furores,
necdum etiam sese quae visit visere credit,   55
utpote fallaci quae tum primum excita somno
desertam in sola miseram se cernat harena.
immemor at iuvenis fugiens pellit vada remis,
irrita ventosae linquens promissa procellae;
quem procul ex alga maestis Minois ocellis   60
saxea ut effigies bacchantis, prospicit, eheu,
prospicit et magnis curarum fluctuat undis,
non flavo retinens subtilem vertice mitram,
non contecta levi velatum pectus amictu,
non tereti strophio lactentis vincta papillas,   65
omnia quae toto delapsa e corpore passim
ipsius ante pedes fluctus salis alludebant.
sed neque tum mitrae neque tum fluitantis amictus
illa vicem curans toto ex te pectore, Theseu,
toto animo, tota pendebat perdita mente.   70
a misera, assiduis quam luctibus externavit
spinosas Erycina serens in pectore curas,
illa tempestate, ferox quo ex tempore Theseus
egressus curvis e litoribus Piraei
attigit iniusti regis Gortynia templa.   75
nam perhibent olim crudeli peste coactam
Androgeoneae poenas exsolvere caedis
electos iuvenes simul et decus innuptarum
Cecropiam solitam esse dapem dare Minotauro.
quis angusta malis cum moenia vexarentur,   80
ipse suum Theseus pro caris corpus Athenis
proicere optavit potius quam talia Cretam
funera Cecropiae nec funera portarentur.
atque ita nave levi nitens ac lenibus auris

magnanimum ad Minoa venit sedesque superbas.   85
hunc simul ac cupido conspexit lumine virgo
regia, quam suavis exspirans castus odores
lectulus in molli complexu matris alebat,
quales Eurotae progignunt flumina myrtus
aurave distinctos educit verna colores,   90
non prius ex illo flagrantia declinavit
lumina, quam cuncto concepit corpore flammam
funditus atque imis exarsit tota medullis.
heu misere exagitans immiti corde furores
sancte puer, curis hominum qui gaudia misces,   95
quaeque regis Golgos quaeque Idalium frondosum,
qualibus incensam iactastis mente puellam
fluctibus, in flavo saepe hospite suspirantem!
quantos illa tulit languenti corde timores!
quam tum saepe magis fulgore expalluit auri,   100
cum saevum cupiens contra contendere monstrum
aut mortem appeteret Theseus aut praemia laudis!
non ingrata tamen frustra munuscula divis
promittens tacito succepit vota labello,
nam velut in summo quatientem brachia Tauro   105
quercum aut conigeram sudanti cortice pinum
indomitus turbo contorquens flamine robur
eruit (illa procul radicitus exturbata
prona cadit, late quaeviscumque obvia frangens),
sic domito saevum prostravit corpore Theseus   110
nequiquam vanis iactantem cornua ventis.
inde pedem sospes multa cum laude reflexit
errabunda regens tenui vestigia filo,
ne labyrintheis e flexibus egredientem
tecti frustraretur inobservabilis error.   115
sed quid ego a primo digressus carmine plura
commemorem, ut linquens genitoris filia vultum,
ut consanguineae complexum, ut denique matris,

quae misera in gnata deperdita laeta<batur>,
omnibus his Thesei dulcem praeoptarit amorem;   120
aut ut vecta rati spumosa ad litora Diae
<venerit,> aut ut eam devinctam lumina somno
liquerit immemori discedens pectore coniunx?
saepe illam perhibent ardenti corde furentem
clarisonas imo fudisse e pectore voces,   125
ac tum praeruptos tristem conscendere montes,
unde aciem in pelagi vastos protenderet aestus,
tum tremuli salis adversas procurrere in undas
mollia nudatae tollentem tegmina surae,
atque haec extremis maestam dixisse querellis,   130
frigidulos udo singultus ore cientem:
"sicine me patriis avectam, perfide, ab aris,
perfide, deserto liquisti in litore, Theseu?
sicine discedens neglecto numine divum,
immemor a! devota domum periuria portas?   135
nullane res potuit crudelis flectere mentis
consilium? tibi nulla fuit clementia praesto,
immite ut nostri vellet miserescere pectus?
at non haec quondam blanda promissa dedisti
voce mihi, non haec miseram sperare iubebas,   140
sed conubia laeta, sed optatos hymenaeos,
quae cuncta aerii discerpunt irrita venti.
nunc iam nulla viro iuranti femina credat,
nulla viri speret sermones esse fideles,
quis dum aliquid cupiens animus praegestit apisci,   145
nil metuunt iurare, nihil promittere parcunt;
sed simul ac cupidae mentis satiata libido est,
dicta nihil meminere, nihil periuria curant.
certe ego te in medio versantem turbine leti
eripui, et potius germanum amittere crevi   150
quam tibi fallaci supremo in tempore dessem.
pro quo dilaceranda feris dabor alitibusque

praeda, neque iniacta tumulabor mortua terra.
quaenam te genuit sola sub rupe leaena,
quod mare conceptum spumantibus exspuit undis, 155
quae Syrtis, quae Scylla rapax, quae vasta Charybdis,
talia qui reddis pro dulci praemia vita?
si tibi non cordi fuerant conubia nostra,
saeva quod horrebas prisci praecepta parentis,
attamen in vestras potuisti ducere sedes, 160
quae tibi iucundo famularer serva labore,
candida permulcens liquidis vestigia lymphis,
purpureave tuum consternens veste cubile.
sed quid ego ignaris nequiquam conqueror auris,
exsternata malo, quae nullis sensibus auctae 165
nec missas audire queunt nec reddere voces?
ille autem prope iam mediis versatur in undis,
nec quisquam apparet vacua mortalis in alga.
sic nimis insultans extremo tempore saeva
fors etiam nostris invidit questibus auris. 170
Iuppiter omnipotens, utinam ne tempore primo
Gnosia Cecropiae tetigissent litora puppes,
indomito nec dira ferens stipendia tauro
perfidus in Creta religasset navita funem,
nec malus hic celans dulci crudelia forma 175
consilia in nostris requiesset sedibus hospes!
nam quo me referam? quali spe perdita nitor?
Idaeosne petam montes? at gurgite lato
discernens ponti truculentum dividit aequor.
an patris auxilium sperem? quemne ipsa reliqui 180
respersum iuvenem fraterna caede secuta?
coniugis an fido consoler memet amore?
quine fugit lentos incurvans gurgite remos?
praeterea nullo colitur sola insula tecto,
nec patet egressus pelagi cingentibus undis. 185
nulla fugae ratio, nulla spes: omnia muta,

omnia sunt deserta, ostentant omnia letum.
non tamen ante mihi languescent lumina morte,
nec prius a fesso secedent corpore sensus,
quam iustam a divis exposcam prodita multam
caelestumque fidem postrema comprecer hora.
quare facta virum multantes vindice poena
Eumenides, quibus anguino redimita capillo
frons exspirantis praeportat pectoris iras,
huc huc adventate, meas audite querellas,
quas ego, vae misera, extremis proferre medullis
cogor inops, ardens, amenti caeca furore.
quae quoniam verae nascuntur pectore ab imo,
vos nolite pati nostrum vanescere luctum,
sed quali solam Theseus me mente reliquit,
tali mente, deae, funestet seque suosque."
has postquam maesto profudit pectore voces,
supplicium saevis exposcens anxia factis,
annuit invicto caelestum numine rector;
quo motu tellus atque horrida contremuerunt
aequora concussitque micantia sidera mundus.
ipse autem caeca mentem caligine Theseus
consitus oblito dimisit pectore cuncta
quae mandata prius constanti mente tenebat,
dulcia nec maesto sustollens signa parenti
sospitem Erectheum se ostendit visere portum.
namque ferunt olim, classi cum moenia divae
linquentem gnatum ventis concrederet Aegeus,
talia complexum iuveni mandata dedisse:
"gnate mihi longa iucundior unice vita,
gnate, ego quem in dubios cogor dimittere casus,
reddite in extrema nuper mihi fine senectae,
quandoquidem fortuna mea ac tua fervida virtus
eripit invito mihi te, cui languida nondum
lumina sunt gnati cara saturata figura,

190

195

200

205

210

215

220

non ego te gaudens laetanti pectore mittam,
nec te ferre sinam fortunae signa secundae,
sed primum multas expromam mente querellas,
canitiem terra atque infuso pulvere foedans;
inde infecta vago suspendam lintea malo, 225
nostros ut luctus nostraeque incendia mentis
carbasus obscurata dicet ferrugine Hibera.
quod tibi si sancti concesserit incola Itoni,
quae nostrum genus ac sedes defendere Erecthei
annuit, ut tauri respergas sanguine dextram, 230
tum vero facito ut memori tibi condita corde
haec vigeant mandata, nec ulla oblitteret aetas;
ut simul ac nostros invisent lumina collis
funestam antennae deponant undique vestem
candidaque intorti sustollant vela rudentes, 235
quam primum cernens ut laeta gaudia mente
agnoscam, cum te reducem aetas prospera sistet."
haec mandata prius constanti mente tenentem
Thesea ceu pulsae ventorum flamine nubes
aerium nivei montis liquere cacumen. 240
at pater, ut summa prospectum ex arce petebat,
anxia in assiduos absumens lumina fletus,
cum primum inflati conspexit lintea veli,
praecipitem sese scopulorum e vertice iecit,
amissum credens immiti Thesea fato. 245
sic, funesta domus ingressus tecta paterna
morte, ferox Theseus, qualem Minoidi luctum
obtulerat mente immemori, talem ipse recepit.
quae tum prospectans cedentem maesta carinam
multiplices animo volvebat saucia curas. 250
at parte ex alia florens volitabat Iacchus
cum thiaso Satyrorum et Nysigenis Silenis,
te quaerens, Ariadna, tuoque incensus amore.
....

quae tum alacres passim lymphata mente furebant
euhoe bacchantes, euhoe capita inflectentes.   255
harum pars tecta quatiebant cuspide thyrsos,
pars e divolso iactabant membra iuvenco,
pars sese tortis serpentibus incingebant,
pars obscura cavis celebrabant orgia cistis,
orgia quae frustra cupiunt audire profani;   260
plangebant aliae proceris tympana palmis,
aut tereti tenuis tinnitus aere ciebant;
multis raucisonos efflabant cornua bombos
barbaraque horribili stridebat tibia cantu.
talibus amplifice vestis decorata figuris   265
pulvinar complexa suo velabat amictu.
quae postquam cupide spectando Thessala pubes
expleta est, sanctis coepit decedere divis.
hic, qualis flatu placidum mare matutino
horrificans Zephyrus proclivas incitat undas,   270
Aurora exoriente vagi sub limina solis,
quae tarde primum clementi flamine pulsae
procedunt leviterque sonant plangore cachinni,
post vento crescente magis magis increbescunt,
purpureaque procul nantes ab luce refulgent: 275
sic tum vestibuli linquentes regia tecta
ad se quisque vago passim pede discedebant.
quorum post abitum princeps e vertice Peli
advenit Chiron portans silvestria dona:
nam quoscumque ferunt campi, quos Thessala magnis   280
montibus ora creat, quos propter fluminis undas
aura parit flores tepidi fecunda Favoni,
hos indistinctis plexos tulit ipse corollis;
quo permulsa domus iucundo risit odore.
confestim Penios adest, viridantia Tempe,   285
Tempe, quae silvae cingunt super impendentes,
Haemonisin linquens claris celebranda choreis,

73

non vacuus: namque ille tulit radicitus altas
fagos ac recto proceras stipite laurus,
non sine nutanti platano lentaque sorore   290
flammati Phaethontis et aeria cupressu.
haec circum sedes late contexta locavit,
vestibulum ut molli velatum fronde vireret.
post hunc consequitur sollerti corde Prometheus,
extenuata gerens veteris vestigia poenae,   295
quam quondam silici restrictus membra catena
persoluit pendens e verticibus praeruptis.
inde pater divum sancta cum coniuge natisque
advenit caelo, te solum, Phoebe, relinquens
unigenamque simul cultricem montibus Idri: 300
Pelea nam tecum pariter soror aspernata est,
nec Thetidis taedas voluit celebrare iugalis.
qui postquam niveis flexerunt sedibus artus,
large multiplici constructae sunt dape mensae,
cum interea infirmo quatientes corpora motu   305
veridicos Parcae coeperunt edere cantus.
his corpus tremulum complectens undique vestis
candida purpurea talos incinxerat ora,
at roseae niveo residebant vertice vittae,
aeternumque manus carpebant rite laborem.   310
laeva colum molli lana retinebat amictum,
dextera tum leviter deducens fila supinis
formabat digitis, tum prono in pollice torquens
libratum tereti versabat turbine fusum,
atque ita decerpens aequabat semper opus dens,   315
laneaque aridulis haerebant morsa labellis,
quae prius in levi fuerant exstantia filo;
ante pedes autem candentis mollia lanae
vellera virgati custodibant calathisci.
haec tum clarisona vellentes vellera voce   320
talia divino fuderunt carmine fata,

carmine, perfidiae quod post nulla arguet aetas.
"o decus eximium magnis virtutibus augens,
Emathiae tutamen, Opis carissime nato,
accipe, quod laeta tibi pandunt luce sorores,   325
veridicum oraclum; sed vos, quae fata sequuntur,
    currite ducentes subtegmina, currite, fusi.
adveniet tibi iam portans optata maritis
Hesperus, adveniet fausto cum sidere coniunx,
quae tibi flexanimo mentem perfundat amore,   330
languidulosque paret tecum coniungere somnos,
levia substernens robusto brachia collo.
    currite ducentes subtegmina, currite, fusi.
nulla domus tales umquam contexit amores,
nullus amor tali coniunxit foedere amantes,   335
qualis adest Thetidi, qualis concordia Peleo.
    currite ducentes subtegmina, currite, fusi.
nascetur vobis expers terroris Achilles,
hostibus haud tergo, sed forti pectore notus,
qui persaepe vago victor certamine cursus   340
flammea praevertet celeris vestigia cervae.
    currite ducentes subtegmina, currite, fusi.
non illi quisquam bello se conferet heros,
cum Phrygii Teucro manabunt sanguine <campi>,
Troicaque obsidens longinquo moenia bello   345
periuri Pelopis vastabit tertius heres.
    currite ducentes subtegmina, currite, fusi.
illius egregias virtutes claraque facta
saepe fatebuntur gnatorum in funere matres,
cum incultum cano solvent a vertice crinem   350
putridaque infirmis variabunt pectora palmis.
    currite ducentes subtegmina, currite, fusi.
namque velut densas praecerpens messor aristas
sole sub ardenti flaventia demetit arva,
Troiugenum infesto prosternet corpora ferro.   355

currite ducentes subtegmina, currite, fusi.
testis erit magnis virtutibus unda Scamandri,
quae passim rapido diffunditur Hellesponto,
cuius iter caesis angustans corporum acervis
alta tepefaciet permixta flumina caede.   360
   currite ducentes subtegmina, currite, fusi.
denique testis erit morti quoque reddita praeda,
cum teres excelso coacervatum aggere bustum
excipiet niveos perculsae virginis artus.
   currite ducentes subtegmina, currite, fusi.   365
nam simul ac fessis dederit fors copiam Achivis
urbis Dardaniae Neptunia solvere vincla,
alta Polyxenia madefient caede sepulcra;
quae, velut ancipiti succumbens victima ferro,
proiciet truncum summisso poplite corpus.   370
   currite ducentes subtegmina, currite, fusi.
quare agite optatos animi coniungite amores.
accipiat coniunx felici foedere divam,
dedatur cupido iam dudum nupta marito.
   currite ducentes subtegmina, currite, fusi.   375
non illam nutrix orienti luce revisens
hesterno collum poterit circumdare filo,   377
anxia nec mater discordis maesta puellae   379
secubitu caros mittet sperare nepotes.   380
   currite ducentes subtegmina, currite, fusi."
talia praefantes quondam felicia Pelei
carmina divino cecinerunt pectore Parcae.
praesentes namque ante domos invisere castas
heroum, et sese mortali ostendere coetu,   385
caelicolae nondum spreta pietate solebant.
saepe pater divum templo in fulgente residens,
annua cum festis venissent sacra diebus,
conspexit terra centum procumbere tauros.
saepe vagus Liber Parnasi vertice summo   390

Thyiadas effusis evantis crinibus egit,
cum Delphi tota certatim ex urbe ruentes
acciperent laeti divum fumantibus aris.
saepe in letifero belli certamine Mavors
aut rapidi Tritonis era aut Amarunsia virgo   395
armatas hominum est praesens hortata catervas.
sed postquam tellus scelere est imbuta nefando
iustitiamque omnes cupida de mente fugarunt,
perfudere manus fraterno sanguine fratres,
destitit extinctos natus lugere parentes,   400
optavit genitor primaevi funera nati,
liber uti nuptae poteretur flore novellae,
ignaro mater substernens se impia nato
impia non verita est divos scelerare penates.
omnia fanda nefanda malo permixta furore   405
iustificam nobis mentem avertere deorum.
quare nec talis dignantur visere coetus,
nec se contingi patiuntur lumine claro.

65

Etsi me assiduo confectum cura dolore
    sevocat a doctis, Hortale, virginibus,
nec potis est dulcis Musarum expromere fetus
    mens animi, tantis fluctuat ipsa malis -
namque mei nuper Lethaeo gurgite fratris   5
    pallidulum manans alluit unda pedem,
Troia Rhoeteo quem subter litore tellus
    ereptum nostris obterit ex oculis;

. . . .

    numquam ego te, vita frater amabilior,   10
aspiciam posthac? at certe semper amabo,
    semper maesta tua carmina morte canam,
qualia sub densis ramorum concinit umbris

Daulias, absumpti fata gemens Ityli -
sed tamen in tantis maeroribus, Hortale, mitto 15
    haec expressa tibi carmina Battiadae,
ne tua dicta vagis nequiquam credita ventis
    effluxisse meo forte putes animo,
ut missum sponsi furtivo munere malum
    procurrit casto virginis e gremio, 20
quod miserae oblitae molli sub veste locatum,
    dum adventu matris prosilit, excutitur,
atque illud prono praeceps agitur decursu,
    huic manat tristi conscius ore rubor.

66

Omnia qui magni dispexit lumina mundi,
    qui stellarum ortus comperit atque obitus,
flammeus ut rapidi solis nitor obscuretur,
    ut cedant certis sidera temporibus,
ut Triviam furtim sub Latmia saxa relegans 5
    dulcis amor gyro devocet aerio:
idem me ille Conon caelesti <in> lumine vidit
    e Bereniceo vertice caesariem
fulgentem clare, quam multis illa dearum
    levia protendens brachia pollicita est, 10
qua rex tempestate novo auctus hymenaeo
    vastatum finis iverat Assyrios,
dulcia nocturnae portans vestigia rixae,
    quam de virgineis gesserat exuviis.
estne novis nuptis odio Venus? anne parentum 15
    frustrantur falsis gaudia lacrimulis,
ubertim thalami quas intra limina fundunt?
    non, ita me divi, vera gemunt, iuerint.
id mea me multis docuit regina querellis
    invisente novo proelia torva viro. 20

at tu non orbum luxti deserta cubile,
  sed fratris cari flebile discidium,
cum penitus maestas exedit cura medullas.
  ut tibi tunc toto pectore sollicitae
sensibus ereptis mens excidit! at <te> ego certe   25
  cognoram a parva virgine magnanimam.
anne bonum oblita es facinus, quo regium adepta es
  coniugium, quod non fortior ausit alis?
sed tum maesta virum mittens quae verba locuta es!
  Iuppiter, ut tristi lumina saepe manu!   30
quis te mutavit tantus deus? an quod amantes
  non longe a caro corpore abesse volunt?
atque ibi me cunctis pro dulci coniuge divis
  non sine taurino sanguine pollicita es,
si reditum tetulisset. is haud in tempore longo   35
  captam Asiam Aegypti finibus addiderat.
quis ego pro factis caelesti reddita coetu
  pristina vota novo munere dissoluo.
invita, o regina, tuo de vertice cessi,
  invita: adiuro teque tuumque caput,   40
digna ferat quod si quis inaniter adiurarit:
  sed qui se ferro postulet esse parem?
ille quoque eversus mons est, quem maximum in oris
  progenies Thiae clara supervehitur,
cum Medi peperere novum mare, cumque iuventus   45
  per medium classi barbara navit Athon.
quid facient crines, cum ferro talia cedant?
  Iuppiter, ut Chalybon omne genus pereat,
et qui principio sub terra quaerere venas
  institit ac ferri stringere duritiem!   50
abiunctae paulo ante comae mea fata sorores
  lugebant, cum se Memnonis Aethiopis
unigena impellens nutantibus aera pennis
  obtulit Arsinoes Locridos ales equus,

isque per aetherias me tollens avolat umbras 55
    et Veneris casto collocat in gremio.
ipsa suum Zephyritis eo famulum legarat,
    Graia Canopeis incola litoribus.
inde Venus vario ne solum in lumine caeli
    ex Ariadnaeis aurea temporibus 60
fixa corona foret, sed nos quoque fulgeremus
    devotae flavi verticis exuviae,
uvidulam a fluctu cedentem ad templa deum me
    sidus in antiquis diva novum posuit.
Virginis et saevi contingens namque Leonis 65
    lumina, Callisto iuncta Lycaoniae,
vertor in occasum, tardum dux ante Booten,
    qui vix sero alto mergitur Oceano.
sed quamquam me nocte premunt vestigia divum,
    lux autem canae Tethyi restituit, 70
(pace tua fari hic liceat, Rhamnusia virgo,
    namque ego non ullo vera timore tegam,
nec si me infestis discerpent sidera dictis,
    condita quin vere pectoris evoluam)
non his tam laetor rebus, quam me afore semper, 75
    afore me a dominae vertice discrucior,
quicum ego, dum virgo quondam fuit, omnibus expers
    unguentis, una vilia multa bibi.
nunc vos, optato quas iunxit lumine taeda,
    non prius unanimis corpora coniugibus 80
tradite nudantes reiecta veste papillas
    quam iucunda mihi munera libet onyx,
vester onyx, casto colitis quae iura cubili.
    sed quae se impuro dedit adulterio,
illius a! mala dona levis bibat irrita pulvis: 85
    namque ego ab indignis praemia nulla peto.
sed magis, o nuptae, semper concordia vestras,
    semper amor sedes incolat assiduus.

tu vero, regina, tuens cum sidera divam
    placabis festis luminibus Venerem,   90
unguinis expertem non siris esse tuam me,
    sed potius largis affice muneribus.
sidera corruerint utinam! coma regia fiam,
    proximus Hydrochoi fulgeret Oarion!

67

O dulci iucunda viro, iucunda parenti,
    salve, teque bona Iuppiter auctet ope,
ianua, quam Balbo dicunt servisse benigne
    olim, cum sedes ipse senex tenuit,
quamque ferunt rursus gnato servisse maligne,   5
    postquam es porrecto facta marita sene.
dic agedum nobis, quare mutata feraris
    in dominum veterem deseruisse fidem.
"Non (ita Caecilio placeam, cui tradita nunc sum)
    culpa mea est, quamquam dicitur esse mea,   10
nec peccatum a me quisquam pote dicere quicquam;
    verum isto populo ianua quid faciat,
qui, quacumque aliquid reperitur non bene factum,
    ad me omnes clamant: ianua, culpa tua est."
Non istuc satis est uno te dicere verbo,   15
    sed facere ut quivis sentiat et videat.
"Qui possum? nemo quaerit nec scire laborat."
    Nos volumus: nobis dicere ne dubita.
"Primum igitur, virgo quod fertur tradita nobis,
    falsum est. non illam vir prior attigerit,   20
languidior tenera cui pendens sicula beta
    numquam se mediam sustulit ad tunicam;
sed pater illius gnati violasse cubile
    dicitur et miseram conscelerasse domum,
sive quod impia mens caeco flagrabat amore,   25

seu quod iners sterili semine natus erat,
ut quaerendum unde <unde> foret nervosius illud
    quod posset zonam solvere virgineam."
Egregium narras, mira pietate, parentem,
    qui ipse sui gnati minxerit in gremium. 30
"Atqui non solum hoc dicit se cognitum habere
    Brixia Cycneae supposita speculae,
flavus quam molli praecurrit flumine Mella,
    Brixia Veronae mater amata meae,
sed de Postumio et Corneli narrat amore, 35
    cum quibus illa malum fecit adulterium.
dixerit hic aliquis: quid? tu istaec, ianua, nosti,
    cui numquam domini limine abesse licet,
nec populum auscultare, sed hic suffixa tigillo
    tantum operire soles aut aperire domum? 40
saepe illam audivi furtiva voce loquentem
    solam cum ancillis haec sua flagitia,
nomine dicentem quos diximus, utpote quae mi
    speraret nec linguam esse nec auriculam.
praeterea addebat quendam, quem dicere nolo 45
    nomine, ne tollat rubra supercilia.
longus homo est, magnas cui lites intulit olim
    falsum mendaci ventre puerperium."

68A

Quod mihi fortuna casuque oppressus acerbo
    conscriptum hoc lacrimis mittis epistolium,
naufragum ut eiectum spumantibus aequoris undis
    sublevem et a mortis limine restituam,
quem neque sancta Venus molli requiescere somno 5
    desertum in lecto caelibe perpetitur,
nec veterum dulci scriptorum carmine Musae
    oblectant, cum mens anxia pervigilat:

id gratum est mihi, me quoniam tibi dicis amicum,
    muneraque et Musarum hinc petis et Veneris.   10
sed tibi ne mea sint ignota incommoda, Manli,
    neu me odisse putes hospitis officium,
accipe quis merser fortunae fluctibus ipse,
    ne amplius a misero dona beata petas.
tempore quo primum vestis mihi tradita pura est,   15
    iucundum cum aetas florida ver ageret,
multa satis lusi: non est dea nescia nostri,
    quae dulcem curis miscet amaritiem.
sed totum hoc studium luctu fraterna mihi mors
    abstulit. o misero frater adempte mihi,   20
tu mea tu moriens fregisti commoda, frater,
    tecum una tota est nostra sepulta domus;
omnia tecum una perierunt gaudia nostra
    quae tuus in vita dulcis alebat amor.
cuius ego interitu tota de mente fugavi   25
    haec studia atque omnes delicias animi.
quare, quod scribis 'Veronae turpe, Catulle,
    esse, quod hic quisquis de meliore nota
frigida deserto tepefactat membra cubili',
    id, Manli, non est turpe, magis miserum est.   30
ignosces igitur si, quae mihi luctus ademit,
    haec tibi non tribuo munera, cum nequeo.
nam, quod scriptorum non magna est copia apud me,
    hoc fit, quod Romae vivimus: illa domus,
illa mihi sedes, illic mea carpitur aetas;   35
    huc una ex multis capsula me sequitur.
quod cum ita sit, nolim statuas nos mente maligna
    id facere aut animo non satis ingenuo,
quod tibi non utriusque petenti copia posta est:
    ultro ego deferrem, copia siqua foret.   40

Non possum reticere, deae, qua me Allius in re
    iuverit aut quantis iuverit officiis,
ne fugiens saeclis obliviscentibus aetas
    illius hoc caeca nocte tegat studium;
sed dicam vobis, vos porro dicite multis   45
    milibus et facite haec carta loquatur anus.

    ....

    notescatque magis mortuus atque magis,
nec tenuem texens sublimis aranea telam
    in deserto Alli nomine opus faciat.   50
nam mihi quam dederit duplex Amathusia curam
    scitis et in quo me torruerit genere,
cum tantum arderem quantum Trinacria rupes
    lymphaque in Oetaeis Malia Thermopylis,
maesta neque assiduo tabescere lumina fletu   55
    cessarent tristique imbre madere genae;
qualis in aerii perlucens vertice montis
    rivus muscoso prosilit e lapide,
qui cum de prona praeceps est valle volutus,
    per medium densi transit iter populi,   60
dulce viatori lasso in sudore levamen,
    cum gravis exustos aestus hiulcat agros;
hic, velut in nigro iactatis turbine nautis
    lenius aspirans aura secunda venit
iam prece Pollucis, iam Castoris implorata,   65
    tale fuit nobis Allius auxilium.
is clausum lato patefecit limite campum,
    isque domum nobis isque dedit dominae
ad quam communes exerceremus amores.
    quo mea se molli candida diva pede   70
intulit et trito fulgentem in limine plantam
    innixa arguta constituit solea,

coniugis ut quondam flagrans advenit amore
  Protesilaeam Laodamia domum
inceptam frustra, nondum cum sanguine sacro   75
  hostia caelestis pacificasset eros.
nil mihi tam valde placeat, Rhamnusia virgo,
  quod temere invitis suscipiatur eris.
quam ieiuna pium desideret ara cruorem
  docta est amisso Laodamia viro,   80
coniugis ante coacta novi dimittere collum,
  quam veniens una atque altera rursus hiems
noctibus in longis avidum saturasset amorem,
  posset ut abrupto vivere coniugio,
quod scibant Parcae non longo tempore abesse,   85
  si miles muros isset ad Iliacos.
nam tum Helenae raptu primores Argivorum
  coeperat ad sese Troia ciere viros,
Troia (nefas!) commune sepulcrum Asiae Europaeque,
  Troia virum et virtutum omnium acerba cinis,   90
quaene etiam nostro letum miserabile fratri
  attulit. ei misero frater adempte mihi,
ei misero fratri iucundum lumen ademptum,
  tecum una tota est nostra sepulta domus;
omnia tecum una perierunt gaudia nostra,   95
  quae tuus in vita dulcis alebat amor.
quem nunc tam longe non inter nota sepulcra
  nec prope cognatos compositum cineres,
sed Troia obscena, Troia infelice sepultum
  detinet extremo terra aliena solo.   100
ad quam tum properans fertur <lecta> undique pubes
  Graeca penetralis deseruisse focos,
ne Paris abducta gavisus libera moecha
  otia pacato degeret in thalamo.
quo tibi tum casu, pulcerrima Laodamia,   105
  ereptum est vita dulcius atque anima

coniugium: tanto te absorbens vertice amoris
    aestus in abruptum detulerat barathrum,
quale ferunt Grai Pheneum prope Cyllenaeum
    siccare emulsa pingue palude solum,   110
quod quondam caesis montis fodisse medullis
    audit falsiparens Amphitryoniades,
tempore quo certa Stymphalia monstra sagitta
    perculit imperio deterioris eri,
pluribus ut caeli tereretur ianua divis,   115
    Hebe nec longa virginitate foret.
sed tuus altus amor barathro fuit altior illo,
    qui tamen indomitam ferre iugum docuit.
nam nec tam carum confecto aetate parenti
    una caput seri nata nepotis alit,   120
qui, cum divitiis vix tandem inventus avitis
    nomen testatas intulit in tabulas,
impia derisi gentilis gaudia tollens
    suscitat a cano volturium capiti;
nec tantum niveo gavisa est ulla columbo   125
    compar, quae multo dicitur improbius
oscula mordenti semper decerpere rostro,
    quam quae praecipue multivola est mulier.
sed tu horum magnos vicisti sola furores,
    ut semel es flavo conciliata viro.   130
aut nihil aut paulo cui tum concedere digna
    lux mea se nostrum contulit in gremium,
quam circumcursans hinc illinc saepe Cupido
    fulgebat crocina candidus in tunica.
quae tamen etsi uno non est contenta Catullo,   135
    rara verecundae furta feremus erae,
ne nimium simus stultorum more molesti;
    saepe etiam Iuno, maxima caelicolum,
coniugis in culpa flagrantem contudit iram,
    noscens omnivoli plurima furta Iovis.   140

atqui nec divis homines componier aequum est

....

....

ingratum tremuli tolle parentis onus.
nec tamen illa mihi dextra deducta paterna
    fragrantem Assyrio venit odore domum,
sed furtiva dedit mira munuscula nocte   145
    ipsius ex ipso dempta viri gremio.
quare illud satis est, si nobis is datur unis
    quem lapide illa dies candidiore notat.

hoc tibi, quod potui, confectum carmine munus
    pro multis, Alli, redditur officiis,   150
ne vestrum scabra tangat robigine nomen
    haec atque illa dies atque alia atque alia.
huc addent divi quam plurima, quae Themis olim
    antiquis solita est munera ferre piis.
sitis felices et tu simul et tua vita,   155
    et domus in qua <nos> lusimus et domina,
et qui principio nobis terram dedit auspex,
    a quo sunt primo omnia nata bona,
et longe ante omnes mihi quae me carior ipso est,
    lux mea, qua viva vivere dulce mihi est.   160

69

Noli admirari, quare tibi femina nulla,
    Rufe, velit tenerum supposuisse femur,
non si illam rarae labefactes munere vestis
    aut perluciduli deliciis lapidis.
laedit te quaedam mala fabula, qua tibi fertur   5
    valle sub alarum trux habitare caper.
hunc metuunt omnes, neque mirum: nam mala valde est
    bestia, nec quicum bella puella cubet.

quare aut crudelem nasorum interfice pestem,
    aut admirari desine cur fugiunt.   10

70

Nulli se dicit mulier mea nubere malle
    quam mihi, non si se Iuppiter ipse petat-
dicit. sed mulier cupido quod dicit amanti,
    in vento et rapida scribere oportet aqua.

71

Si cui iure bono sacer alarum obstitit hircus,
    aut si quem merito tarda podagra secat,
aemulus iste tuus, qui vestrum exercet amorem,
    mirifice est apte nactus utrumque malum.
nam quotiens futuit, totiens ulciscitur ambos: 5
    illam affligit odore, ipse perit podagra.

72

Dicebas quondam solum te nosse Catullum,
    Lesbia, nec prae me velle tenere Iovem.
dilexi tum te non tantum ut vulgus amicam,
    sed pater ut gnatos diligit et generos.
nunc te cognovi; quare, etsi impensius uror,   5
    multo mi tamen es vilior et levior.
qui potis est, inquis?   quod amantem iniuria talis
    cogit amare magis, sed bene velle minus.

73

Desine de quoquam quicquam bene velle mereri
    aut aliquem fieri posse putare pium.

omnia sunt ingrata, nihil fecisse benigne <est>;
   immo etiam taedet, <taedet> obestque magis;
ut mihi, quem nemo gravius nec acerbius urget   5
   quam modo qui me unum atque unicum amicum habuit.

74

Gellius audierat patruum obiurgare solere,
   si quis delicias diceret aut faceret.
hoc ne ipsi accideret, patrui perdepsuit ipsam
   uxorem et patruum reddidit Harpocratem.
quod voluit fecit: nam, quamvis irrumet ipsum   5
   nunc patruum, verbum non faciet patruus.

75

Huc est mens deducta tua mea, Lesbia, culpa
   atque ita se officio perdidit ipsa suo,
ut iam nec bene velle queat tibi, si optima fias,
   nec desistere amare, omnia si facias.

76

Si qua recordanti benefacta priora voluptas
   est homini, cum se cogitat esse pium,
nec sanctam violasse fidem, nec foedere nullo
   divum ad fallendos numine abusum homines,
multa parata manent in longa aetate, Catulle,   5
   ex hoc ingrato gaudia amore tibi.
nam quaecumque homines bene cuiquam aut dicere possunt
   aut facere, haec a te dictaque factaque sunt.
omnia quae ingratae perierunt credita menti.
   quare cur tete iam amplius excrucies?   10
quin tu animo offirmas atque istinc te ipse reducis

et dis invitis desinis esse miser?
difficile est longum subito deponere amorem,
    difficile est, verum hoc qua lubet efficias;
una salus haec est, hoc est tibi pervincendum,   15
    hoc facias, sive id non pote sive pote.
o di, si vestrum est misereri, aut si quibus umquam
    extremam iam ipsa in morte tulistis opem,
me miserum aspicite et, si vitam puriter egi,
    eripite hanc pestem perniciemque mihi,   20
quae mihi subrepens imos ut torpor in artus
    expulit ex omni pectore laetitias.
non iam illud quaero, contra me ut diligat illa,
    aut, quod non potis est, esse pudica velit:
ipse valere opto et taetrum hunc deponere morbum.   25
    o di, reddite mi hoc pro pietate mea.

77

Rufe mihi frustra ac nequiquam credite amice
    (frustra? immo magno cum pretio atque malo),
sicine subrepsti mi atque intestina perurens
    ei misero eripuisti omnia nostra bona?
eripuisti, eheu nostrae crudele venenum   5
    vitae, eheu nostrae pestis amicitiae.

78A

Gallus habet fratres, quorum est lepidissima coniunx
    alterius, lepidus filius alterius.
Gallus homo est bellus: nam dulces iungit amores,
    cum puero ut bello bella puella cubet.
Gallus homo est stultus, nec se videt esse maritum,   5
    qui patruus patrui monstret adulterium.

sed nunc id doleo, quod purae pura puellae
   savia comminxit spurca saliva tua.
verum id non impune feres: nam te omnia saecla
   noscent et, qui sis, fama loquetur anus.

79

Lesbius est pulcer; quid ni? quem Lesbia malit
   quam te cum tota gente, Catulle, tua.
sed tamen hic pulcer vendat cum gente Catullum
   si tria notorum savia reppererit.

80

Quid dicam, Gelli, quare rosea ista labella
   hiberna fiant candidiora nive,
mane domo cum exis et cum te octava quiete
   e molli longo suscitat hora die?
nescio quid certe est: an vere fama susurrat   5
   grandia te medii tenta vorare viri?
sic certe est: clamant Victoris rupta miselli
   ilia, et emulso labra notata sero.

81

Nemone in tanto potuit populo esse, Iuventi,
   bellus homo, quem tu diligere inciperes,
praeterquam iste tuus moribunda ab sede Pisauri
   hospes inaurata pallidior statua,
qui tibi nunc cordi est, quem tu praeponere nobis   5
   audes, et nescis quod facinus facias?

91

Quinti, si tibi vis oculos debere Catullum
    aut aliud si quid carius est oculis,
eripere ei noli, multo quod carius illi
    est oculis, seu quid carius est oculis.

Lesbia mi praesente viro mala plurima dicit;
    haec illi fatuo maxima laetitia est.
mule, nihil sentis? si nostri oblita taceret,
    sana esset; nunc quod gannit et obloquitur,
non solum meminit, sed, quae multo acrior est res,   5
    irata est. hoc est, uritur et loquitur.

Chommoda dicebat, si quando commoda vellet
    dicere, et insidias Arrius hinsidias,
et tum mirifice sperabat se esse locutum,
    cum quantum poterat dixerat hinsidias.
credo, sic mater, sic liber avunculus eius,   5
    sic maternus avus dixerat atque avia.
hoc misso in Syriam requierant omnibus aures:
    audibant eadem haec leniter et leviter,
nec sibi postilla metuebant talia verba,
    cum subito affertur nuntius horribilis,   10
Ionios fluctus, postquam illuc Arrius isset,
    iam non Ionios esse sed Hionios.

Odi et amo. quare id faciam, fortasse requiris.

nescio, sed fieri sentio et excrucior.

86

Quintia formosa est multis. mihi candida, longa,
   recta est: haec ego sic singula confiteor,
totum illud "formosa" nego: nam nulla venustas,
   nulla in tam magno est corpore mica salis.
Lesbia formosa est, quae cum pulcerrima tota est,   5
   tum omnibus una omnis surripuit veneres.

87

Nulla potest mulier tantum se dicere amatam
   vere, quantum a me Lesbia amata mea est.
nulla fides ullo fuit umquam in foedere tanta,
   quanta in amore tuo ex parte reperta mea est.

88

Quid facit is, Gelli, qui cum matre atque sorore
   prurit et abiectis pervigilat tunicis?
quid facit is, patruum qui non sinit esse maritum?
   ecquid scis quantum suscipiat sceleris?
suscipit, o Gelli, quantum non ultima Tethys   5
   nec genitor Nympharum abluit Oceanus:
nam nihil est quicquam sceleris, quo prodeat ultra,
   non si demisso se ipse voret capite.

89

Gellius est tenuis: quid ni? cui tam bona mater
   tamque valens vivat tamque venusta soror
tamque bonus patruus tamque omnia plena puellis

cognatis, quare is desinat esse macer?
qui ut nihil attingat, nisi quod fas tangere non est,   5
  quantumvis quare sit macer invenies.

90

Nascatur magus ex Gelli matrisque nefando
  coniugio et discat Persicum aruspicium:
nam magus ex matre et gnato gignatur oportet,
  si vera est Persarum impia religio,
+gnatus+ ut accepto veneretur carmine divos   5
  omentum in flamma pingue liquefaciens.

91

Non ideo, Gelli, sperabam te mihi fidum
  in misero hoc nostro, hoc perdito amore fore,
quod te cognossem bene constantemve putarem
  aut posse a turpi mentem inhibere probro;
sed neque quod matrem nec germanam esse videbam   5
  hanc tibi, cuius me magnus edebat amor.
et quamvis tecum multo coniungerer usu,
  non satis id causae credideram esse tibi.
tu satis id duxti: tantum tibi gaudium in omni
  culpa est, in quacumque est aliquid sceleris.   10

92

Lesbia mi dicit semper male nec tacet umquam
  de me: Lesbia me dispeream nisi amat.
quo signo? quia sunt totidem mea: deprecor illam
  assidue, verum dispeream nisi amo.

93

Nil nimium studeo, Caesar, tibi velle placere,
  nec scire utrum sis albus an ater homo.

94

Mentula moechatur. moechatur mentula? certe.
  hoc est quod dicunt: ipsa olera olla legit.

95A

Zmyrna mei Cinnae nonam post denique messem
  quam coepta est nonamque edita post hiemem,
milia cum interea quingenta Hortensius uno
....
Zmyrna cavas Satrachi penitus mittetur ad undas,   5
  Zmyrnam cana diu saecula pervoluent.
at Volusi annales Paduam morientur ad ipsam
  et laxas scombris saepe dabunt tunicas.

95B

Parva mei mihi sint cordi monimenta....,
  at populus tumido gaudeat Antimacho.

96

Si quicquam mutis gratum acceptumve sepulcris
  accidere a nostro, Calve, dolore potest,
quo desiderio veteres renovamus amores
  atque olim missas flemus amicitias,
certe non tanto mors immatura dolori est   5
  Quintiliae, quantum gaudet amore tuo.

Non, ita me di ament, quicquam referre putavi
    utrumne os an culum olfacerem Aemilio.
nilo mundius hoc, nihiloque immundius illud,
    verum etiam culus mundior et melior;
nam sine dentibus est. hoc dentis sesquipedalis,   5
    gingivas vero ploxeni habet veteris,
praeterea rictum qualem diffissus in aestu
    meientis mulae cunnus habere solet.
hic futuit multas et se facit esse venustum,
    et non pistrino traditur atque asino?   10
quem siqua attingit, non illam posse putemus
    aegroti culum lingere carnificis?

98

In te, si in quemquam, dici pote, putide Victi,
    id quod verbosis dicitur et fatuis.
ista cum lingua, si usus veniat tibi, possis
    culos et crepidas lingere carpatinas.
si nos omnino vis omnes perdere, Victi,   5
    hiscas: omnino quod cupis efficies.

99

Surripui tibi, dum ludis, mellite Iuventi,
    saviolum dulci dulcius ambrosia.
verum id non impune tuli: namque amplius horam
    suffixum in summa me memini esse cruce,
dum tibi me purgo nec possum fletibus ullis   5
    tantillum vestrae demere saevitiae.
nam simul id factum est, multis diluta labella
    guttis abstersti omnibus articulis,

ne quicquam nostro contractum ex ore maneret,
    tamquam commictae spurca saliva lupae.   10
praeterea infesto miserum me tradere amori
    non cessasti omnique excruciare modo,
ut mi ex ambrosia mutatum iam foret illud
    saviolum tristi tristius elleboro.
quam quoniam poenam misero proponis amori,   15
    numquam iam posthac basia surripiam.

100

Caelius Aufillenum et Quintius Aufillenam
    flos Veronensum depereunt iuvenum,
hic fratrem, ille sororem. hoc est quod dicitur illud
    fraternum vere dulce sodalicium.
cui faveam potius? Caeli, tibi: nam tua nobis   5
    perspecta est igni tum unica amicitia,
cum vesana meas torreret flamma medullas.
    sis felix, Caeli, sis in amore potens.

101

Multas per gentes et multa per aequora vectus
    advenio has miseras, frater, ad inferias,
ut te postremo donarem munere mortis
    et mutam nequiquam alloquerer cinerem.
quandoquidem fortuna mihi tete abstulit ipsum,   5
    heu miser indigne frater adempte mihi,
nunc tamen interea haec, prisco quae more parentum
    tradita sunt tristi munere ad inferias,
accipe fraterno multum manantia fletu,
    atque in perpetuum, frater, ave atque vale.   10

Si quicquam tacito commissum est fido ab amico,
  cuius sit penitus nota fides animi,
meque esse invenies illorum iure sacratum,
  Corneli, et factum me esse putum Harpocraten.

103

Aut sodes mihi redde decem sestertia, Silo,
  deinde esto quamvis saevus et indomitus;
aut si te nummi delectant, desine quaeso
  leno esse atque idem saevus et indomitus.

104

Credis me potuisse meae maledicere vitae,
  ambobus mihi quae carior est oculis?
non potui, nec, si possem, tam perdite amarem;
  sed tu cum Tappone omnia monstra facis.

105

Mentula conatur Pipleium scandere montem:
  Musae furcillis praecipitem eiciunt.

106

Cum puero bello praeconem qui videt esse,
  quid credat, nisi se vendere discupere?

107

Si quicquam cupido optantique obtigit umquam

    insperanti, hoc est gratum animo proprie.
quare hoc est gratum nobisque est carius auro
    quod te restituis, Lesbia, mi cupido.
restituis cupido atque insperanti, ipsa refers te   5
    nobis. o lucem candidiore nota!
quis me uno vivit felicior, aut magis hac quid
    optandum vita dicere quis poterit?

108

Si, Comini, populi arbitrio tua cana senectus
    spurcata impuris moribus intereat,
non equidem dubito quin primum inimica bonorum
    lingua exsecta avido sit data vulturio,
effossos oculos voret atro gutture corvus,   5
    intestina canes, cetera membra lupi.

109

Iucundum, mea vita, mihi proponis amorem
    hunc nostrum inter nos perpetuumque fore.
di magni, facite ut vere promittere possit,
    atque id sincere dicat et ex animo,
ut liceat nobis tota perducere vita   5
    aeternum hoc sanctae foedus amicitiae.

110

Aufillena, bonae semper laudantur amicae:
    accipiunt pretium, quae facere instituunt.
tu, quod promisti, mihi quod mentita, inimica es;
    quod nec das et fers saepe, facis facinus.
aut facere ingenuae est, aut non promisse pudicae,   5

Aufillena, fuit; sed data corripere
fraudando officiis, plus quam meretricis avarae est,
quae sese toto corpore prostituit.

111

Aufillena, viro contentam vivere solo
    nuptarum laus ex laudibus eximiis;
sed cuivis quamvis potius succumbere par est,
    quam matrem fratres ex patruo.....

112

Multus homo es, Naso, neque tecum multus homo est qui
    descendit: Naso, multus es et pathicus.

113

Consule Pompeio primum duo, Cinna, solebant
    Maeciliam; facto consule nunc iterum
manserunt duo, sed creverunt milia in unum
    singula. fecundum semen adulterio.

114

Firmano saltu non falso Mentula dives
    fertur, qui tot res in se habet egregias,
aucupium omne genus, piscis, prata, arva ferasque.
    nequiquam: fructus sumptibus exsuperat.
quare concedo sit dives, dum omnia desint;   5
    saltum laudemus, dum modo ipse egeat.

Mentula habet lustra et triginta iugera prati,
    quadraginta arvi: cetera sunt maria.
cur non divitiis Croesum superare potis sit,
    uno qui in saltu tot bona possideat,
prata, arva, ingentes silvas altasque paludes   5
    usque ad Hyperboreos et mare ad Oceanum?
omnia magna haec sunt, tamen ipse est maximus ultro;
    non homo, sed vero mentula magna minax.

Saepe tibi studiose, animo venante, requirens
    carmina uti possem mittere Battiadae,
qui te lenirem nobis, neu conarere
    tela infesta <meum> mittere in usque caput,
hunc video mihi nunc frustra sumptum esse laborem,   5
    Gelli, nec nostras hic valuisse preces.
contra nos tela ista tua evitabimus acta,
    at fixus nostris tu dabis supplicium.

Commentary

1

On one level, a simple dedication to Cornelius Nepos of Catullus' new volume of poems (1-51); on another level, a programmatic poem which introduces the reader to the kind of verse created by Catullus. As a programmatic piece, poem 1 is a part that is accurately representative of the whole: it not only names but also displays those qualities of newness, charm and polish which set poems 1-51 apart from traditional Roman poetry as it was written prior to the arrival of the New Poets.

Cornelius Nepos (ca. 94-24 B.C.) was, like Catullus, a native of Cisalpine Gaul, and appears to have taken the role of the young poet's mentor. While his fame today is based on his historical works (*i.e.*, *De Viris Illustribus* in sixteen volumes, and *Chronica* in three volumes), Nepos also wrote light verse, so his interest in Catullus' poetry is quite understandable. Whether he is the Cornelius mentioned in poem 102 is presently unclear.

As is typical of poems 2-51, poem 1 displays a carefully considered structure: it begins with a two-line question, continues with a five-line response to that question, and concludes with a three-line formal dedication of the *libellus* mentioned in line 1.

Meter: hendecasyllabic.

1. *dono*: the present tense serves to emphasize that here is the actual moment of dedication.

lepidum   novum   libellum: three   key   programmatic
words,   referring   not   only   to   the   external   appearance
of   the   volume,   but   also   to   its   internal   contents.   It
displays *lepos* (grace,   charm,   wit),   novelty,   and   compactness (the   diminutive *libellus* — a   "little   book").

2.   *arida...pumice*:   the   use   of   pumice   to   smooth   the
edges   of   a   papyrus   roll   is   well   attested;   while *pumex*
is   normally   treated   as   a   masculine   noun,   Catullus
idiosyncratically   treats   it   as   feminine.

expolitum: also   referring   to   internal   as   well   as   external   "polish".   The   "rough   edges"   have   been   removed
both   from   the   physical   book   and   from   the   verse   itself.
Worthy   of   note   in   lines   1-2   is   the   dominance   of *um*
sounds;   indeed   four   sounds   dominate   the   ends   of   the
lines   in   this   poem: *um, as, is*, and *o* — presenting   a
kind   of   end   rhyme   throughout   the   piece.

3.   *Corneli*:   the   second   section   of   the   poem   immediately
supplies   the   answer   to   the   question   raised   in   the   first
section.

4.   *esse   aliquid*:   a   colloquial   phrase: "of   some   worth".
The   appearance   of   colloquialisms   in   poem   1   foreshadows   the   kind   of   "common"   language   that   Catullus
will   employ   in   the   rest   of   his   volume.

nugas: another   colloquial   term,   taken   to   mean
"worthless   stuff"   or   "junk".   The   poet   here   adopts   a
self-depreciatory   tone   that   will   be   picked   up   again   in
the   final   section   of   the   poem.

5.   *unus   Italorum*:   Cornelius,   like   Catullus,   is   a

ground-breaker of sorts; he alone among all the Italians has dared to write a compact universal history. If Catullus sees himself as a poetic innovator, he makes it clear that Cornelius is also doing something "new and unheard of".

6. *tribus...cartis*: the reference is to Cornelius' *Chronica.*

explicare: "to give an account of".

7. *doctis...et laboriosis*: also programmatic terms; *doctrina* was valued greatly by the New Poets, and *doctus* is a coveted compliment; *laboriosis* conveys the hard work that goes into anything done well.

8. *quidquid hoc libelli*: the first line of the last section of the poem picks up the *libellum* of line 1 and treats it in a self-effacing manner, both here and in the following line. The sense of the phrase is something like "this poor excuse for a book".

9. *qualecumque*: "such as it is"; the last of a string of colloquialisms in lines 8-9. Note also the dominance of *q* sounds in these two verses.

patrona virgo: this MSS. reading has come under attack by critics who find no reason for Catullus to introduce another addressee to the poem, and who are troubled by this unusual adjectival use of *patronus*; they favor the emendation *qualecumque quidem est, patroni ut ergo* ("because of its patron"). This reading, however, presents us with a most awkward and inexplicable word order, as well as a choppy rhythm. Given the fact that a reference to a Muse is not out

105

of place at the beginning of a book of poems, it is probably wiser to retain the MSS. reading.

10. *perenne*: "for all time".

   saeclo: "generation".

2A

Given the dedicatory and programmatic nature of poem 1, Catullus' book of lyric poems really begins with this address to Lesbia's pet bird (hence Martial's references to the *Passer Catulli*). It is appropriate that, as the book begins physically, the affair which will be its thematic keynote begins as well: poem 2 is essentially a poem set at the earliest stages of the relationship. Here the poet wishes that his passionate torment could be assuaged as easily as that of his beloved—a first hint that passion may not be equal on both sides.

While there are some textual problems in the poem, its structure is quite clear: an initial group of four verses dealing with *what* Lesbia is doing, a second group of four verses which explains *why* she is doing that, and two final verses in which the poet expresses, first, *what he* would do, and second, *why he* would do it. Thus the concluding verses complete the poem by echoing its preceding sections.

Meter: hendecasyllabic.

1. *Passer*: much ink has been expended on what type of little bird Lesbia has as a pet. Most editors have taken the word in its usual sense of "sparrow", but some find it unlikely that such an ordinary bird

106

would be meant, and have suggested more exotic creatures, such as the blue rock-thrush. However, given the fact that tastes change from period to period as to what constitutes an acceptable pet, there is no real reason for rejecting the common meaning of "sparrow" here. Indeed Sappho's reference (Fr. 1 LP) to Aphrodite's conveyance by sparrows should warn us against being too quick to dismiss a bird associated in antiquity with love and passion.

deliciae: "pet".

meae puellae: note that, at this stage in the relationship, Catullus refrains from naming the object of his affections, so that, for the reader, an initial sense of mystery is created. Note also the repetitive *ae* sounds in this first line (comparable to the *um* sounds in poem 1.1).

2. *ludere...tenere*: these infinitives (like *dare* and *incitare* to come) are dependent upon the *solet* of line 4.

sinu: "lap".

3. *primum digitum*: "finger-tip". Note that the *d* and *t* sounds of this line are appropriate to the action of a pecking bird.

4. *incitare*: "provoke".

5. *cum*: not the preposition, but the conjunction. Catullus now begins to explain why his lady plays with her pet bird.

desiderio meo nitenti: a phrase that has caused a great deal of debate; *desiderium* seems best taken here in the sense of "an object of longing or desire" (*cf.* poem 96.3, where "sense of longing" seems intended). The best English equivalent might be "my heart's radiant (*nitenti*) desire". The dative case here is governed by the *lubet* of line 6.

6. *carum nescio quid*: "some pleasant pastime".

7. *ut solaciolum*: the MSS. reading is *et solaciolum*, but this has created some uncertainty as to the grammatical function of *solaciolum* (in apposition with *carum nescio quid?*); the emendation of *et* to *ut* provides a more meaningful statement: Lesbia uses her pet as a source of comfort.

8. *ut tum ... acquiescat*: textual problems continue here, as V apparently read *ut cum...acquiescet*. In this case *ut* must go with the *possem* of line 9, and the resultant train of thought is garbled. Better to accept the emendation *ut tum...acquiescat* and see the clause as dependent on line 6: not only does this give the passage a clearer sense (Lesbia plays with the bird so that her passion may abate), but it also adheres to the 4 + 4 + 2 structure of the poem.

9. *tecum ludere...possem*: the focus of the poem shifts now to the poet; the *tecum ludere* of this line echoes the *quicum ludere* of line 2, so that, structurally, this line responds to the first 4-line section of the poem. *Possem* here is optative.

ipsa: here in the sense of "your mistress"; *ipse* was

commonly used by slaves in reference to their master. Even now the term "Himself" is sometimes applied to people of great pretensions or arrogance.

10. *tristis...curas*: compare the *gravis ... ardor* of line 8; line 10 responds to the second 4-line section of the poem: Lesbia can ease her cares simply by playing with the bird, but Catullus remains tormented by his *curas*.

2B

There is no break in the MSS. between these lines and poem 2A, yet it was clear even to early editors of Catullus that these three lines do not easily follow, either grammatically or conceptually, upon the final lines of poem 2A; hence, as early as the Renaissance, scholars considered 2B a separate fragment of another (now lost) poem. Some editors have, alternatively, postulated a lacuna of one or more lines here that, were they extant, would afford a transition between poem 2A.10 and these verses. Few modern editors argue for simply taking these lines as the conclusion of poem 2A without at least such a lacuna.

It should be noted that the lack of a break in the MSS. here is not by itself a significant argument for the unity of these lines with poem 2A, since many other poems in the MSS. follow upon each other with no clear break indicated.

Given the carefully balanced nature of poem 2A and the fact that poem 2A is thematically complete as it now stands, it would seem anticlimactic to append these lines, with or without a lacuna; hence it is better to see in these

109

lines a fragment of an originally separate poem that stood between poems 2A and 3. This hypothesis is supported by the fact that Catullus has a tendency to separate poems on similar themes by intervening poems on variant themes (see, for example, the separation of poems 5 and 7 by poem 6): a practice known as *variatio*.

What this lost poem was about is, of course, almost impossible to determine: the extant lines present us only with a comparison—something is as pleasing to *mihi* (the poet?) as the golden apple was to Atalanta. The mythical tale involved Hippomenes throwing golden apples to distract Atalanta and thus prevent her from winning a race with him; Atalanta got the apples, and Hippomenes got her as his wife.

Meter: hendecasyllabic.

1. *est*: the mood of the verb here is another argument for the separation of these lines from the end of poem 2A.

2. *aureolum*: a colloquial term: "golden".

3. *zonam*: "girdle"; a reference to Atalanta's loss of virginity.

3

A "companion piece" to poem 2A: if the preceding poem presented the pet bird as a source of comfort for Lesbia, poem 3 reverses the picture; here, the death of the *passer* is a source of grief for its mistress, and, in a different way, for the poet himself. But the tone of the piece is less than serious, so that it takes on the appearance of a mock dirge, with the bird playfully portrayed as Lesbia's heroic lover. The delicate charm of the poem becomes most apparent at its conclusion, where the mock dirge is transformed into an understated love poem: while the ostensible subject of the piece is the bird, its true focal point is Lesbia.

The poem is divided structurally into four segments: lines 1-5 present the call to mourning and the announcement of the *passer's* death; lines 6-10 provide a *laudatio* of the bird in a sketch of its behavior in life; lines 11-15 in turn portray the bird in death, wending its way to the Underworld—which becomes the object of a *maledictio*; and, finally, lines 16-18 "cap" the poem with an unexpected change of focus from the bird to its bereaved mistress.

Meter: hendecasyllabic.

1. *Veneres Cupidinesque*: various explanations for the plural forms have been offered, from "proverbial expression" (Quinn) to a literal belief in there being more than one Venus; but the most probable explanation is the simplest: the poet uses a "poetic plural" (with the added incentive of the meter) to call all potential mourners together, to do emphatic homage to the deceased in keeping with the mock heroic tone of the poem. A similar use of the emphatic plural can be found at poems 13.12 and 86.6.

2. *quantum est hominum venustiorum*: a partitive genitive construction, also used for added emphasis in the mock heroic style. *Venustus*, which makes its first appearance in the corpus here, is a Catullan

111

"keyword": it encompasses the qualities of grace, charm, refinement—what we might call "class" today. Here the word obviously picks up the *Veneres* of the preceding line.

3. *meae puellae*: the poet continues in this poem the mystery of who his beloved is; *cf.* poem 2A.

4. *passer, deliciae meae puellae*: a complete repetition of poem 2A.1, and a partial repetition of the preceding line in this poem—the latter for added pathos.

5. *oculis suis*: a conceit found elsewhere in the Catullan corpus (*cf.* 14A.1, 82.2 and 4, 104.2). Here it (in conjunction with the *deliciae* of the previous line) signals the poet's playful personification of the bird as a human lover; the reference to eyes also prepares us for the concluding two lines of the poem.

6. *mellitus*: "sweet as honey"; the word appears again in poems 48 and 99 in reference to Juventius.

   norat: *i.e., noverat*; a sexual meaning (like the Biblical "know") is relevant to the personification of the bird as lover; *cf. nosse* at poem 72.1.

7. *ipsam*: "mistress", to be taken with *suamque* in the preceding line (*cf.* poem 2A.9). Note also the dominant *m* and *n* sounds of lines 6-7.

8. *gremio*: "lap"; *cf.* the *sinu* of 2A.2. It has been noted that, at 67.30, *gremium* is used to stand for a woman's genital parts, so the word here is also appropriate to the bird-as-lover motif.

illius: the second *i* is short.

9.   *circumsiliens*: "hopping about".

10.   *ad solam dominam*: "to its mistress alone"; *domina* is a term elsewhere used by Catullus of Lesbia as his beloved (for example, at 68B.68 and 156), hence it also supports the conceit that the bird has a love relationship with Lesbia.

     usque pipiabat: "constantly chirped".

11.   *it per iter*: note the play on words.

12.   *negant*: an impersonal "they" as subject.

     redire: a word that will be repeated shortly in poem 5, and then disappear from the corpus.

13.   *vobis male sit*: "a curse be on you". From this line to the end of the poem, Catullus indulges in mock heroic language, *e.g.*, *malae tenebrae/Orci*. The repetition of *male...malae* provides added emphasis; Orcus was an old name for the Underworld.

14.   *devoratis*: the image is that of the Underworld "gobbling up" the beautiful little bird.

     bella...bellum: a parallel to *male...malae* above; *bellus* here makes its first appearance in the poems of Catullus, and will serve as another "keyword": it alludes to the quality of "smartness" as well as to physical beauty.

113

16. This line is corrupt in the MSS., with V apparently reading *bonum factum male bonus ille passer*. While many editors accept the emendation *o factum male! o miselle passer!*, G.P. Goold has argued persuasively in favor of reading *o factum male, quod, miselle passer* on both metrical and contextual grounds (in *Phoenix* 23 [1969] 186-203). A key support for his reading comes from a parody of poem 3 written in the second century A.D. Directed towards a pet dog called Myia, this poem's 4th and 7th lines read *o factum male, Myia, quod peristi.* Most important, however, is the fact that the context of the Catullan poem seems to require a connective of some sort to join *o factum male* with the *tua nunc opera* of the following verse.

17. *tua...opera*: literally "by your doing", like our "thanks to you".

18. *turgiduli*: "slightly swollen".

   ocelli: cf. line 5 above. The diminutives used in lines 16-18 create an intimacy of tone between the poet and his *puella*.

4

A portrait of a ship, now retired after providing good service to its master. Like the famous Argo of myth, this vessel has the ability to speak, and here tells its life story through an interlocutor, who conveys its tale to unnamed visitors. Much of the poem is an exotic geographical excursus, and the poem itself is the first of several in the *Passer* focusing on travel and distant places.

Given the fact that Catullus once travelled to Bithynia, there has been an inclination among critics to see the poem as fact: the ship is that which brought Catullus home from the East, and it is now resting in Lake Garda, where the poet had a villa. But the poet presents no such clear picture in the poem itself, and the piece may well be a pure poetic fiction.

At first sight, poem 4 seems to provide an example of *variatio* in the *Passer*, since its theme diverges greatly from those of poems 3 and 5, both of which are concerned in some way with Lesbia. Yet, it should be noted that poem 4, in at least one respect, grows out of its preceding piece: where poem 3 presented us with a sparrow personified in human terms, poem 4 similarly features the personification of the ship. Moreover, the last journey of the bird in poem 3 is paralleled here by the motif of the ship's last journey, and in both poems the tone adopted by the poet is playful.

Poem 4 is structurally composed of two units of 12 lines each, "capped" by a 3-line conclusion: lines 1-12 are addressed to the unnamed visitors (*hospites*) and focus upon the ship's claim to fame; lines 13-24 are addressed to the birthplace of the ship and present its "life story" in capsule form; the concluding three lines bring us from the past to the present, and to the retired state of the vessel.

Meter: pure iambic trimeter.

1. *Phaselus*: a Greek word that originally meant "bean pod", but which came to signify a light sea-faring ship having a bean pod shape.

hospites: the unnamed "visitors" addressed by the speaker.

2. *ait*: the ship can talk, just like a human being: the playful personification begins here.

    celerrimus: the nominative case here follows Greek rather than Latin practice, not surprising for a ship born in the East. The gender agrees with the *phaselus* of the preceding line.

3. *ullius natantis...trabis*: "of any bark afloat". The double negative in *neque ... nequisse* is paralleled by the *negat ... negare* of lines 6 and 7; in both cases the ship is being emphatic in its boasting.

    impetum: object of *praeterire*.

4. *palmulis*: normally "oars", but here also retaining its original sense of "palms" for the personified vessel.

5. *linteo*: "sail".

6. *hoc*: take as object of *negare* in the next line.

    Hadriatici: the Adriatic Sea between the modern Balkans and Italy, famous for its sudden storms.

7. *Cycladas*: the Cyclades islands which dot the Aegean Sea between Asia Minor and Greece. Note the dominance of *a* sounds in lines 6 and 7.

8. *Rhodumque nobilem*: the "famous" island of Rhodes, not far from the coast of Asia Minor.

116

horridamque Thraciam/Propontida: if the reading *Thraciam* is correct, translate as "the rough Thracian Propontis"; however, it should be noted that V seems to have read *tractam* here. *Propontida* is a Greek accusative singular, and refers to the Sea of Marmora.

9. *Ponticum sinum*: the "Pontic bay" was the Black Sea.

10. *iste post phaselus*: a colloquialism: "that ship to be", or perhaps "that later-day ship".

11. *comata*: "leafy".

 Cytorio in iugo: Cytorus was a mountain in Paphlagonia, in Asia Minor, not far from Bithynia.

12. *loquente...coma*: even before becoming a ship, this wood could speak.

 sibilum: "whistling". The *s* sounds in *saepe sibilum* are obviously appropriate to the sense.

13. *Amastri...Cytore*: vocatives. Both places were in Paphlagonia and were port towns.

 buxifer: "famous for box-trees". The word appears only here in Latin literature.

14. *tibi*: singular, despite the address to two places.

 haec: refers back to the preceding lines.

cognitissima: "exceedingly well known". Again, *s* sounds are dominant in this line.

15. *ait phaselus*: picks up the first two lines of the poem, and continues the personification of the ship.

   ultima ex origine: "from the very moment of birth".

16 - The paralleling structure of these lines is noteworthy:
17. line 16 features the original tree on the mountain-top, line 17 the newly-made ship in the water.

17. *imbuisse*: "dipped". The word is appropriate both to oars and to human palms.

18. *freta*: "straits".

19. *erum*: "master", as though the ship were a slave to its owner.

   laeva sive dextera: take with *aura* in the next line (another *sive* is implied before *laeva*).

20. *utrumque*: with *pedem* in the following line.

   Iuppiter: modified by *secundus*; "a following Jupiter" = "a following wind". Jupiter was, of course, associated with many aspects of the weather, including winds.

21. *pedem*: a nautical word, indicating a rope which made fast the lower corners of a sail.

22. *litoralibus deis*: "the gods of the sea-shore". The

118

implication is that the ship was never in enough danger to warrant the making of such vows for her safety.

23. *sibi*: dative of agent.

24. *novissime*: "recently". If, however, the reading *novissimo* be retained, *mari novissimo* would mean "the last sea to be travelled", that is, the Adriatic.

   ad usque: "all the way up to". Whether the *limpidum lacum* is indeed Lake Garda is outside the set of the poem.

25. *haec*: as in line 14, the reference is to the preceding material.

   recondita: "secluded".

26. *senet*: the personification continues as the ship grows old. *Seneo* is an uncommon, archaic verb: *senescit* would be more common.

   tibi: singular (compare line 14), despite the double vocative to come in the next line.

27. *gemelle Castoris*: the twin of Castor was Pollux; together these gods were known as the Dioscuri, and were the protectors of sailors and ships.

5

A call to Lesbia to join with the poet in living and loving to the fullest. For Catullus, life *is* his love, which is both to be indulged and protected from malevolent outside forces. The poet here adopts the pose of the lover whose passion makes him (and his love) vulnerable to external but intrusive forces that seek somehow to negate his passion.

This is the first poem in the corpus to cite Lesbia by name. Poems 2A and 3 had already informed us of the existence of *mea puella*, and now the mystery created by the two preceding poems is dramatically resolved.

The juxtaposition of this poem with poem 4 is also thematically significant: the previous poem had ended on a note of quiet resignation (*senet quiete seque dedicat tibi*), as if the ship were saying farewell to its very life; here, in poem 5, life is vigorously affirmed at the very start, and the *senum* of line 2 are dismissed. In musical terms, a contrapuntal relation is thus established between poems 4 and 5.

The poem has a carefully balanced structure: lines 1-3 present the call to love in the face of malicious gossip; lines 4-6 provide the rationale for such an indulgence of passion in the approaching finality of death; lines 7-9 express this *carpe diem* theme in an ecstatic piling up of kisses; and lines 10-13 conclude the poem with an attempt to avert any "evil eye" likely to be cast on such indulgence. Thematically, the poem is best compared to poem 7, often termed its "companion piece".

Meter: hendecasyllabic.

1 - *Vivamus...amemus...aestimemus*: the subjunctives are
3.   hortatory.

1. *Lesbia*: a pseudonym that is metrically identical to "Clodia"; it not only hides the true identity of the lover (a common convention), but also compliments Clodia by associating her with the famous poetess Sappho of Lesbos (*cf.* poem 51). Note also the prominent *a* sounds in this line: the poet immediately sets an enthusiastic tone.

2. *severiorum*: *severus* in the sense of stern, *i.e.*, "of the sterner sort"; *cf.* poem 27.6. In lines 2 and 3, the poet emphasizes the sound of *s*: thus his censure of the *senum severiorum* is conveyed by both sound and sense. *Cf.* lines 12 and 13.

3. *omnes unius*: a dramatic juxtaposition of words; *unius...assis* is a genitive of price (the *as* being a Roman coin of very low value, *cf.* today's penny).

4 - The repetition of *occidere...occidit* stresses the crucial
5. distinction between eternal nature and ephemeral mankind.

5. *lux*: the unusual monosyllabic ending emphasizes the shortness of man's life (*cf.* the emphatic *tacet nox* at 7.7); for the theme, *cf.* Horace *Odes* IV.7.13ff.

6. *nox*: another monosyllable, the "night" balancing the "light" of the immediately preceding *lux*. Another arresting juxtaposition in this line is *perpetua una*.

7. *basia*: this word and its derivatives first appear in Latin in Catullus (*cf.* poems 7, 8, 16, and 48). It is generally assumed that the term is one that was common in Northern Italy.

7   The piling up of *deinde* ... *dein* reflects the ecstatic
10. piling up of kisses: Catullus is insatiable. It has
been suggested by H.L. Levy (*American Journal of Philology* 62 [1941] 222-224) that Catullus is to be imagined as using an abacus for his computations in these lines.

9. *usque*: "right on to".

10. *dein*: the final segment of the poem begins with the dominant word of the previous segment.

11. *conturbabimus*: a mercantile term, meaning to "throw into confusion" one's accounts; *illa* may refer to both verbs in this line.

12. *invidere*: "to cast an evil eye upon" (*cf. fascinare* at 7.12). It was believed that precise knowledge had special powers: knowing the exact number of kisses exchanged by the lovers would enable malevolent outsiders to cast a spell on them.

6

Flavius is having an affair, and Catullus wants to hear all the details. If Flavius refuses to talk, only one conclusion is possible: his girl is not "up to standards".

The Flavius to whom the poem is addressed is otherwise unknown; Neudling's suggestion that Catullus refers to L. Flavius the *consul suffectus* of 33 B.C. cannot be substantiated.

The position of this poem after poem 5 seems significant: in the latter poem, Catullus has harsh words for those who seek to intrude upon others' passion; yet here the poet himself plays the role of the inquisitive outsider who wants to uncover the secrets of the lovers. Roles have been reversed, and now Flavius (like Catullus in poem 5) is the lover who tries to keep his love a private matter.

In structure, poem 6 falls into three unequal segments: lines 1-5 depict Flavius' silence about his liaison; lines 6-14 present the poet's evidence for that liaison; and lines 15-17 contain Catullus' plea for more information.

Meter: hendecasyllabic.

1. *delicias*: "sweetheart". *Cf.* 2A.1, 3.4, and 32.2.

2 - *ni sint...velles...posses*: a "mixed" condition; rather
3. than the more normal imperfect in both clauses, the poet employs the present subjunctive in *sint* to stress present time.

2. *illepidae atque inelegantes*: in the poet's circle *lepos* and *elegantia* are the desirable qualities in a lover, in a friend, and in poetry (see line 17).

3. Note the carefully balanced word order: verb, infinitive, conjunction, infinitive, verb (*a b c b a*).

4. *febriculosi*: "feverish" in an uncomplimentary sense; the only appearance of the word in the Catullan corpus.

123

5. *scorti*: *cf. scortillum*, 10.3.

6. *viduas...noctes*: "lonely nights".

7. *nequiquam*: with *tacitum*; the bed may not have the power of speech, but it lets Flavius' secret out nonetheless.

8. *olivo*: "perfume".

9. A skilful play on sounds: alliterative *p*, repetitive *que* and *et*.

10. *quassa*: "broken".

11. The impressive nouns lend a mock heroic tone (*cf.* poem 3): *argutatio* appears nowhere else in Latin literature and may have been created by Catullus to complement the equally formidable *inambulatio*; translate as: "creaking and moving".

12. Haupt's reading: the line in the MSS. is corrupt. *Nil...nihil* intensifies the negative.

13 - *non...pandas...ni...facias*: the present subjunctives are
14. used to stress the present time; *cf.* lines 2-3 above. *Not* a present contrary to fact condition.

13. *ecfututa*: "fucked out"; Catullus uses the vulgar word to emphasize the vulgarity of the situation.

14. *ineptiarum*: another Catullan catchword, whether as a noun (*cf.* also 14B.1), a verb (8.1), or an adjective (12.4, 17.2, 25.8, 39.16). *Cf.* line 2.

15. With this line, the poet begins a three verse summa-
    tion that echoes, in reverse order, lines 2-4; the *quid-*
    quid...boni malique of this line recalls intentionally the
    nescio quid febriculosi of line 4: both, of course, refer
    to the new girl in Flavius' life.

16. *Cf.* line 3: *velles dicere* there is now echoed by
    dic...volo.

17. *Cf.* line 2: *illepidae* is now contrasted with *lep-*
    ido...versu; the girl may be lacking in *lepos*, but not
    so the poetry of Catullus. The poet concludes with a
    mock heroic ending, intending to raise to the heavens
    this sordid little liaison.

7

The dramatic completion of poem 5: Catullus' impas-
sioned plea for kisses in that poem has resulted in Lesbia,
perhaps in playful exasperation, wanting to know just how
many kisses will satisfy her lover. Yet the two poems are
vastly different in tone: whereas poem 5 presents the
poet's passionate call to love, poem 7 shows us Catullus in
a more thoughtful pose, considering his passion in a more
intellectual manner. Thus we find in this piece Alexandrian
conceits, *doctrina*, and even a reference to the poet's literary hero, Callimachus (*cf.* Introduction).

It must also be noted that poem 7 dramatically completes not only poem 5, but also poem 6. In poem 5,
Catullus had adopted the pose of the secretive lover trying
to hide his passion from ill-willed outsiders; then, in poem
6, we saw roles reversed, as Catullus became a nosey outsider seeking to spy upon the passion of his friend Flavius;

125

finally, in poem 7, we find a dramatic fusion of the poet's roles in both preceding poems: now Catullus brings back the image of himself and his love wanting to be kept apart from the *curiosi*, and yet, as S. Commager has written, "by the act of writing such a poem Catullus forces himself to become, in part, one of the *curiosi*, a detached observer of the passion he proclaims" ("Notes on Some Poems of Catullus" in *Harvard Studies in Classical Philology* 70 [1965] 86). Thus, Catullus is still the threatened lover of poem 5, but he is also (paradoxically) the threatening observer of poem 6.

Structurally, poem 7 is as complex a creation as poem 5: there is a carefully controlled division of the poem into four units of 2 + 4 + 2 + 4 lines.

Meter: hendecasyllabic.

1. *Quaeris quot*: note the arresting alliteration of the initial *q* sounds.

   basiationes: a Catullan modification of *basia*, designed to invest that term with an artificial formality appropriate to the *doctrina* of this poem; *basiationes tuae* = "kissings of you" (*cf.* lines 9-10).

2. *sint satis superque*: here the initial *q* sound is combined with strong alliterative *s* sounds; *satis superque*: "enough and more than enough".

3 - The first two lines have presented Lesbia's question;
6. now Catullus offers his first response by way of poetic commonplace (as many kisses as the sands of the desert) adorned with Alexandrian *doctrina*, including

the setting of the desert in Cyrenaica, birthplace of the Alexandrian poet Callimachus. For a similar image, not tinged with Alexandrianisms, *cf.* 61. 199 ff: *ille pulveris Africi/siderumque micantium/subducat numerum prius,/qui vestri numerare volt/multa milia ludi.*

4. *lasarpiciferis...Cyrenis*: *laserpicium* is silphium, a plant whose juices provided a powerful antispasmodic drug (*cf.* Pliny, *NH* 19.38); the plant had been common around Cyrene and was at one time a major export of the city; so important was it that it appeared on the coins of Cyrene. *Lasarpiciferis* is, like *basiationes* above, a word devised by the poet for this poem; translate as "silphium-bearing".

Cyrenis: in the plural this term is commonly used to represent not only the city of Cyrene, but also its surrounding territory.

5. *oraclum Iovis*: in the Libyan desert, at the Siwah oasis, stood the temple and oracle of Ammon, whom the Romans equated with Jupiter. To mention Jupiter-Ammon here, immediately after a reference to silphium, seems especially appropriate as the coins of Cyrene not only bore the silphium plant, but also on the other side the head of Jupiter-Ammon (*cf.* G.K. Jenkins, *Ancient Greek Coins* [1972] # 264, 265). *Aestuosi*: where the reader might normally expect to learn that the oracle itself is hot (not surprising in a desert), the poet instead tells us here that Jupiter-Ammon is "hot", and a sexual meaning might be implicit.

6. *Batti*: in mentioning Battus (a native of Thera who was supposedly the founder of Cyrene and whose tomb seems to have been located within the city), Catullus is in fact paying homage to his poetic mentor Callimachus, who called himself Battiades in his epigram 35; Catullus also refers to Callimachus by that name at poems 65.16 and 116.2. By this point in the poem we seem to be far indeed from Lesbia and her question for the poet!

7 - In these two lines, Catullus provides Lesbia with his
8. second response to her question of how many kisses: as many as the stars. *Cf.* again poem 61.199 ff.

7. *cum tacet nox*: "when the night is still"; for the rhythm of the phrase, *cf.* poem 5.5. *Nox* here also recalls the *nox est perpetua una dormienda* of 5.6, but, in this poem, night is not an image of death, but an image pertaining to the *furtivos amores* of lovers.

8. *furtivos*: "stolen", a word particularly appropriate to the liaison between Catullus and Lesbia.

9 - In the last segment of the poem, Catullus completes
12. his answer to Lesbia's question and at the same time returns the reader to a theme prominent in poem 5: the stern old men and the *ne quis malus* of the latter poem are now transformed into the *curiosi* who want to count the kisses of the lovers and so bewitch them. Thus, in poem 7, the poet's image of the lover as somehow threatened by external forces is reiterated.

9. *te basia...basiare*: the emphasis here on *basia* brings the poem full circle from the *basiationes* of the opening line; *basiare* is used here with two accusatives, one a direct object (*te*), the other a cognate internal accusative (*basia*).

10. *vesano...Catullo*: the reference to himself in the third person increases the analytical sense of detachment which permeates the entire poem—Catullus can indeed recognize his own madness.

    satis et super: as the *basia* of the previous line referred back to the *basiationes* of line 1, so here *satis et super* picks up the *satis superque* of line 2.

11. *pernumerare*: "to count up", a word which appears only here in the Catullan corpus, and which, in conjunction with *curiosi*, recalls the final lines of poem 5.

12. *fascinare*: like *invidere* at 5.12, a word which signifies the casting of an evil spell, "to bewitch"; a *fascinum* was apparently an amulet worn around the body to protect a person from an evil spell.

    lingua: nominative case.

8

Vale, puella: the poet enjoins himself to stand firm and stop playing the fool in his pursuit of a woman who is no longer interested in him; he must learn to accept the fact that his affair is over. But even his rational understanding of this cannot erase the emotional pain he experiences.

At first glance, poem 8 seems to provide an abrupt break, thematically and metrically, from the preceding poems. And yet, dramatically speaking, the poem grows out of those earlier pieces: poems 5 - 7 especially set the stage for it. Poem 7, for example, hints at Lesbia's inability to comprehend the true depth of the poet's passion (*quaeris quot mihi basiationes/tuae, Lesbia, sint satis superque*, l. 1-2) and depicts Catullus as *vesano* (l. 10) — a madness that has turned into misery (*miser Catulle*) now that the poet can no longer "cure" himself with Lesbia's love. Poem 6 is also dramatically relevant: the programmatic word of poem 8, *ineptire* in line 1, takes our minds back to Catullus' suggestion that Flavius is making a fool of himself in *his* affair (*ni tu quid facias ineptiarum*, l. 14); in poem 8, of course, it is Catullus who plays the fool. Finally, poem 5 with its initial injunction to live and love (*vivamus...atque amemus*) finds a contrasting injunction in poem 8's initial *desinas ineptire*; the *soles* of 5.4 become the *soles* of 8.3 and 8, while the many *basia* of the earlier poem find an echo in the *basiabis* of 8.18. Thus, while poem 8 does indeed strike a new note of despair, it still remains an integral part of its poetic context.

There has been some controversy over the years as to whether the poet had written this piece "tongue in cheek" after some minor spat with Lesbia. Two schools of thought have emerged: one, especially advocated by A. L. Wheeler in his *Catullus and the Traditions of Ancient Poetry* (1934), sees the poet playfully adopting the pose of an irresolute comic *amator* seeking a reconciliation with his mistress; the other school of thought reads the poem as an essentially serious soliloquy untempered by any comic posing (*cf.* E. Fraenkel's "Two Poems of Catullus" in the *Journal of Roman Studies* 51 [1961] 51-53).

It would seem that part of the problem here stems from the meter used by Catullus in this poem, the choliambic - a meter traditionally associated with comedy or satire. Its use here is especially set off by the fact that poems 5-7 have all been in the hendecasyllabic meter. Thus a "comic element" of some kind has been sought for in poem 8. Fortunately, a possible way out of this interpretive dilemma has been put forward by M.B. Skinner, who suggests that "it is possible to argue that both perspectives exist simultaneously in the 'Miser Catulle': the poet's emotions are powerful, sincere, and unequivocal, yet he employs the *topos* of the foolish lover as a means of sardonic commentary upon his own folly" ("Catullus 8: The Comic Amator as Eiron" in *Classical Journal* 66 [1971] 298).

Structurally, the poem falls into three main segments of 8 + 3 + 8 lines. The first segment is composed of a two-line statement of the main theme, followed by a six-line reminiscence of past happiness; the central segment of three lines (9-11) portrays the present misery experienced by the poet; the final segment begins with a two-line farewell to Lesbia, followed by a six-line warning to Lesbia composed mainly of a series of rhetorical questions (*cf.* L.A. Moritz, "Miser Catulle: A Postscript" in *Greece and Rome* 13 [1966] 155-157).

Meter: choliambic.

1. *Miser Catulle*: the initial word sets the tone of the poem, while the self-address of *Catulle* seems a further development of the detachment already noted in poem 7; this is the first time in the corpus that the poet addresses himself, but it will not be the last. This

sense of detachment will continue throughout the poem, as the "rational" side of Catullus seeks to gird up the more vulnerable "emotional" side of himself.

ineptire: "to play the fool", a serious failing in the eyes of the poet; elsewhere he generally uses the adjective *ineptus* in a contemptuous manner (*cf.* 12.4; 25.8; 39.16). See also poem 6.14.

2. Catullus here adapts an apparently proverbial expression (*cf.* Plautus' *Trin.* 1026: *quin tu quod periit periisse ducis*); not only is the sense appropriate, but even the sounds of the line (the *d, p, s*) possess a harsh quality suitable to the general tone of the poem.

3. *fulsere*: perfect. This line begins the poet's reflection on his past happiness (*quondam*) and will be repeated almost exactly at line 8. The *soles* of this line hark back to the *soles* of 5.4.

4. *puella*: Catullus' pain is so great that he is unable to speak Lesbia's name; he returns to the anonymity used previously in poems 2 and 3. That Lesbia is indeed meant here seems clear from the next line.

5. A similar line appears at 37.12; here the symmetry of words and sounds is especially skilful. *Nobis*: dative of agent.

6. *ibi*: "then" (*cf. quondam* above); the *ibi...cum* of this line also prepares us for the *nunc iam* of line 9. The contrast between past and present is made abundantly clear.

iocosa: a term with obvious sexual connotations.

7.   The symmetry of this line is also noteworthy: *tu volebas...puella nolebat*; the words themselves are common, everyday terms, yet Catullus has transformed them into poetry by his arrangement. This is indeed true of the language of this poem in general: it is not intrinsically poetic, but becomes so under the poet's guidance.

8.   This near repetition of line 3 closes this segment on the poet's past happiness; the single different word, *vere*, is indeed significant: Catullus emphatically asserts, for one last time, the joys of the past, as he is about to turn in the next line to the torment of the present (*nunc iam*).

9.   *inpotens noli*: this reading has been accepted by most editors, despite some uncertainty as to the exact implications of *inpotens* here; perhaps "headstrong" is the best translation.

10. *sectare...vive*: the poet features here a series of imperatives, most of which are addressed to himself in the hope of strengthening his resolve. The *miser* of this line recalls the first word of the poem.

11. *obstinata*: "resolved".

     perfer, obdura: the asyndeton emphasizes the poet's resolve to rid himself of his present misery.

12. *vale*: this imperative provides a transition to the

133

final segment of the poem, Catullus' rhetorical leave-taking of Lesbia; note also the repetition in *obdurat*: Catullus' command to himself in the previous line has taken hold, or so he hopes.

13.   *invitam*: "against your will".

14.   *cum rogaberis nulla*: the *nulla* is an emphatic negative, in the sense of "not at all"; translate as "when you will be wooed not at all".

15.   *scelesta*: "unlucky"; as the series of rhetorical questions which follows will show, Lesbia will suffer as a result of the poet's new resolve (or so he hopes?). The gist of the following questions is "whose girl will you be now?" — the answer is "not Catullus'".

16.   *adibit*: "approach". This line and the next two are composed of short questions of similar structure, giving this section a somewhat staccato sound.

17.   *cuius esse diceris*: "whose (girl) will you be called?" since she is no longer the "Lesbia Catulli".

18.   *basiabis*: cf. poems 5 and 7.

19.   *at tu, Catulle*: cf. line 14, of Lesbia; the poet makes a contrast between what awaits Lesbia and what awaits him. The self-address again brings our minds back to the opening line, as if the poem has come full circle.

    destinatus: "steadfast"; while this word recalls the *obstinata* of line 11, it has a slightly different sense:

it implies an on-going process rather than one just begun.

obdura: the thematic key-note of the poem, repeated for emphasis at the very end; *cf.* lines 11 and 12.

9

A welcome to Veranius upon his homecoming from Spain. Learning of his friend's arrival home, the poet looks forward not only to seeing Veranius again, but also to hearing him relate his adventures abroad.

The Veranius of the poem remains enigmatic: he appears elsewhere in the Catullan corpus (12, 28, 47) in the company of one Fabullus; here he has obviously been in Spain, but he must have already been an experienced traveller (1.8). The main point stressed in this poem is simply that Veranius is the poet's "best friend".

Poem 9 resumes a theme already struck by poem 4: Veranius, like the ship of the earlier poem, comes "home" and relates the details of his travels; both poems are indeed united by the general theme of the "homecoming". As noted by T.P. Wiseman, poems 4 and 9 (along with the upcoming 10 and 12) present "a coherently developing picture of Catullus' travels and those of his friends" (*Catullan Questions* [1969] 13); this theme of travel serves as an effective counterpoint to the Lesbia theme in this early part of the *Passer*.

Poem 9 is composed structurally of a four-line question, with a single-line answer; a four-line statement of the poet's expectations, and a two-line concluding (rhetorical) question.

Meter: hendecasyllabic.

1. *Verani*:   just as poem 4 begins with the well-travelled *phaselus*, poem 9 begins with the well-travelled Veranius, only here in direct address.

2. *antistans mihi*: *antesto*, meaning to "be superior to", normally takes a dative. Here, with *milibus trecentis*, translate as: "more valuable to me than three hundred thousand (friends)". *Milibus trecentis* simply serves here to indicate a large number of friends, and is not to be taken literally.

3. *penates*:   the Roman tutelary gods of the household.

4. *unanimos*:   commonly translated as "loving" by editors, a translation which fails to catch the sense of "single-minded devotion" implicit in the term; modern translators might do well to consider some adjectival use of the term "soul-mate".

    anumque: used as an adjective: "aged".

5. *nuntii*:   nominative case in an exclamation (although the accusative is more common in Latin).

    beati: a term to be repeated at lines 10 and 11.

6. *visam*:   "I shall go and see".

    Hiberum: genitive plural of *Hiber*:   "of the Spaniards".

7.   *narrantem*:   with *te* (line 6): "describing".

      nationes: "tribes".

8.   *ut mos est tuus*:   Veranius had clearly been abroad
      before, and had returned to tell the poet of his
      experiences; Catullus now expects a similar sharing to
      take place.

      applicansque collum: the picture is one of the poet
      clasping the neck of Veranius in order to draw him
      physically closer; the poet depicts himself as one of
      the family in Veranius' home.

9.   *os oculosque*:   a play on the sound *os*, akin to the
      play on *an* in *unanimos anumque* in line 4 above.

10.   *Cf.* 3.2:   *et quantum est hominum venustiorum*, also
      partitive genitive.

11.   *quid*:   "who".

10

An anecdotal account of the poet's encounter with a
scortum who calls his bluff after a rash boast. The piece
presents a generally comic tone, reinforced by its use of
colloquial language throughout.

Catullus offers us no clue as to the identity of the
woman involved, and even the identity of Varus is unclear:
one suggestion is that we are dealing here with Quintilius
Varus, a friend of both Horace and Vergil (and possibly the
Varus addressed by the poet in poem 22); another

suggestion is that Catullus refers to Alfenus Varus, a well-known lawyer who might also be the focus of poem 30.

Given the poet's reference to his sojourn in Bithynia, it seems logical to place the dramatic date of the poem in 56 B.C. Thematically, then, this poem also partakes of the "homecoming" motif already seen in poems 4 and 9, now with respect to the poet himself. But, if poem 10 can be related to poems 4 and 9, it also bears a resemblance to poem 6: as C.P. Segal noted many years ago ("The Order of Catullus, Poems 2-11" in *Latomus* 27 [1968] 305-321), both 6 and 10 are alike in being light pieces centered upon a *scortum*; in each the woman is presented as the current mistress of one of the poet's friends; both women are described in similar terms; and in both poems a decrepit bed has a curious role to play.

Given the anecdotal and informal nature of poem 10, it is not surprising that the poem's structure is also of a loose, free-flowing type: the poem begins with a four-line introduction to the *scortum*; the next four lines depict the conversation that took place among the three characters with its questions about Bithynia; a five-line segment then presents Catullus' cynical response. The poem then takes the form of a direct question-and-answer exchange (lines 14-20), followed by a three-line parenthetical aside from the poet. The concluding segment (lines 24-34) paints the embarrassing scene that arises when the woman calls the poet's bluff and Catullus has to "own up".

Meter: hendecasyllabic.

1. *Varus me meus ad suos amores*: note the jingle-like sound and rhythm of this initial verse. For *suos*

amores, *cf.* 6.16; translate as "girl-friend".

2. *visum duxerat*: *visum* has been taken either as the supine of *video*, or the supine of *viso* (*cf.* 9.6). The latter seems to provide a smoother sense here: Varus had taken the poet to "go and see" his mistress. It is often pointed out that *viso* with *ad* commonly refers to visiting the sick; if the girl is indeed not well, this might explain her up-coming request to visit the temple of Serapis, a god connected with healing (lines 24 ff.).

    otiosum: "at leisure".

3. *scortillum*: diminutive form of *scortum* (*cf.* 6.5); translate as "little whore".

    repente: "at first glance".

4. *non sane illepidum neque invenustum*: the adjectives are key terms in Catullus' vocabulary; *illepidae* has already appeared at poem 6.2, while the phrase *illepidum neque invenustum* will be picked up again later in the corpus, at 36.17. *Non sane*: "not very".

5. *huc*: *i.e.*, where the woman was to be found.

    incidere = *inciderunt*. The sense is that "various topics of conversation befell us".

6 - *quid esset/iam Bithynia*: "what was Bithynia like
7. these days?".

    quo modo se haberet: "how was it holding up?".

139

8. *et quonam*: if this reading is correct, translate as "and with what cash it had lined my pockets"; some editors, however, prefer to accept the reading *ecquonam*.

9. *id quod erat*: Catullus told "it like it was".

   ipsis: referring to the natives of the province (but some editors take *ipsis* with *praetoribus* in the next line).

10. *praetoribus*: the officials ("governors") in charge of the province.

    cohorti: the staff of the provincial governor, partly other officials, partly unofficial hangers-on.

11. *cur*: introduces an indirect question dependent on the *nihil* of line 9. The loose grammar reflects the colloquial nature of the conversation.

    caput unctius: a well-greased head was a sign of personal prosperity—ointments were rather expensive items.

12. *irrumator*: a vulgar term for a sexual pervert.

13. *praetor*: in this case the praetor at issue is C. Memmius, governor of Bithynia from 57-56 B.C., and also famous as the patron of the poet Lucretius (*De Rerum Natura*). He had served as praetor in Rome in 58 B.C. prior to taking up his duties in the East.

    faceret pili: cf. 5.3; translate as "nor did he give a

damn for his cohort". *Pilus* literally refers to a hair, or something of very small size or value.

14. *inquiunt*: apparently both Varus and his mistress question the poet about his fortunes in Bithynia. Catullus thus gives us the gist of their statements.

15. *natum*: "native" to the place. Bithynia seems to have been famous for its litters and litter-bearers.

   comparasti = comparavisti.

16. *lecticam*: "litter".

17. *me facerem*: "make myself out to be".

   unum...beatiorem: "one of the luckier sort". For *beatus, cf.* poem 9.5, 10, and 11.

18. *non...mihi tam fuit maligne*: a colloquial phrase: "I was not so badly off".

20. *parare*: "to procure".

   rectos: "strapping" fellows.

21. *at*: the poet takes the reader into his confidence.

   nec hic neque illic: neither at Rome nor in Bithynia.

22. *grabati*: apparently a small, cheap bed.

23. *collo...collocare*: also a jingle-like line; for *collum, cf.* 9.8.

24. *hic*: here in the sense of "at this point".

cinaediorem: another vulgar term (quite in contrast to the poet's concept of the girl in line 4); a modern equivalent might be "a rather shameless slut".

25. *quaeso*: "please".

paulum: "for just a little while".

26. *commoda*: imperative form (here with the final *a* short).

Serapim: Serapis was an Egyptian divinity with reputed healing powers; *ad Serapim* = to the temple of Serapis.

27. *mane*: "hold on!". The final *e* is short.

28. *modo*: "just now".

29. *fugit me ratio*: something akin to our "I lost my head".

sodalis: a term for a close companion, here with the additional sense that this friend was also on Memmius' staff; like the English "mate".

30. *Cinna est Gaius*: the awkward syntax reflects the awkwardness of the situation the poet finds himself in. Gaius Helvius Cinna was also a poet of note (*cf.* poem 95).

31. *utrum illius an mei*: "whether they are his or mine".

quid ad me: "what's it to me?"; further examples of Catullus' very colloquial language in this poem.

32. *quam...pararim = quam si paraverim.*

33. *insulsa male et molesta vivis*: "you are very dumb and disagreeable"; *vivis* here = *es*. Catullus' initial opinion has now been changed.

34. *neglegentem*: the poet tries to excuse himself: he was, after all, only being "careless" in his statements!

11

A farewell to Lesbia, but with a tone of finality that sets this piece apart from the earlier goodbye of poem 8. One senses that the veil has lifted from the eyes of the poet, who now sees Lesbia for what she really is.

Poem 11 is thematically most complex as it unites in its six stanzas the three themes so far developed in this part of the *Passer*: Lesbia, the *scortum*, and travel-homecoming. Its participation in the "Lesbia cycle" is obvious (despite the fact that Lesbia is not directly named); perhaps less obvious is the poem's treatment of Lesbia as if she were a *scortum* like those of poems 6 and 10, a treatment that only becomes clear in the final two stanzas of the piece. Finally, the poem begins on a note of exotic travel, but ends "at home" — where Catullus dismisses Lesbia from his world. Thus, the three thematic "streams" of the initial poems in the *Passer* here come together in a climactic flow.

The structure of the poem also reinforces its thematic complexity: the first half (stanzas 1-3) focuses on the poet's relations with Furius and Aurelius as his would-be companions on an exotic journey; contrasting dramatically is the second half (stanzas 4-6), in which the poet's relationship with Lesbia comes to the fore, and the romance of the far away yields to the ugliness of the "home" world. For Catullus there is no escape from the horror which is Lesbia.

The fact that Furius and Aurelius also appear in other poems (15, 16, 21, 23, 24, and 26), but as targets of the poet's abuse, has led some critics to find irony and contempt in Catullus' address to them here; in the context of poem 11 itself, however, there is no clear-cut reason for rejecting a sincere tone, and other critics have pointed out that Horace, in echoing these lines at *Odes* II.6, did not take them as ironical.

The references in lines 10-12 of the poem would seem to argue for a date of composition some time after 55/54 B.C.

Meter: Sapphic stanzas (*cf.* poem 51).

1. *Furi et Aureli:* the identities of these two men remain uncertain, although it is often suggested that Furius could be the poet Furius Bibaculus.

   comites Catulli: a *comes* is a companion in the *cohors* of a provincial governor (*cf.* poem 10); the term is less intimate than *sodalis* (used of Cinna in poem 10), and the phrase *comites Catulli* may hint that the poet is here playing the role of the provincial governor with Furius and Aurelius as his subordinates.

2. *sive*: the first in a series of *sive/seu*, dependent on the implied sense of movement in *comites*, setting out the possible itineraries.

    extremos...Indos: "the Indians living at the world's end".

    penetrabit: "make his way", although the verb also has a sexual connotation that might foreshadow the sexual explicitness of later verses.

3. *ut*: here locative, *i.e.*, "where".

    longe resonante Eoa: taken with the *unda* of the next line; *Eoa*: "eastern". Note the assonance of these words.

4. *tunditur unda*: again the poet has effectively used sound to echo the sense of his words.

5. *Hyrcanos Arabasve molles*: the Hyrcanians lived by the southeast shore of the Caspian sea; *Arabasve* is a Greek accusative, and these people were considered effeminate (*molles*) because of their alleged love of luxury.

6. *Sagas...Parthos*: the Sagae (or Sacae) were Scythian nomads, while the Parthians were, of course, one of the most persistent, and most feared, enemies of Rome in the East.

    sagittiferosve: a word with an epic flavor; *cf.*

septemgeminus in the next line. The poet's possible travels have an epic quality about them. Note also the effective use of *s* sounds in lines 5 and 6.

7. *quae*: taken with *aequora* in the following line.

    septemgeminus: with *Nilus*; the "sevenfold" Nile refers to the seven mouths of the river.

    colorat: "darkens" or "muddies".

8. *aequora*: while some editors translate *aequora* as the "plains" or "level areas" flooded by the Nile, it is more likely that Catullus is here referring to the discoloration of the Mediterranean "waters" where the Nile enters that sea.

9. *gradietur*: the verb basically means "to make one's way on foot"; here the sense is that of hiking or marching. With this stanza the poetic scene shifts from the East to the West.

10. *visens*: "going to see"; the word has already played a part in the two preceding poems (9, 10) and acts as a verbal thread linking these three poems (it will now disappear until poems 62, 63 and 64).

    Caesaris: the great Julius Caesar, whose exploits in the West had captured the public imagination.

11. The reading of this line is in doubt. The MSS. read *horribilesque ulti-mosque*, which makes appropriate sense, but provides a metrical hiatus that troubles editors. Some editors thus prefer the emendation

horribile aequor in reference to the English Channel; this avoids the hiatus, but detracts from the sense of the line, and provides an awkward repetition of the word *aequor*. Thus the MSS. reading is to be preferred, with the hiatus seen as a sound effect, perhaps to emphasize the breath-taking horror of the Britons.

Rhenum: the Rhine river.

11 -   *ulti-mosque*:   an uncommon, but not unprecedented
12.   line division; translate as "at the end of the world" (*cf. extremos* in line 2).

13.   *omnia haec*:   a summary statement, referring to all the travels just outlined in lines 2-12. The governing verb here is *temptare* in the next line.

14.   *caelitum*:   genitive plural of *caelites*, an archaic word for the gods; its use maintains the epic tone set for the poem so far.

parati: the subjects are Furius and Aurelius.

15.   *nuntiate*:   rather than travel with Catullus all over the face of the earth, Furius and Aurelius are asked only to take a message to Lesbia (*meae puellae* — the poet's decision not to call her by name indicates the distance he has come from her). Messages (*nuntii*) had earlier brought good news in poem 9, but this message is quite different, as the next line makes clear.

16.   *non bona dicta*:   "no kind words", almost a male- diction. These *dicta* are the words which follow in

the next two stanzas.

17. *vivat valeatque*: a rather formal renunciation of Lesbia, in great contrast to the *vivamus...atque amemus* of poem 5.

 moechis: "adulterers".

18. *simul complexa*: a picture of Lesbia as a profligate and voracious lover of men now takes clear form; for an interesting contrast, *cf.* *simul parati* in line 14 in reference to Furius and Aurelius.

 trecentos: *cf.* 9.2 and the upcoming 12.10.

19. *identidem*: "again and again"; *cf.* 51.3, where the word also appears in a poem to Lesbia in Sapphic stanzas.

 omnium: hypermetric: the final syllable is elided before the initial vowel of the next line. *Prati* in line 22 will also show this kind of elision.

20. *ilia rumpens*: a graphic picture of the wanton Lesbia; *ilia* here in the sense of "balls".

21. *respectet*: "look round for".

22. *illius culpa*: "by her fault".

23. *ultimi*: *cf.* lines 11-12; the flower is located at the far edge of the field.

24. *tactus*: just barely nipped, or "grazed" by the

careless plough (Lesbia). There is a similar image in
a fragment by Sappho (LP 105c), in which a flower in
the mountains is crushed under foot by herdsmen; it
is likely that Catullus wanted to close his poem in
Sapphic stanzas with an echo from Sappho herself.
For the poet's most obvious Sapphic echo, see poem
51.

12

A demand that a stolen dinner napkin be returned to
the poet. While the occasion for the poem might seem trivial, Catullus employs the situation to offer comments not
only on "smart" behavior, but also on friendship—in this
case, his relationship with Veranius and Fabullus. Indeed,
a poem which begins as an attack on the thievery of Asinius ends as a sincere compliment to the poet's two comrades.

Poem 12 belongs to the same poetic world as poems 6
and 10 in attempting to define for the reader the qualities
of *lepos* and *venustas*; in fact the verbal similarities
between this poem and poem 10 make it clear that poem
12 is a "follow up" to the previous piece in presenting
another vignette of unacceptable behavior. The appearance
of Veranius also ties poem 12 to poem 9, in which that
friend was introduced for the first time.

The poem can be divided into four structural segments: lines 1-5 castigate Asinius for his theft; lines 6-9
support the poet's disapproval of Asinius by pointing to the
disapproval displayed by the thief's own brother; lines 10-13
demand the return of the napkin which has "sentimental
value" for the poet; and lines 14-17 explain what that value

in fact is.

Meter: hendecasyllabic.

1.   *Marrucine Asini*:   aside from this poem, nothing is known about this person. From lines 6-7 we infer that he was the brother of C. Asinius Pollio, a famous critic and historian; but it is not even certain whether Marrucinus is his cognomen, or just a geographical epithet.   The Asinii seem to have been from Teate, which was located in the territory of the Marrucini, on the east coast of central Italy.

manu sinistra: ablative after *uteris* in line 2; in antiquity (as now) the left hand tended to be associated with theft and "dirty tricks" (*cf.*   poem 47.1).

2.   *belle*:   "smartly".

in ioco atque vino: as we might say "over jokes and wine". Here the poet provides the setting for Asinius' theft.

3.   *tollis*:   "lift".

lintea: *linteum* basically refers to a linen cloth of some kind; here a dinner napkin is meant. The Romans customarily brought their own napkins to dinner parties.

neglegentiorum: *cf.*   10.34.

4.   *salsum*:   "smart" in the sense of clever or witty; *cf.* *insulsa* at 10.33.

fugit te: *cf.* 10.29.

inepte: a Catullan keyword in the vocabulary of bad taste, akin to our "fool" (*cf. ineptire* at poem 8.1).

5. *quamvis*: in its primary sense, with an adjective, "as...as you like"; here translate as "it is as vulgar and unattractive a thing as you like" — although a more modern equivalent might be "it is as vulgar and unattractive a thing as can be".

6. *non credis mihi*: the poet dramatically looks about for support for his opinion.

    Pollioni: there seems to be no good reason to doubt that this is the C. Asinius Pollio well known to both Vergil and Horace; Pollio was born ca. 76 B.C., and critics have seen in his description as *puer* evidence for poem 12 being composed around 60-58 B.C.

7. *vel talento*: "for even as much as a talent"; *talento* here (ablative of price) stands for any large sum of money, which Pollio would gladly pay to wipe out his brother's foolish actions.

8. *mutari*: best taken in the sense of "redeem" or "undo". Pollio wants to redeem the family's honor.

    velit: a potential subjunctive.

8 - *leporum/differtus...facetiarum*: the MSS. here read
9. *disertus*, which presents problems both of sense and grammar; thus many editors accept the emendation

differtus, in the sense of "chock full of". The genitives would then be grammatically explicable. *Leporum* and *facetiarum* both refer to a charming kind of wit, highly valued by the poet, and a quality obviously missing in the napkin thief.

10. *hendecasyllabos trecentos*: *trecentos* again (as in poems 9 and 11) refers to a very large number; here Asinius is warned to expect a great deal of poetic abuse should he fail to return the napkin (this poem itself is, of course, a partial fulfillment of this threat).

12. *quod*: referring to *linteum* in the previous line.

   aestimatione: ablative of cause.

13. *verum*: "but".

   mnemosynum: a Greek word for keepsake or souvenir.

   sodalis: singular, but applicable to both of the poet's friends, soon to be named. *Cf.* 10.29.

14. *sudaria Saetaba*: a *sudarium* was a piece of cloth generally used for wiping the face, *i.e.*, another word for napkin here; Saetabis was a town in the region of Spain known to the Romans as Tarraconensis, and was famous for its linen. We already know, from poem 9, that Veranius had been in Spain on his travels.

15. *miserunt mihi muneri*: note the alliteration here.

Fabullus: the first appearance in the corpus of this close friend; *cf.*   poem 13.

16.   *haec*:   in reference to the *sudaria*.

amem: the mood is governed by *necesse est* (*ut* omitted).

17.   *ut*:   "just as".

Veraniolum: the diminutive as a sign of affection (but note that Fabullus' name is already in a diminutive form).

meum: as with *sodalis* in line 13, this word refers to both men.

13

A mock dinner invitation to Fabullus: the poet won't mind at all if Fabullus comes to dine—as long as he brings all the necessities for dinner!   The "invitation poem" was a recognized type of ancient poetry, and it is likely that Catullus is here parodying the genre.   The Fabullus who is the recipient of the poem is no better known to us today than the Veranius with whom he is often associated. It is clear, however, that both men were considered close friends by the poet.

The relation of poem 13 to the preceding poem in the *Passer* is obvious: poem 12 not only introduces Fabullus for the first time, but even ends with his name; then poem 13 picks up the same figure at once in its initial verse. Even the setting of the *cena*, or dinner party, is common to both poems: in poem 12 Catullus' napkin (a gift from Veranius and Fabullus) is stolen at dinner; in poem 13 a dinner invitation is the focus of the entire piece. Indeed, it has been suggested that these two adjoining poems, along with the earlier poem 9, form a "mini-cycle" in the corpus: all are concerned with Veranius and/or Fabullus, and all seem to celebrate the poet's friendship with these men.

Structurally the poem falls into three segments: lines 1-5 set out the comic "invitation" to dinner, complete with a "shopping list" for Fabullus; lines 6-8 explain the reason for such a peculiar invitation in the poet's poverty; and lines 9-14 offer amends by means of a "gift" that the poet can give his friend.

Meter: hendecasyllabic.

1. *apud me*: "at my place".

2. *paucis...diebus*: the very vagueness of the dinner date implies that the poet has tongue in cheek.

   si tibi di favent: "if the gods are good to you". The phrase has a rather pretentious, mock heroic tone, and is ironical in terms of the following lines. Note also that here we have the initial *si* of a series, all expressing the very conditional nature of the invitation.

4. *candida puella*: "a fair young lady".

5. *et...et...et*: the repetition gives this line the tone of a shopping list.

sale: a pun is intended here: after *vino* one would expect *sale* to maintain its usual sense of "salt", but once we see the *omnibus cachinnis* that follows, we realize that *sale* can also be taken as "wit" here.

omnibus cachinnis: "all kinds of jokes"; *cf.* poem 12.2: *in ioco atque vino*.

6. *venuste noster*: a term of endearment: Fabullus possesses that quality of *venustas* so valued by the poet; *cf.* 3.2.

7. *cenabis bene*: an emphatic repetition of the first words of the poem; now the poet must offer his friend an explanation of his odd invitation.

8. *sacculus*: a small bag, or "purse".

plenus...aranearum: Catullus' purse is "full—of cobwebs"; the delaying of *aranearum* until the end of the verse lends an air of surprise: the poet's purse *is* full, but not of cash! For the motif of Catullus as impoverished, *cf.* poem 10.21-23.

9. *contra*: "in return"; the poet now offers something to his "guest".

meros amores: "pure, undiluted love". Some editors prefer to read *meos amores*, but this reading presents problems of sense: in Catullus *meos amores* usually refers to the object of the poet's affections and it is difficult to see in what way Fabullus can here "receive" that beloved. Besides, the next lines make it clear that Fabullus is about to receive, not a person,

155

but an unguent.

10. *seu = vel si.*

   elegantiusve: "more attractive".

11. Catullus now clarifies what his "gift" is to be:
   unguentum. *Unguentum* normally refers to a per-
   fumed ointment of the kind used at elegant dinner
   parties, but critics have wondered whether Catullus is
   here using the term in some less obvious sense; by far
   the most controversial suggestion has been that of
   R.J. Littman ("The Unguent of Venus: Catullus 13"
   in *Latomus* 37 [1977] 125-128), who argues that
   Catullus is in fact alluding to Lesbia's "vaginal secre-
   tions". This interpretation, however, gives the poem
   a rather inelegant twist and also presents problems of
   sense.

   meae puellae: undoubtedly Lesbia; poem 13, then,
   takes us back to a time when the affair was still in
   full bloom.

12. *donarunt = donaverunt.*

   Veneres Cupidinesque: *cf.* poem 3.1.

14. *totum...nasum*: as in line 8, the delaying of the key
   word until the end of the line creates suspense and
   surprise. The poem ends in the comic image of
   Fabullus turned into one huge nose. It should be
   noted that the poem, while addressed to Fabullus,
   becomes an indirect compliment to Lesbia.

A poem about poetry, in the guise of a wry acknowl-
edgement of a book of poetry given Catullus as a gift by
Calvus. The occasion was the Saturnalia, a Roman festival
that began on December 17th, and which featured the
exchange of gifts among friends; the giver of the gift, C.
Licinius Calvus, was a close friend of Catullus as well as
an accomplished poet and lawyer (*cf.* poems 50, 53, and
96).

Like the preceding poem in the *Passer*, poem 14A
turns upon the motif of a gift: whereas in poem 13 Fabullus was asked to bring "dinner gifts" to Catullus' place in
order to receive in turn the poet's unique gift of *unguentum*, here Calvus has given a gift which compels the poet
to seek out an appropriate gift in response. Both poems,
moreover, bear the air of practical jokes played by friends
upon each other, and both certainly share a similar comic
tone.

First and foremost, however, poem 14A is concerned
with standards of poetry, and in this respect both looks
back to poem 1 and forward to fragment 14B.

Structurally, the poem falls into five segments: lines
1-5 set out the problem, namely, Calvus' gift of an anthology of bad poetry; lines 6-11 focus upon the identity of the
person who first gave the book to Calvus; lines 12-15 disclose the effect the gift had on Catullus; lines 16-20 reveal
the poet's intended revenge; and lines 21-23 offer a final
dismissal of the offensive poetry.

Meter: hendecasyllabic.

1. *plus oculis meis*: an image that appears several times in the corpus: *cf.* 3.5; 82.2 and 4; 104.2. A modern analogy might be the assertion that "I would give my right arm" — that is, the part of myself that I value the most.

2. *iucundissime Calve*: "my most congenial Calvus". *Cf.* 50.16, also to Licinius Calvus.

    munere isto: "because of that present of yours"; *isto* here has its common derogatory sense.

3. *odissem*: imperfect subjunctive.

    odio Vatiniano: Calvus had prosecuted Publius Vatinius, a generally unpopular politician (*cf.* poem 53), and had thus earned that man's fervent hatred; translate as "with a hatred like that Vatinius feels for you". For a similar phrase, see 53.2-3: *Vatiniana...crimina*. Note also the emphatic repetition in *odissem...odio*.

5. *cur*: "on account of which".

    male perderes: "you would damn near destroy me"; for *male* in this intensive sense, *cf.* 10.33.

    tot: with *poetis*.

6. *isti...clienti*: like the *isto* of line 2, *isti* here is derogatory; *clienti* may indeed refer to a "client" (in the modern sense) defended by Calvus in court, but the term technically could merely refer to a *cliens* in the common *patronus-cliens* relationship. Note that the

158

sounds in this line are appropriate for a curse, emphasizing *i*, *d*, and *m*.

7. *tantum...impiorum*: partitive genitive; *cf.* 5.13. Translate as "such a mass of sinners".

8. *quod si*: "but if".

   novum ac repertum: taken together as "newly discovered"; the anthology is a "new find" sent enthusiastically to Calvus by his *cliens*.

9. *Sulla litterator*: Sulla is unknown, but *litterator* usually refers to an elementary schoolteacher in a somewhat disparaging manner. The poet would seem to be implying "what else can one expect from a person of this sort?", that is, one with no real literary taste.

10. If Sulla the schoolteacher did in fact send Calvus this book, then "it's not such a bad thing in my view, but actually good, and even fortunate".

11. *dispereunt*: "wasted". The *labores* of this line would refer to Calvus' efforts on behalf of Sulla.

12. *di magni*: *cf.* 53.5, also a poem about Calvus, and 109.3.

    sacrum: "detestable". The construction here is an accusative of exclamation. For *libellum*, *cf.* poem 1.

13. *scilicet*: "to be sure", an ironical comment.

14. *misti = misisti*.

continuo: although some editors take this as an adjective with *die* (and translate "on the very next day"), it seems probable that *continuo* here is an adverb, meaning "without delay". The image is one of Calvus getting rid of the offensive volume as quickly as he could.

14 - *ut die periret/Saturnalibus optimo dierum*: take
15. *die...optimo dierum* in apposition with *Saturnalibus*; the day referred to would be December 17th.

16. *non non*: repeated for added emphasis: Calvus cannot expect to get off scot-free!

salse: "you funny fellow"; the poet sees himself as the victim of a practical joke.

abibit: in the sense of "get away with" or "be allowed to pass".

17. *si luxerit*: with a sense of impatience: "if dawn ever gets here". Catullus will procure the means of his revenge first thing in the morning.

librariorum: "booksellers".

18. *scrinia*: cylindrical receptacles for books.

Caesios, Aquinos: generalizing plurals, to indicate that the poet intends to collect the poems of all bad poets like Caesius and Aquinus; obviously Catullus saw these men as typical of the poets he despised.

160

19. *Suffenum*: a poet who is also discussed by Catullus in poem 22. The appearance of his name in the singular may be solely the result of metrical demands.

venena: descriptive of all those poets just named.

20. *his suppliciis*: "with these instruments of torture", *i.e.*, the poems.

21. *vos*: the poet turns now to the book sent him by Calvus, which he apparently intends to "return to sender".

valete abite: "goodbye and get away from" here; Catullus omits the expected connective.

22. *illuc*: go back to where you came from.

malum pedem: a play on words: in addition to the literal sense of "foot", *pedem* here also refers to the metrical "foot" — that is, to the poor rhythms in these collected verses.

23. *saecli incommoda*: "you afflictions of the modern age".

14B

A fragment of what looks like a programmatic poem. In being about poetry, these lines pick up the theme of poem 14A, but clearly do not belong with it despite the lack of a break in the MSS.

It seems possible that this fragment was intended to

look ahead in the *Passer* to the cycle of poems about Furius, Aurelius and Juventius which ensues. The self-disparaging tone of these lines might then be explicable as a kind of mock apology for the nature of the poems to follow.

Meter: hendecasyllabic.

1. *ineptiarum*: "nonsense"; cf. *nugas* at 1.4. In both of these programmatic poems, Catullus ironically plays down the value of his poetry.

3. *horrebitis*: also self-disparaging; translate as "shudder to".

   admovere: "apply".

15

A request and accompanying warning to Aurelius: keep safe the *puer* of the poet, or suffer unpleasant consequences. The thematic coarseness of this poem (and some of those to follow as well) has minimized editorial commentary in the past, and has led critics to debate whether or not Catullus is to be taken seriously here: do we accept the poem at face value, or is it really a light-hearted "lampoon" intended to scandalize?

Aurelius has appeared already in poem 11 along with Furius; these two men, either together or singly, also appear in poems 15, 16, 21, 23, 24, and 26 — a group of poems often referred to as Catullus' Furius and Aurelius "cycle". This cycle revolves around sexual themes, and Skinner has gone so far as to call Furius and Aurelius

162

"Siamese twins of depravity" (*Catullus' Passer* [1981] p. 45). It is likely that fragment 14B served as a mock apology in introducing these poems.

Poem 15 is composed of two uneven segments: lines 1-13 present the poet's request to Aurelius, while lines 14-19 threaten the man with mayhem should he fail to honor the request.

Meter: hendecasyllabic.

1. *Commendo*: the verb conveys a sense of entrusting someone or something to another for protection.

    me ac meos amores: in entrusting Aurelius with his *amores*, the poet is also entrusting himself, so close is the bond involved; the identity of *meos amores* is not clear at this early point in the poem, but see line 5.

2. *peto pudentem*: cf. *puto pudenter* at line 13 below; it has been suggested that *pudenter* also be read in line 2, but the MSS. offer *pudentem*, which makes good sense: the poet is seeking a "decent favor", and *pudentem* here suggests, in the words of the Oxford Latin Dictionary, "having a due sense of what one's position requires" — the position involved being that of a kind of guardian for a young man.

3. *ut*: take with *conserves* at line 5.

    cupisti = *cupiisti*.

4. *quod*: referring back to *quicquam* in line 3.

castum...et integellum: "pure and unblemished".

5. *puerum*: at last we discover the object of the poet's concern, an unnamed boy, the identity of whom will become clear as the "cycle" progresses.

   pudice: with *pudentem* in line 2, it is clear that a major theme of this poem is that of *pudor*, the sense of decency.

6. *populo*: the "common folk", the "man in the street".

   nihil: with adverbial force: "not at all".

7. *modo huc modo illuc*: cf. 3.9.

8. *in re...sua*: "in their own affairs".

   praetereunt: cf. 11.23, in a very different context.

9. *verum*: "but".

   pene: the first real "shocker" in the poem; Catullus now takes the poem along an explicitly coarse road.

10. *infesto*: with *pene*: his organ is "harmful" to boys; the adjective also has the sense of something "poised to strike" or "pointed towards" — obviously appropriate in this context.

11. *quem*: referring to *pene*.

    qua lubet: locative: "where you wish".

ut lubet: "as you wish".

12.   *quantum vis*: "to what degree you wish".

       ubi: here the temporal indefinite adverb: "at any time", "whenever".

       foris: "among the people" at large; contrasts with *hunc unum* in the next line.

13.   *excipio*: "I set apart" from the people at large.

14.   *quod si*: "but if"; *cf.* 14A.8.

       vecors: "frenzied".

15.   *sceleste*: "you villain".

16.   *nostrum...caput = me*.

       insidiis: "by a treacherous attack".

       lacessas: "provoke".

17.   *te miserum*: accusative of exclamation.

       malique fati: genitive of description.

18.   *attractis pedibus patente porta*: how Aurelius is to be punished is now made clear; *attractis pedibus*: "with your feet drawn up"; *porta* here = *ano*. Note the alliteration in this line.

19.   A particularly painful punishment, also alluded to in

Aristophanes' *Clouds* 1083 and in Juvenal 10. 317. The fins and scales of the mullet apparently could do great damage on their extraction from the body.

16

A threat to Aurelius and Furius, who have inferred from Catullus' verse that the poet has a sexual problem—a charge Catullus will refute by direct action. Out of this coarse attack, however, comes an important observation about poetry: the reader cannot judge a poet's personal life by what he writes in his verse.

The poem combines two themes which are treated by the preceding poems in the *Passer*: poetry (14A, 14B) and sex (15). Its relation to poem 15 is especially close, both in theme and in language, and, like poem 15, this piece may be a "tongue-in-cheek" lampoon meant to raise eyebrows. Indeed, the poet's very statement about poetic license in lines 5-6 warns us against taking Catullus' graphic threats too literally.

The poem has a tripartite structure: lines 1-4 present the poet's complaint and intended revenge; lines 5-11 are the heart of the poem, and offer Catullus' views on his *versiculi*; finally, lines 12-14 restate the opening complaint and threat.

Meter: hendecasyllabic.

1. *Pedicabo...irrumabo*: graphic terms belonging to the world of sex; *pedicabo* literally refers to the insertion of the penis into the anus, while *irrumabo* pertains to its insertion into the mouth. However, in addition to

these literal meanings, these verbs also had the colloquial sense of the modern "screw you". Catullus
undoubtedly had both literal and colloquial usages in
mind here, and a poem beginning with such language
was bound to raise some eyebrows in conservative cir-
cles.

2. *pathice et cinaede*: also sexual terms; a *pathicus* and
   a *cinaedus* were often objects of contempt for the
   passive, "female" role they assumed in sexual relation-
   ships. The poet is thus calling Aurelius and Furius
   unmanly queers, fitting recipients for the punishment
   he proposed in the first line.

3. *versiculis*: what might be called "light verse" now;
   cf. nugae and *ineptiae*.

4. *molliculi*: from the primary meaning of "tender" or
   "delicate", the adjective came to mean "unmanly".
   The inference is, of course, that the composition of
   tender poetry is the mark of an effeminate poet.
   Even now, tenderness is not often seen as the trade-
   mark of a "macho man".

   parum pudicum: "not terribly decent"; *cf.* poem 15,
   where *pudor* was an important theme.

5. *castum*: *cf.* 15.4. Here virtually a synonym for *pudi-*
   cum above.

   pium poetam: *cf.* 14A.7.

6. *nihil*: *cf.* 15.6: "not at all". The phrase *esse castos*
   is understood here.

7. *tum denique*: "precisely" if (*si* in line 8).

   salem ac leporem: both terms have already appeared in the corpus (12.8 and 13.5) and are key words in the Catullan vocabulary of good taste.

8. Note the reiteration, with minor variation, of line 4. His verses may be "unmanly and not terribly decent", but that is what gives them their charm and wit.

9. *quod pruriat*: "a sexual urge".

   incitare: "rouse".

10. *non dico*: another verbal echo of poem 15 (line 6).

    pilosis: in its primary sense, "hairy", but secondarily as "virile". *Cf.* the modern connection of hair on the chest with a sexy man. It has been suggested that the *pilosi* here are in fact Aurelius and Furius, but both the language and the context make it more likely that the poet is generalizing.

11. *duros...lumbos*: *lumbos* probably refers here to the male genitals; *duros* has the sense of "slow" or "sluggish". The seemingly sexy fellows (*pilosi*) who cannot get an erection are affected by Catullus' *versiculi*.

    movere: *cf.* 15.11.

12. *vos*: the poet returns to Aurelius and Furius and their inferences.

    milia multa basiorum: the most controversial phrase

in the poem, with critics equally divided over whether
the poet is here alluding to poem 5 or poem 48.
But, if Catullus did indeed arrange the poems in his
Passer, might he not have had both pieces in mind?
As Skinner has written, "With the Lesbia cycle fresh
in his mind, the reader...would naturally understand
milia multa basiorum as a straightforward reference to
poems 5 and 7 and assume that Catullus is absolving
himself from the conventional *mollitia* of the erotic
poet.   When he came to poem 48, however, ... he
would realize that he had been duped again: now the
homosexual connotations of *mollis* come into play, and
the particular threats leveled at Furius and Aurelius
take on a sinister importance.   Naturally, Catullus
has anticipated this delayed recognition" (*Catullus'
Passer*, 54).

13.   *Cf.* lines 3-4.

14.   The final line closes the poem by echoing its initial
verse, with the *literal* meanings of both verbs now
emphasized.

17

A poem which begins as a wish for a decent bridge
for the town of "Colonia", but ends as an attack on a
lethargic townsman who is unable to cope with his active
young wife.   The complex relationship in the poem among
the town, the bridge, the husband and his wife was best
elucidated by N. Rudd ("Colonia and her bridge: A note
on the structure of Catullus 17" in *TAPA* 90 [1959]
238-242); according to Rudd the decrepit old bridge is akin
to the inadequate husband, while the festival-loving town

resembles the merry wife.

The poem apparently takes its hypothesis from an actual custom at Rome which involved the throwing of rush effigies of aged men from a bridge; it has been suggested that such effigies served as propitiatory victims for the river god. Catullus, however, has set his poem not in Rome, but at "Colonia" — most likely to be Verona, although some editors prefer the modern Cologna not far from Verona. The identities of the husband and wife remain enigmatic, although J.W. Zarker ("*Mule, Nihil Sentis*: Catullus 83 and 17", *Classical Journal* 64 [1968/9] 172-177) has put forward a case for seeing Lesbia and her husband, Q. Metellus Celer, as the real-life figures involved.

At first glance, poem 17 seems out of place within the Furius and Aurelius "cycle" of this part of the *Passer*. A closer inspection, however, reveals that the poem is thematically connected to the preceding poem 16. That earlier piece ended with the poet's defence of himself against the charge of "not being man enough" (*male me marem putatis*, 13); poem 17 then takes up the theme of sexual inadequacy, and presents us with a man who (unlike the poet) clearly *does* have a sexual problem! The poem also has ties with poems 6, 10 and 12 in focusing upon unacceptable social behavior.

The poem falls into three distinct segments: lines 1-11 introduce the situation in Colonia and the lethargic townsman whom the poet wants to throw off the bridge; lines 12-22 explain the offense committed by the man; and lines 23-26 recapitulate the poet's wish.

Meter: priapean.

1. *Colonia*: the identification of Colonia with Verona is supported by *municipem meum* in line 8; Catullus, of course, was a native of Verona.

   ludere: here in the sense "to celebrate games"; later, in line 17, the verb will convey a more sexual sense.

2. *salire paratum habes*: "are prepared to leap about" in dance; this use of *habeo* almost as an auxiliary verb is not uncommon in classical Latin. A literal translation would be "have made ready your dancing".

   inepta: while the translation "shaky" or "ill-fitting" is often suggested, the primary sense of "silly" or "stupid" is also appropriate.

3. *crura*: the bridge is personified with human legs (the legs of inanimate objects are normally called *pedes*), and this personification looks ahead to the identification of the bridge with the lethargic townsman.

   ponticuli: most likely the same as the *ponte...longo* of line 1, with the diminutive form applying not to the length of the bridge, but to its piteous condition; translate as "miserable old bridge". Note also that diminutives have a prominent role throughout the poem as a whole.

   axulis...in redivivis: "on poor second-hand planks". *Axulis* is a diminutive form of *axis*, and again the diminutive expresses pity or contempt.

4. *supinus eat*: "fall flat".

cavaque: "deep". The bridge in the swamp looks ahead to the man in the swamp of line 10.

5. *sic*: here emphasizing a conditional wish: let Colonia have its fine bridge—as long as the poet gets *his* wish!

   ex tua...libidine: "according to your desires". The noun has a sexual nuance that looks ahead to the sexually attractive wife.

6. *vel Salisubsali sacra*: a bridge on which "even the rites of Salisubsalus" could be celebrated. While the identity of the deity is uncertain (Mars is one suggested candidate), it is clear that the rites in question must have been very vigorous, and taxing to any bridge.

7. *munus*: here in the sense of "gift".

8. *municipem meum*: "a fellow-townsman of mine".

9. *ire praecipitem*: "fall headlong". *Cf.* the falling of the bridge in line 4.

   per caputque pedesque: "head over heels".

10. *verum...ut*: "but only where". The ensuing genitives of this line are dependent on the *vorago* of line 11.

    putidaeque paludis: "of the stinking swamp"; *cf.* line 4.

11. *lividissima*: "murkiest".

maximeque: with *profunda*.

vorago: "quagmire". *Cf.* line 26.

12. *insulsissimus est homo*: "he is the stupidest chap imaginable".

pueri instar/bimuli: "like a two-year-old child". While it has been argued that the townsman is being compared to his *own* child, Catullus is more likely to be generalizing here.

13. *tremula...in ulna*: the meaning of *tremula* here will depend on our interpretation of the *puer* in line 12: if the child is that of the townsman, then "trembling" would appropriately describe the shaky ineptitude of the man; if, however, Catullus *is* generalizing here, then "rocking" would be more logical.

14. *cum*: concessive.

viridissimo...flore: ablative of description: "in the freshest flower" of life. Note the unusual number of superlative adjectives in lines 11-16.

15. *et*: here in the sense of "indeed".

delicatior: in association with a young goat this adjective takes on the sense of "more playful" with a definite sexual overtone; goats, after all, were known for their lusty behavior. Note the double diminutive in *tenellulo*.

173

16. *nigerrimis...uvis*: "ripest grapes". When grapes are ripest, they (like the wife) demand the most careful attention.

17. *ludere*: here with sexual activity implied.

   nec pili facit uni: cf. 10.13. *Uni = unius*.

18. *se sublevat*: while the phrase could mean "bestir himself" in general, the implied sense is that the townsman was unable to get an erection and thus satisfy his wife's desires.

   ex sua parte: "on his own behalf".

19. *Liguri*: the Ligurians were a people of Cisalpine Gaul famous for their talents as woodsmen.

   suppernata: "ham-strung", that is, cut down from below.

20. *tantundem*: "just as much", with *quam*.

   quam si nulla sit usquam: "as if it (that is, the tree) had no existence at all"; *nulla* here in the sense of *non*.

21. *meus stupor*: "that idiot of mine". The man is so stupid that he is *stupor* itself, personified. A few editors prefer to read *merus stupor*, that is, "he is pure, unadulterated stupidity", but the MSS.' *meus* makes perfect sense.

22. The man's lack of awareness exactly parallels the

tree's unconscious state in line 20.

23. *nunc*: the poet returns to the matter at hand, his wish.

   de tuo ponte: *cf.* line 8.

   pronum: "head first".

24. *si pote*: "to see if he can"; *pote* = *potest*. We now learn that the poet's motivation is honorable: he hopes a plunge into the swamp will arouse the man from his lethargy, and that he will emerge from the muck "born again".

   stolidum...veternum: "dull lethargy".

25. *supinum*: "sluggish".

   caeno: "slime".

26. Apparently Roman mules were shod with leather slippers having metal soles. For *mula*, *cf.* 83.3, of Q. Metellus Celer.

(18-20)

In the manuscripts of Catullus' poems, poem 17 is at once followed by what is now called poem 21. However, in the sixteenth century, an editor inserted three poems between them which he believed were also by Catullus. At present, the critical consensus is that the three interpolated poems must be removed and the MSS. order of poems restored. Nonetheless, editors have kept the numbering of the poems that resulted from the interpolation.

21

To Aurelius: stop being so "friendly" with my boy—
or else! Aurelius is here attacked not only for his relationship with the boy, but also for his poverty, which has left
him bereft of food and drink.

The poem is a companion-piece to poem 15, much as
poem 7 is a follow-up to poem 5. It would seem that, as
the poetic drama of the Furius and Aurelius cycle unfolds,
Aurelius has not taken the poet's warning in poem 15 to
heart, necessitating poem 21. Like its companion-piece,
poem 21 is a deliberate "shocker", perhaps not to be taken
too literally.

Structurally, the poem is composed of five uneven
sections: lines 1-4 state the charge against Aurelius; lines
5-6 present the evidence in support of the charge; lines 7-8
announce the poet's intended punishment; lines 9-11 break
the logical sequence by presenting the particular aspect of
the affair that perturbs the poet; and lines 12-13 return to
the poet's threatened punishment.

Meter: hendecasyllabic.

1. *pater esuritionum*: to be called the "father" of something was normally an honor, but here the poet per-
   verts the title for a perverted person: Aurelius is not
   just a hungry man—he is the very father of hungers;
   cf. 23.14.

2. *harum*: with *esuritionum*. A close echo of lines 2-3

176

may be found at 24. 2-3, another member of this poetic cycle.

4. *pedicare*: cf. 16.1.

    meos amores: cf. 15.1; the logical assumption is that the same lad is meant. The poet, however, has not yet clearly identified the lad.

5. *simul es*: "you are in his company".

6. *haerens ad latus*: "sticking to his side".

7. *insidias*: cf. 15.16.

    instruentem: "planning".

8. *prior*: temporal; the poet will get Aurelius first, before he can "get" the poet.

    irrumatione: cf. 16.1.

9. *atque*: here in the sense "and yet". The poet departs from his threat for a moment in order to explain what it is about Aurelius' actions that really bothers him.

    id: referring back to lines 4-6.

    satur: "well fed".

10. *nunc*: "as it is now".

    esurire: "to experience hunger".

11. *a te mi*: the text here is in doubt; the MSS. apparently read *me me*. Some editors prefer the emendation *meus iam (puer)*.

sitire: "to experience thirst". The "Father of Hungers" teaches his "art" to the boy.

12. *pudico*: for stress on *pudor*, *cf.* poem 15. The poet advises Aurelius to get away while he can—with his honor intact.

13. *irrumatus*: for an emphatic position as the final word, *cf.* 16.14.

22

Addressed to Varus, but really a poem about Suffenus, one of the poisonous poets mentioned in poem 14A. The man is a prolific and enthusiastic versifier, but without much talent: while his books look attractive, their contents are boorish.

The poem clearly has points of contact with poems 1, 14A, and 16—all of which deal with poetry and poetic standards. Less obvious, but no less real is its connection with poem 17: in both, a person and an object become identified; in the earlier poem, the husband resembles the bridge and the wife the town, while in poem 22 Suffenus appears to be very much like his books—attractive and polished on the outside, but internally rather crude.

Placed between a poem on Aurelius and one on Furius, poem 22 seems to provide a good example of *variatio* (the separation of two similar poems by a third, dissimilar one); yet it should be noted that poem 22 partakes of the same invective/satirical tone found in all those poems apparently introduced by 14B.

The poem has a tripartite structure: lines 1-11 present Suffenus and his books, and draw the contrast between appearance and reality; lines 12-17 express the poet's amazement at this violent contrast; finally, lines 18-21 soften the criticism with an observation about mankind's propensity towards Suffenus' kind of self-deception.

Meter: choliambic.

1. *Vare*: the same Varus as in poem 10.

   probe: "well".

   nosti = *novisti*.

2. *venustus...dicax...urbanus*: Catullan adjectives of approval. Suffenus is "charming, witty, sophisticated".

3. *idemque*: "yet this very same person" scribbles an incredible number of verses; this fact contradicts the charm, wit and sophistication noted in line 2.

   longe: "by far".

4. *aut decem aut plura*: with *milia* understood. Note the unusual number of elisions (5) in this line, perhaps intended to suggest the haste with which Suffenus works in churning out his thousands of lines.

5. *sic ut fit*: "in the usual way".

   palimpsesto: palimpsest was parchment that had been erased for reuse: hence "recycled paper". *Referre in* as an idiom normally takes an accusative, for which reason some editors prefer *palimpseston* here; however, it is possible that Catullus did use the ablative, with *in palimpsesto* being the common writer's slang of the day. In either case, the sense remains clear.

6. *relata*: "written down" on palimpsest.

   cartae regiae: referring to the best quality papyrus available.

   libri: cf. the modest *libellum* of poem 1.

7. *umbilici*: papyrus was rolled around a stick or cylinder to make a *liber*, and the *umbilici* were the ornamental knobs at the ends of the cylinder.

   lora: "thongs" (see next note).

   membranae: wrappers of parchment were used to cover the papyrus roll; the *lora* would presumably be the straps used for fastening the wrapper. The grammatical problem here is whether *membranae* is nominative plural, or a genitive or dative with *lora rubra*. The punctuation adopted here favors the first possibility, but, of course, the original manuscripts had no such punctuation to serve as a guide.

8. *derecta plumbo*: "ruled with lead" (take with *omnia*); the Romans employed small lead disks and rulers to

mark lines on papyrus.

pumice...aequata: *cf.* poem 1.2; *aequata* here in the sense of "made smooth".

9.   *tu*: indefinite here, not specifically pertaining to Varus; translate as "one".

    bellus...urbanus: "that fine and sophisticated" fellow; *cf.* line 2.

10.   *unus caprimulgus aut fossor*: the fine and sophisticated man about town is transformed into a country bumpkin; translate as "an ordinary goatherd or ditch-digger".

11.   *rursus*: "on the contrary".

    abhorret: he "differs" from his other self (*a se* understood).

12.   *putemus*: deliberative subjunctive.

    scurra: "man about town".

13.   *scitius*: the MSS. reading of *tristius* makes little sense, and two emendations have won adherents of late: one is *tritius*, in the sense of "more polished", the other is *scitius*, meaning "more clever" or "more attractive". While the former emendation has the merit of being closer to the MSS. reading, the latter makes better sense in the context. For the construction in this line, *cf.* poem 13.10.

14. *inficeto...inficetior*: *inficetus* (or *infacetus*) here has the sense of "boorish" or "insensitive". The countryside was considered (especially by urban-dwellers) the realm of boorish clods.

15. *simul* = *simul ac*.

   idem: here in the sense of "at the same time"; note how often this word has appeared in the poem, emphasizing the fact that such a great contrast has been found within one and the same person.

16. *aeque...beatus*: "equally as happy".

17. *gaudet in se*: "delights in himself".

   se...miratur: "marvels at himself". Suffenus is obviously blind to his own shortcomings as a poet.

18. *nimirum*: "without doubt"; the poet moralizes a bit, broadening his view from Suffenus to mankind in general. We are, he says, all "Suffenuses" in one way or another.

   idem: with *fallimur*: "we deceive ourselves the same way".

20. *possis*: indefinite; *cf.* line 9.

   attributus: "allotted".

   error: a "defect" or "imperfection".

21. *manticae quod in tergo est*: "that part of the

knapsack which is on our back"; the phrase refers to a fable of Aesop in which man is said to carry two knapsacks slung over his shoulder: the one in front (which he can see) is full of his neighbor's defects or failings, the one in back (which he can't see) contains his own.

23

To Furius, on the subject of a loan: the man should stop hitting the poet for cash, since he's rich enough, in his own way.

Thus far in the Aurelius-Furius cycle, Catullus has focused on the former figure; now begins a set of poems concerned with the latter, especially with his poverty. This set of poems in its arrangement echoes the previous set about Aurelius: in each set, we find two initial poems separated from the third member of the triad by a poem not involved directly with either Furius or Aurelius.

The theme of poverty has appeared before, in respect to the poet himself, in poem 13. The reader cannot be certain that Furius' poverty in this poem is any more real or serious than that of Catullus in the earlier poem.

Poem 23 falls into four segments: lines 1-6 introduce Furius and his poverty; lines 7-11 enunciate the general blessings which that poverty brings; lines 12-23 then focus on specific bodily blessings; and lines 24-27 conclude the poem with the poet's advice to stop pleading for a loan.

Meter: hendecasyllabic.

1 - It has been suggested that Catullus is here quoting
4. Furius' own words about his poverty; indeed, the poet's focus on certain items lacked by Furius would have more bite if those items were ones used by the man himself in illustrating his need for a loan. However, we cannot be certain that the poet is turning Furius' own words against him in this manner.

1. *neque*: the repetition of *neque* in lines 1-2 emphasizes Furius' lack of material possessions, while the similar repetition of *non* in lines 9-11 emphasizes the blessings which such a lack of possessions brings.

   arca: there may be a play here on two common meanings of *arca*: as a money-box, and as a coffin; Furius, it appears, has neither a box for his cash nor a box for himself!

2. *cimex*: a bed-bug; Furius is so poor that he doesn't even have what everyone has.

3. *verum*: "but" (that is, "what you *do* have ...").

4. *vel silicem comesse*: "to chew up even hard rock"; it would seem that Furius' father and step-mother tended to eat everything in sight—thus perhaps accounting for Furius' extreme poverty.

5. *est pulcre tibi*: "you have a good time"; *est* is the main verb, delayed by the long parenthesis of lines 1-4.

6. *lignea*: literally "wooden", but here more in the sense of "tough".

7.   *nec mirum*: "and no wonder".

8.   *pulcre concoquitis*: "you digest your food very well".
     Cf. pulcre in line 5.

9.   *graves ruinas*: "massive collapses" of buildings they
     own.

10. *dolos veneni*: "plots of poison" from those who would
     like to inherit their possessions.

12. *atqui*: introduces a change of focus, from the general
     to specifically physical blessings of poverty; translate
     as "and what is more".

     cornu: ablative of comparison.

13. *aut siquid, etc.*: *cf.* 13.10 and 22.13. *Aridum* here =
     siccum.

14. *sole...frigore...esuritione*: these are the agents that
     cause Furius' dryness; translate as "heat, cold, and
     hunger". For *esuritione*, *cf.* 21.1, of Aurelius.

15. *bene ac beate*: *cf.* 14A.10. The phrase is also akin to
     the *est pulcre tibi* of line 5.

17. *mucusque*: the English "mucus" seems the best
     translation.

     pituita: "discharge" of the nose; our "nasal drip"
     might be an appropriate equivalent.

19. *culus* = *anus*.

purior salillo: "cleaner than a salt-cellar"; salt-cellars were kept highly clean and polished in the Roman world of etiquette.

20. *decies*: "ten times".

   cacas: "shit".

21. *id*: refers back to the excrement deposited in the previous line.

   faba: "bean".

   lapillis: "pebbles"; some prefer to read *lupillis* here ("lupin-seeds").

22. For *tu* with the subjunctive here, *cf.* 22.9.

   teras: "crush".

23. *inquinare*: "befoul".

24. *commoda*: "benefits" of poverty; object of *noli spernere* in the next line.

25. *nec = aut.*

   putare parvi: genitive of price; *cf.* 5.3. Translate as "make light of".

26. *sestertia*: with *centum* in the next line; "one hundred thousand sestertii".

soles: implying that Furius was a regular moocher.

27.   *desine*: take with *precari* in the previous line.

sat es beatus: editors unhappy with *sat* = *satis* here prefer the MSS. reading *satis beatus*, with *est* understood. The sense in either case is the same.

24

The poet rebukes the boy Juventius for his liaison with Furius. While Catullus may be jealous of the relationship between the two, he is also disappointed in Juventius for choosing such an impoverished lover; indeed, the poem is as much an attack on Furius as a rebuke of Juventius.

This is the first poem in which Juventius is named, although he is presumably the *meos amores* of poems 15 and 21 (*cf.* the suppression of Lesbia's name until poem 5). Nothing really is known about the boy aside from what Catullus tells us in his poems; the Juventii, by all accounts, seem to have been a well respected Roman family.

The poem is clearly a follow up to the preceding poem on Furius' poverty, but it also has verbal connections with poems 21 and 22.

Structurally, poem 24 can be divided into two uneven sections: lines 1-6, which rebuke Juventius for giving his love to Furius; and lines 7-10, which pretend to respond to Juventius' puzzlement over that rebuke.

Meter: hendecasyllabic.

1. *flosculus*: "little flower"; a term of endearment suggesting a young man; *cf. puer* at 21.11.

2 - *Cf.* 21.2-3, where a very similar statement was made
3. about Aurelius.

2. *horum*: with *Iuventiorum* understood; translate as
"not only of these present-day" Iuventii.

3. *posthac*: "hereafter".

4. *Midae*: genitive case; Midas was a Phrygian king
famous in Greek legend for his wealth and for his
"golden touch". The "riches of Midas" here stand for
a very large sum of money in general.

5. *isti*: identified as Furius by the phrase which follows
(repeated from the preceding poem).

6. *sic*: take with *sineres*.

7. *qui*: Juventius responds to the poet's rebuke with a
surprised "what do you mean?".

   homo bellus: *cf.* 22.9.

   est: "yes, he is".

9. *hoc*: refers to the fact that Furius has neither a
slave nor a money-box; object of both *abice* and
eleva.

quam lubet: "as much as you like".

abice elevaque: "belittle and make light of".

10. *tamen:* "still".

25

To Thallus the thief: return the items you stole from me, or face the lash of punishment.

The poet here returns to a concept already examined in poem 12, but the punishment proposed for the *inepte* in this poem is physical rather than poetical (*cf.* 12.10-11). Poem 25 is thus the next member of a group of poems (6, 10, 12, 17) which sketch improper social behavior; in its position within the Aurelius-Furius cycle, indeed, poem 25 resembles poem 17: whereas the earlier poem followed two pieces belonging to the cycle and was followed by another Aurelius poem, poem 25 follows two poems on Furius and precedes another on the same figure. Another resemblance to poem 17 found in this piece is the theme of sexual inadequacy—here in respect to Thallus (lines 1-3, 10). Sexuality in general, of course, is the focal point of the surrounding Aurelius and Furius poems.

The poem has a tripartite structure: lines 1-5 sketch Thallus and his activities; lines 6-8 describe the particular offense against the poet; and lines 9-13 elaborate upon the punishment awaiting Thallus if he does not make up for that offense.

Meter: iambic tetrameter catalectic.

1.   *Cinaede*: *cf.* 16.2.

    Thalle: a person who appears only here in the corpus; attempts to identify him or to argue that the name is a pseudonym for either Juventius or the Asinius of poem 12 have not been successful.

    mollior: for its connotations of effeminacy, *cf.* 11.5 and 16.4.

    capillo: "fur". Note the predominance of *l* sounds in this and the following lines of the poem: perhaps the name Thallus itself suggested such a play on a "soft" sound to the poet.

2.   *anseris medullula*: "the liver of a goose". Goose liver was, and still is, considered a great delicacy in the culinary world.

    imula oricilla: "ear-lobe"; *oricilla* = *auricilla*.

3.   *situque araneoso*: literally, "dust full of cobwebs".

4.   *idemque*: "at the same time"; *cf.* 22.15.

    rapacior: this comparative adjective provides the counterpoint for the *mollior* of line 1. Thallus is a study in contradiction.

    procella: "gale". *Cf.* line 13.

5.   The reading of this line has been the subject of much debate, with numerous emendations having been

proposed. The MSS.' *cum diva*, and the resultant attempts to find a goddess in the line have given rise to much confusion, and the substitution of *laeva* for *diva* seems attractive (the left hand especially was connected with theft; *cf.* 12.1); *ostendit oscitantes* at the end of the line is here changed to *offendit oscitantes*, after Guarinus. The sense of the line at this point seems to be that Thallus' left hand strikes some persons when they are off their guard. The remaining problem is to identify the victims involved: they must be hidden in the MSS.' *mulier aries*; proposals have included *munerarios*, *mulierarios*, *balnearios*, and *nummularios*, none of which have won critical acceptance.

6. *pallium*: an outer cloak.

   involasti: "have pounced upon".

7. *sudariumque Saetabum*: *cf.* 12.14.

   catagraphosque Thynos: what these items were is unclear; both words are adjectives, and "Bithynian painted (or figured)" somethings are meant. In context, a cloth item of some sort would seem to be indicated.

8. *inepte*: *cf.* 12.4.

   palam...habere: "to display openly".

   avita: "ancestral possessions", *i.e.*, family heirlooms.

9. *unguibus*: "claws"; the image is one of Thallus as a

bird of prey.

10. *laneum*: "woolen", but here more in the sense of "soft" or "downy".

   mollicellas: "tender"; *cf.* line 1.

11. *inusta*: "branded"; take with *turpiter*.

   conscribillent: "mark" or "marr".

12. *insolenter*: two meanings are possible here: "contrary to custom" and "unrestrainedly". Perhaps both meanings are implied, although, in view of the image to come, the latter meaning makes more sense.

   aestues: "are tossed about".

   minuta magno: a good example of antithesis.

13. *deprensa*: "overtaken", *i.e.*, by a gale.

26

On the country house of Furius: the drafts that it is vulnerable to are not of the windy sort.

The poem, written in a 4 + 1 structure, is essentially a pun on the verb *opposita est*, which can mean both "be exposed to" and "be mortgaged". Like the other poems of this Furius triad (23 and 24), poem 26 is founded upon the alleged poverty of this man, and it is possible (as was suggested in the case of poem 23) that the poet is using Furius' own words in lines 1-3; in any event, with this piece the Aurelius and Furius cycle of the *Passer* comes to an end.

    Meter: hendecasyllabic.

1.   *vestra*:   the reading of manuscript O; other MSS. read *nostra*, a reading championed by those who think that Catullus is alluding to his own poverty in these lines. *Vestra*, however, makes more sense in the context of the Furius triad as a whole, and the plural form can be explained as including the father and step-mother of poem 23.

    Austri: the south wind.

2.   *flatus*:   "blasts" of wind.   *Cf. ventum* in line 5.

    opposita est: in lines 1-3 the sense of the verb is clearly "is exposed to"; when we come to line 4, however, we find that the poet is punning on the verb.

    Favoni: the west wind.

3.   *Boreae*:   the north wind.

    Apheliotae: the east wind.

4.   It might be noted that 15,200 sesterces does not seem to have been a very large amount in the context of the Roman housing market; *cf.* Furius' request for 100,000 in poem 23. However, even such a relatively modest amount might be too much for poor Furius!

5.   *ventum*:   a possibility exists here for an English pun

on the term "draft", *i.e.*, both wind and a bank draft.

pestilentem: also a play on words: as a real wind, "unhealthy", but as a bank draft, "obnoxious", or "disgusting".

27

A skolion, or drinking song, calling for stronger wine; a type of poem with many parallels in Greek lyric verse.

Such is an interpretation of the poem on its surface level; there is, however, another level to it: as T.P. Wiseman has argued (*Catullan Questions*, 7-8), poem 27 seems to serve as a programmatic poem introducing a unit of bitterly invective pieces (hence the *amariores* in line 2). Wiseman himself asks, "Could it be that 28-47 form a unit beginning and ending with [Memmius and] Piso, continuing the theme of foreign travel [from the first part of the *Passer*] but with the added *amaritudo* forecast in poem 27?" (p. 14). The role of poem 27 as a programmatic announcement has also been advocated by Skinner (*Catullus' Passer*, 27-29).

The poem is easily divided into two sections: lines 1-4 contain the request for stronger wine, while lines 5-7 banish the water that keeps wine from its true strength.

Meter: hendecasyllabic.

1. *vetuli...Falerni*: editors often suggest "good old Falernian" (wine), but in the context of wine it is also possible to see in *vetuli* the sense of "ageing".

194

Falernian wine was a highly respected brand originating in northern Campania.

2. *inger* = *ingere* (imperative); the verb signifies the pouring out of a liquid in great quantity.

    amariores: a programmatic term, pertaining not only to wine, but also to poetry; the essential meaning of *amarus* is "bitter". Catullus is announcing poems of a more invective nature.

3. It was customary at a drinking party to name a master of ceremonies who would prescribe the kind of wine to be consumed and also how strong it was to be. Unfortunately, it is not clear here who Postumia is, although it has been argued that Catullus is alluding to the Postumia who was the wife of Servius Sulpicius Rufus (consul in 51 B.C.), a rather notorious woman who was once the mistress of Julius Caesar. *Cf.* F. Cairns, "Catullus 27" in *Mnemosyne* 28 (1975), who states that this identification "gains further support from Wiseman's observation that 27 has a programmatic function. 28 and 29 are attacks on Caesar's father-in-law...on Caesar himself, and on Caesar's henchman Mamurra. What better *magistra bibendi* to preside over the serving of this harsher wine than Caesar's mistress?" (p.27).

4. The elisions in this line mimic the slurring of speech often associated with strong drink.

    acino: "grape".

    ebriosioris: in agreement with *Postumiae*. For the

play on words in this line, *cf.* 22.14.

5. *Cf.* 14A.21. The *lymphae* are the water that Romans normally added to their wine, and which thus diluted its strength. Accordingly, the poet sends them into banishment here.

6. *vini pernicies*: water as "the bane of wine".

    ad severos: water should depart and head for those who value it: the sober, puritannical sort; *cf.* 5.2.

7. *hic merus est Thyonianus*: the most controversial line in the poem, with numerous interpretations offered. The first problem is the meaning of *hic*: "here", or "this"; if the latter, who is the "this" meant? Some have argued that *hic = ego*, and that the poet is calling himself *merus Thyonianus*. However, the appearance of *hinc* in line 5 makes it more probable that *hic =* "here": water must go away from here, because here is the realm of *merus Thyonianus*.

    The next problem is *merus Thyonianus*: the origin of the proper name seems to be the Thyone, better known as Semele, who gave birth to Bacchus (Dionysus). Is *Thyonianus*, then, an adjective meaning "of Bacchus" or a name for Bacchus himself? "Here is undiluted Bacchus" would make sense, while treating *Thyonianus* as an adjective necessitates the identification of an unstated noun with which it agrees. Were the name neuter, one could assume that *Thyonianum =* wine (*cf. Falernum* in line 1); the masculine ending, however, leaves the problem very much intact.

28

An invective poem in the guise of a letter to Veranius and Fabullus: the poet conveys his condolences for their poor faring abroad in the train of Piso; his sympathy is increased by the fact that he, too, had the bad luck to serve under a good-for-nothing governor.

Although addressed to Veranius and Fabullus, the poem has as its true target both Piso and Memmius, the former the governor of Macedonia, the latter of Bithynia; it is thus an example of Catullan political invective, and a harbinger of the invective poems to come in the *Passer*.

For Veranius and Fabullus, see poems 9, 12, and 13; it should also be noted that poem 47 is concerned with Veranius and Fabullus and how they fared under Piso. For the "unit" thus framed by poems 28 and 47, see the comment of T.P. Wiseman quoted in the introduction to poem 27.

It is often remarked that Veranius and Fabullus serve as counterpoints to Furius and Aurelius in the *Passer*: the true friends of the poet vs. friends whose loyalty is in doubt. In this regard, it is interesting that poems concerned with Veranius and Fabullus are prominent both at the start and finish of the Aurelius-Furius cycle (9, 12, 13, and 28), forming a kind of frame around that unit.

Structurally, poem 28 falls into three segments of five lines each: the first five lines present the predicament of Veranius and Fabullus; the next five lines compare that predicament with that of the poet himself; and the final five lines put both predicaments together and curse the men responsible.

Meter: hendecasyllabic.

1. *Pisonis*: most likely the L. Calpurnius Piso Caesoninus who governed Macedonia from 57-55 B.C. He had earlier served as consul, and was the father-in-law of none other than Julius Caesar. Attempts to find a governor of Spain by this name (on the assumption that Veranius and Fabullus made but one trip abroad, to Spain) have not been successful. Moreover, the well documented character of Caesoninus (in Cicero's *In Pisonem*) matches the characterization of "Piso" in this poem.

   comites: *cf.* 11.1, where the term is used of Furius and Aurelius.

   inanis: "penniless"; the theme of poverty, so prominent in the preceding Furius poems, thus reappears.

2. "With suitable light baggage at hand" — no point in large packs when there's nothing to fill them with!

4. *quid rerum geritis*: a colloquial greeting, appropriate in a letter to friends, and akin to our "what have you been up to?"; *quid rerum*: a partitive genitive construction.

5. *vappa*: literally, "wine that has gone flat"; here, in a figurative sense, a "good-for-nothing" person.

   frigoraque et famem: not things expected by members of a *cohors*; traditionally, such a posting meant a year or more of living well, usually at the expense of the native population.

6. *ecquidnam...lucelli*: "any small gain at all". *Cf.* 10.8.

   tabulis: "account books" or "ledgers".

7. *expensum*: not the expected *acceptum* (as editors have long pointed out); *expensum* refers rather to money paid *out*. The poet may thus be asking whether his friends have gained anything of a non-monetary nature (such as a belated awareness of the true nature of provincial governors) from their expenditures (so Kenneth Quinn, *Catullus: The Poems*, pp. 173-174).

   ut mihi: "as was the case in my ledgers".

8. *praetorem*: provincial governor; Memmius, as we learn in the next line.

   refero datum: the hypothesis that *datum = expensum* lacks supporting evidence; it seems more likely that *refero datum* is here used in the commercial sense of "I enter as advanced" on my account books. Merrill's "set down to my credit" seems a valid translation, and, on this interpretation, the next two lines would represent what the poet set down in his ledgers—namely, his own realization that Memmius was screwing him. Such a reading would harmonize nicely with Quinn's interpretation of *expensum* above.

9. *o Memmi*: a sudden address to Memmius seems

awkward here, but fits in logically if we take lines 9-10 as the poet's quotation of what he recorded in his account books. Memmius had been a praetor in 58 B.C., then set out to govern Bithynia; his interest in literature is attested by Lucretius' dedication of the *De Rerum Natura* to him.

10. *trabe*: usually a tree-trunk, or shaft; here a penis.

   lentus irrumasti: "you took your time in screwing" me; Catullus, one might say, was the victim of a "slow shaft". *Cf.* 10.12.

11. *quantum video*: "as far as I can see".

12. *casu*: "misfortune" here.

   verpa: another term for the penis.

13. *farti estis*: "you are stuffed". Veranius and Fabullus were screwed in the same way Catullus was.

   pete nobiles amicos: spoken with great bitterness; the singular *pete* indicates not a specific injunction to Veranius and Fabullus, but one to people in general.

14. *at vobis*: with *at* the change in address from Veranius and Fabullus to both provincial governors takes place; *cf.* the similar transition at 3.13 and at 27.5.

   mala multa di deaeque/dent: the play on *m* and *d* sounds is quite obvious here; *cf.* 14A.6.

15. *opprobria Romuli Remique*: "you disgraceful scions of

Romulus and Remus".

29

A series of questions for Pompey and Caesar about their henchman Mamurra: can they really tolerate the man's gross behavior in matters monetary and sexual? If so, then they are no better than their subordinate!

Like the preceding poem, poem 29 is a piece of bitter political invective, and is aimed at the most powerful men of the day; it also resembles poem 28 in focusing upon wealth gained from the provinces: here, however, we meet a character (Mamurra) who obviously did well abroad, as opposed to the impoverished Veranius and Fabullus. The poet seems to be saying, in the juxtaposition of these two poems, that the good come back from the provinces empty-handed, while the bad return enriched.

Poem 29 is dated to the period 55—early 54 B.C. by its references to Britain and by its allusion to Pompey as Caesar's son-in-law (Julia, Caesar's daughter and Pompey's wife, died in 54 B.C.).

The structure of the poem is quite precise: a first segment of 10 lines addressed to Pompey is followed by a second segment of 10 lines addressed to Caesar; then the concluding 4 lines address both triumvirs together.

Meter: iambic trimeter.

1. The repetition of *quis potest* emphasizes the poet's indignation—how can *anyone* tolerate what is going on?

2. *impudicus*: one with no sense of shame or moral outrage; the word also could be used of immoral behavior in a homosexual context, and this meaning may well be implied here.

   vorax: "insatiable".

   aleo: "a gambler" — a disreputable activity in the eyes of most Romans. Thus only the most unsavory people could put up with a man like Mamurra.

3. *Mamurram*: a native of Formiae who made a name (and a fortune) for himself in the service of both Pompey and Caesar; he served with the former in the East, and with the latter in Gaul (as chief engineer) and in Spain.

   Comata Gallia: Transalpine Gaul, so called because the natives affected long hair.

4. *ante*: an emendation of the MSS.' *cum te*; some editors prefer *uncti*.

   ultima Britannia: *cf.* 11.11-12, and line 12 below.

5. *cinaede Romule*: whereas it was once traditional to see in this phrase a reference to Julius Caesar, it now seems more likely that Catullus actually refers to Pompey; a clear statement of the case for Pompey may be found in Alan Cameron's "Catullus 29" in *Hermes* 104 (1976) 158-163. Romulus was the first king of Rome, and to call someone a "Romulus" imputed regal ambitions anathema to a Roman. *Cf.* poem 28.15.

haec videbis et feres: *cf.* line 1.

6. *ille* = Mamurra.

    superbus et superfluens: note the play on *super*, a word connected with excess; Fordyce's "overbearing and over-flush" is perhaps the best we can do in English.

7. *perambulabit*: "will make the rounds of".

8. *columbus aut Adoneus*: both connected with Venus, the goddess of sex; Mamurra obviously thinks of himself as the darling of Venus, and of other females (and males?) as well. *Adoneus* = Adonis.

9 - The two concluding lines of this first segment of the
10. poem pick up lines 5 and 2, thus "capping" this address to Pompey, who is now branded as much a disgrace as Mamurra is.

11. *eone nomine*: "was it on this account that" or "was it for this reason that"; the phrase forms a transition from the address to Pompey to the address to Caesar, which immediately ensues.

    imperator unice: a sarcastic "one and only *imperator*"; the title was one normally given to a victorious general by his jubilant troops.

12. *ultima occidentis insula* = Britain. *Cf.* line 4.

13. *ut*: "so that".

ista vestra: cf. 17.21; *vestra* is best explained as pertaining to both Caesar and Pompey.

diffututa mentula: Catullus pulls no punches here: "fucked out prick" = Mamurra.

14. *ducenties...trecenties*: with *centena milia sestertium* understood; *i.e.*, 20 or 30 million *sestertii*.

comesset: "devour"; imperfect subjunctive. Mamurra the glutton "eats up" all that wealth.

15. *quid est alid*: "what is this other than"; *alid* = *aliud*.

sinistra liberalitas: Caesar was famous for his generosity, but this particular type of generosity is "perverted".

16. *parum*: "not enough".

expatravit: "squandered".

helluatus est: a deponent verb which refers to the act of spending too much on such things as eating.

17. *primum*: so the MSS. reading; some editors prefer *prima* (in the belief that the poem is written in pure iambic trimeters—for the metrical controversy involved, *cf.* J.D. Minyard, "Critical Notes on Catullus 29" in *Classical Philology* 66 [1971] 174-181).

lancinata sunt: "are wasted".

18. *praeda Pontica*: what Mamurra got while in the East with Pompey.

19. *Hibera*: the loot of Spain, taken under Caesar.

    scit: "knows about".

    aurifer Tagus: a river in Spain, a province valuable as a source of gold.

20. *nunc*: a generally accepted emendation of the MSS.' *hunc*. Its long syllabic value need not deter one once the assumption that the poem is written in pure iambic trimeters is placed aside.

    Gallicae timetur et Britannicae: with *praedae* understood; E. Badian's emendation of the MSS.' garbled *gallie timet et britannie* (in *Classical Philology* 72 [1977] 320-322). Another popular version is *nunc Galliae timetur et Britanniae*, but this suffers from the fact that Gaul and Britain have already been taken over (*cf.* lines 3-4).

21. *hunc malum*: some editors set *malum* off with commas and interpret it as an expletive ("by the devil"); but the more natural interpretation is to see *malum* modifying *hunc*.

    fovetis: "indulge". This final segment of the poem addresses both Pompey and Caesar.

    quid hic potest: *cf.* the phrasing in line 1.

22. *uncta...patrimonia*: "rich estates".

devorare: cf. *comesset* in line 14.

23. *eone nomine*: cf. line 11.

urbis o potissimi: an emendation of the MSS.' *opulentissime*, which, however, has been defended by Minyard (*cf.* note on line 17).

24. *socer generque*: Pompey had married Julia in 59 B.C.

30

A bitter complaint to Alfenus, who has betrayed the trust of the poet. While the details of the betrayal are not made clear, the language of the poem is that of erotic love (as has been pointed out by D.W. Vessey, "Thoughts on Two Poems of Catullus" in *Latomus* 30 [1971] 48-55), and it is quite probable that a homosexual liaison had existed between the two men.

This poem, while different from poems 28 and 29 in its focus upon a private liaison, still resembles those preceding pieces in two respects: first, it also has a political dimension, only here that dimension lies in the poet's use of a political vocabulary (*cf.* David Ross' *Style and Tradition in Catullus* [1969] 88); second, and more important, it shares the same bitter tone, as Catullus assumes the same accusatory stance he had used in poems 28 and 29.

Poem 30 falls into two equal sections: the first six lines present a series of plaintive questions for Alfenus, while the final six lines focus on Alfenus' actions and the punishment awaiting them.

Meter: greater asclepiadean.

1. *Alfene*:   Who Alfenus was is unknown, although past editors have often suggested that he was the lawyer Alfenus Varus, and that he thus may be the Varus of poems 10 and 22.

   immemor: here in the sense of "heedless of obligations" rather than simply "forgetful".

   unanimis: *cf.*   9.4.

2. *iam*:   the repetition of *iam* in lines 2-3 seems to imply a sudden reversal on the part of Alfenus.

   te nil miseret: "have you no pity at all for"; with the genitive.

   dure: "hard-hearted man".

   dulcis amiculi: the adjective and the diminutive combine to depict the poet as the innocent victim of a treacherous knave.

3. *prodere...fallere*:   "to betray" and "to deceive", both dependent on *non dubitas*.

4. *nec*:   while this may mean "and yet...not" (implying some kind of contrast), the apparent awkwardness of *nec* here has led some to postulate the loss of one or two lines at this point in the MSS. It is unlikely that *nec* simply = *non*.

   fallacum: echoes both the *false* of line 1 and the

fallere of line 3.

caelicolis: a word with an epic flavor, perhaps to stress the sheer awfulness of what Alfenus has done.

5. *quae*: as in the case of *nec* in the preceding line, *quae* seems awkward, lacking a clear antecedent; as it stands, the best that one can do is to translate it as "which facts" and make it refer to the general statement of line 4. It may be that some hypothetical missing lines are also relevant here.

in malis: "in dire straits".

6. *fidem*: looks ahead to the *Fides* of line 11. The question is a rhetorical one.

7. *tute*: an emphatic *tu*.

tradere: "to entrust".

inique: "unfair", a vocative; *cf. dure* in line 2.

me: added to complete an otherwise one syllable short verse.

8. *inducens*: "enticing".

tuta: "safe and secure".

9. *idem*: *cf.* 22.3.

retrahis te: "back away".

10. *irrita*: "null and void"; the image is a traditional one in both Greek and Latin poetry, and also appears in a similar context at 64.59 and 142, 65.17, and 70.4.

ferre: "to carry away".

aerias: "lofty".

11. *oblitus es*: cf. *immemor* in line 1.

at: "nonetheless".

Fides: there was a very old cult of Fides ("Good Faith") at Rome; keeping one's word was clearly a very important obligation. The repetition in *meminerunt, meminit* emphasizes that importance.

12. *quae* = Fides. Note the dominance of *t*, *p*, and *f* sounds in this rather prosaic line.

31

A reunion with Sirmio, after the poet's travels abroad. Although it is in reality a humble isthmus of land, Sirmio is greeted by Catullus as if it were his closest human friend, and the poem in many ways reminds one of the reunion between Catullus and Veranius in poem 9 (on this, see R.M. Nielsen's "Catullus 9 and 31: The Simple Pleasure" in *Ramus* 8 [1979] 165-173).

Poem 31 obviously continues the motif of travel that has run through the *Passer*, but, just as obviously, it presents a break with the bitter tone of poems 28, 29 and 30 which precede it; the negative emotions of these pieces now give way to the more positive emotions of relief and joy. But, if poem 31 is not invective, it curiously presents itself in a meter traditionally connected with satire and invective. It thus seems to be a transitional poem, taking the reader smoothly from the preceding invectives to a series of poems that tend to strike a lighter note.

Skinner, indeed, has argued (in *Catullus' Passer*, 30f.) that poems 31 and 44 form a frame around a poetic unit in which there is "a succession of balanced contrasts between pairs of poems associated by meter and subject matter".

Structurally, poem 31 falls into three segments: lines 1-6, the greeting to Sirmio; lines 7-11, the poet's reflections on his homecoming; and lines 12-14, the resumption of the greeting and an injunction to rejoice.

Meter: choliambic.

1. *Paene insularum*: *paene* is here used adjectivally; literally, "almost islands", *i.e.*, peninsulas.

   Sirmio: the modern Sirmione, a narrow finger of land projecting into Lago di Garda from the south; it is roughly 32 kilometers from Verona. Note how the position of *Sirmio* between *paene insularum* and *insularumque* reflects its natural condition as an isthmus narrow enough to be intermediate between a peninsula and an island; indeed, a high water level in the lake could turn the former into the latter easily enough.

2. *ocelle*: "jewel" in a figurative sense, akin to our "apple of my eye" as a term of endearment—the first indication that Sirmio is here being treated as a living

human being; *cf.* 50.19, where the term is applied to Calvus.

liquentibus stagnis: "clear lakes".

3. *uterque Neptunus:* an allusive reference to Neptune as the god of both fresh and salt waters (*stagnis* and *mari*); the poem may impress the reader by its apparent simplicity, but it is full of *doctrina* nonetheless.

4. *libenter...laetus:* adverb and adjective, both in an adverbial sense: "gladly and joyfully".

    inviso: another indication of the personification of Sirmio: *inviso* is commonly used in the sense of "come to see" someone.

5. *vix mi ipse credens:* "scarcely believing myself", like our "I can hardly believe my eyes"; *mi = mihi.*

    Thyniam atque Bithynos...campos: both refer to the province of Bithynia; more of a learned play on words than a serious question of ancient geography. Perhaps the doublet was poetically in keeping with the dual statements that permeate the poem, *e.g.,* *paene insularum* and *insularum; stagnis* and *mari; uterque Neptunus; quam libenter* and *quamque laetus,* etc.

6. *liquisse:* "left behind".

    in tuto: cf. 30.8; the "safety" of this poem stands in contrast to the ephemeral safety of the previous piece.

7. *solutis:* "cast off".

beatius: *cf.* 9.11 for the general sentiment.

8. *reponit*: "lays down".

9. *larem*: the guardian divinity of the Roman household, here equivalent to "house" itself. The reference, of course, is to the villa of the poet at Sirmio.

10. *desideratoque*: "longed for".

11. *hoc est quod unum est pro*: "this is what is, by itself, recompense for".

12. *salve...venusta*: both terms belong to the human realm, *i.e.*, Sirmio is greeted as a dear old friend and retainer.

    ero gaude/gaudente: "rejoice in your master's joy". *Gaudente* is an emendation of the MSS.' *gaudete*, which some editors keep, associating it with the ensuing *undae*.

13. *Lydiae*: the MSS. read *lidie*; *Lydiae*, if correct, would be a learned reference to the Etruscan history of this part of Italy (Etruscans being thought to have come from Lydia). Some editors prefer to read *lucidae* or *limpidae*.

14. *ridete quidquid ... cachinnorum*: "let sound all the laughter you have in stock"; *domi* here in a more general sense, common in Roman comedy. For *cachinnorum*, *cf.* 13.5; it seems fitting that such a joyous poem end with the sound of laughter.

32

A plea for relief: the poet is aroused and in need of a sexual partner, right away! Whereas Merrill found the contents of this poem "execrable", others see here a light-hearted satire at the expense of the lady involved; indeed, the satire to some extent is equally aimed at the poet himself, with his "macho man" pose of the final verse. As a result, it is hard to see in this poem what may be called a serious "level of intent".

The poem has a balanced structure: the initial three lines make the request, the middle five lines make some suggestions to facilitate the assignation, and the final three lines repeat the request and point out the poet's urgent need that it be granted.

Meter: hendecasyllabic.

1.   *Amabo*:   "please"; the poem begins as a polite request in an epistle form.

   Ipsitilla: the MSS. do not agree on the spelling of this name; other versions suggested include Ipsithilla, Ipsimilla, Ipsicilla, and Ipsissima. It also remains unclear whether this is to be taken as a real name or a pseudonym.

2.   *meae deliciae*: cf. 2A.1. This phrase and *mei lepores* are obviously terms of endearment, although the latter phrase finds no parallel elsewhere in the text.

3.   *iube*:   a word repeated again at lines 4 and 9, thus appearing in each of the structural segments of the

poem in order to stress the poet's urgent request.

ad te = *apud te.*

meridiatum: supine after *veniam*; the verb means "to take a siesta", but Catullus has something else in mind too.

4. *illud adiuvato*: a future imperative (*cf. iubeto* in line 9); translate as "help things along" in the following ways.

5. *liminis...tabellam*: the house door; literally, the "wooden panel of the entrance".

   obseret: "bar" or "bolt".

6. *foras*: "outside", as opposed to the *domi* in the next line.

8. *fututiones*: a Catullan mock heroic term for the sex act; that the poet expects nine in a row alerts us to the heroic atmosphere of what is about to take place.

9. *si quid ages*: the sense is "if you're up to this kind of activity".

   statim: there's no time to be lost; the next two lines explain.

10. *pransus iaceo*: "I'm lying down stuffed with my mid-day meal"; a siesta after lunch remains a common practice in the Mediterranean world.

satur supinus: a nicely alliterative phrase, "flat on my back, filled to the gills".

11. *pertundo*: the verb literally means "to bore a hole through"; this is no average erection, to be sure! It is well known that there was a goddess named Pertunda who was in charge of the marriage bed and saw to it that the bride's hymen was broken. See M.B. Skinner, "*Pertundo Tunicamque Palliumque*", *Classical World* 73 (1980) 306-307.

33

To an unsavory father and son: get out of town, maybe even go to hell!

The Vibennius *pater* and his *filius* are otherwise unknown to us; all that is clear from the poem is that one is a thief, the other a sexual pervert.

Although it is tempting to compare this poem with poems 12 and 25, which also deal with thieves, it should be noted that poem 33 lacks the bitter personal tone of those earlier pieces; indeed, poem 33 is more of a public lampoon than a private complaint of the poet.

Structurally, the poem falls into two equal parts: lines 1-4 introduce the targets of the poet's satire; and lines 5-8 convey the poet's advice and the reasons for it.

Meter: hendecasyllabic.

1. *optime*: Vibennius is good at what he does, but what he does is not good at all: he is a "prince" of thieves.

balneariorum: the Roman baths were notoriously good places for a talented thief.

2. *Vibenni pater*: both vocatives; so also *cinaede fili*.

3. *dextra...inquinatiore*: a descriptive ablative: Vibennius the elder is characterized by his "dirty right hand". That the poet focuses on the right rather than the left hand normally associated with theft (*cf.* poems 12.1 and 25.5) is puzzling, but may suggest that Vibennius was more flagrant than others about his thefts.

4. *culo...voraciore*: the son is characterized by his "rather insatiable rear", responding, of course, to the *cinaedus* of line 2.

5. *exilium malasque in oras*: the preposition *in* seems to govern both nouns; the *malas oras* are literally "the evil shores", but correspond imaginatively to our "hell".

6. *rapinae*: "thefts".

7. *notae sunt populo*: "are well known to the public", *i.e.*, they are public knowledge.

   natis pilosas: "hairy buttocks"; young men tended to lose their attractivenes to other men once they started growing facial and body hair.

8. *fili*: vocative, as in line 2.

   asse venditare: "put up for sale at a penny"; the low price indicates the son's lack of success.

34

A hymn to the goddess Diana, performed by a chorus of boys and girls. Despite this format, there is no evidence in favor of the old theory that Catullus was commissioned to write this piece for actual performance at some religious celebration.

The appearance of this somewhat "un-Catullan" poem between poems 32, 33 and 35, 36 has recently been analysed by Skinner (*Catullus' Passer*, 30-31) as follows: "Those lighthearted pasquinades [32 and 33] are set off from the next set of poems by a solemn, highly conventionalized hymn to Diana...Following upon such enthusiastic bawdry, the invocation of a chaste goddess by a chorus of chaste boys and girls marks one of the most arresting juxtapositions in the entire *corpus*. A second pair of hendecasyllabic pieces [35 and 36] then counters the gross scurrility of 32 and 33 with urbane wit."

The structure of the poem is quite formal, and follows the expected conventions of the hymn: the initial stanza introduces the chorus and the goddess they invoke; the second stanza, in invoking the goddess, recounts her birth on Delos; the next three stanzas then elaborate upon the various functions of Diana—as goddess of the woodlands and mountains, as goddess of childbirth, and as Hecate and the Moon; the concluding stanza presents the actual request of the chorus to Diana.

Meter: each stanza is composed of three glyconic verses followed by one pherecratean.

1.   *Dianae*:   the goddess for whom the hymn is sung is

the Roman version of Artemis, as the ensuing description of her functions makes clear.

in fide: "under the protection of".

2. *integri*: "chaste" or sexually innocent; although technically modifying *pueri*, the adjective refers to both boys and girls. Note the use of repetition in this initial stanza, as the first two lines are echoed closely by the next two lines.

5. *Latonia*: "daughter of Latona"; a matronymic for Diana (Latona = the Greek Leto). The appearance of this matronymic sets the stage for the account of the goddess' birth which follows.

maximi/magna: the juxtaposition emphasizes the greatness of the goddess.

6. *progenies*: "offspring".

7. *Deliam*: adjective with *olivam* in the next line; the reference is to one version of the goddess' birth, in which Leto bore her and Apollo on the island of Delos; in the course of her labor, Leto held on to an olive tree for support.

8. *deposivit* = *deposuit*; translate as "brought forth".

9 - This stanza is notorious for the dominance of the *um*
12. sound: "the genitive plural is a little overworked in this stanza" (Quinn, *Catullus: The Poems*, 192). Still, the play on such a sound is not inappropriate for a formal hymn of this sort.

10. *virentium*: "clothed in green".

11. *saltuumque reconditorum*: "of secluded glades"; the last syllable in the line is elided before the initial vowel of the next verse.

12. *sonantum* = *sonantium*.

13. *Lucina*: the various names by which the goddess is known now begin to be listed; Iuno Lucina, a goddess associated with childbirth, came to be identified with Diana-Artemis who had a similar association.

14. *dicta*: the goddess is "named" as Iuno Lucina, *etc.* by those who invoke her.

    puerperis: "women in labor".

15. *Trivia*: the goddess Hecate, commonly associated with crossroads; another manifestation of Diana.

    notho: with *lumine* in the next line; the Moon shines with "counterfeit light", *i.e.*, the light borrowed from the Sun.

16. *lumine Luna*: note the play on words here. *Cf.* Lucina above.

17. *cursu...menstruo*: "in your monthly movement", a reference to the phases of the moon.

18. *metiens iter annuum*: "measuring out the circuit of the year".

20. *exples*: "fill up".

21. *sis...sancta*: "may you be revered".

   quocumque...nomine: in case the names mentioned in the hymn are not all inclusive; a way of ensuring that the goddess does not take offense at any omission.

22. *Romulique*: the final syllable is elided before the initial vowel of the following verse; *cf.* line 11.

23. *antique*: "in the old style", that is, as you did in days gone by.

24. *sospites*: the request of the hymn: "preserve" or "make prosper".

35

A letter to Caecilius: come to Verona, for there's something I must tell you. Despite its playfully enigmatic tone, the poem suggests that Catullus wants to talk to Caecilius about his promising poem on the goddess Cybele; of Caecilius himself, nothing is known outside this poem.

Both this piece and the following poem are concerned with poetry and mistresses: here the poet imagines that Caecilius' lady has been so affected by his poem that she cannot bear to lose sight of him, and thus may prevent him from journeying to Verona; in the next poem, it will be Catullus' mistress who has been strongly affected by his verse.

A balanced tripartite structure is featured: the first

six lines present the invitation to come to Verona and the reason for it; the next six lines introduce the *puella* who could thwart Caecilius' journey; and the final six lines explain how Caecilius' poem has made her ardor so powerful.

Meter: hendecasyllabic.

1. *Poetae tenero*: a "tender" poet was, by convention, a love poet.

    meo sodali: but Caecilius is not only a love poet, he is a close friend of Catullus; *cf.* 10.29, 12.13, and 30.1.

2. *papyre*: Catullus addresses the papyrus which bears the invitation; an indirect approach that will be carried through the remainder of the poem, as the poet enigmatically hints at what is on his mind rather than speak out bluntly. It should be noted that in poem 36 the poet will also address papyrus (*cacata carta*).

3. *Veronam veniat, Novi*: a predominance of *v* sounds which occurs also at lines 7-9.

    relinquens: "leaving behind".

4. *Comi*: in 59 B.C. the town of Comum was renamed Novum Comum when it received 5000 new settlers; the modern Como, it is located at the southwestern extremity of the Lago di Como (= *Larium litus*).

5. *quasdam...cogitationes*: the poet continues to be

vague; translate as "certain thoughts".

6. *amici...sui meique*: more deliberate vagueness: is there really a third party involved, or (more likely) is this "mutual friend" none other than Catullus himself? *Cf.* poem 30.2, where Catullus refers to himself as *amiculi*.

7. *si sapiet, viam vorabit*: "if he is wise, he will devour the road" in his haste to reach Verona; we might say today that he will "eat up the miles". Catullus clearly suggests that something important is up—that Caecilius would be a fool not to respond to the invitation.

8. *quamvis*: "in spite of the fact that".

   candida...puella: cf. 13.4.

   milies = *miliens*, *i.e.*, a thousand times.

9. *euntem*: "as he departs".

   collo: dative with *iniciens* in the next line.

10. *roget morari*: normally one would expect *ut* and the subjunctive after *roget*; *cf.* 13.13.

11. *quae* = *puella*.

    si mihi vera nuntiantur: more mystery; what rumors are coming to Catullus' ears?

12. *illum deperit*: "is hopelessly in love with him".

13. *nam*: as the final segment of the poem begins, the poet starts to shed some light on what it is that concerns him.

quo tempore: "from the very moment when".

legit: the subject is the *puella*.

incohatam: "not yet finished". *Cf.* line 18 below.

14. *Dindymi dominam*: a poem about the goddess Cybele, to whom Mt. Dindymus in Phrygia was sacred; Catullus, too, wrote a poem about her and her consort Attis—poem 63.

ex eo: refers back to *quo tempore*.

misellae: a common adjective for the love sick (*puellae* understood).

15. *ignes*: the fires of love.

edunt: cf. *vorabit* in line 7.

medullam: technically the marrow of the bones, but figuratively the "vitals" or "heart" of a person. The *puella* is being consumed by the fires of her passion.

16. *ignosco tibi*: probably both for being in love with Caecilius and for thus being reluctant to let him leave.

16 - *Sapphica...musa doctior*: the *puella* (here vocative) is
17. "more discriminating than the Sapphic muse"; a

223

somewhat ambiguous statement: does the poet mean
that she is more *docta* (a Catullan keyword) than the
Muse who inspired Sappho, or than Sappho herself,
who was sometimes called the Tenth Muse in antiquity? Perhaps the distinction was non-existant.

17. *venuste*: another Catullan keyword; the poem is
charming (but not yet finished).

18. *Magna...Mater*: Cybele; note the way in which the
two terms embrace two words crucial to the poem:
Caecilio (since he is the author), and *incohata* (since
there's more work needed, despite how promising the
poem seems). It is not until one reaches this final
verse, with its repetition of *incohata*, that a clear picture emerges: Caecilius apparently considers his poem
finished; Catullus has bad news for him—but, as a
sodalis, he couches it in delicate terms.

36

A vow fulfilled: Lesbia had promised to incinerate
some specially selected poetry, and Catullus helps her out
by burning the *Annales* of the poet Volusius.

Like poem 35, this piece works on two levels at once:
on a literary level, it provides a neat dig at Volusius and
the kind of poetry he wrote; on the personal level, it plays
a joke on Lesbia, who had apparently intended to burn the
poems of Catullus rather than those of Volusius.

But if poem 36 reminds one of the immediately preceding poem in its combination of these two motifs, it also
echoes poem 34 in its second half, where a hymn to Venus

is featured, and it also may look ahead to poem 37 in its reference to *truces iambos* (line 5). Thus the poems from 34 to 37 seem to form a mutually supportive poetic unit.

Poem 36 is easily divided into two segments: lines 1-10 set the stage by introducing both the *Annales* of Volusius and the vow of Lesbia; lines 11-20 then fulfil that vow by tossing the *Annales* into the flames after an appropriate prayer to the goddess involved.

Meter: hendecasyllabic.

1. *Annales Volusi*: both the poem and the poet will appear again in poem 95A; from its title, it would seem that the poem was a verse chronicle along the lines of the venerable *Annales* of Ennius, and thus a type of poetry not appealing to the Novi Poetae; as for Volusius, the best suggestion so far has been that of Neudling, who points to Q. Volusius, a lawyer and orator who was a friend of Cicero.

   cacata carta: the verb refers to the evacuation of the bowels, and so we might say that this papyrus is defiled by the crap written on it; it is tempting to translate the phrase as "toilet paper".

2. *solvite*: "pay" or "discharge".

   mea puella: undoubtedly Lesbia.

3. *Veneri Cupidinique*: *cf.* 3.1 and 13.12; the mention of these particular deities would turn our minds at once to love (and to Lesbia).

225

4. *restitutus*: "restored" in the sense of "reconciled"; a lovers' disagreement seems to be indicated. This line and the next two are dominated by *s* sounds.

5. *truces vibrare iambos*: "launching savage lampoons"; what these *iambi* were is controversial: T.P. Wiseman has argued that Catullus is alluding to poems 28, 29 and 33—his political invectives (*Catullan Questions*, 40), but other critics and editors prefer to see an anticipatory reference to poem 37. The latter seems more likely in view of Lesbia's apparent dislike of such *iambi*. Part of the problem lies in determining whether Catullus restricts the term *iambi* to poems in iambic meters (such as 37), or uses it in a more general sense to refer to poems of satirical or invective content (in any meter).

6. *electissima*: "choicest" or "pick of the crop", with *scripta*.

    pessimi poetae: "the worst of poets"; in the context of the poem so far, it would seem that Lesbia had Catullus in mind here, but was being playfully vague.

7. *tardipedi deo*: the lame-footed god was Vulcan, husband of Venus and god of fire; the adjective lends a mock-solemn note to the line.

    daturam: with *se* understood.

8. *infelicibus...lignis*: a reference to the ancient practice of burning evil things on sterile (*i.e.*, barren of fruit) wood; *cf.* G.W. Clarke's "The Burning of Books and Catullus 36" in *Latomus* 27 (1968) 575-580. As Quinn

points out, however, the common meaning of "unlucky" for *infelicibus* is also operative here: "to end its days helping to burn the *Annals* of Volusius was bad luck for any piece of wood" (*Catullus: The Poems*, 200).

9. *hoc*: with *vovere* in the next line, "this vow".

   pessima puella: "the worst of mistresses"; if Lesbia can call him *pessimi poetae* (line 6), then Catullus can return the favor to her! (Neither, however, seems to be too serious about the name-calling.)

10. *iocose lepide*: the lack of a connective need not indicate corruption in the text, as some have postulated; Lesbia made her vow "jokingly" and "charmingly", especially in that the very vagueness of it (lines 6-8) made for great fun, and avoided any overt threat against the poems of her lover.

    divis: the *Veneri Cupidinique* of line 3.

11. *nunc*: the second half of the poem begins to fulfil the vow, first with a prayer to Venus. One thus assumes that the wished for reconciliation took place.

    caeruleo creata ponto: a reference to the myth of Venus' birth from the foam of the sea. This is appropriately to be followed by a listing of cult places associated with the goddess; *cf.* the listing of Diana's functions and names in poem 34.

12. *Idalium*: a site in Cyprus (the island most closely associated with Venus) famous for a cult of

Venus—Aphrodite.

Uriosque: *Urios* seems to represent the Urium that stood on the coast of Apulia in Italy, although there was also an inland town called Uria located between Brundisium and Tarentum; the plural is troublesome, however, and a connection with Venus-Aphrodite is unknown.

apertos: "exposed" to the winds, more suitable to a coastal than an inland site. Note the numerous elisions in this line.

13. *Ancona*: Ancon (or Ancona) was a town on the Adriatic coast of Italy which featured the head of Venus on its coinage; the form is a Greek accusative.

Cnidumque harundinosam: Cnidus in Asia Minor was especially famed in antiquity for its temple to Aphrodite which contained Praxiteles' notorious nude statue of the goddess. It was also famous for its reeds (*harundinosam*).

14. *Amathunta*: Amathus was another cult site on Cyprus.

Golgos: also on Cyprus.

15. *Dyrrhachium*: once known as Epidamnus, a town on the coast of Illyria. Given its close location to Brundisium across the strait, Dyrrhachium became a busy point of transit; hence Catullus here calls it *Hadriae tabernam* (the inn of the Adriatic). We know nothing, however, of a cult of Venus-Aphrodite here.

16. "consider the vow as received and paid in full"; the poet uses commercial language in his dealings with the goddess.

17. *illepidum*: picks up the *lepide* of line 10.

    invenustum: note the pun on the name of Venus here. *Cf.* 10.4.

18. *at vos interea*: after prayer, the poet turns to the actual sacrifice, addressing once more the *Annales* of Volusius; *cf.* 14A.21 and 27.5.

19. *pleni ruris*: "full of country boorishness"; *cf.* 22.14. V read *pleni turis* (full of incense), and this reading has been defended by M.C.J. Putnam, in "Catullus 36.19", *Classical Philology* 64 (1969) 235-236.

    inficetiarum: "crudities".

20. The poem comes full circle with a repetition of its initial line.

37

On Egnatius and company, the steady customers of a low-life inn, who have been enjoying of late the favors of Lesbia. The poet promises revenge, a promise that is indeed fulfilled both by this poem and by poem 39 to come.

While poems 37 and 39 seem inextricably bound together, it is tempting to speculate that this piece is an example of the *truces iambos* mentioned in poem 36;

229

certainly the depiction of Lesbia here as a common tavern whore would not endear itself to the lady.

Like the preceding piece, poem 37 falls into two readily recognizable segments: the first ten lines introduce the regulars of the *taberna*, castigating them and promising punishment; the second ten lines then provide us with the reason for the poet's anger: Lesbia has been associating with them.

Meter: choliambic.

1.   *Salax*:   "lusty" or "over-sexed"; the *taberna* is here personified.

   taberna: an uncommon word in the Catullan corpus, appearing only here and in the preceding poem (36.15), thus forming a verbal link between the two.

   contubernales: "comrades-in-arms", or perhaps even "inn-mates".

2.   *pilleatis...fratribus*:   Castor and Pollux, so called because of the felt caps they commonly wore in representations; the reference is specifically to the Temple of Castor and Pollux in the Forum Romanum, three columns of which remain today.

   nona...pila: nominative, in apposition with *taberna* in the preceding line; the *pila* was a pillar often used as a sign post in front of businesses. Note the play on *pilleatis...pila*.

3.   *solis*:   repeated at the beginning of the next line, to

230

emphasize the arrogance of the *taberna*'s habitués.

mentulas: cf. 29.13.

4. *quidquid est puellarum*: in the sense of "all the girls in the world".

5. *confutuere*: "to screw", after *licere* in line 4.

    hircos: literally "he-goats", and most likely here referring to foul smell; these men think they have it all, while others are crude creatures worthy of their contempt.

6. *an*: "or perhaps".

    continenter: "in an unbroken line".

    sedetis: the image of sitting is again picked up at lines 8 and 14, the latter in regard to Lesbia.

    insulsi: cf. 17.12.

7. *centum an ducenti*: "a hundred, or even two hundred" of you.

    putatis: echoing the *putatis* of line 3.

8. *una*: "at the same time".

9. *atqui*: "and yet" you'd better think about it.

10. *sopionibus*: apparently "penises" or "phalli".

231

scribam: the tendency of the ancients to mark walls with graphic drawings (especially of genitalia) is amply attested by many archaeological remains today; here the poet, by the magic of such drawings, will effect the punishment he threatens.

11. *puella nam*: as the second movement of the poem begins we are at last given the reason for Catullus' anger at the *contubernales*. That the girl is Lesbia seems certain.

12. This line bears a striking similarity to poem 8.5. Note the dominant *a* sound of both this and the next line.

14. *consedit istic*: "has settled down in that place", though the idea is closer to her having "sunk down" to their level.

   boni beatique: a political phrase, meaning "men of rank and fortune", here undoubtedly used with sarcasm.

15. *indignum*: "shameful".

16. *pusilli et semitarii moechi*: "small-time alley-cat fornicators"; it seems that Lesbia is accused of having two distinct groups of lovers, and while fornicating with the *boni beatique* is bad enough, fooling around with the *pusilli et semitarii* is even worse. For *moechi*, *cf.* 11.17.

17. *praeter omnes*: of all these lovers, one man in particular stands out, a long-haired (*capillatis*) wimp from

Spain.

une: vocative, here in the sense of "you paragon".

18. *cuniculosae*: "rich in rabbits", a reference to a long-haired breed found in Spain.

   Celtiberiae: in the northeastern part of central Spain.

19. *Egnati*: a man who appears only here and in poem 39; there has been much speculation about his identity, but with little result. The best examination of the possibilities is that of Neudling in *A Prosopography to Catullus*.

   opaca: "bushy" or "thick".

   bonum facit: *cf.* line 14 above; Egnatius affects a bushy beard that he thinks makes him look like one of the *boni beatique* - he obviously has social pretensions.

20. *defricatus*: "rubbed clean".

   urina: as is common in the corpus, Catullus ends the poem with his sharpest barb: Egnatius, for all his social pretensions, has at least one very unsavory habit, to be elaborated upon in poem 39.

38

The poet's appeal to Cornificius: please send some

verse to console me in my troubles.

What kind of troubles plague the poet is left unclear. Some editors see in line 6 a reference to Lesbia, and postulate that Catullus is requesting a poem that will alleviate his love-sickness; if this is correct, then poem 38 will complement the surrounding poems, which are also concerned with Lesbia and love. Other editors, however, hypothesize that Catullus is physically ill, perhaps even on his deathbed, and that the poem has little to do with Lesbia. To complicate matters even more, a few editors and critics find the entire poem less than serious, and suggest that the poet is wryly upbraiding his friend for some small oversight.

Should line 6 not refer to Lesbia, the placement of poem 38 in this part of the *Passer* still makes sense: like poems 35, 36, 40 and 42, poem 38 is concerned with poetry, and these poems taken together form a thematic "cluster".

In structure, poem 38 falls into three units: lines 1-3 typically introduce the poet's situation; lines 4-6 upbraid Cornificius for doing nothing to help; and lines 7-8 make the poet's request for poetic consolation.

Meter: hendecasyllabic.

1. *Malest*: "things are going badly" for Catullus; *cf.* 14A.10. The repetition in the next line makes this quite emphatic.

   Cornifici: apparently Q. Cornificius (died 41 B.C.), a poet, politician and general; best known from the letters of Cicero, Cornificius was ranked by Ovid (*Tr.* II. 435-6) along with Catullus, Calvus and Cinna, although only a few fragments of his work survive today.

2. *me hercule*: "by Hercules", as we might say "by God"; there is a metrical hiatus between *hercule* and *et*, which some editors remove by reading *me hercule, et est laboriose*.

   laboriose: the appearance of this word after a reference to Hercules has led some to see a pun here which indicates that the poet is less than serious in his complaining. Translate as "uphill all the way".

3. *magis magis*: more repetition to stress how bad things are.

   in dies et horas: "day by day and hour by hour".

4. *quod minimum facillimumque est*: "something that is no trouble at all, very easily done in fact"; for the phrase, *cf.* 37.15.

5. *allocutione*: "words of comfort"; a comforting poem is in Catullus' mind.

6. *sic meos amores*: the most enigmatic line in the poem, interpreted sometimes as a reference to Catullus' affair with Lesbia; in the immediate context of the poem itself, however, another interpretation is that Catullus is rebuking Cornificius (*irascor tibi*) for not repaying the poet's own affection for him — *i.e.*, "is this how you reward my love for you".

7.   *paulum quid lubet allocutionis*:   give me "any little word of comfort you like"; for anything is better than nothing at all.   A verb of giving is understood.

8.   *maestius*:   "and let it be more sorrowful".

   Simonideis: a reference to the Greek poet Simonides of Ceos (*ca.*   556-467 B.C.); he was most famous in antiquity for poems of pathos and lamentation.

39

   The ever-grinning Egnatius, a man with no *savoir faire*.   That omnipresent grin, however, has a little secret behind it!

   A companion-piece to poem 37, this developed attack on Egnatius might well be another of the *truces iambos* of Catullus.   That Egnatius is one of the lovers of Lesbia is not reiterated here, but is information that we carry over from poem 37 and that helps to explain why the man becomes the object of Catullan ridicule in this piece.

   Poem 39 has a tripartite structure, with lines 1-8 serving to introduce Egnatius and his annoying habit; lines 9-16, with their implied comparison of Egnatius to men of various territories, then set us up for the climax of lines 17-21, where Egnatius' Spanish origin serves to explain what is so offensive about him and his grin.

   Meter: choliambic.

1. *dentes*: Egnatius' teeth had been the last of his physical traits remarked upon in poem 37 (line 20), and they now become the subject of a long invective piece.

2. *renidet usque quaque*: "grins everywhere, in every conceivable situation"; the verb *renideo* will be repeated in lines 4, 6, 7, and 15 to emphasize the constancy of that grin.

   si...cum: the same construction will be repeated in lines 4-5.

   rei: "defendant".

   ventum est: note the impersonal construction, and compare *lugetur* in line 5, and *monendum est <te> mihi* in line 9.

3. *subsellium*: "bench"; one of the wooden benches to be found in a Roman court.

   fletum: "tears"; contrasts with the *renidet* of the next line: Egnatius grins at the most inappropriate times (*cf. flet* in line 5, which is also followed by *renidet*).

4. *ad pii rogum fili*: "at the funeral pyre of a devoted son".

5. *orba*: "bereaved".

   unicum: "only son"; to lose an only son was an especially tragic event, but Egnatius grins nonetheless.

6. *quidquid est*: "whatever is going on".

7. *quodcumque agit*: "whatever he's engaged in".

   morbum: he has a "social disease".

8. *urbanum*: in this line the word means "smart" or "sophisticated" (*cf.* 22.2 and 9), but in line 10 it will take on its literal meaning "man of the town", *i.e.*, a city-dweller.

9. This line is short by one syllable in the MSS., and most editors add *te*, usually after *est*; the construction is an impersonal one, with *monendum* taking *te* as its direct object. Translate *monendum est te mihi* as "I must warn you".

   bone: used sarcastically: "my good" Egnatius; *cf.* 37.19.

10. *urbanus*: here specifically a "man of Rome". The poet begins at Rome, but expands to include the surrounding territories in his comparison; note that the theme of travel already prominent in the corpus is picked up here.

    Sabinus: the Sabines inhabited the mountains of central Italy.

    Tiburs: a "Tiburtine" would come from Tibur (now Tivoli) to the ENE of Rome. Sabine and Tiburtine territories were close together; *cf.* poem 44.

11. *pinguis*: the MSS. read *parcus*, considered suspect

238

because the other adjectives in this section of the poem all pertain to physical traits; if *pinguis* is the correct adjective, it must mean "fat" in this context. *Parcus*, however, could well be retained, if Catullus is using it here in the sense of "thin".

Umber: an Umbrian would live east of Etruria, and NE of Rome.

Etruscus: the most famous of Rome's neighbors, the Etruscans inhabited a vast region north of the city commonly called Etruria.

12. *Lanuvinus*: a native of Lanuvium, a town in the western part of Latium.

   ater: "dark-skinned".

   dentatus: "endowed with a fine set of teeth".

13. *Transpadanus*: a native of the region north of the Po River; Catullus, as a native of Verona, was himself a Transpadane.

   meos: "my own people".

   attingam: "mention".

14. *quilubet*: "anyone else you care to name".

   puriter: "in a cleanly fashion".

15. *renidere usque quaque*: an echo of line 2 above.

16. For the construction here, *cf.* 22.14. *Ineptus* has already appeared in the corpus as a Catullan keyword (*cf.* 12.4, and 25.8), denoting something or someone socially unacceptable.

17. *nunc*: in the sense of "as things stand".

   Celtiber: see note on 37.18. As this line is short by one syllable, most editors insert *es* after *Celtiber*.

18. *minxit*: from *meio*; translate as "has pissed".

   hoc: ablative case.

19. *russam...gingivam*: "reddened gums".

   defricare: *cf.* 37.20.

20. *quo...expolitior*: "the more polished".

   iste vester...dens: "those teeth of you and your countrymen".

21. *amplius*: "a great amount".

   loti: *lotium* seems to have been a colloquial term for urine. It is worth noting that the geographer Strabo (at 3.164) supports Catullus' assertion about the Spaniards with his statement that Iberians both bathe and wash their teeth with urine.

40

A series of questions—and a threat—to a rival. Ravidus had apparently been "making a move" on the poet's lover, and Catullus threatens a poetic revenge.

The poem combines the themes of love and poetry that have dominated the *Passer* since poem 35, although editors are divided over whether the specific love involved here is that for Lesbia (which would be in keeping with the prominence of Lesbia in this cluster of poems) or that for Juventius. Moreover, poem 40 maintains the invective tone of poems 37 and 39, and of the poems to follow in the corpus.

Structurally, the poem is a series of questions in two-line units (1-2, 3-4, 5-6) followed by the poet's promise of revenge and the explanation of his ire (7-8).

Meter: hendecasyllabic.

1.   *mala mens*: "madness"; *cf.* 15.14. Those editors who believe that the poet's affair with Juventius lies at the heart of this poem point out the verbal similarities between poems 40 and 15.

    miselle Ravide: for the ironic use of an adjective, *cf.* 39.9: *bone Egnati*. The name Ravidus has caused problems here, since the meter demands that it be pronounced as dissyllabic (as Raude), or that its final syllable be elided before the initial vowel of the next line (unlikely in the hendecasyllabic meter). Of the man himself, nothing is known beyond what this poem tells us.

2.   *praecipitem*: "headlong".

   meos iambos: if the poet is using *iambos* simply to mean invective verse, poem 40 itself may be meant here; there are no iambic poems addressed to a "Ravidus" in the rest of the corpus. *Cf.* 36.5.

3.   *non bene advocatus*: "not properly invoked", a reference to the belief that a god called upon improperly might well become angry and punish the offender.

4.   *vecordem...rixam*: "an insane quarrel"; *cf.* 15. 14-15.

5.   *an ut*: "or are you acting this way so that"; if an angry divinity cannot explain Ravidus' behavior, perhaps the man actually *wants* to provoke Catullus.

   in ora vulgi: "onto the lips of the crowd".

6.   *quid vis*: "well, what do you want?".

   qualubet: "in any way possible".

   notus: here in the sense of "notorious".

7.   *eris*: with *notus* understood.

   meos amores: from the context of the poem itself, it is unclear whether Lesbia or Juventius is meant; given the surrounding poetic context, however, Lesbia seems the more likely. But see comments on line 1 above.

8.   *cum longa...poena*: "at the risk of a long-lived punishment", *i.e.*, poetic immortality of an unpleasant

kind. *Cf.* the poetic immortality conferred on Egnatius by poems 37 and 39.

41

An attack on one Ameana, the lover of Mamurra: that a girl so unattractive would demand a large sum for her favors argues her insanity, and her unfamiliarity with a mirror!

After an eight-line lampoon against Ravidus in the preceding poem, we encounter this eight-line satire which seems to mark the beginning of a new "cluster" of thematically related poems: 41, 42, and 43. That poems 41 and 43 are closely related has been acknowledged for some time, and they have often been compared to the similar "pair", 37 and 39, on Egnatius; but poem 42 is also thematically a part of this new cluster, as it concerns a similar (if not the same) woman: *cf.* my "The Ameana Cycle of Catullus" in *Classical World* 70 (1977) 445-450.

The thematic difference between this new cluster and the preceding one is that the latter focused upon Lesbia and the "other men" in her life, while the former will direct our attention to Catullus and the "other women" in *his* life.

Poem 41 falls into two equal halves: lines 1-4 provide us with the requisite background information about Ameana, while lines 5-8, by means of an address to her kinsmen, complete the attack by questioning her sanity.

Meter: hendecasyllabic.

1. *Ameana*: the name finds no parallels in ancient literature, but this does not necessarily mean that an
emendation is required, as some have argued. In any
case, the precise spelling of the name is not crucial to
an understanding of the poem.

   puella defututa: the girl has been "all fucked out" by
the excessive intercourse in which she engages; *cf.*
29.13, where a similar term is applied to Mamurra.
The repetition of the word *puella* in the poem (lines
1, 3, 5, and 7) is noteworthy, and may be intended to
contrast her image of herself as a high-class lady with
the fact that all she really is is a common *amica* (line
4).

2. *tota milia*: the girl demands "all of 10,000 sesterces"
or "a full 10,000", a rather exorbitant sum.

3. *turpiculo...naso*: "with a nose that is really rather
ugly".

4. *decoctoris...Formiani*: "of the bankrupt man of Formiae"; the reference is to the Mamurra already
encountered in the *Passer* (poem 29) as a man who
ran through money in an alarming fashion. He will
appear in connection with Formiae also in poems 43
and 57. The town itself was located in southern
Latium.

5. *propinqui*: the poet turns to address the girl's kinsmen, who have the duty of looking after her since she
is so obviously insane.

quibus est...curae: the so-called "double dative" construction, common after *sum*.

7. *rogare*: take with *solet* in the next line.

8. *qualis sit*: "in what condition she is", that is, how
she looks.

aes imaginosum: the "image-filled bronze" is, of
course, a mirror.

42

A dramatic vignette, with overtones from Roman
comedy: an unnamed woman has some of the poet's writing-tablets, and refuses to return them. To get them back,
Catullus marshalls his hendecasyllabics (as foot-soldiers) to
pursue the woman.

As E. Fraenkel made clear in "Two Poems of Catullus", *Journal of Roman Studies* 51 (1961) 46-53, the poem
is based on a custom known as the *flagitatio*, in which a
person is subjected to public ridicule by someone who has a
complaint against him.

The placement of this poem between two poems concerned with Ameana probably indicates that the same
woman is involved here; but even if Ameana's presence is
denied, the theme of the offensive woman and the general
tone of this piece bind it to poems 41 and 43 nonetheless.

Structurally, poem 42 falls into two equal halves, each
of which can be further subdivided: the first twelve lines

are composed of lines 1-6, the usual introduction to the dramatic situation, and lines 7-12, in which the poet and the poems perform the *flagitatio*; the final twelve lines are composed of lines 13-14, an aside to the woman when she fails to react to the demand, lines 15-20, in which the *flagitatio* is repeated with greater vigor, and lines 21-24, in which the poet is forced to admit defeat, and to change his tactics quite radically.

Meter: hendecasyllabic.

1. *hendecasyllabi*: this meter has already demonstrated its utility for invective in the *Passer*; indeed, in poem 12 another thief had been threatened with hendecasyllabics by the poet. Here, however, the metrical feet become personified as the troops of Catullus, called together for a battle, and it should not be forgotten that the poem itself is in this meter and hence is part of the battle.

   quot: "as many as".

2. *undique*: while this can mean "from all sides", it can also mean "from both sides", and in this latter sense can refer to poems 41 and 43, which frame this piece and are written in the hendecasyllabic meter. Such an interpretation, of course, requires that Ameana be the woman in poem 42.

   quotquot: "however many". The repetitions in lines 1 and 2 (*quot-quotquot, omnes*) intensify the picture of the poet marshalling his forces.

3. *moecha turpis*: a coarse expression, akin to

"disgusting slut"; *cf.* *turpiculo* at 41.3. The *flagitatio* itself was probably a pretty coarse affair.

4. *vestra*: the reading of the MSS., but changed by some editors to *nostra*; *vestra*, however, makes perfectly good sense in the context, as Catullus would use the writing-tablets in the composition of his poems. Moreover, the troops need to be convinced that they have a large stake in the battle about to be joined: they will fight for their own possessions.

   reddituram: with *se* understood.

5. *pugillaria*: small writing-tablets, made of wood and coated with wax; apparently identical with the *codicillos* mentioned later in the poem.

   si pati potestis: "if you can bear that". The poet continues to appeal to the self-interest of the *hendecasyllabi*.

6. *reflagitemus*: "demand them back".

7. *quae sit, quaeritis*: in a comic-style interruption, the poems are depicted as asking who exactly their target is.

   illa, quam videtis: *cf.* 4.1, in a very different context.

8. *turpe incedere*: she walks in a shamefully suggestive way, echoing the *turpis* of line 3.

   mimice: "in the manner of a mime actress"; these women were generally held in contempt and would be very out of place in the poet's world of smart sophistication.

moleste: to complement *mimice* in both sound and sense; translate as "in an offensive manner".

9. *ridentem*: "laughing" with her mouth wide open, in the manner of a puppy.

catuli...Gallicani: the comparison of the woman to a dog was no more complimentary then than now. *Gallicani* = "of the Gaullish type", a breed used for hunting; the image would have a special relevance were the woman a provincial (*cf.* poem 43).

10. The poems now surround their target and make the *flagitatio*.

11. *putida*: "rotten" or "stinking".

codicillos: "writing-tablets".

12. The repetition of line 11 with some change in word order reminds one of children's taunting songs even now.

13. *non assis facis*: an address to the woman after the *flagitatio*; she has apparently ignored it. For the construction, *cf.* 5.3.

lutum, lupanar: terms of abuse; the former refers to mud or filth, and a modern equivalent might be "shit"; the latter means "brothel" and characterizes the woman as a whore. Note the alliteration: even coarse words can share in poetic sound.

14.   *perditius*: "more degraded".

15.   The poet now turns his attention back to the *hende-casyllabi*: they must intensify their efforts.

16.   *quod si*: "but if".

       non aliud potest: "nothing else can be done".

       ruborem: "a blush"; note how the sound of *r* becomes prominent here and in the next line, so that the words seem to growl in imitation of a dog (*canis*, line 17).

17.   *ferreo*: the best equivalent in English is "brazen".

       canis: *cf.* line 9 above.

       exprimamus: "let us extract", namely by another *flagitatio*.

18.   *altiore*: "louder".

19 - The *flagitatio* repeated, as in lines 11-12, but (as we
20.   see in the next line) with equal lack of success.

21.   *nil proficimus*: "we are making no headway at all".

22.   *ratio modusque*: "manner and method" must be changed.

       vobis: the MSS. read *nobis*, but *vobis* seems required, especially by the *potestis* of the next line.

24. *pudica et proba*: a total turn about! If insults got nowhere, perhaps flattery (no matter how insincere) will get the tablets back?

43

To Ameana, the girl who rates 0 on a scale of 1-10. The poet carefully lists her failings, then condemns the taste that would compare this creature to Lesbia.

The poem is clearly a companion-piece to poem 41, and completes the "Ameana cluster" of poems in this part of the *Passer*. While her lover Mamurra will continue to play a role in other Catullan poems, Ameana now disappears from the corpus.

In structure, poem 43 echoes poem 41 in being divisible into two parts of four lines each: the first four lines concentrate on the poet's "catalogue" of her flaws, while the second four lines criticize even the thought that Ameana is comparable to a real beauty like Lesbia in any way.

Meter: hendecasyllabic.

1. *Salve*: the poem begins as a verse epistle to Ameana.

   nec: the repetition of *nec* throughout the first half of the poem emphatically stresses what Ameana simply does *not* have!

   naso: Ameana's nose had also come in for criticism

250

in poem 41.3, as a *turpiculo...naso*. It must have been one of her most prominent physical features.

2. *bello pede*: in Roman eyes small feet were beautiful, so one assumes that Ameana's feet, like her nose, were large.

3. *longis digitis*: "long and slender fingers".

    ore sicco: commentators offer "lips" for *ore*, but tend to ignore what Catullus means by this phrase: how were "dry lips" attractive in a woman? If we compare poem 42.9, however, we might come to the conclusion that Ameana's mouth, like that of our canine friends, tended towards wetness caused by unsightly drooling. But there is an even more sinister reference possible: *cf.* poem 80.

4. *nec...nimis elegante*: "not very refined"; is this a reference to her coarseness of speech, or, on a lower level, to her use of her tongue in unrefined activities? Perhaps the poet is being deliberately vague.

5. *Cf.* 41.4. Making this line the first verse in the second part of the poem is the suggestion of K. Quinn (*Catullus: The Poems*, 220); other editors put a period after this verse, thus dividing the poem into segments of five, then three lines.

6. *ten = tene*.

    provincia: most likely a reference to Cisalpine Gaul. Whether Ameana was a native of the region, or just there with Mamurra is difficult to say. *Cf.* 42.9.

8. "O what a senseless and tasteless world we live in!"

44

A paean of appreciation to the poet's country estate, which provided refuge after he fell ill reading an oration by Sestius. Despite its praise for the estate, however, the poem remains at heart a piece of literary criticism, with Sestius' "frosty style" of writing the butt of Catullus' humor.

That poem 44 is a clever parody has been argued by both E.S. DeAngeli ("A Literary Chill: Catullus 44", *Classical World* 62 [1969] 354-356) and C.P. Jones ("Parody in Catullus 44", *Hermes* 96 [1968] 379-383); the former critic, however, sees the poem as written in a bombastic style meant to imitate the style of Sestius, while the latter critic finds the poem to be a parody of the religious language of prayer. Both are most likely on the right track: while the poem does parody a formal prayer, it probably does so in the awkward and stilted style of Sestius—that is, it is a mock-prayer *à la Sestius*. But only discovering examples of Sestius' works would prove this conclusively.

While poem 44 has something in common with poem 31 (both are concerned with a country location dear to the poet and providing him with rest and tranquility) and poem 36 (both share a prayer format and are concerned with literature), its main function is to signal the start of what will become a unifying theme in the last section of the *Passer*: the relationship between the concepts of *otium* and *negotium*. Here, we encounter the *otium* (line 15) which

252

enables the poet to recuperate from an illness, but *otium* and its opposite (*negotium*) will be viewed from many angles in the poems to come.

Structurally, poem 44 is composed of three segments: lines 1-9 address the estate and introduce the poet's illness; lines 10-15 explain how Catullus became ill in the first place, and how he was cured; finally, lines 16-21 offer his thanks to the estate and a closing wish of an unexpected kind.

Meter: choliambic.

1. *O funde noster*: the poet begins by personifying his estate; *cf.* poem 31.

    Sabine seu Tiburs: for the geography involved, *cf.* 39.10; both are vocatives, by attraction to the opening *funde*.

2. The rather jarring parenthesis of lines 2-4 serves two functions: first, as befits a parody of a prayer, it includes all possible names by which the "divinity" addressed was known; and second, it probably mocks the lumbering style of Sestius in his orations.

    autumant: an archaic word appropriate in a prayer; translate as "affirm".

    quibus non est/cordi Catullum laedere: "those who do not have it in their heart to hurt Catullus"; apparently an estate at Tibur was quite fashionable, somewhat of a status symbol. On the other hand, to have a place in Sabine territory was really nothing to

253

brag about.

4. *quovis...pignore...contendunt*: "they swear by whatever pledge you please" that the estate is in Sabine country.

5. The parenthesis ends with an echo of line 1, although the addition of *verius* wryly indicates the address preferred by the poet.

6. *fui libenter*: an idiom with the sense of "I quite enjoyed myself".

7. *villa*: obviously a country-house was part of the general estate (*fundus*).

   pectore: "chest".

8. *non inmerenti*: with *mihi*.

9. *dum...appeto*: the verb is in the present tense, but refers to past action; translate as "while I was seeking". Note the reappearance of *dum* in lines 10 and 14; was this a peculiarity of Sestius' style?

   sumptuosas: "lavish".

   dedit: the placement of this verb in the middle of the subordinate clause has traditionally perturbed editors; the explanation may well lie in Sestius' style.

10. *Sestianus...conviva*: "a dinner-guest of Sestius". Sestius was P. Sestius, a friend of Cicero who was defended by that orator in 56 B.C. He apparently

had the reputation of being a poor public speaker, with a style that Catullus here characterizes as "frigid".

dum volo: *cf.* line 9 above.

11. *orationem in Antium petitorem*: this may well have been the actual title of Sestius' oration; Antius is perhaps the C. Antius who seems to have authored a *lex Antia* which controlled expenditures on meals (a sumptuary law), even to the point of restricting the right of a magistrate to dine out. This identification, if correct, would give an added barb to the poet's reference to seeking *sumptuosas cenas* in line 9. *Petitorem* is here used in the sense of "candidate".

12. *plenam veneni*: *cf.* 14.19.

legi: it would seem that Sestius expected his guests to bone up on his latest effort before coming to dine; *cf.* line 21. Had it not been for his craving belly the poet implies he would never have touched such stuff.

13. *hic*: "thereupon".

gravedo frigida et frequens tussis: "a chilling cold and a hacking cough"; the poet caught a good case of flu, it would appear.

14. *quassavit*: "gave me the shakes".

usque, dum: "constantly, until".

15. *me recuravi*: "cured myself".

urtica: "nettle-tea", the Roman version of chicken soup.

16. *refectus*: "healthy again".

    grates: another archaic word common in religious contexts.

17. *es ulta*: the MSS. reading, but a source of unease since it forces the addressee to change abruptly from the *fundus* to the *villa*. The suggested emendation *ultus*, however, requires the final *s* to drop off (*i.e., es ultu' peccatum*).

    peccatum: "mistake", but also "sin" in the religious dimension of the poem.

18. *nec deprecor*: also religious terminology; translate as "I do not pray to prevent".

    nefaria: "heinous".

19. *recepso*: an archaic future form of *recipio*.

20. *non mi, sed ipsi Sestio*: a surprising twist, going against the expected train of thought.

    frigus: a play on words here, as *frigus* not only refers to physical cold or a chill, but also (in a literary sense) to a "coldness" or "frigidity" of style.

21. *tunc...cum*: "only when".

vocat: "invites" to dinner.

45

Lovers' oaths: a dramatic vignette in which we observe Acme and Septimius swear eternal love to each other, while the god of love expresses his approval. There has been much discussion in recent years as to whether the poet is being totally serious in these lines, or is being ironic — *i.e.*, writing with tongue in cheek, and suggesting that all is not as idyllic as it appears on the surface. For lovers' oaths, *cf.* poem 70.

Poem 45 takes the form of a so-called amoebaean contest (common in pastoral poetry) in which one speaker tries to "cap" the statement of the previous speaker. Thematically, it develops the motif of *otium* in this part of the *Passer* by depicting the *homo otiosus* as Septimius dedicates himself to the service of love; *cf.* H. Akbar Khan's examination of this aspect of the poem in "Catullus 45: What Sort of Irony?", *Latomus* 27 (1968) 3-12.

The structure of the poem is clear and balanced: the first seven lines focus on the oath sworn by Septimius, and are followed by two lines on the reaction of Amor; the next seven lines (10-16) present the corresponding oath of Acme, and are followed by a repetition of lines 8-9 as a refrain; the final eight lines are composed of four two-line units expressing the thoughts of the observing poet.

Meter: hendecasyllabic.

1. *Acmen Septimius*: otherwise unknown, although it seems reasonable to deduce from their names that the

257

woman was Greek and the man Roman; they may well be imaginary characters created for this vignette. *Acmen* is a Greek accusative, object of *tenens* in line 2.

suos amores: cf. **6.16** and **10.1**. Two things should be noted about this opening line of the poem: 1) we plunge *in medias res*: the vignette is in progress; and 2) while the language tells us that Septimius is embracing Acme, the order of the words shows us Acme embracing Septimius: their love seems mutual from the very start.

2. *gremio*: "lap".

3. *perdite amo*: "love desperately"; the phrase is complemented in both sound and sense by the ensuing *amare porro*; note also the elisions of this line.

    porro: "for the rest of time".

4. *omnes...annos*: an elaboration of *porro*, emphasizing Septimius' temporal committment.

    assidue: "incessantly".

5. *quantum qui*: "as much as any man who".

    pote = potest. Cf. **17.24**.

    plurimum perire: "love to greatest desperation"; this verse is noteworthy for its *p* and *q* sounds.

6. *solus*: "all by myself".

Indiaque: Catullus uses "and" where we would normally use "or".

tosta: "parched"; from *torreo*.

7. *caesio*: "blue-eyed".

veniam obvius: "may I come to meet"; Septimius thus concludes his oath of love. Note how here the blue-eyed lion surrounds Septimius in the word order and compare line 1.

8 - The refrain has been the object of much debate,
9. especially with reference to *ut ante*. What is clear is that Amor by his sneeze expresses his approval of what Septimius has just said (*hoc ut dixit*); there is no reason to assume that, before this vignette began, Amor had sneezed unfavorably for the lovers, on the left side (besides, the left was not always considered unlucky; *cf.* the thorough examination of right and left sides in Fordyce's *Catullus*, 205-206). The simplest solution is to take *sinistra ut ante/dextra* as equivalent to *primum sinistra, deinde dextra* - that is, Amor sneezed twice at Septimius' oath, first to the left, then to the right, giving thereby a double blessing. That a sneeze was a good sign goes back as far as Homer's *Odyssey* (17.541), where Telemachus "sneezes a blessing" on the words of his mother.

10. *leviter*: probably "gently" or even "slightly" bending back her head, although those who find irony intended may be tempted towards the meaning "thoughtlessly" or, indeed, "in a fickle manner".

11. *dulcis*: genitive, with *pueri*.

ebrios: his eyes are "drunk with passion".

12. *illo purpureo ore*: "with that radiant mouth of hers".

13. *sic*: with *ut* fashions the oath of Acme, in which she depicts her love for Septimius as being fiercer than his love for her—appropriate especially in an amoebaean format.

mea vita: "my love"; note also the endearing diminutive in *Septimille*.

14. *huic uni domino*: their "one god" is Amor, and the *huic* implies that the lovers know that Amor is present as they speak.

usque: cf. 44.14.

15. While especially noticeable in this line, the sound of *m* dominates the entire speech of Acme; cf. Septimius' use of *p* and *q* sounds. The softer sound seems appropriate to Acme's feminine characterization, the harsher sounds more fitting for the "manly" characterization of Septimius.

16. *ignis...in medullis*: cf. the similar image at 35.15.

mollibus: "tender".

17. Amor blesses Acme's oath with another double sneeze; cf. lines 8-9 above.

19. *auspicio*: "omen", *i.e.*, the sneezes of Amor.

20. *mutuis*: reciprocal in the sense of "belonging to each other". Note the prominence here of the "soft" sounds of *m*, *n*, and *a*.

21. *unam*: *cf. uno* in line 23; there is a careful balance between the couplet in lines 21-22 and that in lines 23-24. Note also how *unam...Acmen* again embraces Septimius in the word order.

misellus: *cf.* 35.14.

22. *Syrias Britanniasque*: Septimius, says the poet, prefers Acme to "all the Syrias and Britains in the world", completing the characterization of a *homo otiosus* who denies the call of *negotium*. The references seem to date the poem to 55 B.C., when Caesar was involved in Britain and Crassus in the East.

24. *facit delicias*: Acme "finds her pleasure" in Septimius alone; ironists, however, are quick to note that the phrase can also mean "have some fun".

libidinesque: sexual "desires". In a modern idiom, one might say that Acme "centers her pleasures and desires on" Septimius alone.

25. The poem ends with a rhetorical question; *cf.* the endings of poems 9, 29, and 47. If the answer is "no one", then some irony may well be intended here: could a love as perfect as this ever really exist?

26. *auspicatiorem*: "more auspicious".

261

46

Spring comes to Bithynia, and the poet feels the powerful urge to head for home. The date would seem to be 56 B.C., when Catullus completed his term of service with Memmius. *Cf.* poem 31.

Poem 46 is more than a "spring song", however, and it is much more than "a poem setting out C.'s plans for sightseeing during the first stage of his return home" (K. Quinn, *Catullus: The Poems*, 228-229). For here the theme of *otium* continues in the poet's leave-taking of Bithynia and its related *negotium* in order to resume the life of *otium* at home: the winter of *negotium* is over.

The poem falls into two unequal halves: in the first six lines we find an initial statement of time (in terms of the seasons) in lines 1-3, followed by another set of three lines (4-6) expressing the urge to travel; in the final five lines we find another statement of time (now in terms of the poet's mental readiness to travel) in lines 7-8, followed by three lines (9-11) of actual leave-taking.

Meter: hendecasyllabic.

1. *Iam:* the repetition of *iam* at the start of lines 1, 2, 7, and 8 emphasizes the realization of the poet that *now* is the time to go.

   egelidos...tepores: "mild days from which all the chill has been removed".

   refert: the idea of "bringing back" is repeated in the final line of the poem by *reportant;* these two verbs of return thus frame the entire poem.

2. *caeli*: literally "sky", but here more in the sense of "weather".

   aequinoctialis: the vernal equinox in March, a time of storms.

3. *iucundis...aureis*: "pleasant breezes" (an instrumental ablative); *aureis = auris*. Pleasant breezes signal the opening of the sailing season.

   Zephyri: the West wind.

4. *linquantur*: subjunctive, as the poet urges himself to be off; *cf. volemus* in line 6.

   Phrygii...campi: Phrygia was a region in Asia Minor; *cf.* 31.5-6: *Bithynos...campos*.

5. *Nicaeaeque...aestuosae*: "sweltering Nicaea" was the major city of Bithynia; for the adjective, *cf.* 7.5. Note also the dominant *ae* sound in the line.

6. *claras*: "famous".

   Asiae: on his way home the poet will pass through the province of Asia, a territory full of associations with the mythical past.

   volemus: expressing the eagerness of the poet to "fly" away.

7. *mens praetrepidans*: his mind is "trembling in

263

anticipation", and "longs" (*avet*) to roam.

8. *laeti...pedes*: from an eager mind we turn to feet that are joyful at the thought of travel; take *studio* with *laeti*.

   vigescunt: "gather strength".

9. *o dulces...coetus*: cf. the ending of poem 31; *coetus* here in the sense of "company".

   comitum: cf. 11.1 and 28.1.

10. *longe*: take with *a domo profectos*; note the echo of 45.19 in *profectos*: the verb appears only in these two juxtaposed poems.

    simul: "together".

11. *diversae...viae*: "different roads"; note again the *ae* sounds.

    varie: "in different ways"; those who set out from home together now scatter, to return home in different ways on different routes. Some editors emend *varie* to *variae*, but the adverb works well and even balances the *longe* of the preceding verse.

    reportant: "bring home" — the final (and key) thought of the poem.

47

Porcius and Socration: two creeps who fare well, while

Veranius and Fabullus are passed over. The poem in reality
is an attack on "the system" which allows such injustice to
occur; it is obvious to the poet that the world of *negotium*
(here in its political aspect) has little to recommend it. The
sentiments expressed are similar to those found in poem 28.

The poem is structured around two rhetorical questions: first, in lines 1-4 the poet asks if Porcius and Socration are preferred by Piso to Veranius and Fabullus; second, in lines 5-7 he asks if they are enjoying lavish feasts
while Veranius and Fabullus scrounge around for invitations. Catullus, of course, knows well the answers to his
questions.

Meter: hendecasyllabic.

1. *Porci et Socration*: there has been much (inconclu-
   sive) speculation about these two characters. Porcius
   would seem to be a real name rather than a pseudonym, but which Porcius is meant is uncertain,
   although some suggest C. Porcius Cato, tribune in 56
   B.C. Socration, however, may be a pseudonym, sati-
   rizing someone as a "little Socrates"; if so, one possible candidate would be the philosopher Philodemus,
   who seems to have been a friend of Piso.

   sinistrae: not "right-hand men" but "left-hand men"
   with the implication that they are crooks; *cf.* 12.1.

2. *Pisonis*: *cf.* poem 28; Piso here represents "the system", much as Cicero will in the upcoming poem 49.

   scabies famesque: obviously terms of insult: Porcius
   and Socration are the "mange and mouth" of the

world.

3. *Veraniolo*: for the diminutive, *cf.* 12.17.

4. *verpus...Priapus ille*: "that circumcised lecher" —
    Piso, of course. For *verpus, cf.* 28.12; Priapus was a
    god of procreation whose name became synonymous
    with lust.

5. *vos*: the repetition of the *vos* in line 3 emphasizes
    the poet's disillusionment, and disbelief.

    convivia lauta sumptuose: "splendid banquets laid on
    at great cost". *Cf.* 44.9.

6. *de die*: "in the day-time" when honest people would
    still be at work.

7. *quaerunt...vocationes*: "hunt after invitations".

    in trivio: "on the streets".

48

Kisses for Juventius: a poem that has much in common with Catullus' other *basia* poems, 5 and 7.

Placed between poems 47 and 49, both of which feature men of political interests, poem 48 at first glance
seems to be an example of simple *variatio*; yet in one sense
it too participates in the *otium-negotium* theme as it
depicts the poet as *otiosus*, concerned only with the private
sphere of passion.

In structure, the poem is one single sentence, divisible into two equal parts, each of which contains a *si* clause.

Meter: hendecasyllabic.

1. *Mellitos*: "sweet as honey"; *cf.* 3.6.

   oculos: for the "kissing of eyes" *cf.* 9.9 and 45. 11-12. Note the *os* sound in this line.

2. *usque basiare*: "to kiss continually"; *cf.* 45.14. Note the repetition of this idea in the *usque...basiem* of the next line.

3. *milia...trecenta*: indicating simply a large, indefinite number; *cf.* 9.2.

4. *nec mi umquam*: an emendation of the MSS.' *nec numquam*; the sense required by the context is clearly "not ever".

   mi...videar satur futurus: "would I think I would be sated".

5. *aridis aristis*: a clever play on sound; translate as "ripe ears of grain". The poet ends his piece with an agricultural image suggesting infinity.

6. *seges*: "crop".

   osculationis: an imposing word appearing only here; *cf.* the similar use of imposing words at 6.11 and, especially, 7.1.

49

To Cicero: an expression of thanks. The occasion of
the poem is quite enigmatic, and many implausible theories
have been put forth: for example, perhaps Cicero sent
Catullus one of his poems for criticism; or perhaps Catullus
is thanking Cicero for keeping his name out of the *Pro
Caelio*; or perhaps Cicero was having an affair with Clodia
(!) and magnanimously yielded his spot in her bed to
Catullus; *etc.*

A complicating factor is that, while it is possible to
take this poem at face value—as a sincere thanks for some
unknown favor, it is also possible to see irony at work here
and to find in the poem a mocking of the "great man". An
ironical interpretation, indeed, is made more likely by the
context of the poem: as Skinner has written, "In the context of the *libellus*, poem 49 offers a last sardonic comment
on Catullus' wasted year in Bithynia and Veranius and
Fabullus' futile pursuit of Piso. The folly of 'seeking noble
friends' is neatly demonstrated by the figure of a powerful
patronus unable to distinguish between flattery and patent
ridicule, unable to recognize the genuine worth of the *pessimus omnium poeta*" (*Catullus' Passer*, 79).

One other point has been neglected: if the final two
lines are indeed ironic, then Catullus is *not* the worst poet
in the world just as Cicero is *not* the best *patronus* in the
world; now, we know that one of Cicero's forensic rivals
was Calvus (see Eric Laughton's "*Disertissime Romuli
Nepotum*", *Classical Philology* 65 [1970] 1-7)—the same Calvus to whom poem 50 is addressed, and it would be curious for these two men to be juxtaposed in this way were
not Catullus "putting Cicero down". Cicero, the man of

extreme *negotium*, comes off as second-best when compared to a man who offsets *negotium* with *otium* as well as the poet-orator Calvus.

Structurally, poem 49 (like the preceding poem) is a single sentence divided into two parts: lines 1-3 introduce the addressee of the poem, while lines 4-7 convey the thanks of the poet to that addressee.

Meter: hendecasyllabic.

1. *Disertissime:* a man "most skilled at public speaking".

   nepotum: "descendants". *Cf.* 58A.5.

2 - Almost identical statements were made at 21. 2-3 and
3. 24. 2-3.

   Marce Tulli: a formal mode of address; Cicero's full name was Marcus Tullius Cicero.

4. The actual statement of thanks (vague though it is) comes in the exact middle of the poem.

5. *pessimus omnium poeta:* would Catullus sincerely think of himself in this light? Poem 36 suggests not, since it is clear there that Volusius has this honor! *Cf.* also poem 14A. The repetition of this phrase in the next line also leads one to question its sincerity.

6. *tanto:* with *quanto:* "as much...as".

7. *optimus omnium patronus:* a phrase that obviously

balances the preceding *pessimus omnium poeta*; there is some ambiguity, however, about *omnium*: is Cicero the best *patronus* of all *patroni*; or, is he the best *patronus* of all and sundry people — *i.e.*, an indiscriminate lawyer? As usual, the answer will depend on whether or not one finds irony in the poem.

50

Poets at play: Catullus recalls a stimulating day spent in poetic improvisation with Calvus. A return engagement is eagerly requested.

The poem presents a portrait of *homines otiosi* who have made love and poetry their way of life; indeed, it is no accident that in this poem Catullus employs the language of love to describe the ecstasy of poetic creation. In its own way, poem 50 is programmatic—placing before the reader all that is held to be important to the Poetae Novi. While technically the poem is an epistle to Calvus, it is in reality an "open letter" to the world.

In its structure, poem 50 falls into four segments: lines 1-6 depict the actual encounter between Catullus and Calvus; lines 7-13 then portray what happened to the former after the encounter was over; lines 14-17 explain how this experience resulted in the creation of the poem at hand; and lines 18-21, finally, present the formal request of the poet.

Meter: hendecasyllabic.

1. *Hesterno...die*: "yesterday".

Licini: Calvus' full name was C. Licinius Calvus Macer; for this poet and orator, *cf.* poem 14A.

otiosi: the key word of the poem, introducing as it does the *otium* that is so vital to the creative process.

2. *multum lusimus*: in keeping with the concept of *otium*, the two poets "played around a great deal"; play is, of course, the antithesis of *negotium*.

tabellis: wooden tablets coated with wax; *cf.* poem 42.

3. *ut convenerat*: "as we had agreed".

delicatos: another key word in the poem; Catullus and Calvus had agreed to be "avante-garde" in modern terms: *delicatus*, in addition to its basic meaning of "delightful" or "sophisticated", has the sense of "wanton" or "risqué". Cicero uses the word with sarcasm to attack the "degenerate youth of today" at *Att.* i.19.8.

4. *versiculos*: "bits of verse"; *cf.* 16.3 and 6. Poem 50 itself, however, is called *poema* in line 16, as if the poet is drawing attention to two differing types of poetic endeavors.

5. *ludebat*: repeated from line 2 to stress the element of play again.

numero modo hoc modo illoc: a reference to the use of different meters in their *versiculi*; *illoc* = *illo* (*cf.*

271

3.9).

6. *reddens mutua*: "improvizing, each in turn", with the sense that the exchange was above all a *mutual* endeavor.

   per: "over"; for the phrase itself, *cf.* 12.2.

7 - Whereas the language of the first segment of the
13. poem centered on poetry, the language of this second segment will draw heavily from the erotic vocabulary.

7. *atque*: "and then".

   lepore: "charm"; a frequent Catullan keyword. For its combination with *facetiae, cf.* 12.8-9.

8. *incensus*: like a lover, Catullus is "on fire" or "aflame".

   facetiisque: "wit".

9. *me miserum*: the poet adopts the pose of the miserable lover. *Cf.* poem 8.

10. *tegeret*: "close".

    ocellos: *cf.* line 19 below.

11. *toto...lecto*: "all over the bed".

    indomitus: "wild".

12. *versarer*: "tossed".

13. *simulque ut essem*: "so that I might be with you"; note that the normal order of events is reversed in this line.

14. *defessa*: "exhausted".

    labore: "suffering".

15. *semimortua*: "half-dead"; the word may have been invented by Catullus.

    lectulo: the diminutive adds to the pathos of the scene.

16. *hoc...poema*: probably a reference to poem 50 itself, although it has been suggested that it refers ahead to poem 51; *cf.* J. Clack, "*Otium Tibi Molestum Est* - Catullus 50 and 51", *Classical Bulletin* 52 (1976) 50-53.

    iucunde: *cf.* 14A.2.

17. *perspiceres*: "thoroughly see".

    dolorem: *cf.* 2A.7.

18. *audax cave sis*: "beware of being reckless"; the final syllable of *cave* is short here.

    precesque: the request is clearly for another meeting between the two men. *Cf.* line 13 above.

19. *cave despuas*: "beware of spurning". The sound of *despuas* reflects well its literal meaning of "spit out".

ocelle: cf. 31.2.

20. *Nemesis*: a Greek deity considered to be the goddess of retribution.

21. *vemens = vehemens*. Translate as "powerful".

laedere: "displease".

caveto: the third *cave* in these final four lines emphasizes the poet's warning to Calvus; here, a future imperative in form.

51

On Lesbia and her effect on the poet; an adaptation of a Greek poem by Sappho. The Greek original read: "To me, he seems to be equal to the gods—that man who sits across from you and listens closely as you speak sweetly and laugh in a charming way; that, alas, has caused the heart within my chest to beat wildly—for when I gaze upon you for even a short time I am unable any longer to make a sound, but my tongue falls silent, and a thin flame at once steals beneath my flesh; I see nothing through my eyes, and my ears hear only a roaring noise, and a cold sweat takes me in its grasp, a tremor seizes me entirely, I am more pale than grass, and I seem to be close to dying. But all this must be borne, since ...." It is clear that Catullus has not slavishly followed Sappho, but has made his adaptation into a unique analysis of love.

In the past, some scholars have argued that the final stanza does not belong with the rest of the poem, but recent work on the poem tends to reaffirm the unity of the piece as we have it in the MSS. See, for example, T.E. Kinsey's "Catullus 51", *Latomus* 33 (1974) 372-378, or E.A. Fredricksmeyer's "On the Unity of Catullus 51", *TAPA* 96 (1965) 153-163. Indeed, the unity of the poem becomes even more apparent when one recognizes in poem 51 an epilogue to the *Passer*: as Skinner has argued, the final stanza, with its stress on *otium* and its naming of the poet (*Catulle*, line 13), forms a fitting conclusion not only to the poems concerned with *otium*, but also to the book as a whole (*Catullus' Passer*, 82-92).

In structure, the poem devotes its initial stanza to a statement of the situation from which the poem springs; the next two stanzas focus on the poet, and on the effect Lesbia has on him; finally, the fourth stanza offers the poet's reflections on the life of *otium* that has allowed such a state of affairs to come into existence.

Meter: Sapphic stanzas (*cf.* poem 11).

1. *Ille*: the identity of the man is irrelevant; he exists within the poem to throw into high relief the poet's reaction to Lesbia.

    mi = *mihi*; *cf.* line 7.

    deo: the comparison of *ille* to a god carries with it a suggestion that Lesbia is herself a goddess: a neat compliment.

2. *si fas est*: a Roman touch, without parallel in the

Greek original; *fas* refers to what is permissible by divine law, and the poet takes care not to offend the gods (*cf.* the ending of poem 50).

superare: "surpass".

3.   *adversus*: "opposite".

identidem: *cf.* poem 11.19. *Ille*, it should be noted, can look at Lesbia "again and again", while just one glimpse is enough to throw the poet into turmoil.

5.   *dulce*: "sweetly", with *ridentem*.

misero: with *mihi* in line 6. *Cf.* 8.1 and 50.9.

quod: "a thing which", in reference to the activities described in the first stanza.

6.   *eripit*: "tears".

simul = *simul ac*; *cf.* 22.15.

7.   *Lesbia*: the appearance of Lesbia's name here is balanced by the *Catulle* of the final stanza; it is, of course, appropriate that both appear in the concluding poem of the *Passer*.

aspexi: from *aspicio*, in the sense of "catch sight of".

est super = *superest*: "remains".

8.   A line is missing here in the MSS. One plausible suggestion is *vocis in ore*, although some prefer

Lesbia, vocis. In either case, *vocis* would be governed by the *nihil* of the preceding line.

9.   *torpet*: "grows numb". Note the prominence of *t* sounds in this stanza.

    tenuis: "thin", with *flamma* in line 10.

    artus: "limbs".

10.   *demanat*: "runs down".

    sonitu suopte: here *s* joins with *t* to suggest the "hissing" in the poet's ears; *suopte* = *suo*.

11.   *tintinant*: "ring".

    gemina: the adjective is transferred from the expected *lumina* to the unexpected *nocte*, resulting in a bold and unusual image.

    teguntur: *cf.* 50.10.

12.   *lumina*: here in the sense of "eyes".

13.   *otium*: the triple repetition of this word in lines 13-15 brings the reader to the conclusion of the *otium* theme developed in the final poems of the *Passer*. It should be emphasized that *otium* as used by Catullus in these poems refers to private as opposed to public duties: "doing your own thing" as opposed to engaging in the service the state; it is not mere idleness or leisure.

Catulle: the insertion of the poet's name furnishes the "seal" which ends the book.

molestum est: "brings you pain".

14. *exsultas*: "run riot".

gestis: "long for".

16. *perdidit*: "has ruined". "Doing your own thing" (says the poet) can indeed bring pain, and some people might even be destroyed by it; but, there is no admonition to turn away from the life of *otium* - for, painful as it may be, it is the requisite of both love and poetic endeavors (*cf.* poem 50). Indeed, out of the pain caused the poet by the sight of his beloved has come this very poem.

52

An attack on two men who seem to have been followers of Pompey and Caesar. The precise circumstances leading to the poem, however, remain obscure (see below).

The poem begins and ends with the same exasperated question; the central lines (2 and 3) explain why the poet feels such exasperation.

Meter: iambic trimeter.

1. *Quid est*: a rhetorical question, perhaps best approximated by the modern "What's going on?".

emori: the generally accepted emendation of V's

278

mori; translate as "pass on", *i.e.*, die.

2. *sella in curuli*: a reference to the so-called curule public offices (the consulship, praetorship, curule aedileship, censorship).

    struma: a "tumor"; Nonius is like a vile, cancerous growth upon the state.

    Nonius: two candidates have been put forward as the objects of Catullus' disdain: L. Nonius Asprenas, an officer serving with Julius Caesar, and M. Nonius Sufenas, a supporter of Pompey who served as a tribune in 56 B.C.

3. *peierat*: "perjures himself".

    Vatinius: P. Vatinius (unlike Nonius) is well known: a Caesarian, he served as a tribune in 59 B.C., a praetor in 55 B.C., and a consul in 47 B.C. There is some debate as to whether Catullus here refers to Vatinius' actual consulship, or to a period earlier when the man was arrogantly assuming the consular office would soon be his. If the actual consulship is meant, this poem would be the latest dated poem in the corpus. On this question, *cf.* A.A. Barrett's "Catullus 52 and the Consulship of Vatinius", *TAPA* 103 (1972) 23-38.

53

An anecdote transformed into a poem in praise of Calvus (*cf.* poems 14A and 50); in form, the first three lines set the stage for the final two which bear witness to the talent of Calvus—of whom it might be said that "good things come in small packages".

Meter: hendecasyllabic.

1. *nescio quem...e corona:*   no one of any importance, just a face in the crowd; the *corona* was the group of bystanders which usually gathered at the site of a trial.

2. *mirifice:*   "wonderfully" (*cf.* 84.3); Calvus was well known as a gifted orator.

    Vatiniana: with *crimina* in the next line; Calvus wrote several speeches against Vatinius (*cf.* poem 52). The prosecution of this poem may well be that which took place in 54 B.C. For *Vatiniana, cf.* 14A.3.

3. *explicasset = explicavisset;* "had set forth".

4. *admirans:*   "in amazement".

    manusque tollens: still a universal gesture of wonder.

5. *di magni: cf.* 14A.12.

    salaputium: emended from the MSS.' *salapantium,* and thought to refer to a person of small stature; some, however, postulate an obscene nuance, perhaps akin to our "little prick".

    disertum: "eloquent" (*cf.* 49.1).

54

Presumably to Julius Caesar, and ridiculing some prominent Caesarians whose precise identities are uncertain. The text is so corrupt, however, that there is little agreement among editors as to specifics, and some believe that "poem 54" is in fact a collage of separate fragments. Even those who accept the poem as one argue that several lines must now be missing, and hence attempts to analyse the structure of the poem seem futile.

Meter: hendecasyllabic.

1. *oppido*: an adverb meaning "quite".

    pusillum: "tiny".

2. In the MSS. line 1 is inexplicably followed by 50.16-17, another indication of how corrupt the text is.

    et eri: the unmetrical MSS. reading; various emendations have been proposed on the supposition that a proper name is required. A popular candidate is C. Lucilius Hirrus, a kinsman of Pompey; some prefer to see the name *Heri*, and I myself have argued for *Atri*, that is, Q. Atrius, an officer in the forces of Julius Caesar.

    semilauta: "half-washed".

3. *subtile*: "delicate".

    peditum: probably "farting" (noun).

4. *si non omnia*: how this fits in grammatically is unclear.

displicere: "displease".

5. *tibi*: Caesar, if lines 6-7 are indeed part of the poem.

Sufficio: so the MSS., but some editors read *Fufficio*.

seni recocto: an "old man rejuvenated", although *recocto* literally means "cooked again".

6. Some have postulated a lacuna of several lines at this point in the MSS.

irascere: future tense.

iambis: cf. 40.2.

7. *inmerentibus*: that is, the poet's iambics do not deserve such an angry reaction.

unice imperator: cf. 29.11.

55

In search of Camerius: the poet traverses the crowded public areas of Rome hoping to find his elusive friend, but to no avail (*cf.* poem 6). Camerius is also the subject of poem 58B, and some editors have advocated attaching that poem to 55, perhaps after line 13. Poem 55 is full of topographical references (indeed the mention of Pompey's Portico makes it certain that the poem was written no earlier than 55 B.C.), the best discussion of which is to be found in T.P. Wiseman's "Looking for Camerius" in the *Papers of the British School at Rome* 48 (1980) 6-16.

Assuming that 58B is not part of poem 55, the latter has a 2 + 10 + 10 structure: the initial two verses ask Camerius for his whereabouts; 3-12 then depict the poet's futile search; and 13-22 conclude the poem with a final appeal.

Meter: modified hendecasyllabic (at least 12 lines are decasyllabic, with the dactyl in the second foot contracted into a spondee).

1. *Oramus, si forte*: the poem begins on a scrupulously polite note; *oramus* has the sense of "please".

   molestum: *cf.* 10.33; 51.13.

2. *demonstres*: subjunctive after *oramus* (*ut* omitted).

   tenebrae: "haunts".

3. *Campo...minore*: the "major" campus of Rome was the famous Campus Martius, and this "minor" one may be the Campus Martialis on the Caelian hill, or perhaps a now unknown campus actually called the "Campus Minor".

4. *Circo*: probably the Circus Maximus, although some have advocated the Circus Flaminius.

   omnibus libellis: "book-shops" from the context, although parallels are not to be found elsewhere.

5. *templo summi Iovis*: the great temple to Jove (Jupiter) on the Capitoline Hill.

6. *Magni...ambulatione*: the "Portico of Pompey" behind the theatre dedicated by Pompeius Magnus in 55 B.C. The term *ambulatione* literally means "walking-place".

   simul: "likewise".

7. *femellas*: diminutive of *femina*; here, of course, really "street-walkers".

   prendi: "grabbed hold of".

8. *sereno*: the MSS. read *serena*, and some editors prefer to emend that to *serenas*; in either case, the sense is similar—the girls do not have guilty expressions.

9. *avelte*: thoroughly corrupt in the MSS. A verb of giving (give me Camerius, girls) seems needed; perhaps *reddite en*.

   flagitabam: "I demanded"; *cf.* 42.6.

10. *Camerium*: there is no agreement as to the scansion of this name; some see a short first syllable, others an initial dactyl.

    pessimae puellae: *cf.* 36.9; playfully indignant.

11. This verse is incomplete in the MSS., but the sense is clear: the girl bares her breasts.

12. *hic...latet*: perhaps a pun is involved, since the Greek

kamarion was a breast-band (like the Roman *stro-phium*).

papillis: "breasts".

13. It has been argued that this line is also part of the quotation in line 12; if so, then *ferre* would have the sense of "carry off" rather than "endure".

   labos = *labor*; the reference, of course, is to the famous Labors of Heracles (Hercules).

14. *fastu*: "disdain" for his friend Catullus.

15. *ubi sis futurus*: "where you will be found".

   ede: "declare", with *audacter* in the next line.

16. *committe*: "entrust" Catullus with this information.

   crede luci: we might now say "bring it to light".

17. *lacteolae...puellae*: the "girls with milk-white skin", of a disreputable type.

18. *Cf.* 6.1-3; note the rather awkward repetition, *tenent...tenes*.

19. *proicies*: "you will forsake".

20. *verbosa...loquella*: ablative after *gaudet*; translate *loquella* as "talk".

21. *si vis*: "if you prefer".

obseres palatum: "close your mouth".

22.   *dum*: "as long as".

vestri sim: V seems to have read *vestri sis*; as emended, the poet asks Camerius at least to let him (Catullus) in on what is going on. *Cf.* poem 6.

56

An anecdote about a surprise sexual assault perpetrated by the poet, who apparently thinks the incident hilariously funny. The Cato to whom it is addressed was probably the poet and scholar Valerius Cato, although some critics have argued on behalf of M. Porcius Cato, the sternly conservative politician (who was unlikely to find the incident funny in any way).

The poem features a 4 + 3 structure, with the first four verses emphasizing the fun to come, and the last three verses depicting the event itself.

Meter: hendecasyllabic.

1.   *O rem*: accusative of exclamation.

iocosam: "full of humor"; *cf.* 8.6.

2.   *tuo*: while technically modifying *cachinno*, *tuo* also goes with *auribus*, *i.e.*, "your ears and laughter".

3.   *quidquid amas...Catullum*: Cato is to laugh as much as he loves the poet; *quidquid* signals the degree of

laughter requested. Note the play on sound in *Cato, Catullum*.

4. *nimis*: "all too"; *cf.* 43.4. *Cf.* also line 1 above.

5. *deprendi*: "I surprised"; *cf. prendi* at 55.7.

    pupulum: "little squirt" of a boy. It has been suggested (rather unsuccessfully) that Clodius is meant here.

    puellae: dative after *trusantem* ("thrusting at") in the next line; Lesbia, if Clodius is the *pupulum*! Some prefer to read *puellam*.

6. *Dionae*: Dione was the mother of Venus, but it is possible that the poet here refers to Venus herself.

7. *pro telo*: scholars debate as to whether this is one word or two; if two, "in place of a weapon", and if one, an adverb (derived from the noun *protelum*) meaning "in succession" or "in turn". It is likely that Catullus was punning here, wanting both meanings implied.

    rigida mea: ablative, with *mentula* understood.

    cecidi: "struck"; the poet makes the punishment fit the crime.

57

A contemptuous attack on both Julius Caesar and Mamurra (*cf.* poems 29, 41 and 43). The two, it seems, are a well-matched pair, rivals in disgusting behavior; they surely deserve each other!

The poem begins with a straightforward statement in lines 1-2; continues with a detailed analysis (lines 3-9); and closes with a repetition of the initial line for emphasis.

Meter: hendecasyllabic.

1. *Pulcre convenit*: it is "beautifully appropriate" that Caesar and Mamurra have found each other.

   improbis: "perverse".

   cinaedis: *cf.* 16.2, 25.1 and (especially) 29.5 and 9.

2. *pathicoque*: given its position between the two names, the adjective seems applied to both men; *cf.* 16.2.

3. *nec mirum*: introduces the explanation; *cf.* 23.7.

   maculae pares utrisque: "on both equal stains"; completed by line 5.

4. *urbana*: since Caesar was based in the city of Rome.

   Formiana: Formiae was the home of Mamurra; *cf.* poems 41 and 43.

5. *impressae*: from *imprimo*, "impress" or "stamp".

   eluentur: "washed away".

6. *morbosi*: "diseased".

gemelli: as Quinn put it, "twin brothers in vice".

7. *lecticulo*: "bed"; with homosexual implications.

erudituli: "somewhat skilled" (ironic understatement); some editors see here a reference to both men's taste for literature and grammar (*cf.* poem 105).

8. *vorax*: *cf.* 29.2 and 10; also 33.4.

9. *rivales socii*: "friendly rivals"; *socii* is an adjective.

puellularum: objective genitive; note the diminutive, and *cf.* 61.57, 175, and 181.

10. For the last line echoing the first, *cf.* poems 16, 36, and 52.

58A

To Caelius: Lesbia has descended to the gutters of Rome. The tone is one of final despair, as the poet realizes the degradation of his beloved. That this outburst is addressed to Caelius seems especially appropriate, as Marcus Caelius Rufus had replaced Catullus (his friend) as Clodia's lover; by now, however, both men saw Clodia for what she was—no illusions remained. *Cf.* poem 11.

The poem takes the form of a single sentence whose main verb—the key word in the poem—is delayed until the final verse. The first three verses form a *cri de coeur*; the last two a straight-talking recognition.

Meter: hendecasyllabic.

1.   *Caeli*:   the basic source for Caelius Rufus' liaison with
     Clodia-Lesbia is Cicero's *Pro Caelio*.   Note how the
     poem begins with three proper names at the forefront:
     the "triangle" of Caelius-Lesbia-Catullus; the central
     figure has her name repeated three times in two lines.

     nostra: usually equals *mea*, but here there is the
     possibility that "our" is indeed meant.

2.   For the sentiment in this and the next verse, *cf.*   8.5
     and 37.12.

4.   *quadriviis*:   "cross-roads".

     angiportis: "back alleys"; Lesbia solicits lovers in
     places frequented by common whores.

5.   *glubit*:   the main verb of the poem paints a graphic
     picture—Lesbia "fondles the balls of" all comers.

     Remi nepotes: the "descendants of Remus " would,
     of course, be the Romans; *magnanimi* is used ironi-
     cally.

58B

A fragment on the same theme as poem 55, and
which some editors attach to that poem (see commentary
on poem 55). It seems to be a parody of the "high style",
but many problems of grammar and sense make complete
comprehension difficult. The situation is not improved when
some editors change the order of lines in the MSS. in order

to "clear up" grey areas; the MSS. order is preserved in the text above.

In structure, poem 58B is basically a seven-line evocation of myth and nature whose point is (imperfectly) provided in the final three verses; see commentary below.

Meter: as in poem 55, modified hendecasyllabic.

1. *Non*: the first of four, which, however, never find the normally expected completion at the end of the poem; *cf.* line 8.

    custos...Cretum: the "guardian of the Cretans" in myth was a bronze giant called Talos; fashioned by Hephaestus, Talos circled Crete three times each day, keeping enemies at bay. *Cretum* is genitive plural.

    fingar: "were formed into".

2. *Pegaseo*: a reference to Pegasus, a winged horse of Greek myth; the adjective modifies *volatu*.

3. *non*: makes sense only if it signals "not if I were".

    Ladas: a famous runner in the Olympic games.

    pinnipesve Perseus: the hero Perseus (slayer of Medusa) had as a secret weapon winged sandals, hence he is here termed "wing-footed".

4. *non*: as in line 3 above.

    Rhesi: Rhesus, King of Thrace, came to the aid of

the Trojans against the Greeks, bringing with him swift and handsome white horses.

bigae: "the chariot and pair".

5. *adde*: the poet moves from mythical figures to natural creations.

    plumipedas volatilesque: the "feather-footed and swift" creatures, *i.e.*, birds.

6. *ventorumque*: the winds, of course, were also associated with speed (*cursum*).

    require: "call for".

7. *cunctos*: some editors prefer either *iunctos* or *vinctos*, but *cunctos* makes better sense in context.

    dicares: from *dico*, *dicare*, "give over".

8. At this point one expects a conclusion that would complete the "not if" sequence, such as "could I find you".

    defessus: "exhausted".

    medullis: *cf.* 35.15, and 45.16.

9. *peresus*: from *peredo*, "consume".

10. *te*: object of *quaeritando*.

    quaeritando: "searching diligently for".

59

On a woman called Rufa (otherwise unknown); the initial line reads like an inscription written on a public wall, but the rest of the poem draws a much more detailed portrait of a rather unsavory character. In form, the poem is but one single sentence.

Meter: choliambic.

1. *Bononiensis Rufa*: Rufa comes from Bononia, the modern Bologna in northern Italy.

   Rufulum: an emendation of the MSS.' unmetrical *Rufum*; some see Caelius Rufus here, but Rufus was a common name.

   fellat: "sucks".

2. *Meneni*: also unknown.

   sepulcretis: "cemeteries".

3. *rapere*: "pilfer".

4. *ex igne*: the bread had been placed with the corpse on the funeral pyre.

   prosequens: "going in pursuit of".

5. *semiraso*: "half-shaven", also not a savory character.

   tunderetur: "beaten"; *cf.* 11.4.

ustore: the job of carrying out the cremation was usually given to a slave.

60

An enigmatic fragment in which the poet complains that his needs are being ignored by a friend (some say Lesbia). The piece shows some similarities with poems 30 and 38, but is written in the "high style" of tragedy. As was the case in poem 59, the fragment as we have it is one single sentence; it expresses the poet's total disbelief at his friend's behavior.

Meter: choliambic.

1.   The poem begins with an old motif: a cruel person must be the offspring of some monster; examples of the type can be found in Homer and in Euripides, and also at 64.154ff.

Num: an incredulous question, "surely not".

leaena: "lioness".

Libystinis: "African".

2.   *Scylla*:   the famous monster of Greek myth, here visualized as a female human whose lower body teems with dogs (*infima inguinum parte*).

3.   *procreavit*:   governs *te* in line 1.

taetra: "hideous", as we might say "a sick mind".

4. *novissimo*: here in the sense of "last".

5. *contemptam haberes*: the modern "hold in contempt"; for the form, *cf. paratum habes* at 17.2.

nimis: *cf.* 43.4 and 56.4.

61

With poem 61 begins that section of the Catullan corpus traditionally called the "Long Poems" (61-68). While these poems differ in many respects (including meter), they are generally united by a pervasive theme of union which is soundly established by the first two members of the group: poems 61 and 62 (sometimes called Catullus' *epithalamia*, or wedding songs). *Cf.* the general introduction.

Poem 61 takes the form of a wedding song written in honor of Manlius Torquatus and Iunia Aurunculeia. Yet it shows no signs of having been composed for an actual performance; rather, it is a sophisticated and elegant fantasy in which the poet assumes the role of an imaginary master of ceremonies organizing the ritual involved. Indeed, the poem depicts many of the actual rituals known to have been associated with the Roman wedding (*cf.* Gordon Williams' "Some Aspects of Roman Marriage Ceremonies and Ideals" in the *Journal of Roman Studies* 48 [1958] 16-29). The genre of the wedding song, however, goes back to early Greek poetry, and is especially associated with

Sappho, whose influence on Catullus can be seen throughout the corpus.

As for the bride and groom in whose honor poem 61 was composed, it is possible (but not certain) that the Manlius Torquatus named was the Lucius Manlius Torquatus who served as praetor in 49 B.C. The bride poses a greater problem, given the fact that she is called both Iunia and Aurunculeia. The most likely solution is to assume that she was born into the *gens* Aurunculeia, but adopted at some point into the *gens* Iunia.

In its form, poem 61 takes on a loose, but logical rhythm structured by the sequence of the events depicted. At the start we have the invocation of Hymen as the god of weddings; then (after a brief address to the assembled *virgines*) the poet provides the traditional praise of the divinity invoked. Next our attention is focused on the seemingly hesitant bride, who needs the poet's encouragement, and on the groom's *concubinus*, soon to be displaced from the side of his master. The groom himself then receives some advice before the poet turns his attention back to the bride, now about to enter her new home. The final section of the poem is focused on the bed chamber of the new couple, where their love is to be consummated and will (if all goes well) soon bring forth a child and heir. The whole composition is also tied together by an effective use of the refrain and verbal repetition.

Meter: stanzas of 4 glyconics and 1 pherecratean (*cf.* the Introduction, and also poem 34).

1. *Heliconii*: Mt. Helicon in Boeotia (central Greece) was traditionally considered the home of the Muses.

2. *cultor*: "inhabitant".

    Uraniae genus: "child of Urania"; Urania was the
    Muse associated with astronomy, but she is impor-
    tant here as the mother of Hymen, god of marriage.

3. *qui rapis*: an apparent allusion to the "marriage by
    abduction" ritual seemingly practised in the early
    years of some ancient societies; *cf.* the Roman leg-
    end of the rape of the Sabine women. Translate
    rapis as "carry off", and *cf.* 62.20-25.

4. *o Hymenaee Hymen*: the Greek god of marriage,
    here addressed in a double name; *cf.* poem 62. The
    full name, whether in this order or reversed, serves
    as a refrain throughout the poem.

6. *cinge tempora*: the god is directed to dress as a
    bride in honor of the occasion.

7. *suave*: adverbial with *olentis*.

    amaraci: probably marjoram.

8. *flammeum*: the orange veil worn by brides in Rome.

    cape: "don".

    laetus: the adjective where an adverb might be
    expected; translate as "in joy".

9. *niveo*: "snow-white".

10. *luteum...soccum*: "a yellow slipper".

11. *excitusque*: "and summoned".

12. *concinens*: "singing" the wedding songs.

13. *voce...tinnula*: "in a ringing voice"; *tinnula* is the first of many diminutives that will pervade the poem.

14. *pelle*: "strike".

15. *pineam...taedam*: a pine torch was a traditional prop at weddings.

16. The names of the bride and groom are appropriately juxtaposed; *Iunia* is the subject of *nubet* in line 21, and *Manlio* is dative after that same verb.

17. *qualis*: "even as"; Iunia is to be compared to Venus herself.

     Idalium: a city in Cyprus, the island sacred to Venus.

18. *Phrygium*: "Trojan"; in myth, the Trojan prince Paris judged Venus to be the fairest of the three goddesses competing for the Golden Apple.

19. *bona cum bona*: in this play on words, the first *bona* modifies *virgo*, the second modifies *alite* (line 20).

20. *alite*: "omen"; the poet refers to the custom of reading the omens at a wedding ceremony.

21. *floridis*: "flowery"; words pertaining to flowers of various sorts will play a large role in the vocabulary of the poem.

   enitens: "gleaming".

22. *myrtus Asia*: *Asia* here is an adjective referring to the coast of Lydia; the myrtle seems to have been commonly associated with the goddess Venus.

23. *Hamadryades deae*: nymphs believed to inhabit trees.

24. *ludicrum sibi*: "as a toy for themselves".

   roscido: "dewy".

25. *nutriunt*: "nourish". This verse is unusual from a metrical point of view in having three long syllables for its second foot.

26. *age*: "come!".

   aditum: "approach".

27. *perge linquere*: "proceed to leave".

   Thespiae/rupis: another name for Mt. Helicon; Thespiae was a settlement at the base of the mountain.

28. *Aonios*: Aonian = Boeotian.

29. *super*: here in the sense of "from above".

30. *frigerans*: "cooling".

Aganippe: the nymph Aganippe gives her name to the stream she inhabits. Note how the use of *Thespiae*, *Aonios* and *Aganippe* lends a learned tone to this stanza; the poet remains "Alexandrian" in style even when dealing with a very "Roman" topic.

31. *ac*: "and then".

33. *revinciens*: "binding fast".

34. *tenax hedera*: "clinging ivy".

35. *implicat*: "entwines".

36. The poet turns from his invocation of Hymen to an address to the *virgines* who participate in the ceremony (like modern bridesmaids).

simul: "at the same time". The poet acts as a choir-master giving instructions to his chorus.

integrae: in the sense of "unmarried"; *cf.* poem 34.2.

37. *advenit*: "arrives" in the near future.

38. *par dies*: "a like day", that is, a wedding day.

agite...dicite: "come sing"; *cf. age* in line 26.

in modum: "rhythmically" or "in time".

39. What the chorus is to sing is in fact the refrain.

41. *lubentius* = *libentius*.

42. *citarier*: "is summoned"; archaic passive infinitive.

   ad suum/munus: "to his duty" as god of marriage.

43. *huc aditum ferat*: *cf.* line 26 above.

44. *bonae Veneris*: love that is properly sanctioned and not illicit. For the collocation of *bonae ... boni, cf.* line 19 above.

45. *coniugator*: "joiner".

46. The invocation of Hymen is completed with a song of praise.

   anxiis: an emendation; the MSS. read *quis deus magis amatis est*, which is metrically impossible.

47. *amantibus*: "lovers".

48. *colent*: future tense.

49. *caelitum*: "of the gods"; *cf.* poem 11.14.

51. *suis*: with *liberis* understood.

   tremulus: "trembling" with the palsy of old age.

53. *zonula soluunt sinus*: to "release the folds (of a garment) from the girdle" is a euphemism for the

surrender of one's virginity.

54. *timens*: the groom is typically nervous.

55. *captat*: "listens for".

56. *fero*: here probably in the sense of "high-spirited";
the bride is, in contrast, *floridam* (line 57).

in manus: according to Roman tradition, marriage
with *manus* was a union in which the wife passed
into the control of her husband.

57. *floridam...puellulam*: the bride is young (note the
diminutive) and "in the bloom" of youth.

58. *Cf.* 62.21.

61. *potest*: with *capere* in line 63.

sine te: that is, apart from marriage.

62. *comprobet*: "approve".

63. *commodi*: genitive after *nil* (line 61); translate as
"profit". *Cf.* 84.1.

65. *compararier*: archaic passive infinitive; *cf. citarier* in
line 42.

ausit = *audeat*.

66. *quit*: "can" (from *queo*).

302

67.   *liberos dare*: "to produce children"; *cf.* line 205.

68.   *stirpe*: "progeny".

      nitier: another archaic passive infinitive; translate as "to depend on" (*quit* is understood).

71.   *quae*: taken with *terra* in line 73.

      careat: note the change in mood; the subjunctive is used here to emphasize a general truth.

      sacris: "sacraments".

72.   *praesides*: "guardians".

76.   The song of praise ends as the bride now appears, apparently hesitating at the door of her house.

      claustra: the "bolts" that lock the door.

      pandite: "throw back", that is, "open".

77.   *virgo, ades*: an emendation of the MSS.' *virgo adest* (maintained by many editors); the second person of the verb, however, seems dictated by the ensuing *viden*.

      viden = *videsne. Cf.* 62.8.

      ut: "how".

      faces: traditionally there were five wedding torches lit during the ceremony.

78. *comas*: in context "plumes" seems the best translation.

79. There is a break in the MSS. at this point, and at least four verses have been lost. It has become traditional for editors to number the next surviving verse as 79.

    ingenuus pudor: the bride's "innate modesty" seems to hold her back.

80. *quem*: refers back to *pudor*.

    audiens: "heeding".

81. *ire necesse est*: that is, she must leave her own home for that of her groom.

82. *Au/runculeia*: the bride's name (*cf.* introduction to poem 61) is spread over two lines; each stanza in the poem is treated as a single metrical unit, so that there is no hiatus between individual lines.

85. *ab Oceano*: take with *venientem* in the next line.

86. *viderit*: perfect subjunctive.

87. *in vario...hortulo*: "in a small garden of many colors"; *cf.* 62.39-44.

89. *stare*: governed by *solet* in line 87; translate as "stand out".

    flos hyacinthinus: there is some uncertainty as to

what plant the poet has in mind here; the most likely candidates are the blue iris and the martagon lily.

90. *abit dies*: "the day passes away", as the bride seems to hesitate.

91. A line is missing in the MSS. here, but, given the context, *prodeas, nova nupta* seems likely; *cf.* lines 92, 96, 106, and 113. *Prodeas* would be more polite than a simple imperative; translate as "you should come forward".

92. *si/iam videtur*: "if it now seems right"; also polite.

94. *viden*: the MSS. read *viden ut*, which conflicts with the demands of the meter; for *viden*, *cf.* line 77.

   faces...quatiunt comas: *cf.* 77-78.

97. *levis*: "fickle".

98. *deditus*: with *in* and the ablative means "devoted to".

99. *probra*: "misdeeds".

   persequens: "pursuing".

101. *secubare*: "to sleep (apart from)".

   papillis: "breasts".

102. *lenta*: "pliant"; modifies *vitis* in the next line.

adsitas: "planted beside"; from *adsero*.

103. *implicat*: *cf.* lines 34-35 above.

105. *complexum*: "embrace".

107. The poet turns from the bride to the marriage bed; there are three lines missing, however, and the sense of the address to the bed is not entirely clear.

108. *candido pede*: the feet of the bed were probably made of ivory.

109. *quae*: with *gaudia* in the next line.

 ero: "master".

110. *vaga/nocte*: "in the rambling night", perhaps an allusion to the Chariot of Night.

111. *medio die*: the time of the mid-day siesta; *cf.* poem 32.

114. The poet now addresses the boys who carry the wedding torches.

115. *flammeum*: *cf.* line 8 above.

116. *in modum*: *cf.* line 38 above.

119. *procax*: "insolent".

120. Fescennine verses were rather bawdy in nature, and

were a traditional part of the wedding festivities; the rationale for their presence was to prevent the happy couple from seeming too fortunate to the gods and thus incurring divine wrath. The name Fescennine may come from *fascinum* (the evil eye), or from the town of Fescennium in Italy.

iocatio: "joking".

121. *nuces*: the scattering of nuts (probably walnuts) was part of the wedding ritual; given the fact that nuts were used as toys by children, the throwing of nuts at a wedding would symbolize the end of childhood.

122. *desertum*: "abandoned".

domini...amorem: "the love of his master" for him (the *concubinus*).

123. *concubinus*: a slave boy.

124. *iners*: usually interpreted as "lazy" or "idle", but here probably in the sense of "impotent"; *cf.* 67.26.

125. *satis diu*: "long enough".

126. *lubet* = *libet*.

127. *Talasio*: Talasius was the native Roman god of marriage; some believe that he was a personification of a ritual cry made at weddings.

129. *sordebant*: "were of no account".

307

vilicae: "the wives of the stewards" of the groom's estate.

130. *hodie atque heri*: the slave boy was disdainful not only in the past, but even up to the present moment.

131. *cinerarius*: "barber".

132. *tondet*: "shaves".

134. The Fescennine joking now turns to the groom; translate *male* as "grudgingly" and take with *abstinere* in line 136.

135. *unguentate*: the groom is "anointed" with perfumes.

   glabris: rather effeminate slaves, usually boys.

136. *abstinere*: "to refrain" from.

139. *quae licent*: "which are permissible".

140. *sola*: "alone".

141. What was permitted a single man is not permitted a married man.

144. The address to the bride lacks the bawdy nature of that given the groom; *tu* is to be taken with *cave* in line 145.

146. *ni = ne*; "lest".

petitum: supine expressing purpose; *cf.* poem 10.2.

aliunde: "elsewhere".

149. *ut potens*: "how well endowed (with possessions)"; *est* is understood.

150. *beata*: "happy".

151. *sine serviat*: "allow it to serve" you.

152. The refrain here interrupts the thought of the sentence.

154. Line 151 is here resumed; translate *usque dum* as "even till".

tremulum: with *tempus* in the next line; *cf.* line 51.

155. *cana...anilitas*: "hoary old age"; *cf.* 108.1.

tempus = *caput*.

156. *annuit*: "affirms"; the shaking of a head was thought to mean the giving of assent, but in old age heads shake for another reason.

159. To the bride, standing at the threshold of the groom's house; translate *transfer* as "bring across".

omine cum bono: *cf.* lines 19-20 above.

160. *limen*: "threshold"; note the double accusative after *transfer*.

161. *rasilemque*: "polished".

   subi: "go under" (from *subeo*).

164. *intus ut*: a generally accepted emendation of the MSS.' *unus ut*; translate *intus* as "within", and *ut* as "how".

   accubans: "reclining".

165. *Tyrio in toro*: the groom is seen reclining on a purple couch; however, from line 184 it would appear that this couch was not the same as the conjugal bed.

166. *totus immineat tibi*: "longs for you with all his heart".

169. *minus ac*: "less than".

170. *uritur*: with *flamma* in the next verse as its subject; translate as "is kept alight".

171. *penite = penitus*; translate as "deeply".

174. *mitte*: "let go". In this section of the poem, the bride is envisaged as entering the marriage chamber.

   brachiolum: the first of several diminutives clustered between lines 174 and 188; all refer to the bride.

   teres: "shapely".

175. *praetextate*: a boy serving as an escort for the

bride; the *praetexta* was the toga worn by boys until reaching adulthood.

puellulae: the bride.

179.   <*vos*>:   refers to *feminae* in the next line.

180.   *cognitae*: *cf.*   line 140.

       feminae: these women would be the "matrons of honor"; ideally such women were *univirae*, that is, married but once. Another Latin term for them was *pronubae*.

181.   *collocate*:   the women are to "arrange" the bride on the wedding bed.

184.   The poet turns here to the groom, summoning him to the wedding bed.

185.   *thalamo*:   "wedding bed".

186.   *floridulo*: *cf.*   line 57 above.

       nitens: "looking beautiful".

187.   *alba parthenice*:   "white camomile"; the name of this plant is particularly appropriate as the Greek *parthenos* means "virgin".

188.   *papaver*:   "poppy".

189.   *ita me iuvent/caelites*:   "so may the gods help me"; a common oath (*cf.* 66.18).

311

190. *nihilo minus*: "nonetheless".

192. *neglegit*: "slight".

193. *perge*: "go on".

   remorare: present imperative passive.

195. *bona...Venus*: properly sanctioned love; *cf.* line 44.

196. *iuverit*: perfect subjunctive, but with a present sense.

   palam: "openly", that is, not furtively or illicitly.

197. *cupis cupis*: an unusual, but highly effective juxta-position.

198. *abscondis*: "conceal" (*cf. palam* above).

199. For the image of this stanza, *cf.* poem 7. 3-8; translate *pulveris* as "dust".

200. *micantium*: "sparkling".

201. *subducat*: "let him count".

203. *ludi*: here in an erotic sense; *cf.* 17.17.

204. *ludite ut lubet*: also *cf.* 17.17.

   brevi: "soon" (*tempore* understood).

205. *liberos date*: *cf.* line 67 above.

206. *tam vetus...nomen*: "so distinguished a name".

207. *indidem*: "from the same origin", that is, as opposed to adoption.

208. *ingenerari*: "be reproduced".

209. The child to be born of this union will complete the picture of marital bliss. Translate *parvulus* as "tiny".

210. *Cf.* line 58 above.

211. *porrigens*: "holding out".

212. *dulce rideat*: cf. poem 51.5.

213. *semihiante labello*: "with his lips half opened"; *semihiante* is scanned as four syllables.

214. *similis*: in physical appearance.

215. This line and the next in the MSS. are apparently defective; the MSS.' reading of *facile insciens* in 215 makes little sense, and is here replaced by *facile omnibus*, although some prefer to read *facile insciis*, placing *omnibus* in line 216.

216. *ab insciis*: an emendation of the MSS.' *ab omnibus*, which presents a metrical difficulty; some prefer to read *ab obviis*. The sense of this passage, however, seems clear: the child, by his physical resemblance to his father, will be easily recognizable even by strangers.

217. *pudicitiam*: "purity"; she knows only one man.

218. *indicet*: "attest to".

219. *talis*: take with *laus* in the next verse.

220. *genus approbet*: "prove his descent"; just as the child inherits the physical appearance of his father, so he inherits the virtuous character of his mother.

221. *qualis*: following up the earlier *talis* in line 219.

    unica: modifies *fama* in line 223.

222. *Telemacho*: the son of Odysseus and Penelope.

    manet: "endures".

223. *Penelopaeo*: an adjective coined from the proper name; Penelope in the *Odyssey* is the archetypal model of the virtuous wife and mother.

224. In the final stanza, the poet concludes his drama with the closing of the doors to the marriage chamber and a final word of advice to the newly-weds.

225. *lusimus*: here without a sexual sense.

226. *bene vivite*: "fare well".

227. *munere assiduo*: "in continual service" to your marital duties; *cf.* line 43 above.

    valentem: "vigorous".

228. *exercete iuventam*: "spend your youth".

62

Despite its apparent kinship with poem 61, this wedding song treats the theme of marriage in quite a different manner. To begin with, instead of featuring a single narrator (as in the preceding poem), poem 62 focuses on two distinct "choruses", one of young men and one of young women, participating in a singing contest as part of a nuptial celebration. As depicted by the poet, both groups have been at a wedding feast, but when the young men see the evening star arise they break off the meal and rise to set the contest in motion; after some preliminary banter within each group, both sing in turn of marriage—the maidens in a negative manner, the youths in a positive one. The contest concludes with the young men victorious as the bride makes her entrance.

It must be noted that the wedding featured here (unlike that of poem 61) is not a specific one in honor of real people; instead, the poet presents us with a totally anonymous bride and groom. Moreover, while there are hints of actual Roman ritual in the poem, as a whole both Roman and Greek elements have been so imaginatively combined that the picture which emerges in the end is more of a conflated fantasy than an historically accurate account.

In structure the poem is formal, but not overly rigid: the stanzas given the two choruses correspond generally to each other, but the poet has not made an effort to equalize the actual number of lines allotted each group. Thus the divisions of the poem are as follows: lines 1-5 (youths), 6-10 (maidens), and 11-19 (youths) are given over to preliminary conversation; lines 20-25 (maidens), 26-31 (youths), 32-? (maidens, with several lines now missing), 33-38 (youths, with some lines also missing), 39-48 (maidens), and 49-58 (youths) form the actual singing contest; and lines 59-66 (youths) present the concluding admonition to the bride. The young men not only win the contest, but also seem to have the greater number of verses (although the missing lines make certainty impossible).

Of historical interest is the fact that this is the only poem of Catullus to have a manuscript tradition apart from the Veronensis (V); it appears in the ninth century codex Thuaneus (T), as part of an anthology. There are, however, quite a few differences in readings between T and our other MSS., and it is difficult to determine which is the more reliable.

Meter: dactylic hexameter.

1. As the poem begins we find ourselves listening in on the conversation of the young men; the time is dusk, when the evening star (Vesper, that is, the planet Venus) has just appeared.

   consurgite: the young men rise from their seats as a group.

   Olympo: here not in the sense of Mt. Olympus, but rather in its general sense of "the sky".

2. *vix tandem*: "at last just barely" shows its light.

3. *iam tempus*: "now it is time"; note the repetition of

iam in this and the next line, giving a sense of urgency to the young men's activities.

pinguis...mensas: a bridal feast has obviously been taking place, most likely at the house of the groom.

4.   *veniet*: "is about to arrive".

hymenaeus: "the wedding song".

5.   The refrain of poem 61 is slightly altered (with the addition of *ades*) to meet the requirements of the meter; *ades* is imperative (*cf. adest* in line 1).

6.   The maidens see the youths rise up, and take that as their cue; *contra* is often taken in a physical sense as "opposite" the youths, but probably also bears the sense of "in reply".

7.   *nimirum*: "certainly".

Oetaeos: from Mt. Oeta in Thessaly; note the learned atmosphere generated by *Oetaeos ...Noctifer* (another name for the evening star).

8.   *sic certest*: the maidens confirm the rise of the evening star; *cf.* 80.7.

viden ut: *cf.* 61.77.

perniciter: "nimbly".

exsiluere: "jump up"; perfect tense.

9. *non temere*: "not for nothing".

   vincere: the MSS. read *visere*, which some editors keep, translating it as "look at"; but *vincere* in the sense of "surpass" or "excel" seems more appropriate to the context. Take *quod* as the object of *vincere*.

   par est: "is right", with *nobis* understood.

10. The refrain, as in line 5, marks the end of a stanza.

11. Our attention returns to the young men, who refer to themselves as *aequales*, "comrades".

    palma: "prize" in the singing contest about to take place.

12. *ut...requirunt*: "how they search for what they have practised", that is, the young women have come prepared for the contest and are well rehearsed.

    meditata: literally, "those things which have been practised".

13. *memorabile quod sit*: "something remarkable"; for the phrasing of the verse as a whole, *cf.* line 9 above.

14. *penitus*: "deep within" themselves.

    quae...laborant: a causal relative clause; translate as "because they toil".

15. *nos*: emphasizing the contrast between the young men and the maidens.

318

alio...alio: "one way ... another way".

divisimus: "we have divided" our attention; the youths have not applied themselves as completely as the maidens have.

16. *iure*: "rightly".

vincemur: *cf. vincere* in line 9 above.

amat victoria curam: note the epigrammatic quality of this phrase.

17. *nunc...saltem*: "now at least"—better late than never.

convertite: "apply" your minds to the job at hand.

18. *iam...iam*: *cf.* lines 3-4 above.

20. The actual singing contest now begins, with each group singing in turn; the traditional name for this type of verse is amoebic poetry. Note how the maidens consistently paint a pessimistic portrait of marriage, while the young men counter with a positive portrayal.

Hespere: another name for Vesper-Venus.

quis...ignis: "what star", since *ignis* here refers to the fire of a heavenly body.

caelo: "in the sky"; *cf. Olympo* in line 1.

21. *qui...possis*: a causal relative clause; *cf.* line 14, where the indicative mood is employed.

natam: "daughter".

complexu...matris: *cf.* 61.58-59.

avellere: "take away"; repeated for emphasis in the next line.

22. *retinentem*: the maiden is "clinging to" her mother.

23. *iuveni ardenti*: "eager youth"; *cf.* 61.56.

castam: note the contrast in the juxtaposed adjectives: where the youth is eager, the maiden is "chaste".

24. *crudelius*: echoes the *crudelior* of line 20 and thus brings the first part of the maidens' song to an end; the motif of the captured city cruelly treated by the enemy seems to be very old.

26. The young men counter the argument of the maidens: Hesperus is not cruel, but rather *iucundior*.

quis...ignis: *cf.* line 20; the youths' stanza is structurally similar to that of the maidens.

lucet: "shines".

27. *desponsa*: "pledged"; the betrothal was called a *sponsio*.

firmes: in a causal relative clause; translate as "confirm".

28.   *quae*: refers to *conubia* in line 27.

      pepigere...pepigerunt: from *pango*, meaning "make"; the difference in form seems dictated by the meter.

29.   *iunxere*: here in the sense of "join together".

      prius quam: "sooner than".

      se...extulit: "has raised itself" in the sky.

30.   *optatius*: "more longed for"; responds to the maidens' *crudelius* in line 24 above.

32.   The answering stanza of the maidens is lost except for its initial line. From the following stanza of the youths, it would seem that the maidens here attack Hesperus as a thief and bringer of fear and harmful actions in the night.

      aequales: *cf.* line 11 above.

33.   The initial verses of the young mens' reply are lost.

      vigilat: "keeps watch".

      custodia: "guard", here in the sense of the night-watch.

34.   *latent*: "lurk".

idem...revertens: the same star (Hesperus) returns as the morning star (but *not* in the same time frame; the poet ignores the true astronomical situation).

saepe: take with *comprendis* in the following line.

35. *comprendis*: "catch" by surprise.

   Eous: the generally accepted emendation of the MSS.' *eosdem*; Eous was a name given the morning star, that is, Venus at dawn.

36. *ficto...questu*: "with pretended complaint".

   carpere: "slander".

37. *quid tum*: "what does it matter".

   si carpunt: with *te* understood.

   requirunt: *cf.* line 12; also 8.13.

39. The maidens' final disparagement of marriage is based on an elaborate simile; *cf.* 61.21-25 and 86-90.

   saeptis...hortis: "walled garden"; *hortus* in the plural often refers to a pleasure garden as opposed to a fruit or vegetable garden.

   secretus: "solitary".

40. *convulsus*: "rooted up"; *cf.* 11.21-24.

41. *mulcent*: "caress".

firmat: "strengthens".

educat: "nurtures".

42. *illum* = *flos*.

optavere: perfect; *cf. pepigere* in line 28.

43. *tenui...ungui*: "with a sharp nail".

carptus: here in the sense of "picked"; *cf.* line 36.

defloruit: "shed its petals".

44. *Cf.* line 42.

45. *dum...dum*: "as long as...so long".

intacta: that is, virginal.

suis: her kin.

46. *polluto*: "defiled"; she is no longer a virgin.

47. *iucunda*: *cf.* line 26 above.

49. The young men respond with a simile of their own, based on the ancient practice of using trees to support vines.

vidua...vitis: a vine that is "unmarried" since it has no tree to support it.

nudo: "bare" of trees.

nascitur: *cf.* line 39; the youths are careful to employ the very words of the maidens in order to refute them.

50. *se extollit*: "lifts itself up".

mitem: "ripe".

educat: *cf.* line 41.

51. *prono*: "sinking downward".

deflectens: "bending down" to the ground.

52. *iam iam*: "now at any moment"; the repetition supplies a greater sense of immediacy.

summum...flagellum: "the top of its shoot".

53. For the structure of this line, *cf.* lines 42 and 44.

coluere: "have cultivated"; oxen (*iuvenci*) were used to loosen the soil around vines.

54. *ulmo...marito*: "to an elm as her husband"; some editors, however, prefer to read *marita*.

55. *Cf.* line 53.

56. *Cf.* line 45; *inculta* means "uncultivated" in a sexual sense.

57. *par conubium*: a marriage that is "proper" in the sense that the partners are suitable to each other.

maturo: "seasonable", neither too early nor too late.

adepta: from *adipiscor*, "attain".

58. *cara*: *cf.* lines 45 and 47.

invisa: "hateful", because she is not yet wed.

A refrain is added by some editors after line 58 to conclude formally the young men's song; there is no refrain, however, at this point in the MSS.

59. *Et tu*: the singing contest over, the young men now offer advice to the bride.

ne pugna = *noli pugnare*; *cf.* line 64 below.

60. *non aequum est*: "it's not right".

cui: to fight "with the man to whom"; *cum eo* is assumed before *cui*. Also understood is *te* after *tradidit*.

61. *quibus*: dative after *parere*.

62. *non tota tua est*: "is not all yours". The thesis here advanced by the youths sounds odd to modern ears.

ex parte: "in part".

parentum: "of your parents", that is, they have a

share in it.

63. *patris est*: some editors prefer *patri est* here.

64. *duobus*: *pugno* with the dative means "contend with"; the two are, of course, the bride's parents.

65. *sua iura*: the parents transfer their shares in their daughter's virginity to their new son-in-law (*genero*).

dote: the "dowry" which played so large a role in ancient marriages.

63

Poem 63 (the "Attis") is not just one of the finest poems written in Latin, it is also one of the most memorable poems ever written, in any language. The "plot" of the piece is deceptively simple: Attis, with his mind in a frenzy of religious ecstasy, castrates himself to become a follower of Cybele, the "Great Mother" of the gods (*cf.* poem 35); his madness, however, dissipates after a night's rest and he regrets what he has done. But there is no escape, for the goddess herself ensures that he is driven back into a state of lasting insanity, to serve her until he dies. In this unequal union of goddess and mortal, Cybele not only deprives Attis of his freedom, but also of his reason and his very humanity. His fanatic devotion has cost Attis everything that had made him a unique human being; he becomes instead more of a wild animal.

If, on the surface, the subject matter of the poem is a particular Greek youth under the spell of a terrifying goddess, on a deeper level poem 63 is a universal tale about the power of passion—how unbridled passion may ultimately defeat our treasured (yet vulnerable) rationality and cost us our identity and freedom. A young man who enjoyed all the blessings Greek civilization could bring ends his days far from home in the wilds of Phrygia as an insane eunuch slave to Cybele; he experiences a perverted kind of marriage that places the marriage theme of the preceding poems in a totally different perspective. Moreover, the poem as a whole ends with the readers' stark and terrifying awareness that Attis' nightmare could easily become their own.

What led Catullus to compose such an awesome poem has long been debated. In the nineteenth century some scholars postulated that Catullus was translating a Greek original now lost—a theory no longer in vogue and for which no substantial evidence was ever brought forward. Others came to believe that Catullus had seen the cult of Cybele in action during his stay in Bithynia; on the other hand, some argued that the cult would have been well known to the poet from its presence in Rome itself (having arrived there during the Second Punic War). Yet, the genesis of such a unique poem must lie deeper—in the poet's own, very personal experience of unbridled passion.

It is obvious from the corpus as a whole that Catullus himself experienced the power of passion in his love for Clodia. Like Attis, he had consecrated himself to a woman, only to come in the end to see the folly of that act (*cf.*, for example, poems 8, 11, 58, and 76). Also, like Attis, he was unable to make a final, lasting escape (*cf.*, for example, poems 72, 75 and 85). Thus one can say that the mental state seen in Attis is also found in the poet himself: both men are driven to a woman by *furor*, both come to regret that *furor*, but both come to their senses too late. Indeed, the awakening of Attis from sleep and his recognition of his desperate situation could be said to reflect the *nunc te cognovi* of Catullus in poem 72. Such an analysis, however, does not argue that Catullus *is* Attis in any literal sense; rather, Attis comes to serve in a general way as a mirror of the poet's own experience. (For a more detailed examination, *cf.* my article "Catullus: the Mythic Persona" in *Latomus* 35 [1976] 555-566.)

It has long been recognized that poem 63 features an alternation of narrative passages with direct speeches (those of Attis and Cybele). But the structure of the poem is more complex than this, and many analyses have been put forward, such as a division of the poem into three basic "movements": 1) the insane frenzy of lines 1-38; 2) the clear-minded repentence of lines 39-73; and 3) the "recapture" of Attis in lines 74-90 (*cf.* Quinn).

A still more complex scheme has been illuminated by E. Schäfer (in *Das Verhältnis vom Erlebnis und Kunstgestalt bei Catull*, 1966): namely, that poem 63 is an example of "ring composition" which takes the form of ABCcba. Schäfer provides the following analysis of lines 1-90:

A. (1-11):   *furor* in action
B. (12-26):   Attis' frenzied speech to the Gallae
C. (27-37):   the rush to Mt. Ida and to sleep
c. (38-49):   the awakening and return to the shore
b. (50-73):   Attis' lament, addressed to his lost *patria*
a. (74-90):   *furor* renewed

It should also be noted that Catullus uses a great

deal of verbal repetition to tie his verses together (*cf.* the commentary on individual lines).

Meter: galliambic.

1. The narrative begins with Attis' arrival in Phrygia, and his subsequent self-mutilation.

    alta: "deep", with *maria*.

    vectus: *cf.* 101.1.

    celeri: words pertaining to speed will play a large role in the poem as a whole; *cf. citato* in the next line.

2. *Phrygium...nemus*: the setting is the wooded area around Mt. Ida; *cf.* line 30 below.

    citato: "swift"; *cf.* line 8.

    tetigit: from *tango*, "reach".

3. *adiitque*: "and entered".

    opaca: "dark".

    redimita: "encircled".

    deae: Cybele, as we soon learn in line 9.

4. *stimulatus*: "spurred on"; *cf.* line 77.

    rabie: words indicating "madness" will repeatedly

occur throughout the poem; the collocation here of *furenti* with *rabie* intensifies the sense of total insanity, which is further emphasized by the following *vagus animis* ("unsettled in his thoughts").

5. *devovit*: an emendation of *devolvit*, the reading of V; the entire line seems to have become garbled in the manuscripts. Translate as "dedicated".

   ili: genitive of *ilium*, "groin"; some editors print *ilei*, a more archaic form of the word.

   pondera: the male genitalia.

   silice: "stone".

6. *itaque*: here in the sense of "accordingly".

   sine viro: "without their manhood"; that Attis is no longer a "man" is made abundantly clear by *citata* in line 8.

7. *etiam...maculans*: "still staining".

   recente: "fresh".

   sola: despite its plural form, translate as "soil"; *cf.* line 40 below.

8. *niveis...manibus*: stresses his new effeminacy; *cf. teneris...digitis* in line 10.

   citata: in this section of the poem, Attis is consistently described by feminine adjectives.

typanum = *tympanum* (*cf.* line 29); the instrument was akin to a small drum and was a common feature of the cult of Cybele.

9. Note the repetitive *t* sounds in both this line and the next, imitating the percussive sounds made by Attis.

    Cybebe = *Cybele*; the meter dictates which form the poet will use.

    mater: Cybele was the "Great Mother" of the gods.

    initia: here denoting the sacred objects used in the cult.

10. *terga*: the "hide" with which the drum was made.

11. *suis...comitibus*: the first indication that Attis was not alone; who these companions are is not made clear, so that all our attention remains fixed on Attis alone.

    adorta est: "she began"; note the gender.

    tremebunda: "trembling" with excitement; feminine singular with *adorta est*.

12. The first speech of Attis shows him to be fully in the power of the goddess.

    agite: "come on!"; *cf.* **61.38.**

    Gallae: the followers of Cybele were known either as

"Gallae" or "Galli"; it is not clear where the name came from, but some trace it to a river in Phrygia.

Cybeles: genitive.

simul: "at once"; speed is so important that *simul* is immediately repeated at the start of the next line.

13. *Dindymenae dominae*: another name for Cybele, from Mt. Dindymus in the eastern part of Phrygia; *cf.* 35.14.

vaga pecora: "wandering herd"; the followers of the goddess become her animals; they have forfeited their humanity.

14. *aliena*: "strange".

quae: feminine plural.

15. *sectam meam exsecutae*: "having followed my way of life"; note the play on sound in this phrase.

duce me: seems redundant to some critics, but effectively stresses Attis' role as leader of the herd.

16. *rapidum*: "swift-moving".

salum...pelagi: the difference between these two terms seems obscure. Both refer to the open sea, but it is possible that *salum* denotes the sea in motion.

truculentaque: "and the ferocities" of the sea.

332

17. *evirastis* = *eviravistis*; "you have castrated".

nimio odio: "because of excessive hatred"; a causal ablative.

18. *hilarate*: "gladden".

citatis erroribus: on the surface, "swift wanderings", but could the sense of *error* as a mistake be latent?

19. *tarda*: take with *mora*.

simul ite: cf. line 13 above.

sequimini: imperative.

20. *Cybebes* = *Cybeles* (genitive).

21. *ubi*: the repetition of *ubi* here and in the following verses lends a hypnotic effect to Attis' speech.

cymbalum = *cymbalorum*; the cymbals were another percussive instrument associated with the cult.

reboant: "re-echo".

22. *tibicen*: "piper".

grave: adverb with *canit*; translate as "in a low pitch".

calamo: "reed"; the instrument ended in a distinct upward curve.

23. *Maenades*: Maenads were women usually associated with the cult of Dionysus; here, however, they are transferred to the worship of Cybele.

vi iaciunt: "violently throw" (literally, "throw with violence").

hederigerae: the Maenads are "wearing ivy"; this is but the first of many elaborate compound adjectives which add vividness to the poem.

24. *sacra sancta*: "holy rites", object of *agitant*, which here takes on the sense of "celebrate".

acutis ululatibus: "piercing yells".

25. *volitare*: "to move with speed".

cohors: *cf.* 28.1.

26. *celerare*: "hurry".

tripudiis: the *tripudium* was a ceremonial dance of an exuberant nature.

27. With Attis' first speech ended, the poet returns to narration: the rush of the cult members towards Mt. Ida.

simul = simul atque; "as soon as".

notha mulier: Attis is a "counterfeit woman" - not really female, but no longer truly male.

28. *thiasus*: here in the sense of a troupe of ecstatic worshippers.

trepidantibus: "quivering".

ululat: *cf.* line 24 above.

29. *remugit*: "bellows" or "roars".

recrepant: "ring out".

31. *furibunda*: "frenzied", in reference to Attis; note the piling up of adjectives in these verses.

anhelans: "gasping for breath".

animam agens: an idiom meaning "almost dead with exhaustion".

32. *dux*: *cf.* line 15.

33. *veluti iuvenca*: a brief simile, ironic because Attis, unlike the heifer, is actually *putting on* a yoke, that of Cybele; *cf.* lines 76 and 84.

indomita: "untamed".

34. *properipedem*: "swift-footed".

35. *tetigere*: perfect tense; *cf.* line 2.

lassulae: we might say today "bone tired"; the Gallae are totally depleted by their rush.

36.   *e*: here in the sense of "after".

    sine Cerere: that is, without food (Ceres was the Roman goddess of grain).

37.   *piger...sopor*: "numbing sleep".

    labante languore: literally, "with faltering fatigue", but loosely "faltering with fatigue".

38.   *quiete*: "slumber".

    rabidus furor: *cf.* line 4.

39.   *ubi*: "when"; the coming of dawn brings a change in the mental condition of Attis.

    oris aurei: with *sol*, a genitive of description; translate as "the sun with its golden face".

    radiantibus: "shining".

40.   *lustravit*: "illuminated".

    aethera: the ether is the "upper air", or more simply, "the sky".

    sola: *cf.* line 7 above.

41.   *pepulitque*: "and put to flight".

    vegetis sonipedibus: "lively steeds".

42.   *ibi*: "then" in this context.

Somnus: sleep personified as a god.

citus: here in an adverbial sense with *abiit*.

43. *trepidante*: with *sinu*; cf. line 28.

    dea Pasithea: in the *Iliad*, one of the Graces, given to Sleep by Hera.

44. *ita*: "so".

    de: "after"; cf. *e* in line 36 above.

    quiete molli...rabie: cf. line 38 above.

45. *simul*: "as soon as".

    sua facta: especially his castration.

    recoluit: "reflected on".

46. *liquidaque mente*: "and with a clear mind".

    quis = quibus; the reference is to his genitalia.

47. *aestuante*: "heaving".

    rusum = rursum.

    vada: "shores".

    tetulit: archaic perfect of *fero.*

48. *maria vasta*: cf. 31.3.

   visens: "looking at".

49. *maestast* = *maesta est*; the *est* completes *allocuta*. Take *maesta* with *voce*.

   miseriter: "sadly"; for the archaic form of the adverb cf. 39.14 and 76.19. In the MSS. this verse is corrupt; the emended version offered here is the one generally accepted.

50. The second speech of Attis expresses his deep regret for what he has done; his mind is now clear, free from the power of Cybele.

   mei creatrix: literally, "father of me"; *mei* is an objective genitive here.

   genetrix: "mother".

51. *quam*: refers to *patria* above.

   miser: note the change in gender; when Attis is in control of himself he reverts to his original maleness.

   erifugae/famuli: "runaway slaves".

52. *solent*: with *relinquere* understood.

   tetuli: cf. line 47 above.

53. *apud*: "near".

stabula: "dens".

54.   *earum*:   that is, the *ferae*.

   opaca: with *latibula* ("lairs").   *Opaca* is an emendation of the MSS.' *omnia*, which some editors retain.

   furibunda: "in my frenzy"; Attis uses the feminine
   form for his possessed self.

55.   *quibus locis*:   "in what regions".

   reor: "am I to think"; present tense (*cf. dono* at
   1.1).

56.   *pupula*:   the "pupil" of the eye.

   sibi: seems redundant to some after *ipsa*; it may in
   fact be metrical "filler".

   derigere aciem: "to direct its sight".

57.   *carens...est = caret.*

   breve tempus: "for a brief time"; Attis seems to feel
   his return to madness inevitable.

58.   This and the next nine lines are noteworthy for a
   great deal of verbal repetition; this repetition points
   to Attis' disbelief of what he has done.

   remota: take with *egone*.

   ferar: future passive.

59. *genitoribus*: "parents".

    abero: immediately repeated for emphasis at the start of the next line.

60. *foro*: the Roman place of gathering is used where one might more realistically expect a reference to the Greek *agora*, or market-place.

    palaestra: the wrestling ground common in Greek city-states.

    stadio: "race-track".

    gyminasiis = *gymnasiis*; the Greek gymnasium was a general area for various sports.

61. *miser a miser*: cf. 61.132.

    etiam atque etiam: "time and time again".

62. *figurae*: "appearance".

    obierim: "have taken on"; perfect subjunctive.

63. *ephebus*: in Greek society, a youth between the ages of 18 and 20.

64. *decus olei*: "the pride of the wrestling ground"; the palaestra was a place where oil was used freely, hence *oleum* came to be another name for it.

65. *frequentes*: "crowded" with his many admirers.

tepida: "warm", because his fans would often stay there all night.

66. *corollis*: "delicate garlands".

   redimita: cf. line 3.

67. *ubi*: "when".

   esset: subjunctive because it happened over and over.

   orto...sole: "at sun-rise".

   cubiculum: "bed-room".

68. The repetition of *ego* reaches a crescendo, as Attis seeks to comprehend his new identity.

   deum = deorum.

   famula: cf. lines 51-2.

   ferar: "be spoken of".

69. *Maenas*: cf. line 23.

   mei pars: only part of what he used to be.

   sterilis: "barren", because he no longer has organs of procreation.

70. *viridis...Idae*: cf. line 30.

   algida...nive amicta: "covered with cold snow".

71. *columinibus*: "summits".

72. *silvicultrix*: "which dwells in the woods".

nemorivagus: "which roams the forests"; the appearance of two elaborate compound adjectives in this line is worth noting. In contrast, the next verse is built around plain, everyday speech.

73. *iam iam*: repeated for emphasis; *cf.* 62.52.

dolet quod egi: "what I have done grieves me".

paenitet: "it brings regret". Attis' speech significantly ends with a word of profound regret.

74. The scene now shifts to the realm of the gods, where Cybele herself hears the lament of Attis.

hinc: "from here", that is, from where Attis stands on the shore.

sonitus <citus> abiit: in the MSS. this verse is too short from a metrical point of view; most editors add *citus* to complete it.

75. *geminas...aures*: "the two ears" of each god; *cf.* 51.11.

nova nuntia: "strange news"; the gods had not expected Attis to rebel.

76. *ibi*: "then".

iuncta: the yoke is "attached" to the lions; myth relates that Cybele's chariot was drawn by lions.

resolvens: "unfastening".

77. *saevumque*: the MSS. read *laevumque*, which is defended by some editors; however, *saevumque* makes more sense in the context of the poem, and a scribal slip in regard to one letter seems easily comprehensible.

stimulans: cf. line 4.

78. The speech of Cybele reveals her ferocity: this is no gentle mother, but a fearsome *domina*.

agedum: "come on!".

<*i*>...<*agitet*>: the line in the MSS. is too short; these are the generally accepted emendations. Translate *agitet* as "persecutes".

fac ut: "bring it about that"; cf. line 79, and also line 82, where the *ut* is omitted.

79. *ictu*: "lash".

reditum in nemora: echoes the *reditum ad vada* of line 47; whereas the shore stands for enlightenment there, *nemora* represents the darkness that is Cybele.

80. *libere nimis*: "all too freely".

81. *caede*: "strike".

terga: "hide"; *cf.* line 10.

verbera: "strokes".

patere: imperative of *patior*; translate as "endure". Cybele has the beast "whip himself" into a frenzy.

82. *mugienti fremitu*: "with a bellowing roar".

retonent: "thunder repeatedly".

83. *torosa*: "muscular".

quate: *cf.* line 10.

iubam: "mane".

84. *religatque*: the only place in Latin literature where *religo* seems to mean "unfasten"; *cf.* line 76 above.

85. *sese adhortans*: "spurring himself on".

rabidum: an emendation of the MSS.' *rapidum*, which seems flat in this context. *Cf.* line 93.

incitat: "rushes".

86. *vadit, fremit, refringit*: the three juxtaposed verbs contribute a sense of speed and tension. The beast not only "makes his way" to where Attis is, he also "roars" and "breaks" the undergrowth (*virgulta*) in his frenzy.

87. *ubi*: "when".

albicantis...litoris: the poet seems to refer here to the covering of white sea foam often seen on a beach.

88. *tenerumque*: some would change this to *teneramque*, but Attis is still "his old self" here, not yet driven back into madness.

marmora pelagi: *marmora* here probably refers to the white, seemingly "marbled" surface of the sea; the entire phrase could simply be translated as "the sea".

89. *illa*: V seems to have read *ille*, but once Attis is again mad (*demens*) it is fitting that feminine forms return.

90. *omne vitae spatium*: "for the whole span of his life", that is, of course, of his remaining life. *Cf. breve tempus* in line 57.

famula: *cf.* line 68 above.

91. The poem concludes with a remarkable coda: speaking in his own voice, the poet prays that Cybele's madness not come to afflict him. Note the *d* sounds in the first line of this prayer: the percussive sound of the instruments associated with the goddess.

Dindymi: *cf.* line 13.

92. *a mea...domo*: *cf.* Attis' statement at line 58.

93. *incitatos*: "aroused".

345

rabidos: as was the case in line 85, some prefer the reading *rapidos*; *rabidos*, however, offers a much more powerful ending to the poem as a whole— which has indeed focused on madness.

64

An "epyllion" (a modern term for a small-scale epic) on the wedding of Peleus and Thetis. As a genre of poetry, the epyllion was the product of Alexandrian literary theory, which considered the traditional (Homeric-style) epic form obsolete. It was Callimachus, himself the author of an epyllion (*Hecale*), who vociferously argued on behalf of the new, more compact genre, proclaiming that "a big book [that is, an epic] is a big evil". In his eyes the epyllion should take the form of a relatively short narrative poem (usually in dactylic hexameter verse) which focused upon the more unfamiliar events in the life of a hero; it should also be erudite, descriptive of detail, and elegantly told. Thus, the *Hecale* (only fragments of which survive today) used the myth of Theseus and the Bull of Marathon as a context out of which came a concentrated examination of the hospitality of an old woman named Hecale for the hero.

There were writers in Alexandria who disagreed with Callimachus' call to abandon traditional epic (for example, Apollonius of Rhodes, who composed his *Argonautica* in a more traditional style), but it was to be the Callimachean view which would come to influence the Roman New Poets of the first century B.C. Not only Catullus, but Cinna, Calvus, Cornificius, and Valerius Cato would try their hands at the genre. It is only Catullus' epyllion, however, which has come down to us intact.

346

Catullus' poem was built around what can be called an "outer" and an "inner" myth. The outer myth was that of the meeting and marriage of the hero Peleus (one of the Argonauts) and the sea-nymph Thetis. The actual first encounter of the pair opens the narrative, but it is their formal wedding that provides the real fabric of the poem, out of which comes the inner myth of Ariadne, daughter of King Minos of Crete, and her ill-fated love for Theseus, son of Aegeus the King of Athens. The mechanism for the movement from outer to inner myth is the marriage couch displayed at the wedding festivities, for this bears a coverlet on which Ariadne is depicted abandoned on the deserted island of Dia. Her tale (which also encompasses the story of Theseus and Aegeus) dominates the poem (lines 50-266), after which the poet returns us to the wedding, and to the nuptial song offered by the goddesses of Fate (the Parcae). This song takes the form of a chilling prophecy pertaining to Achilles, the mighty son to be born to Peleus and Thetis, and thus enables the poet to take his readers to the Trojan War, in which Achilles was to play a major role. The poem then concludes with what has come to be known as the "moralizing epilogue", in which Catullus decries the degeneration of mankind since the allegedly "golden" Heroic Age, a view not without deep irony, given the shabby treatment of Ariadne by a "hero", and the cruel acts of the "heroic" Achilles foretold by the Fates (for detailed examinations of this irony, *cf.* T. E. Kinsey, "Irony and Structure in Catullus 64", *Latomus* 24 [1965] 911-931; L. C. Curran, "Catullus 64 and the Heroic Age", *Yale Classical Studies* 21 [1969] 171-192; and my own "Catullus 64: the Descent of Man", *Antichthon* 9 [1975] 41-51).

Thus the outer myth with its generally optimistic atmosphere (excepting the Achilles' prophesy) contrasts starkly with darker images of love betrayed and of morality disdained. It is this repeated movement from light to dark, in fact, which makes poem 64 one of the more psychologically intriguing poems in the Catullan corpus. Indeed, there are many scholars who would see in the detailed portrait of Ariadne a reflection of Catullus himself; both seem to be victims of an unreciprocated passion which has placed their very existence in jeopardy, shaking the formerly firm foundations on which they stood (*cf.* my article "Catullus: the Mythic Persona", in *Latomus* 35 [1976] 555-566).

Structurally, this epyllion is one of the most complex of Catullus' poems, comparable only to poem 68B. On the surface, the poem has six major movements: 1) the first meeting of Peleus and Thetis; 2) the arrival of the mortal guests at their wedding; 3) the description of the coverlet on the wedding couch, depicting the tale of Ariadne; 4) the departure of the mortal guests and the arrival of the gods; 5) the appearance of the Fates and their prophetic song; and 6) the moralizing epilogue. Yet, as several scholars (such as D.F.S. Thomson in "Aspects of Unity in Catullus 64", *Classical Journal* 57 [1961] 49-57; J.C. Bramble in "Structure and Ambiguity in Catullus LXIV", *Proceedings of the Cambridge Philological Society* 16 [1970] 22-41; and D.A. Traill in "Ring-Composition in Catullus 64", *Classical Journal* 76 [1981] 232-241) have made clear, there is a fine balancing among and within these broader segments (although each of the aforementioned scholars would subdivide the poem in slightly different ways). For example, the initial picture of praiseworthy heroic times (especially at lines 22-24) is echoed at lines 384-396 in the epilogue, just before the poet's strong condemnation of the degenerate present (lines 397-408). The arrival of the mortal guests at lines 31-42 is paralleled by the arrival of the divine guests at lines 278-302. The Ariadne tale with its moving lament (lines 50-201) finds an emotional counterpart in the tale of Theseus' homecoming with its tragic speech of Aegeus (lines 202-248). In turn, the laments of both Ariadne and Aegeus are counterpoised in the outer myth by the song of the Fates (lines 323-381). Thus, whatever precise internal divisions one advocates, poem 64 weaves a complicated pattern of thoughts, images, and words throughout its fabric.

Meter: dactylic hexameter.

1. *Peliaco*: adjective (*cf.* 66.8 and 68B.74); Pelion was a mountain in Thessaly, in central Greece.

   quondam: as modern tales begin with "once upon a time".

   vertice: "on the top" (locative).

   pinus: nominative plural.

2. *dicuntur*: that is, the tale is a traditional one.

   liquidas: here in the sense of "clear"; *cf.* 63.46.

   nasse = navisse (from *no, nare*); note how the poet has personified the pines.

3. *Phasidos*: in form a Greek genitive; the Phasis was the major river of Colchis.

   fines Aeetaeos: "the lands of Aeetes" (the King of Colchis and the father of Medea); *fines* is here treated as masculine, but *cf.* line 217 below. This

349

line is one of thirty in the poem to feature a spondaic fifth foot; it is one of many lines which show a careful balance in the placement of nouns and adjectives.

4. *lecti*: from *lego*, "choose".

   Argivae: "Argive" was synonymous with "Greek" in antiquity, even as far back as the time of Homer.

   robora: here in the sense of "the elite", but *cf.* line 107 below.

   pubis: "youth"; *cf.* 68B.101.

5. *Colchis*: "from the people of Colchis" (dative plural).

   avertere: "to carry away".

6. *vada salsa*: a phrase with an epic turn; translate as "briny seas".

   decurrere: "to traverse", also in epic style.

   puppi: the Argo.

7. *verrentes*: "sweeping".

   abiegnis...palmis: "oars of fir". Note how five of these first seven lines have their final foot begin with a *p* sound, perhaps to echo the oars striking the waters.

8. *diva*:   Athena (Minerva to the Romans).

   quibus: the *iuvenes* of line 4.

   retinens: Athena "who keeps".

   arces: "the heights", that is, the acropolis found in a Greek city.

9. *ipsa...fecit*:   other versions of the myth name Argus as the builder of the ship, but it is much more impressive to have a goddess do the work.

   currum: the ship as a chariot of the seas.

10. *pinea...texta*:   "the framework of pine".

    inflexae...carinae: dative, "to the curved keel".

11. *illa*:   that is, the ship Argo.

    rudem...Amphitriten: "the inexperienced sea" (personified as Amphitrite, the Nereid who was wife to Poseidon, god of the sea); the sea was "inexperienced" at having ships sail through it.

    cursu: here refers to the passage of a ship.

    prima: the MSS. read either *primam* or *proram*; the correction to *prima* is appropriate here, since the Argo was thought to be the first ship ever built, but it also creates problems later in the poem when Theseus appears with a fleet of ships which predates the Argo.

imbuit: "trained", but *cf.* 4.17.

12. *rostro*: the end of a ship's prow.

   proscidit: "ploughed up".

13. *tortaque*: "churned", with *unda*.

   remigio: "the oars"; *cf. palmis* in line 7.

   spumis: take with *incanuit*.

14. *emersere = emerserunt*.

   feri...vultus: their faces are "untamed" since the Nereids belong to the world of nature. Some editors, disturbed at describing the Nereids as untamed or wild, change *feri* (the MSS. reading) to *freti*.

   gurgite: *cf.* 65.5; Catullus uses the word four times in poem 64 (see also lines 18, 178, 183).

15. *aequoreae*: "of the sea"; the Nereids (*cf.* line 11 above) were sea nymphs.

   monstrum: not a "monster", but rather a "marvel"; note the spondaic fifth foot which effectively suggests the awestruck wonder of the nymphs.

16. In the MSS. this line is metrically defective, and most editors add *haud* since a negative seems necessary.

luce: "day".

marinas: with *Nymphas* in the next line.

17. *oculis*: emphatic—"with their own eyes!".

corpore: note the singular where English would expect the plural.

18. *nutricum*: *nutrix* is usually a "wet-nurse", but here it bears the sense of "breasts".

tenus: with the genitive case; translate as "up to".

gurgite: see line 14 above; the word appears in the same metrical position throughout the poem.

19. *tum Thetidis Peleus*: the stage has been carefully set for this crucial moment: Peleus on the Argo and Thetis in the sea behold each other and fall in love. The poet has rejected other versions of the tale, in which the two are already married when the Argo sails, or in which Thetis is an unwilling bride, in order to focus upon that electric moment (*tum*, repeated in the next two verses) when two hearts come together. Note how the collocation of *Thetidis Peleus* visually reinforces their union.

fertur: cf. *dicuntur* in line 2. An *esse* is understood with *incensus*.

20. *humanos...hymenaeos*: "marriage to a mortal".

despexit: "look down on" or "disdain"; the final

353

syllable is scanned as long before *hymenaeos* (*cf.* 62.4 and 66.11).

21. *pater ipse*: Zeus (the Roman Jupiter). In a common version of the myth, Zeus himself loved Thetis, but had to give her up because of an oracle which stated that Thetis' son would be greater than his father.

iugandum: from *iugo*, "marry".

Pelea: Greek accusative.

sensit: "decided".

22. Here the poet injects a song of praise to the heroes of that bygone age.

nimis: "very much", with *optato*; *cf.* 43.4 and 56.4.

saeclorum: some see here a reference to the Five Ages of Man described by Hesiod in the *Works and Days*.

23. *deum genus*: *cf.* 61.2; *deum* is genitive plural.

The line numbered as 23b did not appear in the MSS. Part has been supplied by the Scholia Veronensia commenting upon *Aeneid* V. 80, and part is conjecture.

progenies: "offspring", with *bona* in line 23.

bonarum: with *matrum* in line 23.

24. *vos*: that is, *heroes*.

   compellabo: "address".

25. *teque*: Peleus (*cf.* line 26; and the repeated *tene* in lines 28-29), one of the Heroes; *teque adeo* has the sense of "yes, and *you*".

   eximie: "exceptionally", with *aucte*.

   taedis: the wedding-torch here stands for the wedding itself; *cf.* line 302 below.

   aucte: "blessed"; *cf.* 66.11.

26. *columen*: "pillar".

   Peleu: vocative.

   Iuppiter ipse: *cf.* line 21 above. Note the immediate repetition of *ipse* for emphasis in the next verse.

27. *divum*: genitive plural.

   concessit: "ceded"; *cf.* line 29.

   amores: that is, his love for Thetis.

28. *tenuit*: "hold" in the sense of possess.

   Nereine: V apparently read *nectine* here; *Nereis*, however, would be the usual form of the noun.

29. *Tethys*: wife of Oceanus; she bore Doris, the mother

of the Nereids; *cf.* 66.70.

concessit: here in the sense of "allow"; *cf.* line 27.

ducere: to lead in marriage.

neptem: Thetis was the grand-daughter of Tethys.

30. *Oceanusque*: for Oceanus and Tethys together, *cf.* 88. 5-6.

31. *quae...optatae...luces*: the days to be devoted to the wedding festivities. The connection with the preceding verses seems loose at best.

simul = *simul ac*; *cf.* 22.15 and 63.27.

finito: "determined".

32. *advenere* = *advenerunt*.

domum: the residence of Peleus.

frequentat: "crowds".

33. *Thessalia*: see note on line 1; all the mortal inhabitants of Thessaly pay their respects to Peleus and his bride.

laetanti: "rejoicing".

regia: the royal palace, the *domus* of line 32.

34. *ferunt prae se*: they "display" the wedding gifts

they bring.

35. *Cieros*: an emendation of the MSS.' *syros*; there was a town of this name in Thessaly, but little is known of it. The poet's point, however, is clear: the entire Thessalian country-side is left empty as the residents travel to the palace of Peleus; all normal life is in abeyance.

Pthiotica: adjective with *Tempe* (Greek neuter plural); from Pthia in southern Thessaly.

Tempe: the famous valley of the Peneus river in northern Thessaly.

36. *Crannonisque...Larisaea*: Crannon and Larisa were towns in central Thessaly.

37. *Pharsalum*: the Thessalian town made famous by Julius Caesar's defeat of Pompey the Great. Note how the geographical catalogue in these lines lends an exotic atmosphere to the poem, and also displays the poet's erudition.

coeunt: "gather round".

frequentant: cf. line 32 above.

38. *nemo...iuvencis*: in this and the next three verses the poet will shift his attention back and forth from human to animal activities in the fields of Thessaly.

mollescunt: because they no longer bear the yoke.

39. *non*: for the triple repetition in lines 39-41, *cf.*
lines 19-21 above.

humilis: "low-lying", *i.e.*, not trained on trees.

purgatur: "is weeded".

rastris: "hoes".

40. *glebam* = *glaebam* (a clod of earth).

prono: the ploughshare is "directed downwards" in
order to do its job.

convellit: "breaks up". Note the preponderance of
spondees in this line, reflecting the heavy effort of
the animal at work.

41. *falx*: "pruning-hook".

attenuat: "thins".

frondatorum: those who prune the tree.

42. *desertis*: "abandoned".

infertur: here in the sense of "grows upon".

43. *ipsius*: Peleus.

at: signals the transition from the deserted fields to
the crowded palace.

quacumque...recessit: gives us an impression of the

sheer size of the structure; translate *quacumque* as "in whatever direction".

44. *splendent*: images of brightness dominate this and the following lines.

45. *soliis*: "on the thrones" (dative; *cf. mensae*).

   collucent: "shine brightly".

46. *gaudet*: "takes pleasure"; *cf.* 31.12.

   gaza: "treasure".

47. Our attention now shifts to a very special object: the sacred couch (*pulvinar*) on which it was customary to place images of the gods during festivals; it serves here as a wedding couch since the bride is a goddess. On it is draped the coverlet portraying the tale of Ariadne.

   geniale: "nuptial".

48. *sedibus in mediis*: the Roman wedding couch stood in the atrium of the house.

   Indo...dente: "Indian ivory".

   quod: the *pulvinar*.

   politum: "finished".

49. *tincta*: "colored".

conchyli: a   shell-fish   from   which   the   Romans extracted a purple dye.

purpura: a noun ("purple cloth").

fuco: "dye".

50.   *priscis   hominum...figuris*   =   *priscorum   hominum figuris*.

variata: "adorned with".

51.   *virtutes*:   in the sense of "valorous deeds". There is irony here, as the poet soon shows what kind of valorous behavior these ancient heroes displayed.

52.   *namque*:   "for indeed"; what follows is intended to illustrate heroic *virtutes*.

fluentisono: "wave-echoing".

Diae: the small island of Dia lies to the north of Crete; it is possible, however, that Catullus refers to the larger Cycladic island of Naxos, which seems to have been called Dia at an early time in its history.

53.   *Thesea*:   Greek accusative.

cedentem: "departing"; note the alliteration.

classe: Theseus has a fleet of ships which must predate the building of the Argo; *cf.*   line 11.

54.   *indomitos...furores*:   *cf.*   50.11;   *furores*   are   the

passions of love.

Ariadna: the poet has delayed the proper name for dramatic effect.

55. *necdum*: "and not yet".

quae visit visere: an emendation of the MSS.' *que sui tui se*.

56. *utpote...quae*: "inasmuch as she"; *cf.* 67.43.

fallaci: "deceitful"; words of deception and betrayal will be much used in this section of the poem.

57. *sola*: "lonely"; she is the sole inhabitant of the island.

cernat: "perceives".

58. *immemor*: a thematic word — *cf.* lines 123, 135, and 248; it is similarly used as well at 30.1. Theseus thinks only of himself, with no regard for Ariadne.

at: shifts our attention from Ariadne to Theseus; *cf.* line 43.

vada: *cf.* line 6 above; the dactylic rhythm of this verse reflects the hurried motion of Theseus in his flight.

59. For the general sentiment of this line, *cf.* 30.10.

irrita: a strong word—"null and void".

procellae: dative.

60. *alga*: "sea-weed"; Ariadne stands in the water at the edge of the beach. *Cf.* line 168.

Minois: Ariadne was the daughter of Minos, King of Crete.

ocellis: diminutive for added pathos; *cf.* 3.18.

61. *effigies*: "statue"; she stands motionless, rooted to the shore.

baccantis: in her wild emotion and wild appearance she is akin to a maenad of Bacchus.

prospicit, eheu, prospicit: the repetition also adds pathos.

62. *curarum*: the sorrows of love; *cf.* 2A.10.

fluctuat: "seethes with"; note how the *undis* of her emotion parallel the actual waves in which she stands.

63. *non*: note the triple repetition, and *cf.* 39-41.

subtilem: "dainty".

mitram: a kind of bonnet tied under the chin with ribbons.

64. *contecta*: "covered up", with *pectus* as direct object; this construction appears also in the next verse.

amictu: "dress".

65. *tereti*: "shapely"; *cf.* 61.174.

strophio: the breast-band worn by women.

lactentis: probably here in the sense of "milk-white".

66. *omnia quae*: accusative; refers to all the articles of clothing just described.

67. *ipsius*: Ariadne; *cf.* line 43 above.

alludebant: "were playing with"; spondaic fifth foot.

68. *fluitantis*: "floating" as they are carried about by the waves.

69. *vicem*: "changed state".

toto: repeated for emphasis twice in the next verse; she was totally obsessed with Theseus.

ex te...pendebat: an idiomatic phrase with the sense of "gazed intently at you".

70. *perdita*: nominative.

71. *a misera*: heightens our pity for Ariadne in her desperate plight.

externavit: "has made mad"; *cf.* line 165.

72. *spinosas*: "thorny" in the sense of "difficult".

Erycina: Aphrodite (or Venus), who had a cult site on Mt. Eryx in Sicily.

serens: "sowing".

curas: *cf.* line 62 above.

73. *illa tempestate...quo ex tempore*: slightly awkward, but the poet's meaning is clear; translate as "ever since that time when".

ferox: also used of Theseus at line 247; it implies both being daring and, at the same time, being insolent.

74. *Piraei*: Piraeus is still the major port of the city of Athens.

75. *regis*: King Minos of Crete, here called unjust in anticipation of the tale of the Minotaur about to be related.

Gortynia templa: "Cretan quarters"; Gortyn was a city on Crete, but Minos' true capital was at Knossos.

76. Here begins the famous tale of the Minotaur, a creature half man and half bull, who every year devoured seven Athenian men and seven Athenian

women. These unfortunates were sent as recompense to Minos, whose son Androgeos had been killed by Athenians. It would be prince Theseus who would free Athens from this tribute by slaying the beast, with the help of Ariadne.

nam perhibent olim: a traditional way of introducing a tale; *cf.* line 212 below.

peste: in some versions of the myth, Minos laid seige to Athens, and hunger and disease forced the Athenians to surrender.

coactam: take with *Cecropiam* in line 79.

77. *Androgeoneae*: adjectival form of the proper name.

exsolvere: "pay"; governed by *coactam* in the line above.

78. *electos*: the victims were chosen by lot.

simul et: "and likewise".

decus innuptarum: the "glory of maidens", *i.e.*, the very best young women; we might speak of the "flower" of maidenhood. *Cf.* 63.64. Note that this and the next two verses all feature a spondaic fifth foot, to stress the heavy penalty being paid by Athens.

79. *Cecropiam*: Athens, so called because its first king was Cecrops. *Cf.* lines 83 and 172.

dapem: "as a sacrificial meal".

80.   *quis* = *quibus*; with *malis*.

      angusta: "narrow"; Athens was then a small city.

      vexarentur: "were shaken".

81.   *pro*: "on behalf of".

82.   *proicere*: "bring forward", as a special sacrifice.

      talia: with *funera* in the next line.

      Cretam: "to Crete", with *portarentur* in line 83; note the lack of any preposition.

83.   *funera...nec funera*: "corpses but not corpses"; the poet refers to the fact that the Athenian victims of the Minotaur had their bodies devoured and digested by the monster.

84.   *nave*: *cf. classe* in line 53; Theseus' personal ship was one of a larger group.

      nitens: "pressing on".

85.   *magnanimum*: ironical; *cf. iniusti* in line 75.

      Minoa: Greek accusative.

      superbas: the poet plays on the ambiguity of this adjective—"magnificent", and at the same time "arrogant".

86. The description of Ariadne's falling in love seems to owe a great deal to Apollonius' treatment of Medea's passion in the *Argonautica*. See the Introduction.

conspexit: "looked at".

lumine: "eye".

87. *suavis...odores*: for another fragrant bed, *cf.* poem 6.

88. *lectulus*: the diminutive makes Ariadne seem even more vulnerable in her innocence.

alebat: "was rearing", in the shelter of the quiet women's quarters. For the sentiment, *cf.* 61.58-59 and 62.21.

89. *quales*: picks up *odores* in line 87; the *odores* are "like the myrtles" of southern Greece.

Eurotae: genitive; the Eurotas was a river in the Peloponnese of southern Greece.

progignunt: V seems to have read *pergignunt*, but most editors accept this emendation as appropriate to the context.

90. *distinctos...colores*: "or like the different hues (of flowers)"; note how this expansion of the image seems to drift away from the immediate comparison.

educit: "brings forth".

verna: "of spring".

91. *non prius...quam*: "no sooner...than".

illo: Theseus.

flagrantia: because of her passion.

declinavit: "did she turn aside"; note the spondaic fifth foot, suggesting the effort it took Ariadne to turn her eyes away from Theseus.

92. *concepit*: "absorbed"; *cf.* 2A.8. Note the alliteration of *c* sounds in this verse.

93. For the sentiment here, *cf.* 35.15 and 45.16.

funditus: adverb, "utterly".

imis: "deepest".

exarsit: from *exardesco*, "catch fire".

94. At this point the poet interrupts to address Cupid and Venus as the causes of Ariadne's passion.

misere: adverb, "wretchedly".

exagitans: "inciting".

immiti: "inexorable".

furores: *cf.* line 54 above.

95. *sancte*: "divine".

curis...gaudia misces: the same concept appears at 68A.18; translate *misces* as "blend".

96. *Golgos...Idalium*: in Cyprus; *cf.* 36.12-15.

frondosum: "rich in leaves"; note the spondaic fifth foot.

97. *qualibus*: with *fluctibus* in the next line.

iactastis = *iactavistis*; "have tossed".

mente: take with *incensam*.

98. *in*: here more in the sense of "for".

flavo: "fair-haired"; *cf.* line 63.

99. *tulit*: "endured".

languenti: "faint". The faint *corde* of Ariadne contrasts greatly with the *immiti corde* of Cupid in line 94 above.

100. *quam tum*: emended from the MSS.' *quanto* (which some editors defend). Take with *saepe*: "how often then".

magis...expalluit: "did she turn more pale".

fulgore: "brightness".

101. *cum*: completes *tum* in the preceding verse; the poet here emphasizes *c* sounds to suggest the hard task of Theseus.

monstrum: the Minotaur.

102. *appeteret*: "sought".

103. *non*: taken by some with *ingrata*, but more likely to be taken with *promittens* in the next line; Ariadne did not make promises to the gods in vain.

ingrata: "unwelcome".

munuscula: diminutive for added pathos.

104. *tacito*: she did not voice her prayers aloud, betraying her family as she was.

succepit: V seems to have read *succendit*, but the emendation makes better sense in context; *succepit* = *suscepit*, "undertook".

105. The poet introduces the death of the Minotaur with a Homeric-style simile: the crashing fall of a large tree.

brachia: "branches".

Tauro: the Taurus is a mountain range located in SE Asia Minor.

106. *conigeram*: "cone-bearing".

cortice: "bark"; sweating bark would refer to the resin of the tree.

107.   *indomitus turbo*: a "wild whirlwind"; the main verb is *eruit* in the next line.

   contorquens: "twisting".

   robur: here the trunk of the tree.

108.   *eruit*: "uproots"; its objects are *quercum* and *pinum* in line 106.

   illa: the tree.

   procul: take with *cadit* in the next line.

   radicitus: adverb, "by the roots".

   exturbata: "forced out"; the spondaic fifth foot reflects the force involved.

109.   *late quaeviscumque*: the generally accepted emendation of the MSS.' meaningless *lateque cum eius*; take *quaeviscumque* with *obvia*.

110.   *sic*: signals the end of the simile.

   domito: cf. *indomitus* in line 107; the *indomitus turbo* is now Theseus.

   saevum: used as a noun here; "the savage".

   prostravit: from *prosterno*, "overthrow"; the

counterpart to *eruit* in line 108.

111.   *vanis*: "empty".

      iactantem: agrees with *saevum* in the preceding line.

112.   *sospes*: "safe and sound".

      reflexit: "turned back".

113.   *errabunda*: "wandering"; Theseus was within the maze-like Labyrinth.

      regens: "directing".

      filo: "thread". Ariadne had given Theseus a ball of thread to unravel as he entered the maze; to exit he had only to follow the thread back.

114.   *labyrintheis*: adjective.

      flexibus: "windings".

115.   *tecti*: the Labyrinth.

      frustraretur: "trick"; the object is *eum* understood with *egredientem* in the line above.

      inobservabilis: "untraceable".

      error: here in the sense of "wandering".

116.   *sed quid*: a rhetorical device to end the digression that began at line 76.

primo...carmine: "from the first part of my song", that is, Ariadne on Dia.

117.   *commemorem*:   "relate".

ut: "how"; *cf.* **66.3-6.**

genitoris: Minos.

118.   *consanguineae*:   "sister"; probably Phaedra, although Minos had several daughters.

matris: Pasiphae.

119.   *misera*:   with *gnata*.

deperdita: nominative; Pasiphae is "utterly ruined" by her daughter's decision to betray her family.

laeta<batur>:   V read *leta* here, leaving the line incomplete; if *laetabatur* is in fact correct, then the poet is describing Pasiphae as one who "used to take delight" in her daughter. The emendation would also give us another verse with a spondaic fifth foot.

120.   *omnibus his*:   summing up the preceding lines.

Thesei: genitive; scanned as two syllables.

praeoptarit = *praeoptaverit*, "preferred"; scanned as trisyllabic, with the first two syllables merged.

121.   *aut ut...aut ut*:   "either so that...or so that".

spumosa: "foaming"; with *litora*.

122.   <*venerit*>:   commonly supplied to make up for a lost word here in the MSS.

    devinctam lumina: "having bound her eyes"; for the construction, *cf.* line 64 above.

123.   *liquerit*:   an ironic echo of *linquens* in line 117—she who left her family is in turn left by Theseus.

    immemori: *cf.* line 58.

    coniunx: Ariadne considered Theseus her husband.

124.   We are now given a detailed portrait of Ariadne alone on the beach at Dia.

    ardenti corde: "with her heart ablaze".

    furentem: *cf.* line 54 above.

125.   *clarisonas*:   "clear-sounding"; *cf.* line 320 below.

    fudisse: from *fundo*, "pour".

    voces: here in the sense of "cries".

126.   *tum*:   "at one time"; completed by *tum* ("at another time") in line 128.

    praeruptos: "steep".

conscendere: the present tense makes the action more immediate.

127. *aciem...protenderet*: "extend her gaze".

in: here "over".

128. *tum*: *cf.* line 126 above.

tremuli: "rippling".

adversas: two meanings of *adversus* seem to be played upon here—"hostile" and "lying in one's path".

129. *mollia...tegmina*: "fine coverings"; *cf.* 65.21.

nudatae: in the sense of "thus made bare", *i.e.*, by her action in raising the garment.

surae: "calf" of her leg.

130. *extremis*: "final" since she thinks she is soon to die; *cf.* her comment at line 188 below.

dixisse: note the switch back to the perfect tense.

131. *frigidulos*: "rather faint"; the diminutive adds more pathos to the scene.

udo...ore: ablative of circumstance; translate *udo* as "wet with tears".

cientem: "calling forth".

132. Here begins what is commonly called "Ariadne's Lament" (132-201).

sicine: "is this how"; *cf.* line 134, and also 77.3.

patriis: "native".

perfide: repeated for emphasis in the next line.

133. *deserto*: *cf.* lines 57 and 187.

134. *numine*: here the "power" of the gods (*divum*) to inflict punishment.

135. *immemor*: *cf.* line 58 above.

devota: "accursed". Note the play on the harsh *d* and *p* sounds in this line.

137. *consilium*: "decision".

praesto: "at hand".

138. *immite*: *cf.* line 94 above.

nostri: plural where we would expect singular.

miserescere: "feel pity for", with the genitive.

139. *blanda*: with *voce* in the next line; translate as "smooth".

140. *miseram*: an emendation of V's *misere*; with *me* understood.

sperare: "look forward to".

141. *conubia*: "the ceremonies of marriage".

 hymenaeos: "wedding songs"; the word has a major role to play in poems 61 and 62. *Cf.* also line 20 above.

142. *aerii*: "lofty".

 discerpunt: "disperse".

 irrita: cf. line 59, and also 30.10.

143. *nunc iam*: an emendation of V's *tum iam*; cf. 8.9.

 nulla: emphatically repeated in the next verse.

 iuranti: "who swears an oath".

144. *speret*: here in the sense of "trust"; cf. line 140.

 sermones: "words".

145. *quis* = *quibus* (antecedent is *viri* in line 144); dative of the person interested.

 dum: "as long as".

 cupiens: "covetous".

 praegestit: "is very eager".

apisci: "obtain".

146.   *parcunt*:   "refrain from".

147.   *cupidae*: *cf.*   line 145.

       libido: "desire".

148.   *nihil...nihil*:   echoing the *nil...nihil* of line 146.

       meminere: V seems to have read *metuere*, perhaps
       under the influence of line 146; *meminere* seems
       more logical in context.

       periuria: *cf.*   line 135 above.

       curant: "care about".

149.   *ego te*:   a significant collocation, reflecting the former
       closeness of the two.

       in medio...turbine: "in the midst of the whirlwind";
       cf.   line 107.

       versantem: "twisting".

150.   *germanum*:   the Minotaur,   technically   her   half-
       brother.

       crevi: from *cerno*, "decide".

151.   *fallaci*:   "deceitful"; *cf.*   line 56.

       supremo in tempore: "at the time of greatest trial";

cf. line **169** below.

dessem: from *desum*, "fail"; with the dative case.

152. *dilaceranda:* "to be torn to pieces".

153. *iniacta* = *iniecta*; "thrown on".

tumulabor: "shall I be buried"; the proper burial rites were crucial to the peace of the deceased's soul.

154. For a similar conceit, *cf.* poem **60**.

genuit: from *gigno*, "beget".

sola: ablative, with *rupe*; translate as "deserted", and *cf.* line **57**.

155. *conceptum:* as we might say "after conception".

exspuit: "spit out".

156. *Syrtis:* probably the dangerous shallows at the Gulf of Sidra in North Africa.

Scylla: cf. **60.2**.

rapax: "ravenous".

vasta: refers to the monstrous size of Charybdis, the destructive whirlpool often associated with Scylla. It was traditionally located off the coast of Sicily.

157. *reddis:* "pay back".

pro: "in return for".

158. *cordi fuerant*: for the idiom, *cf.* 44.2-3; 81.5; and 95B.1. The pluperfect tense suggests that Theseus had never been sincere in his promises.

conubia: *cf.* line 141 above.

159. *saeva*: "harsh".

horrebas: "dreaded".

prisci praecepta parentis: likely a reference to Aegeus rather than Minos; Ariadne assumes that Aegeus was "old-fashioned" (*prisci*) and would have forbidden his son to take as bride any daughter of King Minos. Note the play on *p* sounds here.

160. *attamen*: "even so".

vestras: plural, since it was the house of not only Theseus, but also his family. *Cf.* 39.20.

ducere: with *me* understood.

161. *iucundo*: with *labore*.

famularer: "serve" (deponent verb).

serva: "as a slave"; the idea that a woman unable to act as wife to her beloved would gladly serve him as a slave is a conceit also found in Greek literature.

162. *permulcens*: "rubbing".

   liquidis: "pure" or "clear".

   vestigia: here in the sense of "feet".

163. *consternens*: "covering". This line seems intended to remind us of the coverlet on the marriage bed of Peleus and Thetis—on which the tale of Ariadne is depicted. *Cf.* line 47ff.

164. *sed quid*: *cf.* line 116.

   ignaris: "insentient".

165. *exsternata*: "maddened"; *cf.* line 71.

   quae: the *auris* in line 164.

   auctae: "blessed with"; *cf.* line 25, and 66.11.

166. *missas*: "uttered"; with *voces* ("cries").

   reddere: "report"; the winds cannot even convey her laments so that others might hear them.

167. *ille*: Theseus.

   mediis versatur: *cf.* line 149 above; here *versor* bears the sense of "be situated" or simply "be".

168. *apparet*: "show himself"; but if there is no mortal around an immortal (Dionysus) will shortly appear.

alga: *cf.* line 60.

169. *insultans*: "exulting", with *fors* in the next verse.

   extremo tempore: as death approaches; *cf.* line 151.

170. *invidit*: "has begrudged"; *auris* (accusative plural) is the direct object.

   nostris...questibus: dative of the recipient after *invidit*.

171. Ariadne appeals to Jupiter for justice, voicing her vain wish that Theseus had never set foot on Crete.

   tempore primo: as we would say "in the first place".

172. *Gnosia...litora*: that is, the shore of Crete; Knossos was the legendary capital of Minos' realm and site of the Labyrinth.

   Cecropiae: *cf.* line 79; with *puppes*. The collocation of *Gnosia* and *Cecropiae* lends an air of Alexandrian learning to the verse.

173. *dira...stipendia*: the "terrible tribute" is the annual sending of the Athenian youths; *cf.* line 76ff.

   tauro: the Minotaur.

174. *perfidus*: *cf.* lines 132-133; with *navita* (*nauta*).

   religasset = *religavisset*; "made fast" or "moored".

funem: the rope tying the ship to the shore.

175. *malus*: used as a noun here; "the wretch".

celans: "concealing"; the poet emphasizes *c* sounds in this verse in order to reflect the harsh anger of Ariadne.

176. *requiesset = requievisset*; "found rest".

hospes: "as a guest". The trusting relationship between guest and host (a very serious bond in the ancient world) was violated by Theseus.

177. *nam quo*: in this passage, composed of a series of questions, Ariadne employs what could be called the "rhetoric of desperation"; there is no person or place to which she can turn.

me referam: "am I to return".

perdita: "abandoned as I am".

nitor: "depend on".

178. *Idaeosne...montes*: the Ida mountain range on Crete.

gurgite: the "abyss" of the sea.

179. *discernens*: "separating"; with *me* understood.

truculentum: "wild"; *cf.* 63.16. In the MSS. this adjective is followed by an *ubi* which most editors remove.

dividit: also with *me* understood.

aequor: here the surface of the sea.

180. *ipsa*: emphasizes that the decision to leave was hers; no one forced her to do what she did.

181. *respersum*: "stained".

fraterna caede: "the clotted blood of my brother"; *cf.* line 150.

182. *memet*: emphatic form of *me*; there is no one else who would offer consolation.

183. *quine*: picks up *coniugis* in the preceding verse.

lentos: here "pliant".

incurvans: "bending" in his haste.

184. *praeterea*: "and, what is more".

colitur: an emendation of the MSS.' *litus*, which some editors retain, with the verb *patet* understood.

sola: *cf.* line 154.

185. *egressus*: "way out".

cingentibus: "surrounding".

186. *nulla...omnia*: the repetition of these two words in lines 186-187 stresses the bleak situation of Ariadne.

ratio: here in the sense of "means".

nulla spes: for metrical purposes the final syllable of *nulla* is made long by the double consonant which follows in *spes*.

187. *ostentant*: "point the way to".

188. *ante*: with *quam* in line 190.

languescent: "weaken"; future tense. Note the alliteration in *languescent lumina*.

lumina: as often, "eyes".

189. *prius*: with *quam* in line 190.

fesso: "exhausted".

190. *prodita*: "betrayed as I am"; cf. *perdita* in line 177.

multam: "penalty".

191. *caelestumque = caelestiumque*.

fidem: here in the sense of "honor"; if the gods are indeed honorable, they should respond to Ariadne's plea.

postrema: "last".

192. *quare*: Ariadne now launches her curse against Theseus.

virum = virorum.

multantes: "punishing"; *cf.* line 190.

vindice: here used as an adjective; translate as "avenging".

193. *Eumenides*: the Furies (or Erinyes), who were notorious punishers of wrong-doing, especially of perjury, the crime of Theseus. They came to be depicted as loathsome creatures with snakes wreathing their heads.

anguino...capillo: "hair consisting of snakes".

redimita: "crowned".

194. *frons*: "brow".

exspirantis: take with *iras*; translate as "rushing out".

praeportat: here in the sense of "manifests". Note the play on *p* sounds in this line as Ariadne spits out her curse.

195. *huc huc*: *cf.* 61.8-9.

adventate: "come in haste".

196. *extremis...medullis*: *cf.* line 93 above; *extremis* here

386

takes on the sense of "deepest".

197. *inops*: "helpless".

   ardens: *cf.* line 124.

   amenti: "mad".

   furore: the passion of love; *cf.* line 54 above.

198. *quae*: the *querellas* of line 195.

199. *nolite pati*: "do not allow".

   vanescere: "come to nothing".

200. *quali...mente*: translate as "with such a mind as".

201. *funestet*: literally "stain with blood", that is, Theseus is to be an agent of death; this is the curse to which the speech of Ariadne has been leading.

202. *pectore*: note the frequent appearance of this noun throughout this section of the poem—lines 194, 198, 202, and 208. The emphasis on *p* sounds in this line recalls line 194 above.

   voces: *cf.* line 125.

203. *supplicium*: punishment for Theseus.

   anxia: "troubled as she was"; *cf.* 68A.8.

204. *annuit*: from *adnuo*, "assent" or, more literally,

387

"nod in assent"; the nod was the act by which Zeus (Jupiter) granted a request.

caelestum: *cf.* line 191.

numine: *cf.* line 134.

rector: Zeus (Jupiter), the king of the Olympians.

205. *quo motu*: emended from V's *quo modo tunc*; *motu* refers to the gesture made by Zeus in giving consent.

horrida: "rough".

contremuerunt: "tremble all over".

206. *mundus*: "the heavens"; *cf.* 66.1. The image is one of the cosmos being disrupted by the nod of Zeus.

207. *caeca...caligine*: "dark mist".

mentem: governed by *consitus* in the next verse.

208. *consitus*: from *consero*, here in the sense of "cover".

oblito: "forgetful".

209. *Cf.* line 238 below.

mandata: "commands".

constanti: "steadfast".

210. *dulcia...signa*: the white sail; *cf.* lines 233-237.

nec: with *se ostendit* in the next line.

maesto: used of Ariadne in line 202 above; Aegeus and Ariadne are alike in their suffering caused by Theseus.

211.   *sospitem*: "safe and sound".

Erectheum...portum: Piraeus, the harbor of Athens, is termed "Erecthean" after Erectheus, an early king of the city (and an ancestor to Aegeus and Theseus). *Cf.* line 229. (V seems to have read *ereptum*.)

visere: "to look upon".

212.   *namque ferunt olim*: *cf.* lines 1-2 and 76; the poet flashes back to the parting of Aegeus and Theseus.

classi: ablative (*cf.* 66.46); at line 53, however, Catullus employs the more common *classe*.

divae: Athena, the patron of Athens.

213.   *concrederet*: "entrusted".

214.   *complexum*: with *eum* (*i.e.*, Theseus) understood; accusative as subject of the infinitive *dedisse*.

dedisse: governed by *ferunt* in line 212.

215.   For the sentiment, *cf.* 65.10 and 68B.106.

unice: Theseus was the "one and only" son of

Aegeus; *cf.* 39.5 and 73.6.

216. *gnate*: the repetition serves to highlight the importance of his son to the aged king.

dubios: "precarious".

cogor: a word used by Ariadne in line 197 above. *Cf.* note on line 210.

dimittere: "send away"; *cf.* line 208.

217. *reddite*: vocative, agreeing with *gnate*. According to the myth, Theseus arrived in Athens to claim his rightful place when Aegeus was an old man; the father and son had never before met, since Theseus had been raised in Troezen by his mother and maternal grandfather.

fine: here treated as a feminine noun; *cf.* line 3, and 66.12.

218. *Cf.* 101.5; Aegeus sees his son standing on the threshold of death.

fortuna: here in the sense of "misfortune".

mea ac tua: in lines 218-221 words denoting "I" and "you" are juxtaposed to reflect the close bond between Aegeus and his son. *Cf. gnate, ego* in line 216.

fervida virtus: "fiery courage".

219. *invito*: "against my will".

   languida: "feeble" in old age. Note that Ariadne had used the phrase *languescent lumina* in line 188 above.

221. *laetanti pectore*: "happy heart"; the juxtaposition of *gaudens* and *laetanti* puts emphasis on Aegeus' total lack of happiness when Theseus is about to go on his quest.

222. *fortunae signa secundae*: white sails are meant.

223. *expromam*: "bring forth"; *cf.* 65.3. Note the dominant *m* sound in this line—reflecting Aegeus' quiet sadness.

   querellas: also used by Ariadne in line 195 above.

224. *canitiem*: "grey hair".

   foedans: "befouling"; befouling one's person with earth and dust was a sign of grief as far back as Homer's *Iliad*.

225. *infecta...lintea*: "sails dyed" black in mourning.

   vago...malo: "the roaming mast".

226. *nostros* = *meos*.

   incendia: here in the sense of "passions".

227. *carbasus*: "sail"; feminine.

obscurata: "darkened".

dicet: here "proclaim".

ferrugine Hibera: literally, "Spanish rust"; the poet uses the phrase to mean a dark color.

228. *quod...si*: "but if".

concesserit: completed by *ut* in line 230.

incola Itoni: Athena, who seems to have had a shrine at Itonus in Boeotia (some claim the site was in Thessaly).

229. *Erecthei*: genitive; *cf.* line 211.

230. *annuit*: *cf.* line 204 above; for this verb to be completed by an infinitive (*defendere*) is relatively rare.

tauri: genitive with *sanguine*; *cf.* line 173.

respergas: *cf.* Ariadne's speech at line 181.

dextram: "your right arm".

231. *facito*: future imperative; *cf.* 50.21.

condita: agrees with *mandata* in the next line.

232. *vigeant*: "live on", *i.e.*, are not forgotten.

aetas: a period of time; *cf.* 68B.43.

233. *invisent*: "look upon"; *cf.* 31.4.

lumina: "your eyes".

234. *funestam...vestem*: "sorrowful sails" of black; *cf.* line 201 in the speech of Ariadne.

antennae: "yard-arms" of the ship.

deponant: "lower"; subjunctive.

undique: "completely".

235. *intorti...rudentes*: "the twisted rigging"; "twisted" because they were made of plaited rushes.

236. *quam primum*: "as soon as possible"; with *cernens*.

laeta: take with *mente*; *cf.* line 221 above.

237. *agnoscam*: here in the sense of "know once more".

reducem: "brought back".

aetas: *cf.* line 232 above.

sistet: "will present".

238. This and the next two verses recall lines 207-211 above, and mark the end of the flashback which began at line 212.

haec mandata: subject of *liquere* in line 240.

239. *Thesea*: Greek accusative, object of *liquere*.

ceu: "just as"; a brief simile in epic style.

flamine: "blast".

240. *nivei*: "snowy".

liquere: the verb does double duty: first referring to *haec mandata* with *Thesea* as object, and second (within the simile) referring to *nubes* with *cacumen* as object; perfect tense.

241. *pater*: Aegeus.

prospectum: "view" of the ship returning.

ex arce: it is uncertain whether the poet depicts Aegeus looking out to sea from the Athenian Acropolis, or (more logically) from a headland such as Sunion at the southern tip of Attica.

242. *assiduos...fletus*: *cf.* 68B.55.

absumens: "exhausting"; the dominant *a* sound in this line reflects the grief of Aegeus.

243. *inflati*: "swollen" with wind.

lintea: "canvas".

244. *scopulorum*: "rocks".

245. *immiti*: "inexorable"; *cf.* lines 94 and 138.

246. *funesta*: take with *tecta*; the house was "in mourning" because of his father's death. *Cf.* line 201 in the speech of Ariadne.

   domus...tecta: translate simply as "house".

247. *ferox Theseus*: *cf.* line 73.

   Minoidi: Ariadne (Greek dative); for the sentiment of these lines, *cf.* lines 200-201 above.

248. *obtulerat*: from *offero*, "inflict (on)".

   immemori: *cf.* line 58.

249. *quae tum*: the scene now shifts to Ariadne on the beach as depicted by the coverlet.

   prospectans: *cf. prospectum* in line 241.

   cedentem: resumes the picture of Theseus given at line 53.

   maesta: *cf.* lines 60, 130, 202, and 210 (where it is applied to Aegeus).

250. *volvebat*: "was pondering".

   saucia: "wounded" by love.

251. The poet here turns to another section of the coverlet where the god Dionysus is depicted.

   at: signals the new element in the tale.

florens: the god is in the "flower of youth"; *cf.* 17.14.

volitabat: used to suggest frenzied movement; *cf.* 63.25.

Iacchus: a cult name for Dionysus/Bacchus.

252. The proper nouns lend an exotic air to this verse, appropriate to the exotic god himself.

thiaso: a band of devout worshippers; *cf.* 63.28.

Satyrorum: satyrs were youthful woodland creatures who followed the god.

Nysigenis Silenis: Sileni were older members of the god's band who were often depicted as intoxicated; these came from Nysa, a place connected with the cult of Dionysus, but its exact location is unclear (India, Arabia, Asia Minor, Thrace and Naxos have all been suggested).

253. *tuoque...amore*: "love for you"; *cf.* 87.4.

incensus: *cf.* lines 19 and 97.

254. At least one verse seems to have been lost at this point in the MSS. It would have contained a noun (such as *Maenades*) as an antecedent to the *quae* of line 254. Some editors, however, read *cui Thyades* instead of *quae tum alacres*, thus eliminating the need to postulate a missing line.

quae: Maenads were well known female followers of Dionysus.

alacres: they moved in a frenzy; *cf.* line 251.

lymphata: "distracted".

255. *euhoe*: the cry uttered by Maenads; it stands outside the grammar of the verse, as if in quotation marks.

bacchantes: participle; the women are "celebrating the rites of Bacchus".

capita inflectentes: *cf.* 63.23.

256. *tecta...cuspide*: a sharp point swathed with ivy or vine leaves (see next note).

thyrsos: the wand associated with the worship of Dionysus; it was usually wreathed in ivy or vine leaves, or crowned by a fir cone.

257. *pars*: note the repetition of this word in lines 256-259; the women act out their frenzy in different ways.

divolso: from *divello*, "tear apart"; the rending of an animal was part of the rites of Dionysus.

iuvenco: "bullock".

258. *tortis*: "writhing".

259. *obscura...orgia*: normally *orgia* would refer to the "secret rites" of a god, but here, in view of the specificity of the preceding lines, it probably has its secondary meaning of "mystic emblems".

cavis...cistis: the *cista* was a basket-like container for mystic emblems of a cult; note the sharp *c* sound which pervades this verse.

celebrabant: "were crowding round".

260. *audire*: here in the sense of "understand" or "learn about".

profani: those who were not initiates of the cult.

261. Lines 261-264 feature an effective play on the sounds *p*, *t*, *o*, and *i*, with each verse imitating the actual sounds of the action depicted. In this line, for example, the dominant *p* sound reflects the beating of a drum. *Cf.* 63. 21-22.

plangebant: "were beating noisily".

proceris: "extended" or "stretched out".

tympana: "drums", usually of small size; *cf.* 63.8, 9, 21, 29, and 32.

262. *tereti...aere*: that is, cymbals.

tinnitus: "clanging"; accusative plural.

263. *multis*: dative; *cf. pars* in lines 256-259.

raucisonos...bombos: "hoarse boomings".

efflabant: "were blowing out".

264.   *barbaraque...tibia*: the *tibia* was a flute-like pipe; it was *barbara* because it was a Phrygian rather than a Greek instrument.

stridebat: "was shrieking".

265.   The description of the coverlet ends, and we are returned to the wedding of Peleus and Thetis. *Cf.* lines 50-51 above.

amplifice: "splendidly".

266.   *pulvinar*: *cf.* line 47.

complexa...velabat: freely, "enclosed and veiled".

amictu: "drapery".

267.   *quae*: "these things", that is, the scenes on the coverlet; object of *spectando*.

Thessala pubes: here referring to all the mortals in attendance; for their arrival, *cf.* lines 31-34.

268.   *coepit*: the subject is *pubes* in line 267.

decedere: the mortals "make way for" the gods.

269.   *hic*: temporal; translate as "at this point".

qualis: another simile in the epic style begins, one which focuses on the waves and the morning breeze.

flatu...matutino: take with *horrificans* in the next line.

270.   *horrificans*:   "ruffling"; *cf.* line 205 above.

Zephyrus: the west wind; *cf.* 46.3.

proclivas: the waves are "tumbling down" as they move.

271.   *Aurora*:   the dawn; ablative absolute with *exoriente*.

vagi: "wandering"; *cf.* lines 225 and 277.

sub: here in the sense of "up to".

272.   *quae* = *undae*.

tarde primum: take with *procedunt* in the next verse.

clementi: "gentle".

273.   *leviterque sonant*:   "lightly (*i.e.*, softly) sound".

plangore: "plash" or "slapping".

cachinni: genitive singular.

274.   *post*:   temporal.

magis magis: *cf.* 38.3 and 68B.48.

increbescunt: "grow".

275. *purpureaque...luce*: the reddish glow of dawn.

procul: take with *refulgent*.

nantes: "as they float".

276. *sic tum*: marks the end of the simile and the return to the wedding festivities.

regia tecta: *cf.* line 246.

277. *ad se quisque*: "each to his own home".

vago: *cf.* line 271 above.

discedebant: note how this spondaic ending lends a sense of slow movement to the line.

278. *quorum*: the mortal guests.

princeps: Chiron (see below) comes first, at the head of the throng of divinities.

Peli: *cf.* line 1.

279. *Chiron*: the wise centaur (half man and half horse) who would become the mentor of the young Achilles.

silvestria dona: "woodland gifts", that is, flowers, as

the following verses make clear.

280. *quoscumque*: with *flores* in line 282.

281. *ora*: the "region" of Thessaly; *cf.* 66.43.

creat: "produces (on)".

propter: "beside".

fluminis: the river in question is most likely the Peneus; *cf.* line 285 below.

282. *parit*: "gives birth to"; for the image, *cf.* 62.41.

Favoni: the west wind; *cf.* Zephyrus at line 270. Note how the *f* sounds of this line suggest the gentle movement of the wind.

283. *indistinctis...corollis*: "disordered garlands", *i.e.*, the flowers are arranged in no ordered manner; some editors, however, prefer to read *in distinctis...corollis*.

plexos: "plaited".

ipse: Chiron.

284. *quo*: take with *iucundo...odore*.

permulsa: "caressed"; *cf.* line 162 above.

domus...risit: *cf.* 31.14, and line 46 above.

285. *confestim*: "immediately" after Chiron.

Penios: the god of the river Penios (Peneus) in Thessaly.

Tempe: neuter plural; *cf.* line 35 above.

286. *super impendentes*: "overhanging".

287. *Haemonisin*: V seems to have read here *minosim linquens doris celebranda choreis*, a line which defies interpretation; the emendation *Haemonisin* seems the best of many suggested, and would refer to Thessalian women (*cf. Haemonis* in the Oxford Latin Dictionary; the form would be a Greek dative plural). The emendation of *doris* to *claris* seems dictated by the context.

linquens: with *Tempe* as direct object.

celebranda: "to be crowded"; agrees with *Tempe*.

288. *non vacuus*: Penios does not come empty-handed.

ille: emphatic, "he in his turn".

radicitus: "roots and all".

289. *fagos*: beech trees (feminine noun).

recto...stipite: "with a straight trunk"; ablative of description.

laurus: feminine noun.

290. *nutanti platano*: "swaying plane-tree".

lentaque: *cf.* line 183 above.

sorore: the poplar tree. The myth alluded to is that of the sisters of Phaethon, who, after the fiery death of their brother while driving the chariot of the Sun, were changed into poplar trees.

291. *flammati*: Phaethon "who was set on fire".

aeria cupressu: "the lofty cypress"; *cupressu* is also feminine.

292. *haec*: that is, all these trees.

late: take with *locavit*.

contexta: "interwoven"; Penios seems to have woven screens of some sort out of his gifts.

293. *velatum*: "cloaked"; note the *v* sound of this verse.

fronde: "foliage".

294. *sollerti corde*: "clever mind"; Prometheus was the clever god who outwitted Zeus and gave fire to mankind. In return, Zeus had him chained to a desolate rock; he eventually won his freedom by warning Zeus not to marry Thetis, whose son would be greater than his sire. Thus his presence at the wedding of Thetis to Peleus has a kind of irony to it.

295. *extenuata*: "much diminished" due to the passage of

time.

vestigia: "traces".

296.   *silici*:   with   *restrictus*;   Prometheus   had   his   limbs
"bound fast to a rock".

catena: ablative of means.

297.   *persoluit*:   "paid   in   full";   note   the   play   on   sharp   *p*
sounds.

praeruptis: "steep";   *cf.*   line   126.   The   spondaic
ending   gives   the   line   a   slow,   heavy   sound   appropriate to the context.

298.   *pater divum*:   Zeus (Jupiter);   *divum = divorum*.

coniuge: Hera (Juno).

natisque: "children";   this   line   is   hypermetric,   that
is,   the   *que*   in   *natisque*   is   elided   before   the   opening
vowel of the next verse.   *Cf.*   34.22.

299.   *caelo*:   "from the sky".

Phoebe: Phoebus Apollo. Most versions of the myth
show Apollo and Artemis taking part in the wedding
festivities.

300.   *unigenamque*:   Artemis is "of the same parentage" as
Apollo;   *cf.*   66.53.

cultricem montibus: "she   who   dwells   in   the

mountains".

Idri: if the reading is correct (V read *ydri*) this may refer to the Idrus who would seem to have been the founder of the town of Idrias in Asia Minor. The town was a center for the worship of Hecate, a goddess often identified with Artemis.

301. *Pelea*: Greek accusative; note the postponement of *nam* (*cf.* 23.7).

aspernata est: the reason for such disdain is unclear; *cf.* note on line 299 above.

302. *taedas...iugalis*: "nuptials"; *cf.* line 25 above.

celebrare: here in the sense of "celebrate"; *cf.* line 287.

303. *qui*: the gods who did attend.

niveis: "ivory"; *cf.* line 45.

304. *large*: "copiously".

multiplici...dape: a meal of many courses.

constructae: "heaped up".

305. *cum interea*: temporal; *cf.* 95A.3.

infirmo: "feeble".

306. *veridicos*: "truthful".

Parcae: the Roman goddesses of fate and childbirth, traditionally three in number; they appear at the wedding to sing a prophetic song.

edere: "bring forth" or, even more appropriate to their function, "give birth to".

307. *his*: dative of possession; *cf.* line 263 above.

tremulum: because of their extreme old age; *cf.* 61.51.

complectens: "enveloping"; with *vestis*.

308. *candida*: nominative, with *vestis* in the preceding verse.

talos: "ankles".

incinxerat: from *incingo*, "surround".

ora: "edge".

309. *at roseae niveo*: emended from V's *at roseo niveae*; it seems logical for the Parcae to have snowy white hair.

vittae: ritual "head-bands".

310. *carpebant*: used here in a technical sense to refer to the carding of wool; translate as "pull out" or "tease out".

rite: "in the proper manner".

laborem: their wool working.

311.   *laeva*: "the left hand"; nominative.

       colum: "the distaff".

       amictum: "covered"; *cf.* 63.70.

312.   *dextera*: "the right hand".

       leviter: "nimbly".

       deducens fila: the threads are drawn downwards from the distaff; *fila* is understood after both *deducens* and *formabat* (in line 313).

       supinis: "up-turned".

313.   *prono in pollice*: the thumb is pointed downwards during this part of the process.

314.   *libratum tereti...turbine*: "poised on rounded whorl". The *turbo* was a disk at the bottom of the spindle (*fusum*); its function was to control the motion of the spindle.

       versabat: the subject is still *dextera* in line 312.

315.   *atque ita*: here in the sense of "and then", *i.e.*, in the next step of the process.

decerpens: "plucking off"; with *dens*.

aequabat: the subject is *dens* (which imparts an uncommon monosyllabic ending to the verse).

316.   *laneaque...morsa*:   "and little bits of wool".

aridulis...labellis: note the diminutives for added pathos.

haerebant: "were clinging to".

317.   *quae*:   the *morsa* of the preceding line.

fuerant exstantia: translate as "had appeared"; thus the uneven fibres were removed from the woolen thread.

318.   *candentis*:   "bright white".

319.   *vellera*:   the tufts of wool that have not yet been worked; accusative plural after *custodibant*.   Note the alliteration of *v* and *c* in this line.

virgati...calathisci: "baskets made of osiers".

custodibant: archaic form of the imperfect;   *cf.* 68B.85 and 84.8.

320.   *haec* = *hae* (the Parcae); the form is archaic.

clarisona: *cf.* line 125 above.

vellentes: V seems to have read *pellentes*; if the

409

emendation is correct, we have in this line a triple alliteration (*cf.* line 262). Translate *vellentes* as "plucking".

321.   *divino*: here takes on the sense of "prophetic".

     fuderunt: from *fundo*, "utter".

     fata: "oracles".

322.   *carmine*: repeated for emphasis just as the prophecy is about to begin.

     post nulla...aetas: "no age to come"; *cf.* line 232.

     arguet: "will convict of" being dishonest.

323.   *o...augens*: the wedding song (*cf.* poems 61 and 62) begins with praise of Peleus; translate *augens* as "you who increase".

     decus: *cf.* 63.64 and line 78 above.

     magnis virtutibus: ablative of means; *virtutibus* here has the sense of "deeds of prowess" or "heroics".

324.   *Emathiae*: used of Thessaly, but in truth a district of Macedonia.

     tutamen: Peleus is "the defence" of Thessaly. *Cf.* line 26 above.

     Opis...nato: the son of Ops (= Rhea) is Zeus.

325. *accipe*: "hear".

pandunt: "disclose".

luce = die; *cf.* line 16 above.

326. *veridicum*: *cf.* line 306.

vos: the *fusi* of the next verse.

quae: with *subtegmina* in line 327.

327. This refrain will appear twelve times in the song, dividing it into twelve strophes of varying length; *cf.* the refrains in poems 61 and 62.

subtegmina: the "threads" of fate; object of *ducentes*.

fusi: "spindles".

328. *iam*: here in the sense of "very soon".

maritis: "husbands" in this context; dative case.

329. *Hesperus*: the evening star of poem 62.

adveniet: the repetition suggests a sense of impatience on the part of the groom.

fausto: "lucky"; the star is, of course, Hesperus.

coniunx: Thetis.

330. *flexanimo...amore*: "love that sways the mind".

   mentem: here in the sense of "heart"; with *tibi*.

   perfundat: subjunctive in a relative clause of purpose (introduced by *quae*). Translate as "imbue".

331. *languidulosque*: diminutive expressing affection; for the adjective, *cf.* line 219 above.

   paret: "will submit"; the future tense parallels that of *adveniet* in line 329.

332. *levia...brachia*: *cf.* 66.10.

   robusto: "mighty".

334. *nulla...tales*: note the play on *nullus*, *talis* and *qualis* in lines 334-336.

   contexit: from *contego*, "shelter".

335. *foedere*: "covenant"; *cf.* 76.3 and 109.6.

336. *concordia*: refers to the perfect harmony between husband and wife; *cf.* 66.87.

   Peleo: dative; but *cf.* line 382 below. Scan as disyllabic.

338. Here begins a prophecy about Achilles, the son to be born to Peleus and Thetis.

   expers terroris: "without fear" or, more simply,

"fearless".

339. *haud tergo*: that is, he does not turn his back in cowardly flight. This verse amplifies the *expers terroris* of the preceding line.

340. *persaepe*: "very often".

vago: "far-ranging"; for the play on *v* and *c* sounds in this line, *cf.* line 319 above.

certamine cursus: we would say "a running contest"; *cursus* is genitive after *certamine*.

341. *flammea*: "swift as fire".

praevertet: "will outstrip"; in the *Iliad* Achilles is famous for his swiftness of foot. Note that *v* and *c* sounds also dominate this verse.

cervae: "deer".

343. *non...quisquam*: "no one".

illi...se conferet: "will oppose him".

heros: "as a hero".

344. *Phrygii...campi*: the Phrygian fields were at Troy, and it was in the Trojan War that Achilles distinguished himself; *campi* is an emendation of the MSS.' *tenen*. For the phrase, *cf.* 46.4.

Teucro: "Trojan"; Teucer was a legendary Phrygian

king.

manabunt: "will flow".

345.   *obsidens*: "laying siege to". The prominent *o* sound in this verse suggests the great length of the war.

longinquo: "prolonged".

346.   *periuri Pelopis*: a reference to the myth of how Pelops secured his marriage to the daughter of King Oenomaus. He first bribed the driver of the king's chariot to sabotage the vehicle, thus killing the king (who would only give his daughter in marriage to a man who could beat him in a chariot race). He then murdered the driver to secure his new position. This resulted in a curse being laid on the house of Pelops.

tertius heres: Agamemnon, the leader of the Greek forces at Troy.

348.   *illius*: Achilles.

virtutes: *cf.* line 323 above.

claraque: "distinguished".

349.   *fatebuntur*: "will bear witness to".

350.   *incultum*: "unkempt" because they are in mourning; an emendation of the MSS.' corrupt *in civos*.

351.   *putridaque*: "withered" in old age.

variabunt: "will mark" in discoloration; loosening the hair and beating the breast were traditional signs of mourning. Note how the stressed *p* sounds in this line echo the pounding of the hands on the breast.

353. *velut...messor*: the image of the reaper follows epic style; just so Achilles will "reap" his enemies.

praecerpens: "cutting off"; an emendation of V's *precernens*.

aristas: simply "grain".

354. *flaventia*: "golden" with the color of ripe grain.

demetit: "harvests".

355. *Troiugenum*: an epic compound, "those born at Troy"; the form is genitive plural.

infesto: "aggressive".

prosternet: "will strike down".

357. *magnis virtutibus*: *cf.* line 323 above.

unda: the final syllable remains short despite the appearance of a double consonant in the following word; but *cf.* line 186.

Scamandri: the Scamander was one of the major rivers of Troy.

358. *diffunditur Hellesponto*: the water "pours off into the Hellespont" (today sometimes known as the Dardanelles); *Hellesponto* is dative case. Note the spondaic fifth foot.

359. *iter*: the "course" of the river.

 angustans: "narrowing".

 acervis: "heaps".

360. *tepefaciet*: "will make warm".

 permixta: "indiscriminate"; ablative, with *caede*.

362. *testis erit*: cf. line 357 above.

 morti: the corpse of Achilles.

 reddita: "delivered".

363. *teres...bustum*: "rounded tomb"; nominative case. For *teres*, cf. line 314.

 coacervatum: "heaped"; cf. *acervis* in line 359.

 aggere: "mound".

364. *niveos...artus*: "snow-white limbs"; cf. line 303.

 perculsae virginis: the "maiden struck down" was Polyxena, the daughter of King Priam of Troy; she was sacrificed on the tomb of Achilles as a final tribute to that hero. *Cf.* line 368 below.

416

366. *copiam*: "opportunity"; completed by *solvere* in the next line.

Achivis: another name for the Greeks.

367. *urbis Dardaniae*: the "city of Dardanus" was Troy; Dardanus was a son of Zeus who became the ancestor of the kings of Troy.

Neptunia...vincla: a reference to the legendary walling of Troy by Poseidon; *vincla = vincula*. Note the emphasis on exotic names in lines 366-368: *Achivis*, *Dardaniae*, *Neptunia*, and *Polyxenia*.

368. *Polyxenia...caede*: "the slaughter of Polyxena".

madefient: an emendation of V's unmetrical *madescent*; translate as "will be soaked".

sepulcra: cf. *bustum* in line 363 above.

369. *quae*: Polyxena.

velut...victima: just as Achilles was given a simile at line 353, so here Polyxena is likened to a sacrificial animal.

ancipiti: "two-headed"; the ritual weapon.

succumbens: "sinking under".

370. *truncum*: "mutilated".

summisso poplite: "her knee lowered in submission".

372. *agite*: *cf.* 61.38 and 63.12. The Parcae here turn from Achilles to the nuptial ceremony at hand.

optatos: a frequent word in the poem; *cf.* lines 22, 31, 141, and 328.

animi...amores: for this use of *animi*, *cf.* 2A.10, 68A.26, and 102.2.

373. *coniunx*: Peleus; *cf.* line 329.

foedere: *cf.* line 335 above.

divam: Thetis.

374. *dedatur*: from *dedo* in the sense of "yield" or "surrender".

iam dudum: "at once"; take with *dedatur*.

376. *non*: with *poterit* in the next line.

illam: Thetis; object of *revisens*.

orienti luce: at the dawn of the next day.

377. This line seems to refer to an ancient belief that one could determine the virginity (or lack thereof) of a woman by a length of ribbon or thread; in this case, the nurse will find that Thetis' measurements have changed after her wedding night with Peleus.

circumdare: "surround".

418

filo: *cf.* lines 113, 312, and 317.

378. In the MSS. line 378 repeats the refrain in a most intrusive manner; most editors omit it.

379. *discordis*: the girl is "discordant" in the sense that she is in conflict with her husband.

   maesta: completed by *secubitu* in the next verse.

380. *secubitu*: the act of sleeping apart from a spouse; *cf.* 61.101.

   mittet: here in the sense of "will stop". For the general sentiment, *cf.* 66.15-16.

381. The final refrain marks the end of the song of the Parcae, and sets the stage for the moralizing conclusion.

382. *praefantes*: from *praefor*, "predict".

   Pelei: dative and disyllabic; *cf.* line 336 above.

383. *divino*: *cf.* line 321.

   cecinerunt: from *cano*, "sing". Note the strong *c* sounds in this verse.

384. *praesentes*: "in person".

   namque: emphatic, "for indeed"; for its position, *cf.* 66.65.

419

ante: adverbial.

invisere: "visit"; with *solebant* in line 386.

385. *heroum*: genitive plural.

mortali...coetu: such as the wedding of Peleus and Thetis; dative case (*cf.* 66.37).

ostendere: with *solebant* in the next line.

386. *caelicolae*: *cf.* 30.4 and 68B.138.

spreta: from *sperno*, "scorn".

387. *saepe*: rhetorically repeated at lines 390 and 394.

pater divum: *cf.* line 298.

residens: an emendation of the MSS.' *revisens* (defended by some editors); but *residens* makes more sense with *templo in fulgente*.

388. *venissent*: "had come round".

sacra: "rites".

389. *terra*: ablative case; translate as "on the ground". Note how the spondaic movement of this line reflects the bulls ponderously falling on the ground.

390. *vagus*: *cf.* line 271.

Liber: another name for Dionysus.

Parnasi: the imposing mountain to the north of Delphi; it was sacred to both Apollo and Dionysus.

391. *Thyiadas*: female followers of Dionysus; accusative plural.

effusis...crinibus: "with their locks loosened" in ecstasy.

evantis: "crying 'euhoe'" (*cf.* line 255 above); agrees with *Thyiadas*. The dominant *e* sound echoes the piercing cry of the women.

392. *Delphi*: the inhabitants of Delphi.

certatim: "in rivalry" to honor the god.

393. *divum*: accusative case.

fumantibus aris: locative ablative.

394. *letifero*: "death-dealing".

Mavors: Mars (the Greek Ares), god of war.

395. *Tritonis era*: the mistress of Triton (probably a river in Boeotia in central Greece) was Athena, whom the Romans called Minerva.

Amarunsia virgo: Artemis (Diana), who had a cult center at Amarynthus on the island of Euboea. The MSS., however, read either *ramunsia* or *ranusia*, and some editors emend that to *Rhamnusia* (that is, the

421

goddess Nemesis; *cf.* 66.71 and 68B.77). The context favors another Olympian such as Artemis, and, moreover, the appearance of Nemesis in a battle is not paralleled elsewhere in ancient literature.

396. *praesens*: *cf.* line 384 above.

   catervas: here in the sense of "troops".

397. *sed postquam*: there was a wide-spread belief in antiquity that mankind had gradually degenerated; after the perfection of the Golden Age, man had fallen into increasing corruption.

   imbuta: "tainted".

   nefando: "abominable"; *cf.* line 405 below.

398. *de mente fugarunt*: *cf.* 68A.25; *fugarunt = fugaverunt* ("have put to flight").

399. *perfudere = perfuderunt*; from *perfundo*, "drench".

   fraterno...fratres: the repetition serves to emphasize the horror of the act.

400. *destitit*: from *desisto*, "cease".

   extinctos: "deceased".

401. *primaevi*: "youthful".

   funera: "death".

402. *liber*: the father is "free" to do what he wished.

uti nuptae: emended from the MSS.' problematical *ut innuptae*; translate *nuptae* as "bride".

poteretur: from *potior*, "acquire"; its object is the ablative noun *flore*.

novellae: "young". The father would seem to want his son out of the way so that he could freely indulge himself with a young bride. The MSS., however, read *novercae* ("step-mother"), a reading which throws the sense of the line into confusion.

403. *substernens*: *cf.* line 332 above.

impia: repeated in the next line to stress the sin of this act.

404. *verita est*: from *vereor*, "fear" or "be afraid".

scelerare: "desecrate".

penates: the Roman household gods; *cf.* 9.3. The MSS. read *parentes*, which is rejected by most editors.

405. *fanda nefanda*: the conjunction *et* is omitted, but understood; take *fanda* as "right".

permixta: *cf.* line 360 above.

406. *iustificam*: "just-dealing".

avertere = *averterunt*; "turned aside".

407.   *talis...coetus*: *cf.* line 385.

   dignantur: "deign"; deponent verb.

408.   *contingi*: "to be touched".

   lumine: the light of day. The poem ends with a sense of despair for the condition of mankind.

65

Poem 65 is a preface, in the form of a poetic epistle, to poem 66, Catullus' translation of Callimachus' *Lock of Berenice*. It is addressed to Q. Hortensius Hortalus, an orator and author whose name also appears in poem 95A. From poem 65 itself, it would appear that Hortalus had requested some poetry from Catullus, but the unexpected death of the poet's brother had prevented that request from being fulfilled. When Hortalus reminded Catullus of his initial request, the poet sent him a translation (poem 66) and an explanation of his tardiness (poem 65).

Probably because of its prefatory nature, poem 65 is the shortest of the long poems. Its twenty-four lines (assuming the loss of a single verse at line 9) are structured as follows: the first four lines take the form of a concessive clause interrupted by lines 5-14, which function much like an aside and present a lament for the poet's brother; the original train of thought is resumed at line 15, and lines 15-18 provide the apodosis for the concessive clause of lines 1-4. The poem then concludes' with an extended simile in lines 19-24 which may have been inspired by a Callimachean poem (see commentary on line 19); if so, this simile provides a fine transition to poem 66 itself.

Meter: in poem 65 we find, for the first time in the corpus, the elegiac meter which will exclusively characterize poems 65-116. It seems likely, in fact, that poem 65 is programmatic in this respect: at line 12 the poet states *semper maesta tua carmina morte canam*, and the elegiac meter is the rhythm of sadness *par excellence*. (For a more detailed examination of poem 65 as programmatic, *cf.* T.P. Wiseman's *Catullan Questions* [Leicester, 1969] 17ff.)

1. *confectum*: "exhausted"; take with *me*.

   cura: here in the sense of "sorrow".

2. *sevocat*: "calls me away".

   doctis...virginibus: the Muses; *cf.* line 3.

3. *potis est*: "is able"; with *mens animi* in the next line.

   expromere: here probably "to give birth to"; *cf. fetus*.

   fetus: for a poet, the "offspring" of the Muses would be poems.

4. *mens animi*: an idiom best translated simply as "mind".

   fluctuat: "tosses"; *cf.* 64.62. Words connected with water and waves loom large in poem 65.

ipsa = mens animi.

5. *namque*: "for indeed"; the poet turns aside to lament the recent death of his brother, and the thought of line 4 will only resume in line 15.

Lethaeo: a reference to the river Lethe (the river of forgetfulness) in the Underworld.

gurgite: "flood"; *cf.* 64.14, 18, 178, and 183. *Lethaeo gurgite* is an ablative of source after *manans* in line 6; *cf.* line 24 below.

6. *pallidulum*: the diminutive adds to the pathos of the passage.

manans: with *unda*, "streaming"; *cf.* line 24.

alluit = adluit, "washes". Note the soft *l*, *m*, and *n* sounds of this line.

7. *Troia*: take with *tellus*.

Rhoeteo...litore: Rhoeteum was a promontory near Troy.

quem = frater.

subter: "close to".

8. *ereptum*: "torn away", with a clear sense of violence; *cf.* 68B.106 and 82.3.

obterit: "crushes"; its subject is *Troia...tellus* in the preceding line.

9. This line is missing in the MSS., but it must have begun the poet's direct address to his brother. For these lines, *cf.* 68A.20-24, and 68B.92-100.

10. *vita...amabilior*: "more worthy of love than life (is)".

11. *semper*: repeated for emphasis in the next line.

    amabo: picks up the *amabilior* of the preceding line.

12. *maesta...carmina*: "songs made sad".

    tua...morte: "by your death"; take with *maesta*.

    canam: the commonly accepted emendation of the MSS.' *tegam*; *cf. concinit* in the next line.

13. *qualia*: a simile based on the myth of Procne and Philomela; when her husband Tereus rapes her sister Philomela, Procne punishes him by killing their son Itys. Both women are eventually turned into birds by the gods.

    densis: "thick".

14. *Daulias*: there is disagreement among scholars as to which sister is meant here, though Procne seems the more likely; *Daulias* is derived from Daulis, a region in central Greece that was ruled by Tereus. Translate as "the Daulian".

absumpti: "murdered".

Ityli: better known as Itys, the son of Procne and Tereus.

15. *sed tamen*: signals an end to the digression that began with line 5.

maeroribus: "sorrows".

16. *haec...carmina*: that is, poem 66.

expressa: "translated".

Battiadae: a reference to Callimachus of Cyrene; *cf.* poem 7.4-6 and poem 116.2.

17. *ne*: with *putes* in line 18.

nequiquam credita ventis: "vainly entrusted to the winds"; *cf.* 30.9-10; 64.59 and 164-166; 70.4.

18. *effluxisse*: "have run away".

19. *ut*: a simile based on the ancient concept of the apple as a token of love; Callimachus may have served as Catullus' source here, since he wrote a poem (*Cydippe*) that dealt with this theme.

sponsi: here in the sense of "lover".

malum: "apple".

20. *procurrit*: "rushes out".

casto...gremio: cf. 66.56; *gremio* is here "bosom", as is made clear in the next line.

21. *quod*: refers to *malum*.

   miserae oblitae: two adjectives where one might expect *misere oblitae*; we might say "of the forgetful wretch".

22. *prosilit*: "jumps up".

   excutitur: "is shaken out".

23. *illud* = *malum*.

   prono...decursu: "in a downwards descent".

   praeceps: "rapid". Note the spondaic nature of this verse.

24. *huic*: the maiden.

   conscius...rubor: "a guilty blush".

66

Poem 66, the so-called *Coma Berenices*, is a close (but not *verbatim*) translation of a Callimachean elegy (parts of which are still extant) written about 246/245 B.C. The Greek poem was composed as a tribute to Berenice, a princess of Cyrene who had married Ptolemy III (Euergetes) and thus become queen of Egypt. The basis of the poem was a vow made by the queen upon the departure of her new husband to Syria, where he was to engage in military action. Berenice promised to dedicate a lock of her hair in thanksgiving should Ptolemy safely return home; on his return, she did indeed cut off a lock of her hair, perhaps placing it in the temple of Aphrodite Zephyritis near Canopus. The lock, however, apparently disappeared, and Conon of Samos, the court astronomer, claimed that it had been transformed into a constellation, evermore to be known as the "Lock of Berenice".

Given the subject matter, it is no surprise that the Callimachean original was full of learned astronomical lore which has made some parts of the Catullan poem difficult for modern readers to comprehend. In fact, poem 66 stands as a most illustrative example of the scholarly nature of Alexandrian verse. Yet it ought not to be viewed merely as a cold, mechanical translation, valued only as a literary curiosity, for Catullus has adapted his raw material to suit his own style and purposes, and one need only note how the Latin poet has stressed the themes of married love and painful separation in his adaptation, giving the Callimachean poem a new (and thoroughly Catullan) emotional intensity. In this regard, poem 66 indeed shows a great affinity with poem 51, Catullus' adaptation of a Sapphic ode.

In structure, poem 66 falls into three basic segments: lines 1-38 provide the necessary background data, introducing the lock, Conon, Berenice and Ptolemy, and setting out the circumstances of the vow; lines 39-78 depict the severed lock lamenting its transference to the heavens; and lines 79-94 conclude the poem by focusing on the future offerings of unguents to the lock, a poor solace, we learn, for one so miserable at leaving its former home on the head of the

430

queen.

1. *qui*: the poem opens with the lock lauding the achievements of the astronomer Conon (*cf.* line 7 below).

   dispexit: "distinguished".

   lumina mundi: that is, the various constellations; *mundi* here has the sense of "the heavens" (*cf.* 64.206).

2. *comperit*: "came to understand" the daily movements of the stars.

   obitus: "settings".

3. *ut*: "how" (also in lines 4 and 5); governed by *comperit* in line 2.

   rapidi: here in the sense of "scorching".

   nitor: "brightness".

   obscuretur: as in an eclipse; note the spondaic ending.

4. *cedant*: "retreat" (as part of their annual motion).

5. *Triviam*: another name for Diana as the goddess of the Moon; *cf.* 34.13-16.

   sub Latmia saxa: "to the Latmian rocks"; Mt. Latmus was located in Caria and, according to legend, was where the Moon met with her beloved Endymion.

relegans: "banishing".

6. *gyro...aerio*: the Moon's "course in the sky".

   devocet: "calls down".

7. *idem*: the same man who so carefully studied the heavens discovered the lock (*me*) in the sky.

   <*in*> *lumine*: V read *numine* here, but most modern editors print *in lumine* or *in limine* ("on the threshold of the sky"); a similar problem is found later at line 59.

8. *Bereniceo*: an adjective formed from the proper name; translate as "of Berenice".

   caesariem: generally means "hair", but here rather "lock" of hair.

9. *clare*: "brightly".

   quam = *caesariem*.

   illa = Berenice.

10. *levia...brachia*: "delicate arms"; *cf.* 64.332.

    protendens: "stretching out" in prayer.

11. *qua...tempestate*: "at the time when".

novo auctus hymenaeo: "blessed with a new marriage"; the theme of marriage continues to unite all the long poems. There is a metrical hiatus between *novo* and *auctus*.

12. *vastatum...iverat*: "he had gone to lay waste"; *vastatum* is a supine used to express purpose.

Assyrios: here = *Syrios*; Ptolemy went to Syria to avenge the murder there of his sister (the queen of Syria) in 246 B.C., very soon after his marriage to Berenice.

13. *nocturnae...rixae*: in an erotic sense, a "nocturnal tussle".

vestigia: "traces".

14. *de*: "for" after *gesserat* ("had waged").

virgineis...exuviis: the martial image of these lines is completed by reference to the "spoils of a virgin".

15. *estne...Venus*: the lock now reflects upon the behavior of Berenice as her husband went off to war. Translate *novis nuptis* as "brides" (*cf.* 61.91); *novis nuptis odio* is a double dative in construction.

anne: the generally accepted emendation of the MSS.' *atque*.

16. *frustrantur*: "are disappointed".

17. *ubertim*: "copiously".

433

thalami...intra limina: "inside the threshold of the bedroom".

18. *ita me divi...iuerint*: a common oath: *cf.* 61.189-190, and 97.1 (a variation); *iuerint = iuverint* (perfect subjunctive).

    gemunt: "bewail".

19. *querellis*: tearful "complaints".

20. *invisente*: "going to see"; *cf.* 31.4.

    torva: "fierce".

    viro: here in the sense of "husband".

21. *at*: anticipates a false explanation offered by Berenice; "but" (you will say that). Some editors prefer to keep the MSS.' *et* here.

    orbum: "left desolate" by her husband's departure.

    luxti = luxisti (from *lugeo*).

22. *fratris*: Berenice and Ptolemy were first cousins; moreover, it was an ancient tradition in Egypt that royal brothers and sisters marry.

    flebile discidium: a "lamentable separation".

23. *cum*: temporal here.

exedit: "consumed".

cura: here in the sense of "anxiety".

medullas: cf. 35.15; 45.16; and 100.7.

24.   *ut*: "how"; note the dominant *t* sounds in this verse.

tibi: take with *sollicitae* ("worried").

25.   *sensibus ereptis*: cf. 51.5-6.

excidit: "failed".

at...certe: the MSS. here read *at ego certe*, resulting in a line too short for the meter; inserting *te* would solve the problem and provide an object for *cognoram* in the next line.

26.   *cognoram* = *cognoveram*.

magnanimam: "brave".

27.   *facinus*: "deed"; the action referred to is Berenice's role in the murder of her first husband, Demetrius of Macedonia. When he became sexually involved with Berenice's mother, the offended wife arranged his death, and then married Ptolemy to become the queen of Egypt.

28.   *coniugium*: "husband", that is, Ptolemy.

quod: refers back to *facinus* in line 27.

ausit = *audeat*; cf. 61.65.

alis = *alius*; cf. 29.15.

29. *sed tum*: that is, when Ptolemy was setting out for Syria.

maesta: with *verba*.

mittens: "letting go".

30. *Iuppiter*: cf. 1.7, and line 48 below.

tristi = *trivisti* (from *tero*, "rub").

lumina: here in the sense of "eyes".

31. *tantus*: "so powerful".

an quod: "or can it be that".

amantes: "lovers"; cf. 72.7.

32. *longe*: temporal ("for a long time").

33. *ibi*: "then".

cunctis...divis: cf. line 9 above.

pro: "on behalf of ".

34. *taurino sanguine*: "the blood of bulls" offered in sacrifice.

35. *reditum tetulisset*: "made a return"; *cf.* 63.47.

   haud...longo: "not at all long"; *cf.* line 32.

36. *Asiam*: Ptolemy seems to have subdued territory from Asia Minor to India in this particular venture.

37. *quis = quibus*; take with *pro factis*.

   reddita: here in the sense of "delivered".

   coetu: "assembly" (dative case); *cf.* 64.385.

38. *pristina vota*: "yesterday's vows", though not to be taken literally—more than one day had gone by.

   novo munere: balances *pristina vota*; translate as "recent service".

   dissoluo: "discharge"; scanned as four syllables.

39. The lock here begins a formal lament in the high tragic style.

   invita: repeated for emphasis at the start of the next line.

   cessi: "departed".

40. *adiuro*: with the accusative, "I swear by".

   tuumque caput: not just a traditional formula here, since the lock had actually been a part of that head in the past.

41.   *ferat*:   "suffer".

quod: that is, *tuumque caput*; object of *adiurarit* (which provides a spondaic ending to the line; *cf.* line 3 above).

inaniter: "falsely".

42.   *qui = quis.*

postulet: "would claim".

parem: "a match for", with *ferro*.

43.   *eversus*:   "brought down"; the poet refers in these lines to Xerxes digging a canal across the isthmus of Athos at the start of his invasion of Greece in 483 B.C.

oris: probably "region" in this context; *cf.*   64.281.

44.   *progenies Thiae*:   the "descendant of Thia" was Helios, the Sun god (hence the adjective *clara*).

supervehitur: "rides past" in his traditional chariot.

45.   *Medi*:   the Persians.

peperere: from *pario*; translate as "have created".

iuventus: take collectively to mean "soldiers"; modified by *barbara* in the next line.

46.   *navit*:   from *no*, "sail".

Athon: note how the key identifying word is left until the very end of the passage; *cf.* the delaying of Conon's name at the beginning of the poem.

47. *facient*: future tense.

48. *ut*: here introducing a wish.

Chalybon: a Greek genitive plural; the Chalybes were legendary workers in iron (some say they even discovered the metal) who inhabited the shores of the Black Sea.

49. *et qui principio*: "and he who in the beginning".

venas: "veins of ore".

50. *institit*: from *insto*, "apply oneself to"; with the infinitive *quaerere* in line 49.

stringere: if the reading is correct (some prefer to read *fingere*) this is a technical term for "drawing" molten metal into bars to harden.

duritiem: "hardness".

51. *abiunctae*: "detached"; take with *comae*, which in turn should be taken as being in apposition with *sorores*.

52. *Memnonis Aethiopis*: genitive singular; Memnon was the king of Ethiopia who fought on the Trojan side in the great war at Troy. The son of the goddess of

Dawn, Memnon was made immortal after his death at
Troy.

53. *unigena*: "brother"; *cf.* 64.300; the brother of Memnon was Zephyrus, the West Wind.

impellens: "setting in motion".

nutantibus: "flapping".

54. *obtulit*: with *se* in line 52.

Arsinoes Locridos ales equus: the "winged horse of
the Locrian Arsinoe" also identifies Zephyrus. Arsinoe
had been the sister and wife of Ptolemy II, and after
her death she was deified as Aphrodite Zephyritis;
"Locrian" was an epithet of Zephyrus. This elaborate
playing on names is typical of Alexandrian verse.

55. *isque*: that is, Zephyrus.

aetherias: "heavenly".

avolat: "flies away".

56. *Veneris* = Aphrodite Zephyritis = Arsinoe.

57. *suum...famulum*: Zephyrus.

eo: "for that purpose".

legarat = *legaverat*; "had sent".

58. *Graia*: the dynasty of the Ptolemies was Greek in

origin.

Canopeis: an emendation of the MSS.' *canopicis*; the town of Canopus was situated near Alexandria.

incola: "resident"; *cf.* 64.228.

59.   *inde Venus*: this verse in the MSS. begins *hi dii ven ibi*, and many emendations have been proposed; *inde Venus* seems to be the best of the lot.

solum: "only".

lumine: V read *numine*, and some editors prefer *limine*; *cf.* line 7 above.

60.   *Ariadnaeis...temporibus*: "the brows of Ariadne"; for Ariadne, *cf.* poem 64.

61.   *corona*: the crown bestowed on Ariadne by the god Dionysus, which was later transformed into a constellation not far from the Coma Berenices.

fulgeremus: with *ut* understood; another spondaic ending.

62.   *devotae...exuviae*: "the dedicated spoils"; for *exuviae*, *cf.* line 14 above.

flavi verticis: *cf.* 64.63.

63.   *uvidulam*: "a little moist" (the MSS. read *viridulum*).

a fluctu: because Aphrodite's temple was on the

441

coast.

cedentem: "departing".

templa deum: that is, the heavens; *deum* = *deorum*.

64. *sidus*: "constellation".

diva: the Venus of line 59.

65. *Virginis*: the constellation Virgo, which, like Leo, Callisto, and Bootes, lies not far from the Coma Berenices.

contingens: "bordering on".

namque: would normally appear earlier in the line.

66. *Callisto*: a Greek dative; Callisto was an Arcadian princess loved by Zeus and hated by Hera. When Hera transformed her into a bear, Zeus placed her in the heavens as Ursa Major, the Great Bear.

iuncta: "joined to", *i.e.*, close together.

Lycaoniae: Callisto is called "Lycaonian" because her father's name was Lycaon.

67. *vertor in occasum*: "I come round to my setting"; the verb is often used for the motion of heavenly bodies.

Booten: Bootes is another constellation.

68. *vix*: "barely"; take with *mergitur* ("is immersed").

   sero: "late".

69. *premunt*: "press hard on".

   vestigia divum: "the footsteps of the gods".

70. *autem*: here in the sense of "whereas".

   Tethyi: Tethys was a sea goddess, the wife of Oceanus; *cf.* 64.29-30. The form is a Greek dative.

   restituit: with *me* understood.

71. This and the next three lines form a parenthetical aside to the goddess Nemesis.

   pace tua: an idiom translated as "by your leave".

   hic: "at this point".

   Rhamnusia virgo: Nemesis had a shrine at Rhamnus in Attica; she was the goddess who punished people for presumption and arrogance, or simply for excessive good fortune. *Cf.* 64.395.

72. *ullo...timore*: causal ablative.

73. *nec si*: here in the sense of "not even if".

   infestis: "hostile".

   discerpent: "will revile".

74. *condita*: things that have been "stored up" in silence will now be disclosed (*evoluam*).

quin: "but rather", after *non tegam* in line 72.

75. The aside over, the lock resumes its thoughts of line 70.

tam...quam: "so much...as".

me afore: repeated at the start of the next verse, to stress the lock's feelings of separation.

76. *discrucior*: "I am in torment", with an accusative and infinitive; *cf. excrucior* at 85.2.

77. *quicum* = *cum quo*; it refers to *vertice* in line 76.

expers: "having no share in"; take with *ego*.

78. *unguentis*: apparently the costly perfumes used by married women.

una: adverbial; "together".

vilia: the MSS. read *milia*, which some editors defend; however, the lock seems to be making a comparison between the rich perfumes of wives and the inexpensive ones used by maidens—in which case, *vilia* ("cheap stuff") makes better sense.

79. *nunc vos*: here the lock makes a request of all women about to be wed; they are to offer rich scents to it.

quas: the logical correction of the MSS.' *quem*.

lumine: here not in the sense of "day", but in its primary sense of "light", *i.e.*, light from the torch.

taeda: *cf.*   61.15; also 64.25 and 302.

80.   *non* = *ne*.

prius: with *quam* in line 82.

unanimis: *cf.*   9.4 and 30.1.

81.   *nudantes*:   "baring".

reiecta: "cast off".

82.   *iucunda*:   take with *munera*.

libet: from *libo*, "pour".

onyx: a stone vessel used to contain perfumes.

83.   *vester*:   offerings are sought not from every woman, but from the chaste.

colitis: "honor".

iura: in this context, the "laws of marriage".

84.   *sed quae*:   "but the woman who".

impuro: "vile".

85.   *a*:   an interjection.

    levis: with *pulvis*.

    irrita: her gifts are "ineffective" because they are not accepted by the lock.

86.   *praemia*:   here in the sense of "gifts" or "offerings".

87.   *sed magis*:   "but rather" (than being adulterous).

    semper concordia: balanced by *semper amor* in the next line; *concordia* is best translated as "harmony".

    vestras: with *sedes* in line 88.

88.   *sedes*:   "homes".

    assiduus: "continual".

89.   The lock now addresses Berenice one last time.

    tuens...sidera: "gazing at the stars"; *tuens* is the participle of *tueor*.

90.   *placabis*:   "appease" by offerings.

    luminibus: here "days"; contrast line 79 above.

91.   *unguinis expertem*:   "lacking perfume"; *expertem* here takes the genitive of *unguen*, but *cf.* lines 77-78. *Unguinis* is the generally accepted emendation of the MSS.' *sanguinis*.

non = *ne*; *cf.* line 80.

siris = *siveris*, perfect subjunctive of *sino*; the MSS., however, read *vestris*.

tuam me: "I who am yours".

92. *largis*: "copious".

affice: an emendation of the MSS.' *effice*; translate as "endow".

93. *corruerint*: suggested in place of the MSS.' *cur iterent* (defended by some editors); the lock seems to be saying "let the stars fall from the heavens".

coma regia fiam: that is, the lock would return to its mistress' head.

94. *proximus*: "next to", with *Oarion* (Orion).

Hydrochoi: Aquarius (the form is dative).

fulgeret: the sense is clear, but there is some controversy over the form of the verb; while some maintain it to be the imperfect subjunctive of *fulgere*, the majority of editors see it as the present subjunctive of *fulgerare*, which is, in turn, an archaic form of *fulgurare*, "to gleam" or "to flash". The meter would seem to support this last interpretation.

67

A conversation between the poet (in the role of a

passerby) and the door of a house with a poor reputation. The setting is the town of Verona, and the poem is full of local color—making it extremely difficult for a modern audience to comprehend fully. Indeed, it would seem that Catullus intended the poem for a very specific audience which would be knowledgeable about the matters detailed; he purposely employs ambiguous wording in key passages (see commentary below) to prevent "outsiders" from following the details of the piece. As a result, poem 67 has generated a great deal of scholarly disputation and very little consensus.

In general, the "dramatic plot" is as follows: a passerby asks the door for an explanation of its alleged "bad behavior", and receives a scandalous tale of an immoral woman who once lived within; the door claims that it is innocent of any charges of wrong-doing: the fault all lies with the unnamed woman, who certainly must have been well known to the intended audience of the poem.

In keeping with its informal tone, poem 67 has an irregular structure, loosely based on an alternation of speakers. The first eight lines are spoken by the poet to the door and accuse the door of straying from its previously faithful path; in the next six lines the personified door indignantly asserts its innocence. Lines 15-18 feature an exchange between the door and the poet, in which the door is invited to tell its side of the story, which it does in lines 19-28; this ten-line segment focuses on the previous marriage of the unnamed woman and relates a shameful tale of improper sexual activity. The poet interrupts at lines 29-30 with a sarcastic remark, but the door then resumes its tale in lines 31-36; here the additional sexual liaisons of the woman are detailed. In lines 37-44 the door explains the source of its information, thus assuring the poet of the veracity of what it has said, and the poem then concludes (lines 45-48) with an enigmatic allusion to yet another sexual escapade of the woman.

1. The poem begins with two lines that would be appropriate as part of an epithalamium (*cf.* poems 61 and 62), thus maintaining the nuptial motif which runs through the long poems; of course, marriage will continue to be a major theme as the poem develops.

   dulci...viro: not "husband" as the epithalamium-like beginning suggests, but rather "master" as line 3 makes clear; *cf.* 66.33.

   parenti: not the parent of a bride, but the parent of the *viro* just alluded to in this line.

2. *bona...ope*: *cf.* 34.23.

   auctet: literally, "increase", but here in the sense of "make prosper". The words are still appropriate to a bride as part of a marriage song, but with the next line the poet will show that he has been playfully deceiving his audience.

3. *ianua*: the addressee is *not* a woman, but a door! The audience must now "rethink" the preceding couplet.

   Balbo: all we know of this person comes from these lines: he owned the house when he was an old man (*senex*, line 4), and he had a son (line 5).

servisse benigne: cf. *servisse maligne* in line 5.

4. *olim*: "once" (in the past).

    sedes: "house".

5. *ferunt*: cf. *dicunt* in line 3; as befits a poem full of gossip, "they say" plays a large role in the vocabulary of the piece.

    rursus: "on the contrary".

    gnato: the commonly accepted emendation of the MSS.' *voto*; this must be the son of Balbus, but no proper name is furnished here. Given the fact that the first line of the poem referred to a father and son, it seems reasonable to assume (though Catullus does not specifically say so) that this Balbus and his son are also the characters alluded to in that opening verse.

6. *es...facta marita*: emended from V's *postquam est porrecto facta marite sene*; some editors, however, are troubled by the concept of a door being said to become married, and it is tempting to accept Badian's suggestion that we read *postquam est porrecto pacta marita sene* (in "The Case of the Door's Marriage", *Harvard Studies in Classical Philology* 84 [1980] 81-89). If *es...facta marita* is retained, it must refer to the marriage of the door's new owner, indicating per-haps that old Balbus was a widower.

    porrecto: "stretched out" in death; cf. 61.211.

7. *agedum*: cf. 63.78; V apparently read *dic age de vobis*.

   feraris: cf. *ferunt* in line 5.

8. *veterem*: used ambiguously here in that it can modify either *dominum* or *fidem*; the poet seems to want us to apply it to both.

   deseruisse: "to have abandoned", a word appropriate to a personified door.

9. *Caecilio*: one of the basic problems of the poem is the relationship of this Caecilius to Balbus and his son. The door here tells us that it now belongs to Caecilius, and the simplest conclusion for a reader to come to is that this man is the son of the old Balbus, with his full name being Caecilius Balbus. Some editors, however, prefer to see in Caecilius a man who is totally unrelated to the Balbi, who merely happens to own the house formerly in their possession. It must be recognized that Catullus could have made the relationship between Caecilius and Balbus clearer *if* he had so desired.

   tradita nunc sum: the phrase has a nuptial ring, as if the door were a bride coming to the house of her new mate; cf. 62.60 and 66.81.

10. *est*: note that the door uses the present tense—a clue that its alleged wrong-doing lay not in the past but in the present when Caecilius is owner of the house.

11. *peccatum*: "done wrong".

     pote: *cf.* 17.24.

12. "But what is a door to do with those people"; take
     faciat as a subjunctive in a deliberative context. The
     MSS. are corrupt, reading *verum istius populi ianua*
     qui te facit—impossible both metrically and grammati-
     cally.

13. *quacumque*: "whenever"; *cf.* 64.43.

14. *clamant*: "shout".

15. *istuc*: here in the sense of *istud*.

     uno...verbo: "by word alone"; the poet insists that
     the door must prove the truth of its words.

16. *facere ut*: "bring it about (that)".

     quivis: "anyone at all".

17. *Qui*: "how"; the door is characterized as a rather
     pouty creature feeling somewhat sorry for itself.

     quaerit: here in the sense of "makes inquiries".

     laborat: "is anxious".

18. *Nos = ego*; the poet offers himself as a proper audi-
     ence for the door.

     nobis dicere: *cf.* line 7 above.

ne dubita: for similar prohibitions, *cf.*   61.193 and 62.59.

19.   *Primum igitur*:   a breathless beginning to the door's tale; the poet's request for information now releases a flood of unpleasant revelations.

quod: "that".

tradita: *cf.* line 9 above; here the nuptial sense of the word is entirely appropriate.

nobis: probably standing for the house *in toto*, though it is not impossible that it simply equals *mihi*.

20.   *illam*:   so the woman will always be referred to, her name never appearing in the poem.

vir prior: one of the most contentious phrases in the poem. Two interpretations have been argued: first, that the phrase refers to a former husband of the lady in question; second, that *prior* is predicative and means "her husband wasn't the first" to have her. This latter interpretation seems rather strained, however, and the reader's initial instinct would be to take *vir prior* as a former (unnamed) husband who had been sexually deficient; in this case, *attigerit* should be taken as a concessive subjunctive (although some editors prefer to change *attigerit* to *attigerat*).

21.   *languidior*:   "weaker"; *cf.* 25.3.

tenera: in the sense of not being fully mature; with

beta, an ablative of comparison.

sicula: literally, a small dagger; here a euphemism for penis.

22. For this line, *cf.* poem 32.

23. *pater illius*: "the father of that man" (*i.e.*, the *vir prior*); the second syllable in *illius* is long here.

gnati: take with *cubile*.

violasse = *violavisse*; *cf. conscelerasse* in the next line.

24. *miseram*: "wretched".

conscelerasse: "to have disgraced".

25. *sive quod*: the door as analyst tries to comprehend what would lead a father to behave in such an outrageous way.

caeco: his love was "blind" to the moral issue at stake.

26. *iners*: "inactive" in a sexual sense; *cf.* 61.124.

sterili: *cf.* 63.69.

27. *quaerendum unde* <*unde*>: the widely accepted emendation of V's *querendum unde*; *unde unde* would have the sense of "somehow or other".

nervosius: "more vigorous"; *cf. iners* in line 26.

28. *zonam solvere virgineam*: *cf.* 2B.3.

29. The poet interrupts with an ironic comment, with the adjectives *egregium* and *mira* heavily sarcastic in tone.

30. *sui gnati...gremium*: that is, the *gremium* of his son's wife; *minxerit* (from *meio*, "to make water" — *cf.* 78B.2 and 99.10) *in gremium* refers to the sex act.

31. *Atqui*: the door excitedly adds that there is more to come in the way of scandal.

    cognitum habere: translate simply as "knew".

32. *Brixia*: a town originally founded by the Cenomani people in Cisalpine Gaul; the modern Brescia, it lies not far from Verona.

    Cycneae supposita speculae: an emendation of the MSS.' garbled *chinea suppositum specula*; translate as "placed under the watchtower of Cycnus". In myth, Cycnus ("Swan") was a young prince transformed into a swan as he lamented the death of Phaethon (the son of the Sun, who died driving his father's chariot). This and the following verses tell us that the unnamed woman had once lived in Brixia, where she indulged in her sexual peccadilloes.

33. *quam*: refers to Brixia.

    molli: "gentle".

Mella: a river about a mile (2 km) west of Brixia.

34. *Veronae mater amata meae*: another enigmatic phrase; ancient sources do not make Brixia the "Mother City" of Verona, although both were connected with the Cenomani. *Meae* refers to the fact that the door itself is located in Verona.

35. *Postumio et Corneli*: two other lovers of the woman; neither can be identified with any degree of confidence, although some editors suggest that the latter is the Cornelius of poem 102.

36. *malum...adulterium*: "vile adultery"; *adulterium*, of course, implies that the woman was married during her liaisons with Postumius and Cornelius.

37. *dixerit hic aliquis*: the door anticipates someone asking how on earth it (situated in Verona) can know about the woman's life in Brixia; take *hic* as "at this point".

istaec: all the scandals so far related.

nosti = novisti.

38. *cui*: "for whom".

limine: "threshold".

39. *auscultare*: "listen to".

suffixa tigillo: "fastened to the lintel"; *tigillum* literally is a small beam of wood, in which would be set a vertical pivot for the door (the other pivot being set into the sill).

40. *tantum*: here in the sense of "merely".

41. *furtiva*: "hushed".

42. *ancillis*: her female slaves, in whom she tended to confide.

    flagitia: "sins".

43. *quos diximus*: that is, the Postumius and Cornelius of line 35.

    utpote: "inasmuch as".

    quae = illa.

44. *speraret*: V seems to have read *sperent* here; translate as "trusted".

45. *praeterea*: the door comes to the end of its tale, saving the "juiciest tidbit" for the last.

    quendam, quem dicere nolo: in strong contrast to lines 35 and 43, where identities were made clear; the door, however, is about to provide its audience with enough clues to make an identification of this mysterious man.

46. *rubra*: somewhat ambiguous: did the man literally have red facial hair, or are his brows red with anger? The former seems slightly more probable, and would

furnish the audience with a good clue.

47. *longus*: here "tall"; *cf.* 86.1.

   lites: "lawsuits".

48. *falsum...puerperium*: a "false childbirth"; it would seem that an earlier lover of this man accused him (falsely) of making her pregnant.

   ventre: "womb".

68A

In the Catullan manuscripts no break appeared between 68A (1-40) and 68B (41-160), and many scholars in the past have treated these lines as a single poem (for this so-called "unitarian" position, *cf.* the now standard article of H.W. Prescott entitled "The Unity of Catullus LXVIII" in *TAPA* 71 [1940] 473-500). In more recent years, however, a consensus has been growing that 68A and 68B are in fact two separate poems; not only are the names of the respective addressees different (Manlius vs. Allius), but even striking differences in detail mark each work (for example, in 68A the poet has set aside the pleasures of love, but in 68B he has not). Moreover, that the poet would write nearly the same dirge for his deceased brother *twice* in a single poem (20-24 and 92-96) strikes most scholars as inherently unlikely. Finally, lines 1-40 are undeniably complete in themselves, telling a fully coherent tale (for a "separatist" analysis of the poem, *cf.* M.B. Skinner's "The Unity of Catullus 68: The Structure of 68a", *TAPA* 103 [1972] 495-512).

Poem 68A, then, depicts the following scenario: Manlius is in great distress, unable to sleep or even to find solace for his sleeplessness in reading the "classics"; the cause of his suffering is that he presently sleeps alone, with no one to love. He thus writes to Catullus with two requests (line 10): send him gifts of the Muses, and gifts of Venus. The poet, however, is himself in great distress, being in Verona after the unexpected death of his beloved brother, and so he cannot honor either one of Manlius' requests. Poem 68A is basically an apology from Catullus to Manlius, explaining why the poet cannot oblige his friend. As a poetic epistle, it very much resembles poem 65, the difference being that 65 clearly announces its companion poem (66), while 68A in no way points to poem 68B as an accompanying work.

Skinner (*art. cit.*), building on the work of other separatists, has thoroughly demonstrated the structural sophistication of 68A. The poem has three basic divisions: lines 1-14 serve as a prologue, lines 15-26 focus upon the death of the poet's brother, and lines 27-40 present the concluding apology. Thus the poem has a strict 14+12+14 structure, and Skinner also shows that each of the three basic segments can in turn be divided in two. She concludes that 68A "is a finished artistic product....No essential element is lacking, and any attempt at expansion would destroy the perfect balance the poet has already achieved" (p. 509).

1. *casuque*: "and chance".

   oppressus: "crushed".

2. *conscriptum...lacrimis*: "written in tears".

epistolium: a diminutive form—Manlius sent the poet a short note.

3. *naufragum*: the image of a shipwrecked man will soon be applied to Catullus himself in line 13.

    ut: introduces a purpose clause.

    eiectum: "run aground".

4. *sublevem*: "lift up".

    restituam: "bring back".

5. *sancta Venus*: cf. 36.3.

    requiescere: "find rest".

6. *desertum*: here in the sense of "left behind".

    caelibe: this adjective normally is used to refer to someone not having a spouse, either through being unmarried or through being widowed; in the context of this verse, all that is certain is that Manlius now sleeps alone.

    perpetitur: "allows".

7. *veterum...scriptorum*: most likely Catullus refers to the ancient Greek poets.

8. *oblectant*: "delight".

    cum: temporal.

pervigilat: Manlius "stays awake all night" in his torment; *cf.* 88.2.

9.   *id*: used to sum up the preceding lines in general.

gratum: "pleasing".

10.   *muneraque et Musarum...et Veneris*: it would seem that Manlius makes two distinct requests of the poet, one having to do with poetry (*Musarum*) and the other with love (*Veneris*); the exact nature of the latter is much debated, but one of the more logical views is that Manlius asks Catullus for sexual gratification. *Cf.* line 27ff., where Manlius is certainly eager to lure the poet to Rome.

hinc: that is, from Catullus.

11.   *incommoda*: "misfortunes" (*cf. commoda* in line 21); Catullus must make it clear that Manlius is not the only person in torment at the moment.

Manli: the widely accepted correction of V's corrupt *Mali*; that this is the Manlius of poem 61 is risky speculation. It should be noted that some editors prefer to read *Mallius*.

12.   *odisse*: "disdain".

hospitis: whether the poet was host or guest remains unclear; what is more important is that either role was seen to impose an obligation (*officium*) on those involved.

461

13.   *accipe*: "hear".

quis = *quibus*; with *fluctibus*.

merser: "am overwhelmed"; subjunctive in an indirect question.

14.   *amplius*: "any longer".

beata: in the sense that the giver need be "happy" himself in order to offer the present.

petas: *cf.* line 10 above.

15.   *tempore quo*: "ever since the time when"; *cf.* 35.13.

vestis...pura: refers to the all-white *toga virilis* assumed by youths around the age of 16; as boys they wore the *toga praetexta*, which had a purple border.

16.   *aetas*: take here as "life".

florida: *cf.* 61.57.

ageret: "was passing".

17.   *multa satis ludi*: refers to the experience of love; *cf. ludere* at 17.17, and see also 61.203-204.

dea: Venus.

nescia nostri: "unaware of me".

18. *curis miscet*: *cf.* 64.95; that love was bitter-sweet was an old theme even by the time of Catullus.

19. *studium*: his "enthusiasm" for love.

    luctu: "grief".

    fraterna...mors: translate as "my brother's death".

20. For this address to his brother, *cf.* 65.10ff.; 101.5ff.; and especially 68B.92ff. Note how the words *fraterna/frater* are repeated in this segment, and *cf.* the use of *tu/tuus/tecum*.

    adempte: "taken away" (from *adimo*).

21. *mea*: with *commoda*; the preponderance of *m* and *n* sounds in these lines lends them a mournful tone; *cf.* 101.

    fregisti: from *frango*.

    commoda: "everything good"; *cf.* line 11 above.

22. *tecum una*: "along with you"; repeated in the next line.

    est...sepulta: "is buried" (from *sepelio*).

24. *in vita*: that is, while he was still living.

    dulcis...amor: balances *dulcem...amaritiem* in line 18.

    alebat: "used to promote".

25. *fugavi*: from *fugo*, "put to flight".

26. *studia*: *cf.* line 19 above.

    delicias: erotic in nature; *cf.* 45.24 and 74.2.

27. This and the next three lines have generated much debate; the basic problem turns upon whether Catullus is quoting directly from Manlius' note (a theory accepted here).

    Veronae: "at Verona" (locative).

    turpe: with *est* understood.

    Catulle: the reading of the MSS., but those who do not see a direct quotation here change it to *Catullo*.

28. *hic*: if a direct quotation, Rome; if not, Verona.

    quisquis de meliore nota: "anyone who is of better quality"; this may well be an oblique way for Manlius to describe himself.

29. *deserto...cubili*: that Manlius is referring to himself is supported by the fact that his bed had already been described as *desertum* in line 6.

    tepefactat: "tries to warm"; an emendation of the MSS.' *tepefacit*, which is metrically impossible. *Cf.* the commentary on line 10.

30. *id*: sums up the quotation just concluded; *cf.* line 9.

magis: "rather".

31. *ignosces*: "you will pardon (me)".

   luctus ademit: *cf.* lines 19-20.

32. *munera*: *cf.* line 10.

   cum nequeo: in sum, his brother's death has made
   the poet unable to oblige Manlius in the latter's quest
   for sexual stimulation. Catullus, having made it clear
   that he cannot furnish *munera Veneris*, next turns his
   attention to *munera Musarum*. (Students interested
   in the homosexual interpretation of this part of the
   poem may consult T.E. Kinsey's "Some Problems in
   Catullus 68", *Latomus* 26 [1967] 35-53.)

33. *nam, quod*: transitional to a new topic (*i.e.*, the
   request for *munera Musarum*); translate as "moreover,
   as to the fact that".

   scriptorum: ambiguous, since it could be the genitive
   plural of either *scriptor* (author) or *scripta* (writings).
   In context, however, the former seems more probable:
   Catullus needs books in order to fashion a learned
   poem for Manlius (perhaps akin to poem 66).

   copia: here in the sense of "number", but *cf.* line
   40.

34. *hoc*: nominative.

35. *sedes*: "abode".

carpitur: "is passed"; for *aetas*, *cf.* line 16 above.

36. *huc*: that is, Verona.

capsula: a cylindrical container used to store books (as rolls).

37. *quod cum ita sit*: "since this is the way it is".

statuas: "conclude"; subjunctive after *nolim*.

maligna: "unkind"; *cf.* 10.18.

38. *id*: that is, not honor Manlius' request for verse.

ingenuo: here more in the sense of "generous".

39. *utriusque*: indicates the two-fold nature of the request in Manlius' short note; *cf.* line 10.

petenti: with *tibi*.

posta = *posita*; "supplied".

40. *ultro*: "unasked, of my own accord".

deferrem: "I would have offered".

copia: a possible pun here, playing on a secondary meaning of the noun, "opportunity".

68B

The last of the long poems, 68B is in some ways the most innovative, and foreshadows the polished love elegies of such later poets as Propertius and Tibullus. At its surface level, the poem is a panegyric on behalf of one Allius (otherwise unknown), who seemingly came to the poet's aid by providing a safe meeting-place for Catullus and Lesbia (presumably during the early stages of their relationship). But, at a deeper level, poem 68B is not only a thanks-offering to Allius, but also a love poem intended for Lesbia herself, whom it both compliments—by comparing her to the mythical Laodamia who passionately loved a man (Protesilaus) doomed to die at Troy—and cautions—by acknowledging her lack of fidelity to the poet alone. Indeed, the simple number of verses pertaining either directly or indirectly to Lesbia (see below) makes it clear that she dominates the thoughts of the poet in this poem (as she will continue to dominate them in the epigrams which follow). And yet, on a third level, poem 68B also speaks to the death of Catullus' brother—a death which stands at the emotional center of the elegy.

These three themes (Allius, Lesbia, the brother) are most intricately blended in a structure that qualifies as "Alexandrian" and belies any impression of a poem spontaneously "thrown together". As scholars have long recognized, poem 68B has a pyramidal form, best depicted by the following figure:

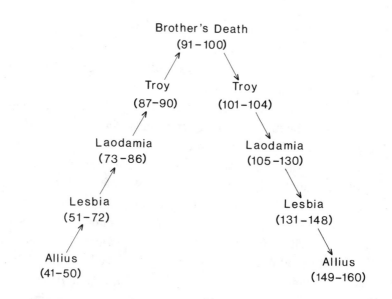

For a similarly complex structure, *cf.* poem 64.

41. The traditional numbering of lines (as if poems 68A and 68B were one piece) is maintained for ease of reference.

reticere: "keep silent".

deae: the Muses.

qua me Allius: V read here *quam fallius*, but the appearance of the name Allius elsewhere in 68B makes its restoration in this line certain.

42. *iuverit...iuverit*: repeated to emphasize Allius' kindness towards the poet (soon to be explained in detail).

officiis: "services"; *cf.* line 150 below.

468

43. *ne*: the commonly accepted emendation of the MSS.'
nec; *cf.* line 151.

saeclis = saeculis.

obliviscentibus: "that bring forgetfulness".

44. *caeca*: here in the sense of "dark".

studium: perhaps "devoted zeal" best conveys the
sense of the Latin here.

45. *vobis*: the Muses again.

porro: "in future time"; *cf.* 45.3.

46. *facite*: "bring it about that".

carta: that is, the paper on which the poem is
written.

anus: with *carta*, "even when it is old"; *cf.* 78B.4.

47. A hexameter line is missing here in the MSS.

48. *notescatque*: the subject seems to be Allius.

magis...magis: *cf.* 38.3 and 64.274.

49. *texens*: "weaving"; note the alliteration of *t*.

sublimis: "up in the air".

telam: "web".

50. *deserto*: here "abandoned in neglect"; the general image is one of a monument abandoned to oblivion.

51. *nam*: the poet begins to explain his debt to Allius.

duplex Amathusia: Amathusia is another name for Venus (taken from a town on her favored island of Cyprus); *cf.* 36.14. Venus is "two-faced" because she brings both blessings and curses; *cf.* 64.95 and 68A.18.

52. *scitis*: the poet is still speaking to the Muses.

torruerit: "scorched"; some prefer the MSS. reading *corruerit* in the sense of "overthrew", but the emendation is supported by *arderem* in the following verse.

genere: "respect".

53. *Trinacria rupes*: Mt. Etna, the fiery volcano of Sicily.

54. *lymphaque...Malia*: the district of Malis in Greece was known for its hot springs.

Oetaeis...Thermopylis: Thermopylae (in Malis) was not far from Mt. Oeta; *cf.* 62.7. The collocation of three proper names gives this verse a very Alexandrian tone.

55. *maesta*: with *lumina* ("eyes" here).

tabescere: "waste away".

56. *imbre*: the rain is that of tears.

   genae: "cheeks"; subject of *madere*.

57. *qualis*: the image which now appears has generated a great deal of controversy: does it refer back to illustrate the tears of the poet, or does it look ahead to the help supplied by Allius (*cf.* line 66)? In truth, it seems to pertain to both, forming a transition from the poet to Allius.

   aerii: "lofty".

   perlucens: with *rivus* in line 58; the mountain brook is "shining out" against the darker stone around it.

58. *muscoso*: "mossy".

59. *prona*: "sloping"; with *valle*. For the phrase *prona praeceps*, *cf.* 65.23.

60. *densi*: in population.

   transit iter: "makes its way".

61. *lasso*: "exhausted"; capable of modifying either *viatori* or *sudore*.

   levamen: "comfort"; the image of the brook as a comfort to the weary traveller was common in Greek poetry.

62. *gravis*: "severe"; with *aestus*.

exustos: "burnt up".

hiulcat: "splits open", that is, cracks appear in the dried out fields.

63.   *hic*: "at this point"; some editors prefer to read *ac*.

velut: a new image now develops, that of a favorable wind suddenly appearing to storm-tossed sailors—another traditional motif in ancient poetry.

turbine: "storm".

64.   *lenius*: "more gently".

secunda: "favorable"; *cf.* 4.21.

65.   *Pollucis...Castoris*: Castor and Pollux were the divine protectors of sailors; *cf.* 4.27. Both names are objective genitives after *prece*.

implorata: nominative, in agreement with *aura* in line 64; note the spondaic ending of this verse.

66.   *nobis = mihi*.

67.   *clausum...campum*: "a closed field"; note how the phrase is balanced in the line by *lato...limite* ("broad path").

patefecit: "opened up"; Allius provided the poet with "access" to Lesbia, as the following lines make clear.

68. *isque...isque*: taken with *is* in the preceding line emphasizes the key role played by Allius.

nobis = *mihi*; completed by *dominae* ("a house for me and my mistress"). Some retain the MSS.' *dominam*, however, thus introducing an unknown woman to the scene.

69. *communes...amores*: a love that was mutual.

exerceremus: "carry on".

70. *quo*: "where".

molli: "delicate".

candida diva: Lesbia is not only "radiant", she has also become a goddess in the eyes of her lover.

71. *trito*: the threshold is "well-worn" because it is used so often by the lovers.

plantam: the sole of the foot.

72. *innixa*: from *innitor*, "rest"; nominative case.

arguta...solea: Lesbia's sandal seems to have made a noise of some kind, and most editors translate *arguta* as "creaking"; *solea* is ablative.

constituit: "set down"; the entire image reminds one of the approach of a bride to her new home; *cf.* 61.159ff.

73. Here begins a lengthy (lines 73-130) simile, comparing Lesbia to the mythical Laodamia, whose newly-wedded husband (Protesilaus) was the first Greek slain at Troy.

coniugis...amore: "love for her husband".

ut quondam: "as once upon a time".

74. *Protesilaeam*: adjectival form of the proper name. The three words of this line symbolize the joining of the two lovers into a single *domus*.

75. *frustra*: "in vain", since Protesilaus was soon to die.

nondum cum: "since not yet".

76. *hostia*: a sacrificial animal.

pacificasset = *pacificavisset*, "had appeased". It would seem that the proper rites had not been performed, and the next lines imply that the reason was simple impatience caused by overwhelming passion.

77. *mihi*: the poet now interjects a prayer of his own, addressed to Nemesis (*Rhamnusia virgo*); for Nemesis, *cf.* 64.395 and 66.71.

tam valde: "so intensely".

78. *quod*: "that".

invitis...eris: that is, against the will of the gods; *cf.* 76.12.

474

79. *quam ieiuna...ara*: "how much the thirsty altar".

80. *amisso*: "lost".

81. *ante*: completed by *quam* in the next line.

   coacta: in agreement with *Laodamia* in line 80.

   dimittere: "let go"; governed by *coacta*.

82. *una atque altera...hiems*: "one and then another winter".

83. *in*: here has the sense of "during".

   saturasset = saturavisset; pluperfect subjunctive after *antequam* (*cf.* note on line 81).

84. *posset ut*: result clause; the subject is Laodamia.

   abrupto: "cut short".

85. *quod*: that is, that the union would be cut short.

   scibant = sciebant.

   Parcae: the Fates; *cf.* 64.306ff.

   non longo tempore abesse: "was not a long time off".

86. *miles*: "as a soldier".

   Iliacos: "of Troy"; Ilium was another name for the

475

city.

87. *raptu*: causal ablative.

primores: with *viros* in line 88; translate as "foremost men", that is, "heroes".

Argivorum = *Graecorum*. Homer frequently refers to the Greeks collectively as Argives in the *Iliad*; Argos was a prominent town of southern Greece.

88. *ciere*: "to summon".

89. *Troia*: note the emphatic repetition of the name in these lines; this dwelling on Troy as a graveyard will next lead the poet to his brother's death there.

(*nefas!*): "shame!"; a parenthetical exclamation.

commune sepulcrum: both Greeks and Trojans died there in great numbers; *cf. communes...amores* at line 69.

90. *acerba cinis*: in the sense of a "premature grave"; note that *cinis* is here treated as a feminine noun, but as a masculine noun (its usual gender) at line 98. *Cf.* also 101.4. The elisions in this line give it a "choking" sound quite appropriate to the sense.

91. *quaene etiam*: an emendation of the MSS.' corrupt *que vetet id*; take *quaene* in the sense of "Troy (was it) which". Here begins not a digression, but the emotional focal point of the poem as a whole.

92. For this verse, *cf.* 68A.20 and 101.6. Note how the *misero frater* of this line becomes *misero fratri* in the next: both brothers are indeed *miser*, though for differing reasons.

93. *lumen*: "light of life".

   ademptum: the repetition reinforces the sense of loss.

94 - *Cf.* 68A.22-24.
96.

97. *quem nunc*: the poet now makes the transition from his brother back to Troy and then to Laodamia.

   tam longe: take with *compositum* in the next line.

   nota: "familiar".

98. *cognatos*: "related".

   compositum: "interred".

99. *Troia...Troia*: both ablatives, with *sepultum*.

   obscena...infelice: Troy was "ill-omened" and "wretched".

100. *detinet*: its object is the *quem* of line 97.

   extremo...solo: "a land far away"; *cf.* 11.2.

101. *ad quam*: we return now to the tale of Protesilaus

and Laodamia, left at line 90.

lecta: in the MSS. this line is incomplete, and *lecta* ("chosen") seems a plausible addition; *cf.* 64.4.

pubes: in a collective sense, the "young men".

102. *penetralis...focos*: the hearths in the inmost part of the homes were symbolic of the homes themselves.

deseruisse: "forsake".

103. *Paris*: the Trojan prince who abducted Helen (here called *moecha*, that is, an adulteress; *cf.* 42.3).

gavisus: from *gaudeo*.

libera: "undisturbed"; modifying *otia* in the next line. *Cf.* 64.402.

104. *pacato*: "tranquil".

degeret: in expressions of time, "pass" or "spend".

105. *quo...casu*: causal ablative; for *casu*, *cf.* 68A.1.

tibi: the poet's attention is now fully on Laodamia.

106. *ereptum est*: with violence implied; *cf.* 82.3.

anima: "breath", *i.e.*, the breath of life.

107. *coniugium*: "husband"; *cf.* 66.28.

tanto: here begins one of the most detailed and striking images in the Catullan corpus, comparing the love of Laodamia to a deep abyss.

absorbens: "swallowing up".

vertice: here a "whirlpool" or "eddy"; note how *amoris* can be taken either with *vertice* or with *aestus* in the next line.

108.   *aestus*:   the "surge" of passion.

abruptum...barathrum: "steep abyss"; *barathrum* seems to have been used in a technical sense to indicate an underground channel used to drain off excess waters, but the poet's main emphasis here is on the *depth* of the abyss (*cf.* line 117 below).

109.   *quale ferunt Grai*:   a specific *barathrum* is chosen to illustrate the point. Take *ferunt* as "say".

Pheneum prope Cyllenaeum: Pheneus was a town in northern Arcadia not far from Mt. Cyllene; *Cyllenaeum* is an adjective formed from the proper name (*cf. Protesilaeam* at line 74). Note the spondaic ending of the verse.

110.   *siccare*:   "dries up".

emulsa: from *emulgeo*, "drain"; take with *palude*.

pingue: "rich".

111.   *caesis...medullis*:   the "insides" of the mountain (Mt.

Cyllene) were "split open" by Heracles when he dug the *barathrum*.

112. *audit*: "is said".

falsiparens Amphitryoniades: an epic-style allusion to Heracles; Amphitryon was the supposed father of the hero, whose actual sire was the god Zeus—hence the term *falsiparens* is applied to the "son" of Amphitryon.

113. *tempore quo*: as in many a Homeric image, the mythical allusion is finely detailed, almost taking on a life of its own.

certa: with *sagitta*.

Stymphalia monstra: Stymphalus was a lake near Pheneus where Heracles (as part of his Labors) killed birds that fed on human flesh.

114. *perculit*: from *percello*, "strike".

imperio deterioris eri: during his Labors, Heracles was the servant of Eurystheus, the king of Mycenae.

115. *pluribus...divis*: since Heracles was to become a god.

caeli: "heaven".

tereretur: "be frequented".

116. *Hebe*: the goddess of youth, who was to become the bride of the new god Heracles.

117. *sed tuus...amor*: the comparison now ends, with the poet's attention back on Laodamia, whose love for Protesilaus was even deeper than that thoroughly described abyss.

118. *qui*: that is, *amor*.

indomitam: Laodamia was, up to this point, "untamed" by love; *tamen indomitam* is the widely accepted emendation of the MSS.' *tuum domitum. Cf.* 63.33.

119. *nam*: a new image appears in a further attempt to convey the depth of Laodamia's passion.

tam carum: with *caput* in the next line.

confecto: "consumed".

parenti: dative after *carum*.

120. *una...nata*: the old man has only one child, a daughter.

seri: "late" in the sense of being born late in the life of his grandfather.

121. *qui*: that is, the *nepos*.

divitiis...avitis: "grandfather's riches"; the child will be his grandfather's legal heir.

vix tandem: "just in the nick of time".

122. *testatas...tabulas*: "the will that has been properly witnessed", *i.e.*, is legally valid.

123. *derisi gentilis*: the kinsman who hoped to inherit (before the birth of the child) now becomes "laughed at".

   tollens: here in the sense of "taking away".

124. *suscitat*: "dislodges".

   volturium: that is, the all too eager kinsman.

   capiti: an archaic form of the ablative.

125. *nec*: another image, comparing Laodamia's passion to that of a dove for its mate.

   gavisa est: *cf.* line 103 above.

   columbo: "dove"; *cf.* 29.8.

126. *compar*: female "mate".

   improbius: "more greedily".

127. *mordenti...rostro*: "nipping beak".

   decerpere: "to snatch".

128. *quam*: after *multo...improbius* in line 126.

   multivola: "lustful".

482

129. *sed tu*: the images completed, the poet speaks directly to Laodamia.

vicisti: "have surpassed".

130. *ut semel*: "when first".

conciliata: "united in marriage".

131. *aut nihil aut paulo*: "either a little or not at all".

cui: Laodamia.

concedere: "yield".

132. *lux mea*: thus our attention returns to Lesbia, whom we had left at line 72. In the depth of her passion, Lesbia matches or almost matches Laodamia. The phrase *lux mea* will again appear in line 160.

se...contulit: "brought herself".

133. *circumcursans*: "running about"; *cf. circumsiliens modo huc modo illuc* at 3.9.

134. *fulgebat*: *cf.* line 71 above.

crocina...tunica: Cupid wears a saffron-yellow tunic, perhaps as if he were an attendant at a wedding; usually the god went naked.

candidus: *cf.* line 70 above.

135. *quae*: Lesbia.

uno...Catullo: "with Catullus alone"; the poet is no longer under the illusion that Lesbia's affections are restricted only to him.

136. *rara...furta*: "the few affairs"; *furta* here = *furtivi amores* (*cf.* 7.8). The poet in these few lines seems to be minimizing the erotic activities of Lesbia, in an attempt perhaps to preserve his self-respect.

verecundae: an adjective that basically signifies one who has a sense of morality, who is "modest" or "restrained"; it is not a term that applies easily to Lesbia, and the poet seems to be assuming a mask of willful ignorance.

137. *simus* = *sim*, that is, the poet.

stultorum: "silly fools".

molesti: "irksome"; *cf.* 10.33. The poet sounds as if he were trying to be "sophisticated" rather than "old-fashioned" in regard to morality.

138. *caelicolum*: genitive plural; *cf.* 64.386 and 30.4.

139. *in*: "at". Juno's husband is, of course, Jupiter (Jove), famous for his many illicit affairs.

contudit iram: V apparently read *cotidiana* here, and various emendations have been put forward; while some write *concoquit* ("digested") *iram*, *contudit iram* (in the sense of "suppressed her anger") seems less strained and closer to the MSS.

140. *omnivoli*: Jupiter "who wants everything"; *cf. multi-vola* at line 128 above.

furta: an emendation of the MSS.' *facta*, which some defend, translating it as "misdeeds"; the appearance of *furta* in line 136, however, favors its repetition here.

141. *atqui*: "and yet"; the poet catches himself.

componier: "be compared"; archaic passive infinitive. *Cf. citarier* at 61.42. (V, however, read *componere*.)

aequum: "fair". There seem to be some lines missing at this point in the MSS.; attempts to tie line 142 to 141 have been unconvincing, and the point of line 142 remains obscure.

142. *tolle...onus*: according to some, "do away with the burden"; according to others, "take up the burden".

143. *illa*: Lesbia.

dextra deducta paterna: not to be taken literally, for the Roman father himself did not lead the bride to her husband (*cf.* poem 61); rather, the point here is that Lesbia's liaison with Catullus had no familial sanction. Take *dextra* as "right hand".

144. *venit*: "approach".

odore: "perfume".

145. *mira...nocte*: "the wonderful night"; some would

change this (the reading of V) to *media* (or *muta*)...*nocte*.

munuscula: note the diminutive, and *cf.* 64.103.

146. *dempta*: "taken away".

   viri: Metellus, the husband of Lesbia.

   gremio: *cf.* line 132 above.

147. *nobis...unis*: "to me alone"; *cf.* line 135.

148. *quem...dies...notat*: "a day which she marks".

   lapide...candidiore: the sign of a good day; *cf.* 107.6.

149. With this verse, we arrive at a poetic postscript to Allius.

   quod potui: a deprecation of his poetry; *cf.* poem 1.

   confectum carmine: "made in verse".

150. *officiis*: *cf.* line 42 above.

151. *vestrum...nomen*: "your family name".

   scabra...robigine: "corroded rust"; *cf.* line 44.

152. A somewhat prosaic line, which nevertheless conveys effectively a sense of time to come (also emphasized

by the heavy elision in the line). Note that *dies* is here feminine, not masculine as it was in line 148.

153. *huc*: that is, to this *munus*.

plurima: with *munera*.

Themis: the goddess associated with Justice.

154. *antiquis...piis*: a reference to the famed "Golden Age" of old (*cf.* 64.384ff.); *piis* is here a noun.

155. *sitis*: the plural is explained by the following *et...et*.

simul: "together".

tua vita: *cf.* 45.13 and 109.1. The actual identity of this woman is unknown.

156. This verse is too short in the MSS. and editors add either *ipsa* (after *domus*) or *nos*, as here. *Cf.* line 68 above.

157. *et qui*: an enigmatic line, with both reading and general sense in doubt. The identity of *qui* is obscure, and is not at all illuminated by the fact that this line in V ended in *terram dedit aufert*, which makes little or no sense. The emendation *auspex* (in the sense of "patron") is a desperate attempt to impose some meaning.

158. The metrical hiatus after *primo* has led many to suspect that this line is also corrupt.

159. *longe ante omnes*: with *sit felix* understood.

carior: *cf.* poem 82.1ff.

160. *lux mea*: as in line 132. It seems fitting that the poem as a whole concludes with a reference to Lesbia.

qua viva: ablative absolute.

69

An attack on Rufus, who, according to the poet, is puzzled by his lack of success with women. The poet, however, has a simple explanation: Rufus stinks. Here, as elsewhere in the corpus, Catullus focuses his invective on bodily functions (*cf.* poem 71).

The identity of the Rufus involved is controversial, but there is the possibility that we are dealing here with M. Caelius Rufus (*cf.* poem 58).

The poem has a 4 + 4 + 2 structure: the first four lines set out the problem experienced by Rufus, the second four lines provide the poet's explanation, and the concluding couplet offers the poet's advice.

1. *admirari, quare*: "wonder why"; *cf.* line 9, where *quare* has the sense of "therefore".

tibi: taken with *supposuisse* in the next line.

2. *Rufe*: for an interesting argument in favor of seeing M. Caelius Rufus here, *cf.* N. Dane, "Rufus

Redolens" in *Classical Journal* 64 (1968-9) 130.

supposuisse: the perfect infinitive used in place of the normal *supponere* (perhaps for metrical reasons).

femur: "thigh".

3. *non si*: "not even if".

   rarae: the literal sense is "loosely woven", but here the translation "exquisite" would be appropriate.

   labefactes: such gifts might "cause to waver" the resolve of a woman.

4. *perluciduli...lapidis*: "a transparent gem".

   deliciis: here "pleasures" or "luxuries".

5. *quaedam mala fabula*: "a certain ugly rumor".

   qua: "according to which".

6. *valle sub alarum*: "under the vale of your arm-pits"; an image appropriate to the personification of Rufus' odor as a goat.

7. *mala*: "ugly", as in line 5 above.

8. *bestia*: Dane argues that this is an allusion to L. Sempronius Bestia, an enemy of Caelius Rufus.

   quicum: an uncommon feminine form.

bella puella: if Rufus is in fact Caelius Rufus, then the poet may be attacking Lesbia here; no *bella puella* would go near stinking Rufus—but Lesbia did!

9. *quare*: note how the words *quare* and *admirari* in lines 9-10 serve to echo the opening line, bringing the poem full circle.

interfice: "kill" that goat—the image continues.

pestem: "pest" in the sense of "nuisance".

10. *fugiunt*: a colloquial use of the indicative.

70

On the credibility of Lesbia's oaths of devotion to the poet: her words of love are received with skepticism. While the motif of the fickleness of lovers is a common one (indeed Catullus seems to be imitating a poem by Callimachus here; *Cf. Palatine Anthology* V.6), Catullus transforms the commonplace into a serious examination of his own unique situation.

The poem falls into two parts: the first couplet presents Lesbia's affirmation, while the concluding couplet expresses the poet's evaluation of that affirmation.

1. *dicit*: a key word in the poem, repeated twice in line 3; Lesbia's affirmations are only words.

mulier: here Lesbia, but, as repeated in line 3, every woman.

490

nubere: "to get married to"; this seems to imply that Clodia's husband was no longer around (we know that Metellus had died in 59 B.C.). Note the play on *m* and *n* sounds in this line.

2. *non si*: "not even if"; *cf.* 69.3.

3. *cupido...amanti*: "to her eager lover".

4. *rapida*: "swift-flowing"; note how the dactyls of this line suggest the quick motion of winds and waves.

71

A gibe at an unnamed man with two afflictions: body odor and gout. Given the appearance of an ill-smelling Rufus in poem 69, one is tempted to see the same man being ridiculed here. The two poems do indeed look like companion pieces.

The poem has a 4 + 2 structure, in which the first two couplets set up the general situation of the *aemulus*, while the final couplet presents the "capping" joke at his expense.

1. *iure bono*: "rightly"; *cf. merito* in line 2.

   sacer: here in the sense of "accursed" or "horrible".

   obstitit: "hindered" his success.

2. *tarda podagra*: "the gout that slows you down"; note the play on sound in this phrase.

secat: "cuts to the quick".

3. *aemulus iste tuus*: while Rufus may be the *aemulus*, the identity of the person actually addressed by the poet remains unclear.

    vestrum...amorem: the use of *vestrum* here implies "the love shared by you and your woman".

4. *apte*: the MSS. read *a te* here, a reading questioned even by those editors who print it in their texts; it seems to disrupt the inner logic of the entire poem. One codex corrected the reading to *apte*, which does indeed make better sense; however, the resultant construction *mirifice...apte* is awkward. For a lucid analysis of the problem, *cf.* R.A. Kaster's "A Note on Catullus, c. 71.4" in *Philologus* 121 (1977) 308-312.

5. *futuit*: "has a screw".

    ambos: both himself and the woman, as is explained further in the next line.

6. Note the careful balance between the two halves of the pentameter: each word in one half is paralleled by a corresponding word in the other half, with *odore* and *podagra* receiving due emphasis.

72

A poem of recognition and disillusionment: the poet sees Lesbia for what she is, and the quality of his love for her is irreparably changed; the passion may still exist, but lost is the concern and respect he once felt for her.

If poem 71 is a companion piece to poem 69, this poem has the same relationship to poem 70: there the poet had his suspicions about his lover—suspicions that are now confirmed.

Structurally there are two movements in the poem: the first half focusing on the past, and the second half on the present; within the first half, couplet one is concerned with Lesbia, while the second couplet describes Catullus' feelings; within the second half of the poem, lines 5-6 again focus on Lesbia, while the final couplet concentrates on the poet.

1. *Dicebas quondam*: the first half of the poem is set in the past, focusing on what Lesbia once said and on how Catullus once felt towards her. For *dicebas, cf.* the *dicit* of poem 70.

    te nosse: *te* is here the subject of *nosse* (= *novisse*); in the context of the poem as a whole, *nosse* must imply intimate sexual "knowledge", although precise parallels are not to be found elsewhere.

2. *prae me*: "in preference to me".

    velle: with *te* as the understood subject.

    tenere: *cf.* poem 11.18.

    Iovem : *cf. Iuppiter* at 70.2.

3. *dilexi*: *diligo* means "to love" but in the sense of "to esteem highly"; it is this "esteem" that the poet tries to express in this and the next line.

tum: emphasizing the "pastness" of the situation.

vulgus amicam: the mainly physical love of the common man for his mistress.

4. A verse that expresses by analogy the spiritual quality of the poet's love for Lesbia: a *pater* does not lust after his sons or sons-in-law, but values and esteems them. Fordyce is probably right in thinking that the poet's inclusion of *generos* here "reflects a traditional attitude which puts the sons-in-law within the head of the family's protective concern" (*Catullus*, p.363). Note also the prominence of *t* sounds in both this and the preceding line.

5. *nunc te cognovi*: the poem now focuses on the present moment, with the heavy spondees of the phrase emphasizing the gravity of the statement; for *cognovi*, cf. *nosse* in line 1, where a different kind of knowledge is meant.

   impensius: "still more immoderately"; the physical passion (*uror*) remains powerful.

6. *mi = mihi*.

   vilior et levior: "of lesser value and of lesser importance".

7. *qui potis est*: "how can this be"—Lesbia fails to comprehend the statement of lines 5 and 6.

   inquis: the poet presents a dramatic scenario in which

Lesbia interrupts the poem, thus precipitating the final explanatory couplet.

iniuria: the most likely "injury" would be infidelity; *cf.* line 1, where Lesbia has promised fidelity to the poet exclusively.

8. *amare magis*: Lesbia's infidelity only makes the poet's lust for her greater.

bene velle minus: while Catullus' physical longing is more intense, his "respect" for Lesbia has faded; he loves her more, but likes her less.

73

A poem on ingratitude, precipitated by a betrayal of friendship. The false friend is not named, but editors find a possible candidate in Caelius Rufus. For a similar expression of dismay, *cf.* poem 30, addressed to Alfenus.

The poem falls neatly into three segments: the first couplet offers some general advice to the reader; the second couplet provides a statement of explanation; and the final couplet furnishes an illustrative example.

1. *de...bene...mereri*: the phrase *bene mereri de* is best translated here as "do a service to".

velle: take with *desine*; note, however, how the collocation of *bene velle* in this verse echoes the *bene velle* of 72.8—indeed, the repeated words effectively tie these two epigrams together, despite the difference in subject matter.

2. *fieri*: here in the sense of *esse*.

   putare: with *desine* understood from the previous line. Note both the repeated *p* sounds and the succession of infinitives in this line.

   pium: "dutiful" in the sense of showing appropriate gratitude.

3. *ingrata*: "thankless".

   fecisse benigne: "to have acted kindly" towards someone; for the conjectured *est* in this line, *cf.* the next note.

4. The reading of this line has long been in dispute: the manuscript reading is *immo etiam taedet obestque magisque magis*, a reading which is unmetrical; most editors see an intruder in *magisque* and remove it from the verse, adding *prodest* at the beginning (printed by Ellis, Fordyce, and Quinn). However, it is difficult to see how an original *prodest* disappeared, and *magisque magis* may hint at an original repetition within the line; hence some editors repeat the internal *taedet*, and add an *est* at the end of the preceding verse to close its thought. If *prodest* is adopted, it would govern the *fecisse benigne* of line 3.

   taedet: to have done a good deed is exhausting.

   obestque: "it is harmful".

5. *ut mihi*: "as in my case"; the poet now provides a specific proof of his general statement of lines 3 and 4.

urget: "vexes".

6.   *modo*: "just now".

me...habuit: "considered me".

unum atque unicum: "one and only"; the elisions of
this line have often been criticized, but the poet probably employs them to create a choking effect: his pain
is so intense that he cannot get the words out clearly.
For Catullus' use of elision, *cf.* M. Owen Lee's "Illustrative Elisions in Catullus", *TAPA* 93 (1962) 144-152.

74

The introductory epigram in the "Gellius Cycle" (74,
80, 88-91 and 116). The first appearance of Gellius establishes him as sexually voracious, and, as the cycle develops,
his sexual perversion will be depicted in all its grossness.

The Gellius so castigated by the poet is most probably L. Gellius Poplicola, a member of the circle of Clodius;
he would become consul in 36 B.C.

Structurally, each couplet comprises a "movement"
within the poem: the first states the problem of a stern
uncle, the second presents Gellius' unique solution to that
problem, and the third depicts the end result.

1.   *audierat* = *audiverat*.

patruum: the dominant word of the poem, appearing
here and also in lines 3, 4 and 6 (twice); this five-fold

repetition makes the poem as much about the uncle as about Gellius.

obiurgare: "scold".

2. *delicias diceret aut faceret*: "say or do anything naughty".

3. *ipsi = sibi.*

perdepsuit: literally, "to knead thoroughly", but here in the sense "to give a good screw to".

4. *reddidit Harpocratem*: "rendered him an Harpocrates"; Harpocrates was a name for Horus, an Egyptian divinity commonly portrayed holding a finger to his lips, a symbol of silence.

5. *quamvis*: "even though".

irrumet: cf. 16.1.

ipsum: note how *ipsum* here echoes the *ipsam* of line 3.

6. *verbum non faciet*: if *irrumet* is taken literally, then Gellius' uncle will be physically unable to speak, since his mouth is obviously full. Catullus is clearly playing with words here.

75

A companion piece to poem 72, where a similar statement of the poet's predicament was made; indeed, poems

70, 72, and 75 form a thematic progression that will find its culmination in poem 76.

The complex thought of the epigram is contained within a simple structure: the first couplet presents the condition in which the poet finds himself, while the concluding couplet depicts the result of that condition.

1. *Huc*: "to such a point".

   mens...mea: some editors prefer to take *mea* with Lesbia, but the noun *mens* seems to require a modifier, and the collocation of "my mind" and "your fault" presents a neat balance.

   deducta: "reduced".

   culpa: cf. 11.22.

2. *officio...suo*: "by its devotion".

   perdidit ipsa: *ipsa* here implies that the poet was, to some extent, the author of his own ruin; not all the blame is placed on Lesbia.

3. *bene velle*: cf. 72.8.

   si optima fias: that is, if Lesbia changes her character totally.

4. *nec desistere amare*: cf. 72.8.

   omnia si facias: "no matter what you do"; note the parallelism in these last two lines.

Reflections on unrequited love: the poem begins as a soliloquy expressing the despair of the poet, and ends as a prayer for his release from a love that has turned into sickness. The poem forms a dramatic climax to the sequence comprised of poems 70, 72, and 75; it also, however, has much in common with poems 73 and 8, the latter of which expresses similar sentiments, although in not so despairing a tone.

Structurally, the poem features two major movements: lines 1-16 and lines 17-26. The first movement contains the poet's self-address in a 6 + 6 + 4 structure: a statement of what is thought to be a general truth is followed by the poet's description of his own behavior and its consequences, which is in turn followed by an expression of his resolve. The second movement invokes the aid of the gods in attaining his sought-for release in a 6 + 4 structure: the prayer proper, capped by a final expression of the nature of the release he seeks.

1. *qua*: take with *voluptas*. Note how *voluptas* here is echoed by *gaudia* in line 6.

    benefacta priora: "good deeds done in the past"; *cf.* 73.3.

2. *pium*: another verbal echo of poem 73 (line 2); *cf.* also line 26 below.

3. *sanctam...fidem*: "sacred trust".

    nec foedere nullo: the double negative has led some

editors to prefer a reading of *nec foedere in ullo*; *foedere* has the sense of "compact".

4. *divum = deorum.*

    numine: "divine power"; governed by *abusum*.

5. *multa parata manent...gaudia*: the sense is that there are many pleasures held in store for the poet (*cf.* line 1).

    in longa aetate: "all the length of your days".

    Catulle: *cf.* 8.1.

6. *ingrato*: "thankless"; *cf.* 73.3. This final line of the poem's first segment reveals that the source of the poet's malaise is his *amor*, and paves the way for what is to follow.

    tibi: take with *parata manent* in the preceding line.

7. *bene*: with both *dicere possunt* and *facere* (*possunt*). The phrase *bene ... facere* reminds us of the *benefacta* of line 1.

    cuiquam: "to anyone".

8. *haec*: picking up the *quaecumque* of line 7; it will in turn be echoed by *quae* in the next line. Note how the language of lines 7-8 seems prosaic rather than poetic.

9. *ingratae...credita menti*: the ungrateful mind is, of

course, that of Lesbia.

perierunt: "have been squandered"; the language of this line is that of commercial activity. *Cf.* 8.2.

10. The reading of the MSS. here is *quare cur te iam amplius excrucies*, which imposes a metrical hiatus after *iam* where elision would normally be expected; the emendation *tete* reasonably resolves the problem. For *tete*, *cf.* 101.5.

excrucies: a word expressing severe torment; the poet has become his own torturer.

11. *animo offirmas*: some take *offirmas* as transitive here and read *animum*; the intransitive use of the verb, however, is well established in Latin literature. For the sentiment, *cf.* 8.11.

istinc: "from the brink" of destruction.

te ipse reducis: the MSS.' reading *istincteque* had led some editors to read *teque reducis*, despite the awkwardness of *-que* following on *atque*; *te ipse* avoids this problem and gives good sense: the poet must become the author of his own salvation; *cf. ipsa* at 75.2.

12. *dis invitis*: the interpretation of this ablative absolute has been controversial; in its immediate context the most probable sense is that the gods are unwilling that the poet continue to be *miser*. R. Freis, however, has argued that a better interpretation is that the gods are unwilling that Lesbia return the poet's

love ("Form and Thought in Catullus 76", *Agon* 2 [1968] 47-48).

desinis...miser: cf. 8.1.

13 - These two lines stand in the very center of the poem, and sum up the poet's dilemma succinctly.

13. *longum subito*: the juxtaposition of these words is a telling one; a *longum amorem* would be a "love of long duration".

deponere amorem: cf. the *deponere morbum* of line 25 below.

14. *hoc* = *deponere amorem*. Cf. lines 15 and 16 below.

qua lubet efficias: "you *must* achieve any way you can".

15. *salus*: "hope of survival".

haec = *deponere amorem*, but drawn by *salus* into the feminine case.

pervincendum: the spondaic ending emphasizes the great effort involved in *deponere amorem*.

16. *facias*: cf. *efficias* in line 14.

pote: "possible".

17. *o di*: the poet turns to the gods for help in achieving his goal — *deponere amorem*.

vestrum: "in your nature" is the best translation for this genitive; the repeated *si* in line 17 is a commonplace in prayers.

18. *extremam...opem*: "aid at the last second"; note how the aid of the gods physically embraces those on the verge of death (*ipsa in morte*).

19. *puriter*: cf. 39.14; the poet means that he has lived his life according to the standards he deems important—standards described at the very beginning of the poem.

20. *pestem perniciemque*: "plague and poison" in English preserve the alliteration here. Love has clearly become a sickness.

21. *quae*: an emendation of the MSS.' *seu*, accepted by most modern editors; it refers, of course, to both *pestem* and *perniciem*. For the language of this line, *cf.* 51.9.

    ut torpor: "like a paralysis".

22. *laetitias*: "all pleasures"; *cf. voluptas* in line 1 and *gaudia* in line 6.

23. *non iam*: "not now" in the sense of "no longer".

    illud: explained by *ut diligat illa*. For *diligat*, *cf.* 72.3-4.

    contra: "in return".

24. *velit*: with *ut* understood from the preceding line.

25. *ipse*: *cf.* line 11 above.

   valere: "to become well".

   taetrum...morbum: love has become a "loathsome disease".

26. *reddite mi hoc*: "grant me this".

   pietate: *cf.* line 2 above. The poet has done everything that should have been done; he has "kept the faith".

77

To Rufus: a complaint on a betrayal of friendship. The poem has affinities with poems 69 (both addressed to Rufus: *cf.* poem 69), 73 (also dealing with a false friend), and 76 (linguistic similarities: *cf.* below). Given the "Lesbia" poems in this segment of the epigrams, it is tempting to see Rufus as the poet's rival for the affections of that woman.

The poem features a 4 + 2 structure, with the initial four lines asking a rhetorical question of Rufus, and the final couplet supplying the poet's own response.

1. *frustra ac nequiquam*: these words reinforce each other; translate as "to no avail and without good reason".

credite amice: in agreement with *Rufe*.

2. *magno cum pretio atque malo*: responds to the second *frustra* - the poet's trust in Rufus was not really "for nothing" since he paid a great price for it; *malo* here is best translated as "painful". For the construction, *cf.* 40.8.

3. *subrepsti*: one of several words in lines 3-6 that seem to echo the language of poem 76 (*cf.* 76.21: *subrepens*). The form of the verb here is a contracted perfect.

    intestina perurens: the poet uses strong language: Rufus has been "scalding his guts" by his treacherous behavior.

4. *ei*: like *eheu* in lines 5 and 6, an exclamation expressing anguish.

    misero: supply *mihi*.

    eripuisti: *cf.* 76.20.

    omnia nostra bona: not "all my possessions" but rather "every blessing I have"; a reference to Lesbia seems likely.

5. *eripuisti*: repeated from the line above in much the same way that *frustra* had been repeated in lines 1 and 2. Note also the repetitions of *nostra(e)* and *eheu*. This amount of verbal repetition serves to stress the poet's disbelieving shock at what Rufus has done.

venenum: Rufus is like a poison that has destroyed the poet's life; *cf. pestis* in the following line.

6. *pestis*: *cf.* 76.20; taken in conjunction with the preceding *venenum, pestis* here takes on the sense of "blight".

78A

A stinging attack on Gallus, who is playing with fire and liable to end up burned. While the subject matter is basically coarse, the language employed by the poet has a sophisticated complexity.

Each couplet in the poem forms a structural unit: lines 1-2 set the scene for the reader; lines 3-4 focus on the activities of Gallus; and lines 5-6 suggest the ultimate consequences.

1. *Gallus*: aside from what Catullus tells us, we know nothing about this character.

   lepidissima: a word of some importance in the polymetric poems (*cf.* 1.1, 6.17, 36.10); it encompasses both physical and non-physical qualities valued by the circle of the poet.

2. *alterius...alterius*: a striking verbal frame for the pentameter; the form is genitive.

   lepidus: echoing the *lepidissima* of the preceding line; the woman and the boy are "two of a kind".

3. *Gallus*: the repetition of the name at the start of the

couplet (*cf.* line 5) centers our attention firmly on the man.

bellus: like *lepidus*, a Catullan keyword, denoting a man of some culture and refinement; *cf.* 22.9. This and the next line play upon this adjective.

4. The pentameter falls into two halves, with the *bellus puer* on one side and the *bella puella* on the other; for *bella puella cubet*, *cf.* 69.8.

5. *stultus*: "foolish"; in this line *stultus* replaces the *bellus* of line 3. *Cf.* 17.12.

6. *qui patruus*: a man who "despite being an uncle" teaches a nephew to engage in sex with an aunt. Could his own wife be next? Note the play on words in *patruus patrui* (*cf.* poem 74).

monstret: "teaches".

78B

A fragment of a poem that once stood between the present 78A and 79 (in the MSS. poems 77-79 are run together); it is probable that the extant lines were preceded by an unreal condition, along the lines of 21.9-11. In its present state, it is difficult to identify the persons involved, although some argue that Lesbia is the *pura puella*.

1. *sed nunc id doleo*: *cf.* 21.10.

purae pura puellae: a striking use of alliteration and juxtaposition.

2. *savia*: "lips". Note the alliterative use of *s* in this line.

   comminxit: his spittle "pisses" her lips.

   spurca: "filthy".

3. *id non impune feres*: "you will not get away with this".

4. *qui sis*: would seem to imply that the addressee was not directly named in the lost verses.

   anus: here used as an adjective.

79

A sarcastic attack on Lesbius, a pseudonym for P. Clodius Pulcer, the infamous brother of Lesbia. But, despite the poem's focus on Lesbius, it is undeniable that Lesbia also has her character blackened. That brother and sister had an unusually intimate relationship seems well attested by such contemporary sources as Cicero.

The poem is structurally simple: the first couplet introduces Lesbius and tells us of his relationship with Lesbia; the concluding couplet provides the "sting" of the epigram by suggesting something unsavory about the man.

1. *Lesbius est pulcer*: the pun on Clodius' cognomen is clearly meant to make Lesbius' identity more than obvious to the reader. For Lesbius/Lesbia as a brother/sister pair, *cf.* Aufillenus/Aufillena in poem 100.

quid ni: "why shouldn't he be?".

2. *gente*: the Claudian *gens* was one of the most distin-
    guished in Rome; Clodius and Clodia might well have
    disdain for someone belonging to such a second-rate
    gens as the Valerian.

3. *hic pulcer*: the pun repeated from line 1.

    vendat: editors disagree on the sense of the subjunc-
    tive here; the form could be a jussive subjunctive, *i.e.*,
    "let him sell" Catullus and his *gens*, in which case the
    poet is saying that Clodius is welcome to sell him and
    his family *provided that* he can come up with three
    friends willing to kiss him in greeting (line 4) — which
    Catullus, of course, doubts; on the other hand, *vendat*
    could mean "would sell", in which case Catullus is
    castigating the man as one who would shrink from no
    crime (no matter how disgusting) to get what he want-
    ed—even if it were something as trivial as three kisses
    of greeting. This ambiguity could well be intentional on
    the part of the poet, who thus attacks Clodius on two
    different levels. For Catullus' effective use of ambigui-
    ties, *cf.* D.N. Levin, "Ambiguities of Expression in
    Catullus 66 and 67", *Classical Philology* 54 (1959)
    109-111.

4. *tria*: here used to signify a trivial number.

    notorum: "friends".

    savia reppererit: if *vendat* in the preceding line is
    taken as a jussive subjunctive, *reppererit* would then
    be a future perfect indicative; but if *vendat* means

510

"would sell", *reppererit* must be a perfect subjunctive in a less vivid condition. This ambiguity is compounded by a possible ambiguity in *savia*: while it normally means "kisses", this word can also mean "mouths", and if the latter meaning is adopted here, the poet is making reference to the deviant sexual practice of *fellatio*: Clodius is looking for three men to indulge him in this way! It should be noted that the next poem in the corpus is most definitely concerned with this sexual practice.

80

On the sexual practices of the Gellius who previously appeared in poem 74. The second piece in the "Gellius cycle", this epigram presents an even more graphic picture of this particular "sexual offender", and at the same time completes a triad of poems (78B, 79, 80) concerned with lips, mouths, and kisses.

The poem has a 4 + 4 structure: the apparently innocent question of lines 1-4 is answered by the gross depiction of *fellatio* in lines 5-8.

1. *Quid dicam...quare*: "what shall I say is the reason why".

    rosea ista labella: the language is that of conventional love poetry in the lyric mode; note especially the diminutive in *labella*: "little lips".

2. *hiberna...nive*: "winter snow"; the image is also appropriate to the lyric mode.

fiant: here in the sense of *sint*.

3. *mane...quiete*: the line begins and ends with the two crucial times of day that Gellius exhibits his oh-so-white lips—early morning and mid-afternoon (after the siesta, *i.e.*, *quiete*). *Cf.* poem 32.

   octava: take with *hora* in the next line.

4. *longo...die*: "in the lengthy day"; most likely a reference to the longer and hotter days of summer when the siesta was a necessity.

5. *nescio quid certe est*: "something is going on, for sure". Now the poet drops the mask of innocence and makes his accusation of *fellatio*.

   fama: a word that appears in the polymetrics and epigrams only here and at 78B.4; it provides one of several links among 78B, 79 and 80.

   susurrat: a word that sounds like its sense—"whispers".

6. The key noun is omitted, but implied by the rest of the verse: what Gellius devours (*vorare*) is large (*grandia*), stiff (*tenta*), and found near the middle of a man's body (*medii viri*).

7. *sic certe est*: picking up the similar start of line 5, now in certain affirmation.

   Victoris: otherwise unknown.

rupta...ilia: *cf.* 11.20.

8. *emulso...sero*: an agricultural image (the drawn off whey) changed by the poet into a sexual image: "sucked out semen".

    labra: *cf. labella* in line 1.

81

A complaint to Juventius: how can you prefer that man from Pisaurum to me? The poem has much in common with poem 24, also addressed to Juventius.

The epigram is structurally a single sentence in which the initial couplet focuses on Juventius, the second couplet on "that man from Pisaurum", and the third couplet on the poet's reaction to such a hideous liaison.

1. *in tanto...populo*: the phrase implies that the setting of the poem is the city of Rome.

2. *bellus homo*: *cf.* 22.9 and 24.7; the appearance of this phrase at 24.7 has led some to speculate that the man from Pisaurum might be Furius, but see line 4 below for another possibility.

    diligere inciperes: "start loving".

3. *praeterquam*: "besides".

    iste tuus: full of contempt, and taken with *hospes* in the next line. *Cf.* 71.3.

Pisauri: the modern Pesaro, a town on Italy's Adriatic coast; in the first century B.C. it would seem to have been a town that had fallen on hard times (indeed, in 43 B.C. new settlers had to be dispatched there).

4. *hospes*: "guest"; the man would appear to be staying with Juventius in Rome.

   inaurata: "gilded"; there is some temptation to see in this word a sly play on the name "Aurelius" — could he be the man from Pisaurum? For Aurelius, *cf.* poems 11, 15, 16 and 21.

5. *cordi est*: *cf.* 44.3.

   nobis: the key word appears at an emphatic position in the line, and we realize that the poet is motivated in this poem by jealousy.

6. *quod facinus facias*: "what an outrageous offense you are committing".

82

An appeal to Quintius to keep his hands off the poet's love. Quintius also appears in poem 100, but the identity of this man remains unclear.

The poem features a 2 + 2 structure, in which the first couplet forms the protasis ("if clause") of a condition, while the concluding couplet forms the apodosis or main sentence; note, however, how the whole poem is bound together by repetition.

1. *oculos debere*: to "owe one's eyes" is a colloquial phrase equivalent to "owing one's very life"; for eyes in this same sense, *cf.* 3.5, 14A.1, and 104.2.

2. *aut aliud si quid* = *aut si quid aliud*; the poet speaks to the possibility that there may be something even more precious than one's eyes. This line finds a close echo in line 4.

3. *eripere ei noli*: "don't take from him"; *eripere* is here used in the sense of "steal", just as it was in poem 77; *ei* is monosyllabic.

   multo quod carius: although the poem itself is vague, it seems likely that Lesbia is meant.

4. *seu* = *vel si*; *cf.* line 2.

83

A poetic diagnosis. Lesbia verbally abuses Catullus in the presence of her husband; the explanation: her abuse is but a sign of her great love for the poet. A later epigram (poem 92) will offer a variation on this theme.

Structurally, the poem is divided between the basic data of Lesbia's abuse and her husband's response to it (lines 1-2) and the poet's own diagnosis of that data (lines 3-6).

1. *mi* = *mihi*. In this dramatic scenario, the poet, the lady and her husband are all present.

   praesente viro: if Lesbia is Clodia Metelli, the poem

must have been written before 59 B.C., when Q. Metellus Celer died; some editors, however, argue that *vir* should not be taken in its usual sense of "husband" here, preferring it to allude to a "beloved male" — an interpretation that seems strained at best.

2. *haec*: in agreement with *laetitia*.

    illi fatuo: "that fat-head".

    laetitia: "source of joy".

3. *mule*: the English phrase "stupid ass" seems an appropriate translation; *nihil sentis* surely indicates some unusual degree of stupidity (*cf. illi fatuo* in the preceding line). *Cf.* 17.20 also.

    nostri oblita: "unmindful of me"; *cf.* line 5 below.

4. *sana*: "in her right mind"; the poet here expresses the conceit that love is a disease.

    quod: "in view of the fact that".

    gannit: commonly used to express the snarling of a dog.

    obloquitur: "can't keep herself from speaking"; *cf. taceret* in line 3.

5. *meminit*: responds to *oblita* in line 3.

    multo acrior: "much fiercer".

6. *irata est*: "she is in a rage"; echoes *mala plurima dicit* in line 1, and at the same time contrasts with *sana* in line 4.

hoc est: "that is to say".

uritur et loquitur: *cf. gannit et obloquitur* in line 4; *et* here should be translated as "and for that reason".

84

On the vulgar and annoying Arrius: a man with many and great aspirations! The fellow apparently overused aspirated vowels and consonants in an affected style of speech that grated on the ears of others.

Two explanations for this style of speech have been put forward: first, that Arrius' family (see lines 5-6) came from the northern part of Italy where such aspiration was common; second, that Arrius was trying to appear sophisticated by adopting (to excess, however) the urban type of Latin which retained aspirates no longer used in rustic Latin. For an examination of the question, *cf.* D.N. Levin's "Arrius and his Uncle" in *Latomus* 32 (1973) 587-594.

The identity of Arrius remains uncertain, but the strongest candidate at present is one Q. Arrius mentioned by Cicero (*Brutus* 242) as a poor orator of humble origin who also happened to be an associate of M. Crassus.

In structure, the poem falls into two equal halves: lines 1-6 introduce Arrius and his excessive aspiration, while lines 7-12 provide the epigrammatic "sting": no one and no place in the world can escape the aspirations of Arrius.

1   *Chommoda...hinsidias*: several scholars have recog-
2.   nized these nouns as belonging to the language of
     oratory (*cf.* R.J. Baker and B.A. Marshall, "*Com-
     moda* and *Insidiae*: Catullus 84. 1-4", *Classical
     Philology* 73 [1978] 49-50); such language would, of
     course, be appropriate for the Q. Arrius mentioned by
     Cicero as an orator. Translate *chommoda* as "hadvan-
     tages" and *hinsidias* as "hambushes".

3.   *mirifice*: "in a wonderful way"; *cf.* 71.4.

     sperabat: Arrius had hopes that he was speaking
     impressively, but instead he was making a fool of
     himself, at least in the eyes of the poet.

4.   *quantum poterat*: "as emphatically as he could".

5.   *credo*: "I expect".

     sic: "in the same such way"; the poet uses this
     couplet (apparently) to get in a dig at Arrius' family
     on the maternal side.

     liber avunculus: editors do not agree on whether *liber*
     is here to be taken as an adjective (implying that the
     family may have had a servile origin), or as a proper
     name (*Liber*: the uncle's actual name, or a nickname
     that might allude to his tendency to indulge too
     much in the juice of Bacchus-Liber). However, the
     fact that Cicero refers to Q. Arrius as *infimo loco
     natus* seems to support the former interpretation.

7.   *hoc misso in Syriam*: Catullus may be alluding here
     to Crassus' journey to the East in 55 B.C.

requierant = *requieverant*; translate as "had a holiday".

8. *audibant* = *audiebant*; the subject is still *aures*.

    leniter et leviter: a play on two words of similar meaning and sound; Fordyce's "smoothly and softly" seems a good English equivalent.

9. *postilla*: "after that time", that is, after Arrius left for Syria.

10. *horribilis*: probably chosen by the poet for its initial aspiration as well as for its meaning. *Cf.* 11.11.

11. *Ionios fluctus*: the Ionian Sea, to the west of the Greek mainland.

12. *Hionios*: the final word of the poem, like the very first word, mocks the offending pronunciation. It is now clear that merely getting Arrius out of Rome (and Italy) is not enough: he spreads his verbal pollution wherever he goes.

85

Self-analysis in a philosophical tone: the poet finds himself in the grip of paradoxical emotions, and if he cannot explain his state, he can nevertheless experience its torture.

It is difficult, especially considering the earlier poems 70, 72 and 75, to exclude the presence of Lesbia from this epigram; yet, it should be noted that the poet does not identify the object of his love and hate, thus elevating the poem from the particular to the universal level.

Despite its form as a single couplet, poem 85 has a complex structure: it is dominated by eight verbs, four in each line, and each verb in each line finds an echo in a verb of the other line. It is no wonder, then, that poem 85 has traditionally been considered one of Catullus' master-pieces — combining complex form and thought in the space of but two verses.

1. *Odi et amo*: the basic paradox, stated bluntly; for the concept, *cf.* poems 72 and 75.

   quare: the poet is *not* asked "who" he loves and hates, but "how" such a state could exist.

   requiris: an indefinite "you" is brought into the poem to question the poet.

2. *nescio*: responds at once to *requiris* above; the final *o* is short here.

   fieri: picks up the *faciam* of line 1.

   sentio et excrucior: in structure balancing the *odi et amo* of line 1.

86

A poem not so much about either Quintia or Lesbia as about what constitutes true beauty; obviously, as far as the poet is concerned, good looks alone are not enough.

Cf. poem 43.

The poem falls into three sections: the first couplet introduces Quintia and acknowledges her physical attractiveness; but the second couplet denies that physical attractions alone constitute being *formosa*; finally, the third couplet introduces Lesbia, and uses her as an example of true beauty.

1. *Quintia*: this woman appears only here in the corpus; it is tempting to see in her the sister of the Quintius of poems 82 and 100.

   multis...mihi: the poet very effectively points out the difference in taste between "many people" and himself by this collocation.

   candida: fair skin seems to have been considered very attractive in a woman. *Cf.* 13.4.

   longa: "tall".

2. *recta*: the adjective would apparently refer to the way Quintia carried herself. Translate as "cuts a fine figure".

   haec...singula: "these (attractions) taken separately".

   sic: here has the sense of "as specified above".

3. *totum illud* "formosa": "that whole concept of beauty"; note that *formosa* stands outside the grammatical construction governed by *nego*.

nego: responds to the *confiteor* of line 2.

venustas: "charm"; *cf.* the poet's use of the adjective *venustus* in the polymetrics.

4. *tam magno*: it would seem that Roman men liked large women.

mica salis: literally, "grain of salt", often interpreted as "wit", but really alluding to "a quality which gives 'life' or 'character' to a person or thing" (*Oxford Latin Dictionary*). Quintia may have a large body, but it does not contain even one grain of this necessity. *Cf.* 13.5.

5. *cum*: "not only".

6. *tum*: "but also".

omnibus una omnis: an effective juxtaposition of words—Lesbia's uniqueness is thus made clear. *Omnibus* would, of course, include Quintia.

omnis...veneres: "all the charms that exist"; true beauty, then, consists of physical attractiveness plus *venustas/veneres*.

87

On the uniqueness of the poet's love for Lesbia (*cf.* poem 86, on the uniqueness of Lesbia's beauty). The epigram is not, as Ellis would have it, "an obviously imperfect fragment", but a perfectly balanced expression of a love that knows no comparison.

Each couplet takes the form of a simple statement: the first stresses the *quantity* of the poet's love, while the second focuses on the *quality* of that love. Verbal repetition ties both couplets together.

1. *Nulla*: *cf. nulla* in line 3.

   tantum...quantum: *cf. tanta...quanta* in lines 3-4.

   amatam: echoed by *amata* in line 2. For the thought of this line, *cf.* 8.5, 37.12.

2. Note the dominant *a* sound of this line.

   est: the reading of the MSS. Some editors, however, read *es* here, making *Lesbia...mea* vocative, despite the intervening *amata*.

3. *fides*: a word that includes the concepts of good faith, trust, and loyalty—the qualities of the poet's love. Note the alliteration of *f* in this line.

   foedere: "covenant"; *cf.* 76.3.

4. *in amore tuo*: "in my love for you"; the appearance of *tuo* here is a major reason for the changing of *est* to *es* in line 2 by some editors.

   ex parte mea: "on my part", seemingly suggesting that Lesbia's other lovers can offer no such love as this. Note the play on sound in *parte reperta*.

   mea est: just as each couplet begins with *nulla*, so each ends with *mea est*.

88

Gellius and incest: an escalation of the attack launched by the poet in poems 74 and 80; this and the following poems emphasize the gross unnaturalness of Gellius' passions.

Structurally, the poem falls into two balancing halves: lines 1-4 pose a series of questions to Gellius, while lines 5-8 answer them for him.

1. *cum matre atque sorore*: the poet makes it immediately clear that the charge is incest, a more serious offense than Gellius' adultery in poem 74 or homosexual liaison in poem 80.

2. *prurit*: "craves to have a screw"; *cf.* 16.9.

   pervigilat: Gellius does not waste his nights sleeping; rather, he stays awake all night to indulge his unnatural lust.

   tunicis: "garments".

3. *quid facit is*: an emphatic repetition (*cf.* line 1). The charge which follows reminds the reader at once of poem 74.

4. *ecquid scis*: "do you have any idea at all?"; the poet, of course, expects a negative answer.

   suscipiat: "incurs".

5. *suscipit...quantum*: in direct response to the question

of line 4; *sceleris* is understood after *quantum*.

ultima Tethys: the poet turns to the heroic style to emphasize the impossibility of cleansing Gellius of his sin. Tethys was a sea-goddess, the wife of Oceanus; for *ultima, cf.* 29.4.

6. *Nympharum*: spirits thought to inhabit water, often considered the daughters of Tethys and Oceanus.

abluit: "wash away".

Oceanus: with the appearance of this major god of water the poet makes it clear that not all the water in the world can cleanse Gellius.

7. *nihil est quicquam sceleris*: "there is no sin at all".

quo prodeat ultra: "to which he might proceed further".

8. *voret*: "devour" in the sense of "suck himself".

89

The continuing saga of Gellius: now exposed as "the family man" *par excellence*! The poet painstakingly builds his portrait of an utterly corrupt man.

The poem features a 4+2 structure: the first four verses detail the incestuous crimes of Gellius, and the concluding couplet adds a pointed summation.

1. *Gellius est tenuis: quid ni ?*: *cf.* 79.1; translate *tenuis*

as "thin" (*cf. macer* in lines 4 and 6).

tam bona: "so accommodating"; note the repetition of *tam* in these initial verses.

2. *valens*: "vigorous", with an implied contrast to Gellius' thinness; take with *soror*.

vivat = est. Note the dominant *v* sound in this line.

3. *bonus patruus: cf.* 74 and 88.

tamque omnia plena: a Latin idiom akin to our "a whole kit and caboodle".

4. *cognatis*: "kindred", a key word, of course, in Gellius' sex life.

5. *ut*: "even though".

attingat: "touch" in a sexual way.

fas: a word with deep religious overtones to a Roman.

6. *quantumvis*: "as much as you like".

quare sit macer: cf. line 4 above.

90

On Gellius' most hideous liaison, which the poet manages to make even more hideous by imagining a child born of it.

The initial couplet provides the basic theme of the poem, while the final four verses provide the explanatory elaboration.

1. *Nascatur magus*: "may a *magus* (magician) be born" from such an incestuous union; the Persian *magi* were associated with incestuous practices in antiquity.

   ex: take with *nefando/coniugio*.

   nefando: "abominable"; *cf. impia* in line 4.

2. *discat*: also a wish: "may he learn".

   aruspicium = *haruspicium*; translate as "divination", that is, the art of reading the divine messages to be found in the organs of sacrificial victims; *cf.* line 6.

3. Note the play on sound in *magus ex matre* and *gnato gignatur*; this line is essentially a restatement of line 1 and begins the poet's explanatory comments.

4. *impia*: here perhaps "perverted"; *cf. nefando* in line 1.

5. *gnatus*: the MSS. reading, but one that seems awkward after the *gnato* (= Gellius) in line 3; some editors read *gratus* instead, but this presents problems of sense.

   accepto...carmine: "with a well-received chant".

6. *omentum*: "bowels" of the sacrificial victim.

   liquefaciens: "dissolving" in the flame.

527

91

Gellius' crime against the poet: we now learn the reason for Catullus' animosity towards Gellius (manifested in the preceding poems)—he had tried to win over the poet's mistress. After this poetic venting of wrath, Gellius will disappear from the epigrams until poem 116.

The poem has a 4+2+4 structure: the first four lines present the poet rejecting possible reasons for placing trust in Gellius; the central couplet focuses on the real (and unflattering) reason for the poet's trust; and the final four verses show how Gellius proved that trust to be foolhardy.

1. *ideo*: "for this reason"; completed by the *quod* of line 3.

2. The elisions of this verse produce an effect of "gulping": the troubled poet can barely get these words out. *Cf.* 73.6.

   nostro = meo.

   perdito: "hopeless"; the poet here has no illusions about his relationship with Lesbia.

3. *cognossem = cognovissem*; Catullus (as line 7 will show) did indeed know Gellius well, but *that* was not why he was willing to trust the man.

   constantemve: "loyal".

4. *posse*: with *putarem* above.

inhibere: "restrain", after *posse*.

probro: "misdeed".

5.   *neque quod*:   take as *quod neque*; now we learn the
     real reason for the poet's trust: Catullus had never
     imagined that Gellius would go after Lesbia simply
     because Gellius' inclinations (sexually speaking) were
     known to lie within his own family.   Theoretically,
     then, Lesbia ought not to have appealed to him.

6.   *hanc* = Lesbia.

     me...edebat: "was eating me up alive"; *cf.*   35.15.

7.   *usu*:   here seems to refer to social intercourse, but
     not at the level of true friendship; translate perhaps
     as "familiarity".

8.   *id*:   refers to *multo coniungerer usu* above; *cf. id* in
     line 9.

     satis...causae: "cause enough".

9.   *satis*:   also with *causae* (understood).

     duxti = *duxisti*.

10. *culpa*:   "wrongdoing".

     sceleris: "villainy", genitive after *aliquid*.

92

A variation of the conceit expressed earlier in poem 83: Lesbia's constant verbal abuse of the poet is but a sign of her love for him. The poet is convinced of this, since he speaks ill of her all the time, but loves her nonetheless.

Structurally, the poem is well balanced: there is verbal and conceptual parallelism between the first and second couplets, with the first couplet focused on Lesbia, and the second on the poet.

1.   *Lesbia*:   the *hanc* of the preceding poem (91.6).

   mi dicit semper male: balanced by *deprecor illam* in line 3; *cf.* 83.1.

   nec tacet umquam: balanced by *assidue* in line 4.

2.   *dispeream*:   a form of oath: "may I drop dead" if Lesbia doesn't love me! The oath is repeated, with slight change, in line 4.

3.   *quo signo*:   "by what evidence" do I know this to be true?

   quia sunt totidem mea: a phrase that has troubled many editors, particularly in respect to the meaning of *totidem*; a likely interpretation is that the poet, in response to *quo signo*, states "because my words (*verba*, understood) are the same in number"—as explained further by the next three words of the poem.

   deprecor illam: here in the sense of "curse her",

balancing the *mi dicit semper male* of the first line.

4. *assidue*: "all the time".

93

The poet's complete indifference to Julius Caesar, expressed in a contemptuous manner; it seems pointless to speculate on whether some particular overture by Caesar precipitated this epigram (*cf.* poems 29, 54, and 57). A similar political theme will continue in poem 94.

Like the earlier poem 85, poem 93 is a tightly constructed couplet in which verbal forms dominate.

1. *Nil nimium studeo*: "I am not very keen at all".

velle placere: sometimes criticized for being redundant, but both verbs are important: the poet not only isn't keen on pleasing Caesar—he cannot even contemplate *wishing* to please the man.

2. *albus an ater homo*: an apparently proverbial expression of total indifference.

94

Doing what comes naturally: a play upon the name of Mentula. The man's name certainly suits his behavior!

Mentula also appears in poems 105, 114, and 115; the name may well be Catullus' nickname for Mamurra, the henchman of Caesar and Pompey mentioned in poem 29 (where he is indeed termed a *diffututa mentula*, line 13).

531

For Mamurra, see also poems 41, 43, and 57.

The couplet takes the form of a statement and resultant question in line 1, followed by a proverbial explanation in line 2.

1.   *Mentula*:   "Prick".

     moechatur: "fucks around", especially in adulterous liaisons.

2.   *hoc est quod dicunt*:   a way of introducing a proverbial expression; *cf.*   100.3.

     ipsa olera olla legit: "the pot itself gathers the potherbs", an expression not otherwise known.   The sense is that Mentula, just like the pot, is doing what is natural to him. Note the play on *olera* (*holera*) *olla*.

95A

An expression of the literary tastes of the New Poets: the *Zmyrna* of Cinna, written in neoteric style, will outlast the *Annales* of Volusius, a work already called *cacata carta* in poem 36.   For Cinna, *cf.*   10.30; only a few lines of his *Zmyrna* are extant today, but the poem seems to have been an epyllion of the type written by Catullus in poem 64.   It is obvious that the loss of line 4 prevents our total comprehension of poem 95A.

Structurally, the poem falls into two equal sections: the first four lines introduce the contrasting poems of Cinna and Volusius (see below, on line 4), while the final four lines compare the ultimate fates of the *Zmyrna* and

532

the *Annales.*

1. *Zmyrna*: the poem apparently dealt with the love of Zmyrna for her own father and her subsequent transformation into a tree; Ovid treated the myth in *Met.* X. 298ff.

    nonam...messem: cf. *nonamque...hiemem* in line 2; a figurative way of emphasizing the great length of time Cinna spent on his creation: it took all of nine summers and winters to write.

2. *edita*: "has been published"; *est* is understood.

3. *milia...quingenta*: probably "500,000 *verses*".

    Hortensius: Q. Hortensius Hortalus, the recipient (poem 65) of Catullus' translation of Callimachus' *Coma Berenices* (poem 66). Hortensius was apparently on good terms with the poet, appreciated the poetry of Callimachus, and composed neoteric verse himself; it thus seems unlikely that he stands here for an over-prolific versifier to be contrasted with Cinna. Perhaps Catullus was not the only poet to send him poems: did Volusius inflict his *Annales* on the man? (See below, line 4).

    uno: probably completed by *anno* in line 4.

4. Did the name Volusius appear in this line? If so, it would neatly balance the *Cinnae* of line 1. Perhaps the poet was telling his readers (in lines 3 and 4) that poor Hortensius was faced with reading innumerable verses by a second-rate poet; Catullus, on the other

hand, was faced with the pleasant task of reading the finely-wrought poem of Cinna.

5. *cavas*: "deep running".

Satrachi: a river in Cyprus, which, according to legend, was associated with Adonis—who happened to be the son of Zmyrna; thus the poem of Cinna will even be read in that part of the world which gave rise to the myth it relates.

penitus: "far away".

6. *Zmyrnam*: the third time within six lines that the title of Cinna's poem begins a verse; the emphasis gives a sense of increasing importance to the poem.

cana...saecula: "the grey-haired generations of the future" will continue to read and value the *Zmyrna*.

pervoluent: the verb refers to the process of unwinding a scroll, *i.e.*, reading; it is quadrisyllabic here.

7. *Volusi Annales*: *cf.* poem 36.

Paduam: the Padua was one of the mouths of the Po river; it presents a contrast with the Satrachus of line 5. The sense is that the poem of Volusius—unlike that of Cinna—will not be known far from home.

morientur ad ipsam: *cf. mittetur ad undas* in line 5.

8. While some editors find in this line a reference to the wrapping of fish in the marketplace, D.F.S. Thomson

has made a strong case for the poet alluding to a method of cooking fish in loose jackets of papyrus ("Catullus 95.8" in *Phoenix* 18 [1964] 30-36).

scombris: "mackerels".

95B

Like poem 95A, a poem concerned with literature and literary tastes. Attempts to join this couplet to that poem, however, have been unconvincing, and it seems best to take this as a separate poem.

The couplet in its original state probably contrasted a neoteric poet in line 1 with the non-neoteric Antimachus of line 2. The loss of the end of line 1, however, makes certainty impossible.

1. *Parva*: a term appropriate to a neoteric poem; Catullus and his associates disliked the long and wordy approach to poetry.

   mei: some editors complete *mei* with an indefinite *sodalis*, but it seems more likely that a proper name has fallen out of the text here.

   monimenta: here used of poetry; *cf.* 11.10.

2. *populus*: in contrast to *mihi* in line 1; the poet's taste is not the same as that of the populace at large.

   tumido: "windy" in the sense of verbose.

   Antimacho: Antimachus of Colophon was an epic poet

(*ca.* 400 B.C.) known for his verbosity; his major epic was the *Thebaid*. He also composed an elegiac poem called the *Lyde* which was disliked by Callimachus; thus Catullus' disdain is to be expected.

96

A poem of consolation for Calvus: Quintilia's premature death is no longer painful for her since Calvus' grief has made clear his great love. It is uncertain whether Quintilia was Calvus' wife or mistress; it is known, however, that Calvus wrote a poem about her death, two fragments of which survive. It is quite likely that Catullus alludes to this poem (see below, line 6), in which case the motif of poetry struck in poems 95A and 95B here continues.

In structure, poem 96 is a single conditional sentence, with the protasis in lines 1-4, and the apodosis in lines 5-6. *Cf.* the structure of 76.1-6.

1. *mutis...sepulcris*: "the silent dead".

2. *accidere*: here in the sense of "touch", almost "impinge on" the senses of the dead.

   dolore: a key word in the poem, found again in line 5: it was Calvus' sorrow that lessened the sorrow Quintilia felt at her own death. By employing *nostro* the poet universalizes the experience.

3. *quo desiderio*: in apposition with *dolore*, further defining that noun; *desiderium* here refers to a longing for someone/something lost or absent (*cf.* 2A.5).

536

renovamus: "rekindle".

4. *olim missas...amicitias*: "friendships once dismi
   reference to Calvus by Ovid (*Tristia* 2. 431-2)
   that Calvus had been unfaithful to Quintilia dত
   life. This would serve to explain why Quiা
   death, is heartened by Calvus' sincere expr৷
   grief (and remorse).

5. *immatura*: "untimely".

   dolori est: a double dative construction wit
   liae; *dolori esse* = to cause pain or sorrow.

6. *quantum gaudet amore tuo*: seemingly a cons
   of Calvus' own words (in his poem for Quint
   tan hoc etiam gaudeat ipsa cinis; the *certe*
   would then respond to Calvus' tentative *forsা*

4

97

An attack on Aemilius, who, despite his
and rear, is quite a success with the ladies. This
of three consecutive epigrams dealing with the ৷   5.
"foul mouth".

The poem falls into three equal units: lin
ent the poet's comparative evaluation of Aem   6.
and ass; lines 5-8 explain the poet's preference
ter; and lines 9-12 examine the inexplicable suc
a disgusting man with women.

1. *ita me di ament*: a parenthetical express৷

the modern "God help me"; *di* is short here and does not elide with *ament*.

referre putavi: "think that it mattered".

culum: "ass".

Aemilio: the identity of this man is uncertain; he may possibly be L. Aemilius Paullus, consul in 50 B.C. (see commentary on poem 98 also).

nilo...nihiloque: in both cases translate as "by no degree".

hoc...illud: *hoc* refers to *os*, while *illud* refers to *culum*.

verum etiam: a corrective statement, expressing the poet's ultimate preference.

mundior et melior: note both the alliteration and the rhythmical balance.

hoc: again refers to Aemilius' *os*.

dentis sesquipedalis: "teeth a foot and a half long".

gingivas: "gums".

ploxeni: a rare word that seems to allude to some kind of wagon-box or carriage-body; perhaps the image is that of Aemilius' gums being torn and bruised.

7. *praeterea*: "in addition".

    rictum: "opening" in the sense of an open mouth; *habet* understood.

    diffissus: from *diffindo*; translate as "spread wide".

8. *meientis*: "pissing".

    cunnus: "cunt", the female pudenda.

9. *hic* = Aemilius.

    se facit: "imagines himself".

10. *pistrino...asino*: the "mill" and the "ass" allude to the task of leading the ass that turns the mill in a bakery; this job was commonly performed by slaves.

11. *attingit*: in a sexual sense; *cf.* 89.5.

    putemus: *cf. putavi* in line 1 above.

12. *aegroti*: "diseased".

    culum lingere: echoes the *os an culum* of line 2 above; translate *lingere* as "lick" and *cf.* 98.4.

    carnificis: "hangman".

98

On a man whose mouth is foul both in a physical and metaphorical sense. The name "Victius" is unknown in

539

Republican Rome, and editors have proposed various emendations to the text, such as Vittius or Viccius; the most attractive emendation, however, is "Vetti", referring to Lucius Vettius, an infamous informer of the Late Republic. This man, in 59 B.C., accused L. Aemilius Paullus and other senators of plotting to assassinate Pompey; thus a poem on Aemilius (97) followed by one on Vettius (poem 98) would have special meaning for the poet's audience. *Cf.* my article "Order and Meaning in Catullus 97-99", in *Classical World* 72 (1979) 403-408.

Poem 98 features a balanced 2+2+2 structure: the initial couplet introduces a man who is a talkative fool; the second couplet focuses attention on his foul tongue; and the final couplet offers some satirical advice.

1. *In...in*: "against".

   pote = *potest*; *cf.* 17.24.

   putide: while the primary meaning is "stinking" or "rotten", a secondary meaning, often used in relation to speech, is "affected"; both meanings seem implied here, especially if "Victius" is really "Vettius".

2. *id quod...dicitur*: introducing a proverbial phrase.

   verbosis...fatuis: translate as "talkative fools".

3. *si usus veniat*: "if the need should arise".

4. *culos...lingere*: *cf.* poem 97.

   crepidas...carpatinas: "sandals made of hide",

presumably quite filthy; note the harsh *c* sound of this line.

5.   *omnino*: repeated for added emphasis in the next line; translate as "absolutely" and take with *perdere*.

omnes: echoing *omnino*: absolutely no one can survive Vettius!

6.   *hiscas*: just "open your mouth". Informers knew the ability of the word to destroy people, and more than "bad breath" is meant here.

99

The last Juventius poem in the collection, and, appropriately, a poem of farewell: the poet has had enough of the boy's cruel treatment.

At first glance, the poem may seem to have little in common with the preceding epigrams against Aemilius and "Victius", but in fact Catullus has continued the "foul mouth" theme, though with an ironic twist: the poet, who has just been castigating Aemilius and "Victius" for *their* foul mouths, is unexpectedly condemned by Juventius for his *own* foul mouth; the proverbial tables have been turned, and Catullus now finds himself put into the same unsavory category as vile Aemilius and "Victius". For the theme, *cf.* poem 78B.

Poem 99 structurally falls into three sections (6+4+6): the first six lines present the poet's theft of the kiss; the next four lines depict the reaction of Juventius; and the final six lines focus upon the poet's suffering and his resolution not to suffer such torment again.

1. *Surripui* = *subripui*; *cf.* 86.6.

   ludis: possibly here in the sense of "tease", but *cf.* 17.17.

   mellite: already used with respect to Juventius at 48.1; *cf.* 3.6.

2. *saviolum*: a "tiny little kiss".

   dulci dulcius: a play on words attractive to Catullus; *cf.* 22.14, and line 14 below.

   ambrosia: famous as the delectable food of the gods.

3. *verum id non impune*: *cf.* 78B.3.

   amplius horam: "more than an hour" (accusative of extent of time).

4. *suffixum*: "nailed".

   me memini: the poet emphasizes his recollection of this past event.

5. *purgo*: the poet tried to "justify" his action to the boy; the term is one of several in this poem taken from the language of medicine.

6. *tantillum*: "a tiny bit".

   vestrae: the plural would seem to imply the cruelty

of "you and your kind".

7. *simul* = *simul atque* ("as soon as").

   id: that is, the stealing of the kiss.

   diluta: "washed".

8. *guttis*: "drops" of water.

   abstersti: from *abstergeo*, here in the sense of "disinfect".

9. *contractum*: the boy treated the kiss as if it were a potential source of disease.

10. *commictae*: "contaminated".

    spurca saliva: *cf.* 78B.2.

    lupae: "whore".

11. *infesto*: "dangerous" to his health.

12. *cessasti* = *cessavisti*.

    excruciare: *cf.* line 4 above, and poem 85.

13. *ut*: introducing a result clause.

    ambrosia: echoing line 2 above.

14. *Cf.* line 2 above; translate *tristi* as "bitter". Hellebore was a potent cathartic used in antiquity to treat

madness.

15. *quoniam*: "seeing that".

   misero: *cf.* line 11 above.

16. *posthac*: "in time to come".

   surripiam: the final word echoes the very first word of the poem.

100

An ironic poem of support for Caelius in his love for Aufillenus. Caelius, says the poet, is in love again! Joined with that rascal Quintius too! (There's a proper pair.) Well, Caelius, good luck to you—you've proved your "good will" towards me already when you "relieved" me of my love.

The above interpretation of the poem assumes, of course, that "Caelius" is M. Caelius Rufus (*cf.* poem 58A), who replaced Catullus in the affections of Lesbia; "Quintius" must be the Quintius of poem 82, a man also involved with Lesbia.

Poem 100 has a 4+4 structure: the first four lines set out the situation of Caelius and Quintius, while the last four lines express the poet's ironic wish on behalf of the former.

1. *Aufillenum...Aufillenam*: a brother and sister; for Aufillena, *cf.* poems 110 and 111. It is worth noting that this line is composed of four proper names.

2. *flos Veronensum*: *cf.* 24.1; the main objection against identifying "Caelius" with M. Caelius Rufus is that we know of no connection the latter had with Verona.

   depereunt: "are desperately in love with"; *cf.* 35.12.

3. *hic...ille*: Caelius and Quintius respectively.

   hoc est, quod dicitur: *cf.* 94.2; the phrase prepares the reader for a proverbial saying.

4. *fraternum...sodalicium*: "brotherly partnership"; a play on the usual meaning of the phrase since Catullus twists it to refer to the fact that a brother and sister are the objects of the men's affections.

5. *cui faveam*: "whom should I support"; note how this verse as a whole recalls poem 1.1ff. Catullus is, in a sense, "dedicating" his support to Caelius.

6. *perspecta est igni tum*: the commonly accepted emendation of the MSS.' *perfecta est igitur*; translate as "was tried by fire then".

   unica amicitia: spoken ironically, since Caelius' unique act of friendship was stealing Lesbia from the poet.

7. *vesana*: *cf.* 7.10; for the image in this line as a whole, *cf.* 35.15.

8. *potens*: "successful"; could it be that the poet wishes Caelius well in this particular love because it is homosexual in nature? Certainly, were Caelius to stick with this type of love Catullus would be less threatened in

545

his relationship with Lesbia.

101

A poem dramatizing the ritual farewell spoken by Catullus at the grave of his brother in the Troad of Asia Minor (*cf.* 65.5-14, 68A.19-26, and 68B.89-100); it is possible that the poet visited this grave during his year in Bithynia.

This short elegy, one of the most famous poems in the corpus, makes skillful use of *m* and *a* sounds to convey the solemnity of the occasion (*cf.* poem 96, which has a similar theme). In structure, the poem presents a four-line prelude (depicting the dramatic situation) followed by a six-line farewell to the deceased.

1. *per...per*: the first of this pair is best translated by "through", the second by "over".

   gentes: "nations".

   vectus: "carried".

2. *advenio*: a formal "I am come".

   frater: the poet addresses his brother three times in the poem (here, lines 6 and 10) in a manner reminiscent of the Roman ritual of speaking the name of the deceased at the corpse in hopes of calling him back to life.

   ad: here indicating purpose; translate as "to perform".

inferias: the ritual offerings traditionally made to the dead; these could include offerings of honey, milk, wine or flowers.

3. *te...donarem*: "present you with"; the tense of the verb reflects the poet's past determination to make the traditional offerings.

    munere mortis: "death gift".

4. *mutam...cinerem*: *cf.* 96.1.

    alloquerer: "address" in a formal manner.

5. *quandoquidem*: "seeing that".

    tete...ipsum: especially emphatic (fortune has taken *you*, yes *you*).

    abstulit: from *aufero*.

6. *indigne*: adverb with *adempte*; translate as "undeservedly".

    adempte: "taken away"; *cf.* 68A.20 and 68B.92.

7. *tamen*: here in the sense of "all the same".

    interea: "however".

    haec: refers to the traditional offerings; governed by *accipe* in line 9.

prisco: "ancient".

parentum: "ancestors".

8. *tristi munere*: "as a sad gift"; *cf.* line 3 above.

    ad inferias: repeated from line 2 above; purpose is again implied.

9. *fraterno*: *cf.* 100.4.

    multum manantia: "thoroughly drenched" with tears.

10. *in perpetuum*: "forever".

    ave atque vale: "hail and farewell"; the poet's formal (and final) goodbye to his brother.

102

A pledge of secrecy to Cornelius: the poet will not betray his confidence. The identity of Cornelius is uncertain, but there is no reason to rule out the Cornelius of poem 67 or the Cornelius (Nepos) of poem 1.

Structurally the poem is a conditional sentence with the first couplet the protasis and the second couplet the apodosis.

1. *Si quicquam*: *cf.* 96.1 and 107.1.

    tacito: dative; translate as "a man of silence".

2. *cuius*: refers back to *tacito* in line 1.

penitus: "intimately".

fides animi: "faith of mind" = "faithful mind".

3. *meque*: some editors take this as equivalent to *me quoque*, but it may be correlative with *et* in the next line ("both...and"). In either case, the construction seems awkward.

    illorum: refers back to *tacito* in line 1.

    iure sacratum: "bound by the oath".

4. *factum me esse*: "I have become".

    putum: an emendation of the MSS.' *puta*, a reading which provides a difficult sequence (future indicative followed by imperative); translate as "a pure, unadulterated" Harpocrates. For Harpocrates, *cf.* 74.4.

103

An attack on Silo disguised as a polite piece of advice: he should either return the poet's money if he insists on behaving badly, or keep the money and stop his offensive behavior.

The poem features a balanced 2+2 structure, with each couplet offering Silo a choice, and with each couplet ending in the phrase *saevus et indomitus*. *Cf.* poem 82.

1. *sodes* = *si audes*; translate as "please". The poem is savage, but polite.

decem sestertia: "10,000 sesterces", a substantial amount of money; *cf.* poem 41.

Silo: the precise identity of the poet's target is unknown; the cognomen is fairly common and seems to be of respectable Italian origin.

2. *esto*: future imperative.

    quamvis: "as you like".

    saevus et indomitus: adjectives often associated with wild animals; Silo's behavior thus is shown to be subhuman.

3. *nummi*: "coins".

    quaeso: "I pray"; a polite word to balance the *sodes* of line 1.

4. *leno*: "a pimp"; it seems unlikely that Silo was really a professional pimp, for the epigram would only have a real sting were the man respectable in the eyes of society. Calling Silo a pimp constitutes the poet's main attack on the man.

    idem: "at the same time"; pimps, says the poet, have no right to such behavior.

104

A rebuke to two men who have misread the poet's feelings towards Lesbia. The epigram is not as enigmatic as some editors suggest: there are clues within the poem that point to the men involved being Quintius and M. Caelius Rufus; *cf.* my article *"Tu Cum Tappone*: Catullus 104" in *Classical World* 70 (1976) 21-24.

The poem is structured as a question (lines 1-2) followed by an insulting response (lines 3-4).

1. *Credis*: the poet avoids directly naming the addressee.

   meae...vitae: Lesbia, although the poet here too avoids the direct name.

   maledicere: "to speak words of abuse"; this must have been the accusation of the two men involved.

2. *Cf.* poem 82; this line suggests that the addressee is the Quintius of that preceding poem.

3. *non potui*: but *cf.* poem 92.

   perdite amarem: *cf.* 45.3.

4. *Tappone*: probably not a reference to a person with that cognomen, but an allusion to a stock figure in Italian farce; thus Catullus is calling the second man a "clown". Given the close association of Quintius and Caelius in poem 100, I have argued that "Tappo" is a derogatory name for M. Caelius Rufus.

   omnia monstra facis: "you turn everything into a monstrous act", that is, he misconstrues the poet's behavior. In so doing he commits a monstrous act himself.

105

Mentula ("Prick") as poet: the Muses take offence. For Mentula-Mamurra, *cf.* commentary on poem 94.

The couplet is finely balanced: the first line begins with Mentula and depicts his poetic pretensions; the second line begins with the Muses and depicts their reactions to Mentula's efforts.

1. *Pipleium...montem*: Pipla (or Pimpla) was a district in northern Greece near Mt. Olympus; it was traditionally held to be sacred to the Muses.

   scandere: "climb".

2. *furcillis...eiciunt*: "throw him out with pitchforks". As Mentula has done violence to the Muses, so the Muses respond with violence towards him.

   praecipitem: "head first".

106

A pretty boy with an auctioneer: love for sale? It is possible that the boy in question is Juventius, but one cannot rule out a disparaging reference to Clodius.

Structurally the couplet features a first line which sketches the scene for the reader, and a second line which draws the disdainful inference.

1. *puero bello*: calling the lad "pretty" may make a veiled allusion to Clodius Pulcer; *cf.* poem 79.

praeconem: a public crier, or "auctioneer".

qui videt: an indefinite "one who sees".

2. *nisi*: "but that".

vendere: the only other appearance of this verb in the corpus is in poem 79, where Clodius is ready to sell the poet and his family.

discupere: "longs very much". The understood subject is *puerum*.

107

An exclamation of joy caused by an unexpected reconciliation with Lesbia; the mood of manic joy is intensified by the unusual amount of verbal repetition in the poem. For a more sedate evaluation of the situation, *cf.* poem 109.

The poem features a 2+4+2 structure: the first couplet makes a general statement about joy; the next two couplets explain the particular situation at hand; and the final couplet expresses the poet's joy by means of a rhetorical question.

1. *Si quicquam*: a favored opening phrase; *cf.* poems 96 and 102.

cupido optantique: "a man eager and wishful"; some have removed the metrical hiatus between these words by adding *que* to *cupido*.

2. *insperanti*: a man "not expecting" his wishes to come true.

   hoc: refers to *quicquam* above.

   proprie: with *gratum*; translate as "particularly".

3. *hoc*: refers to line 4.

   nobisque est: an emendation of the MSS.' *nobis quoque*, an ungainly phrase in the context of the line as a whole.

4. *restituis*: "restore".

   mi = mihi; the change from plural (*nobisque*) to singular is not uncommon in Latin poetry.

5. *cupido atque insperanti*: the words earlier applied to a vague "someone" are now clearly applied to the poet; *atque* here has the sense of "and yet".

   ipsa: "of your own free will"; note the monosyllabic ending of this line, and *cf.* line 7 below.

6. *lucem*: "day"; accusative of exclamation.

   candidiore nota: a day with a white mark was a lucky day; *cf.* 68B.148, and compare the modern phrase "red-letter day".

7. *uno*: here in the sense of "alone".

   hac quid...optandum: an emendation of the corrupt

MSS. reading; *hac* is to be taken with *vita* in line 8.

8. *optandum*: *cf.* *optantique* in line 1; the poem has come full circle.

    vita: ablative.

108

The rending of Cominius: poetic justice. The victim of this vituperation may be one of two brothers, P. Cominius and C. Cominius, notorious as prosecutors in Rome.

The poem takes the form of a single conditional statement, with the first couplet providing the protasis, and the following couplets forming the apodosis.

1. *populi arbitrio*: "by verdict of the people"; the tables are turned as the prosecutor stands trial.

    tua cana senectus: literally "your hoary old age", but modern usage would prefer "you in your hoary old age".

2. *spurcata*: "made foul"; *cf.* 99.10.

    intereat: "be put to death".

3. *equidem*: "for my part".

4. *lingua*: it is fitting that the tongue be dealt with first, given Cominius' profession.

    sit data: "would be given".

5.   *effossos*:   "gouged out".

   voret: "devour".

6.   *intestina*:   "guts"; "devour" is understood in this line.

109

   Lesbia's pledge of love; the poet prays that she is being sincere, but betrays his own sense of doubt. The poem is a companion piece to poem 107. *Cf.* also poems 70 and 72.

   The epigram has a 2+2+2 structure: the initial couplet presents us with Lesbia's promise to the poet; the following couplet features Catullus' prayer that her promise be sincere; and the concluding couplet depicts the result of the promise being kept.

1.   *Iucundum*:   to be taken with *perpetuumque* in the next line; translate as "a thing of joy".

   mea vita: *cf.*   104.1.

   proponis: reiterated by *promittere* in line 3.

2.   *hunc nostrum*:   with *amorem*, "this love of ours".

   inter nos: best taken with *iucundum ... perpetuumque fore*.

   perpetuumque: "everlasting".

3.   *di magni*:   the poet invokes divine aid; *cf.*   76.17.

556

vere: *cf.* *sincere* and *ex animo* in the next verse; it is vital to the poet that Lesbia speak sincerely.

4. *ex animo*: "from her heart".

5. *tota...vita*: "throughout our whole lives"; an ablative, instead of the more common accusative, is used to express duration of time.

perducere: "prolong".

6. *foedus*: the poet conceives of his relationship with Lesbia as a covenant; *cf.* 76.3 and 87.3.

amicitiae: not friendship in the ordinary sense, but a kind of spiritual alliance; *cf.* 96.4.

110

On Aufillena, who takes the money and runs. Aufillena had appeared briefly in poem 100, but here Catullus develops an unflattering portrait of her as a deceitful whore. It is possible that the poet is making a cruel pun on the lady's name: Aufil - *lena*, the procuress, the seductress, a woman akin to the Silo of poem 103. *Cf.* poem 111.

Structurally, the epigram falls into two equal halves: the first four lines compare Aufillena with prostitutes of decent character, who deliver on their promises; the final four lines then brand Aufillena as the lowest type of whore imaginable.

1. *bonae*: here in the sense of "obliging" or "accommodating"; *cf.* 89.1.

   amicae: "mistresses"; *cf. meretricis* in line 7.

2. *quae facere instituunt*: "those things which they undertake to do"; an implied *eorum* exists between *pretium* and the accusative *quae*.

3. *tu*: in contrast to the *bonae amicae*.

   quod...quod...quod: all to be taken as causal; they explain why Aufillena is not a *bona amica*.

   promisti = *promisisti*.

   mihi quod mentita: "because you lied to me"; *es* understood.

   inimica es: *cf. amicae* in line 1.

4. *das et fers*: "give and take"; *et* is an emendation of the MSS.' *nec*.

   saepe: implies that Aufillena is not new at this game.

   facis facinus: *cf.* 81.6.

5. *ingenuae est*: genitive of characteristic; *ingenuae* here bears the sense of "honest".

   pudicae: also genitive of characteristic, with *fuit* in the next line; the past tense is used to imply that once

Aufillena made the offer she gave up all claims to chastity.

6. *corripere*: "carry off".

7. *fraudando officiis*: the MSS. are corrupt here, reading *fraudando efficit*; the emendation can be translated as "by defrauding (men) of your services".

   meretricis: "whore"; another genitive of characteristic with *est*.

8. *toto corpore*: "with every inch of her body".

111

The portrait of Aufillena completed: she is now depicted as a wife, as a mother, and as a woman involved in an incestuous affair with her uncle. For a detailed analysis of this cycle of poems (100, 110, 111), *cf.* my article "Quintius and Aufillena in Catullus", *Classical World* 74 (1980-81) 220-223.

The first couplet focuses upon the Roman ideal of the wife who is sexually true to her legal husband; the second couplet demonstrates that Aufillena's ideals are quite different, and generally offensive.

1. *viro*: "husband" in this context.

   contentam vivere: "to spend one's life satisfied".

2. *nuptarum*: "wives"; perhaps Aufillena is married to the Quintius of poem 100.

laus: we might say *"the* praise"; *est* is understood here. *Cf.* 110.1.

eximiis: "distinguished".

3. *cuivis*: "any man at all"; *cf.* *viro ... solo* in line 1.

    quamvis: if an adverb, to be taken with *succumbere* ("to submit as much as you like"); but perhaps the accusative of *quivis*, and thus the subject of *succumbere* ("that any woman at all submit").

    par est: "it's fitting".

4. *matrem*: Aufillena apparently has children.

    fratres ex patruo: a pun: Aufillena's liaison with her uncle (*patruo*) could produce cousins (*fratres patrueles*) for herself as well as brothers (*fratres*) for her other children. Such a play on words serves to emphasize even more the incestuous horror of Aufillena's affair. The missing word at the end of this verse may have been *parere* (from *pario*, to give birth).

112

Naso under fire: the poet attacks the man on both a political and sexual level; *cf.* my article "Catullus 112" in *Classical World* 77 (1983) 65-68. As the name Naso was fairly common, the exact identity of the poet's victim remains in doubt.

The single couplet of this poem is formed around the

repetition of the adjective *multus*, and "capped" by the sting of the final *pathicus*.

1. *Multus*: an adjective of great breadth, and hence of great ambiguity; take in the sense of "verbose" or "long-winded" throughout the poem.

   neque tecum multus homo: Naso seems to have an unnamed companion who is as silent as Naso is talkative; *neque* = "but not".

   est qui: some editors prefer to read *est quin*, and change the *descendit* of the next line into *te scindat*; for a strong argument in favor of *est qui*, cf. M. Gwyn Morgan's "Catullus 112: A *Pathicus* in Politics", *American Journal of Philology* 100 (1979) 377-380.

2. *descendit*: often used to refer to a politician "going down" to the forum to attend to business or to canvass for election; the verb, however, can also have an obscene meaning pertaining to sexual penetration.

   pathicus: a man who undertook to play the passive, female role in a homosexual relationship, a role which carried with it a great deal of social contempt; the revelation that Naso is a *pathicus* is, of course, the heart of this invective. Only when seeing this word would the reader realize the sexual nuance of *descendit*, and that the unnamed companion is sexually involved with Naso.

113

An attack on Maecilia, a woman whose world has been rapidly expanding! The precise identity of the poet's victim is unknown, but the name is well attested and it is unlikely that (as some have argued) Catullus originally wrote "Mucilla" in reference to Mucia, the divorced wife of Pompey the Great.

The poem is held together by verbal repetition and by the satirical contrast of two lovers *vs.* two thousand; it ends with a pseudo-proverbial phrase meant to sum up the whole situation.

1. *Consule Pompeio primum*: Pompey the Great first served as consul (with Crassus) in 70 B.C. Translate *primum* as "for the first time", and note the juxtaposition of *primum* with *duo*.

   Cinna: cf. 10.29-30 and 95A.1.

   solebant/Maeciliam: there is an infinitive understood after *solebant*; translate as "were accustomed to screw Maecilia".

2. *facto consule nunc iterum*: Pompey became consul again (also with Crassus) in 55 B.C. Translate *iterum* as "a second time".

3. *manserunt duo*: perhaps the same *duo* as in line 1.

   creverunt: "have increased".

   milia in unum/singula: "a thousand apiece for each

one", that is, Maecilia's lovers have grown from 2 to 2000 in fifteen years.

4. *fecundum*: "prolific".

114

On Mentula's estate, which, despite its bounty, cannot make up for the man's excesses. For Mentula (Mamurra) as a profligate spendthrift, *cf.* poem 29. Poem 115 also treats this theme, but in a more graphic manner.

The epigram features a 4+2 structure: the first four lines sketch the situation for the reader, while the final couplet presents the poet's sarcastic evaluation of that situation.

1. *Firmano*: Firmum was a town south of Ancona, on the Adriatic coast of Italy.

    saltu: "estate"; the ablative is causal in nature.

    falso: "wrongly".

    Mentula: *cf.* poems 94 and 105.

2. *fertur*: "is said (to be)".

    egregias: "outstanding"; the poet is not being ironic here—the estate *is* impressive.

3. *aucupium omne genus*: "fowl of every sort" for hunting; *omne genus* is an accusative of specification.

prata: "meadows".

arva: "ploughed fields" for agriculture.

ferasque: "wild game".

4.   *nequiquam*: the richness of the estate in the end does not matter—it still cannot support the excesses of Mentula.

fructus: "revenues", that is, the income of the estate.

sumptibus: "expenses".

exsuperat: the subject is Mentula. *Cf.* 29.13-22.

5.   *concedo*: the poet is willing to let Mentula *appear* to be rich.

dum: "provided that".

6.   *saltum*: *cf.* line 1; the poem begins and ends on the same note.

dum modo: also "provided that". Editors unhappy with the metrical hiatus after *modo* have proposed various emendations, such as *dum modio* and *dum modo homo*; the latter is tempting, as it would provide a pointed contrast between the estate and its owner.

egeat: "is in need".

115

On Mentula and his estate: a further reflection on the theme of poem 114.

The epigram begins with a two-line introduction which supplies the necessary data; the following four lines then provide an elaboration of detail, and the concluding couplet presents the invective "sting".

1. *lustra et*: the attractive emendation of Thomson for the problematical *instar* of the MSS. Translate *lustra* as "bush", that is, uncleared land, and *cf. silvas* in line 5 below.

    triginta iugera: about 20 acres; a *iugerum* was a plot of land roughly 240 X 120 feet.

    prati: *cf.* 114.3.

2. *quadraginta arvi*: about 27 acres of ploughed fields; *cf.* 114.3.

    maria: probably here in the sense of "marshland"; *cf. paludes* in line 5 below. This reference to *maria* is not derogatory in tone, for marshland would be valuable on an estate, especially in providing a habitat for game; *cf.* 114.3.

3. *Croesum*: Croesus was, in legend, an extremely rich king of Lydia in Asia Minor.

    superare: "surpass"; *cf. exsuperat* at 114.4.

4. *saltu*: *cf.* 114.1 and 6.

    tot bona possideat: *cf.* 114.2.

5. Each noun in this line echoes a noun in lines 1-2; *ingentes silvas* = *lustra*, and *altasque paludes* = *maria*. *Altasque paludes* is a commonly accepted emendation of the MSS.' *saltusque paludesque*.

6. *Hyperboreos*: the exotic legendary inhabitants of the extreme north. The reference to both the Hyperboreans and the Ocean in this verse is intended to emphasize the vast extent of Mentula's holdings. The poet's tone in the poem begins to shift here, from serious statement to invective exaggeration.

7. *magna*: to be contrasted with *maximus* in this line, and echoed by *magna* in the next line.

    ipse: the estate is contrasted with its owner; *cf.* 114.6.

    ultro: "in his own right".

8. *homo*: *cf.* note on line 6 in poem 114.

    vero: "in fact".

    mentula magna minax: Ellis' translation of "monstrous menacing Mentula" (Prick) remains attractive; note the repetitive *m* and *n* sounds in this verse. For a detailed analysis of poems 114 and 115, *cf.* P. Harvey's "Catullus 114-115: Mentula, Bonus Agricola", *Historia* 28 (1979) 329-345.

116

The conclusion not only to the Gellius cycle (*cf.* poems 74, 80, 88-91), but also to the elegiacs as a whole; the poet here threatens Gellius with punishment for taking an aggressive stance against him. The *tela* promised Gellius by the poet are most likely the preceding poems in the Gellius cycle. It indeed seems fitting that the elegiacs of Catullus, so concerned with invective, close on such a threatening note. *Cf.* the introduction to poem 65.

The epigram begins with six lines depicting the poet's attempt to soothe Gellius and end his hostility, and concludes with a couplet in which Catullus promises to strike back.

1. *studiose*: "diligently"; the MSS. read *studioso*, which seems awkward whether taken with *animo venante* or with *tibi*.

   venante: the poet "hunts about" for poems to send Gellius.

2. *carmina...Battiadae*: *cf.* 65.16. Catullus refers to translations of Callimachean poems.

   uti: "so that".

3. *qui*: "by which". Note that this verse is composed entirely of spondaic feet.

   nobis = *mihi*; translate as "towards me".

   neu conarere: "and you would not try".

4. *tela infesta*: "hostile barbs".

   meum: this verse is defective in the MSS. and *meum* is commonly inserted.

   mittere: "hurl".

   in usque caput: "all the way to (my) head". For this use of *usque*, *cf.* 4.24.

5. *hunc...laborem*: that is, the work of finding the right translations to send him.

   mihi: here a dative of agent, with *sumptum esse*.

   nunc: take with *video*.

   sumptum esse: "was undertaken".

6. *Gelli*: note how the poet delays the name of the poem's recipient.

   nostras = *meas*; *cf.* line 3 above.

   hic: "in this matter".

   valuisse: "prevail".

7. This verse ends in the MSS. with *evitabimus amitha*, a reading which makes little sense; *evitabimus acta* is one of the more probable emendations, and it requires us to take *contra nos* in the sense of "against us (= me)".

tela: *cf.* line 4 above.

acta: "launched".

8.   *fixus*: "pierced".

nostris: with *telis* understood.

dabis supplicium: "will pay the penalty"; the final *s* in *dabis* is suppressed for metrical purposes, making *tu dabis* a dactyl. Given this metrical peculiarity in line 8, it is tempting to read *evitabimus missa* in the preceding line, and see an identical suppression of final *s*.